A TEXAS FRONTIER

The Clear Fork Country
and Fort Griffin, 1849–1887

BY TY CASHION

UNIVERSITY OF OKLAHOMA PRESS: NORMAN AND LONDON

Published with the assistance of the National Endowment for the Humanities, a federal agency which supports the study of such fields as history, philosophy, literature, and language.

Library of Congress Cataloging-in-Publication Data

Cashion, Ty, 1956–
    A Texas frontier : the Clear Fork Country and Fort Griffin, 1849–1887 / by Ty Cashion.
        p.   cm.
    Includes bibliographical references (p.   ) and index.
    ISBN 0-8061-2791-0 (alk. paper)
    1. Fort Griffin Region (Tex.)—History. 2. Frontier and pioneer life—Texas—Fort Griffin Region. 3. Texas, West—History, Local. 4. Frontier and pioneer life—Texas, West. 5. Violence—Texas—Fort Griffin Region—History—19th century. 6. Violence—Texas, West— History—19th cenury. I. Title.
    F394.F636C37   1996
    976.4'734—dc20   95-41192
                                                                    CIP

The paper in this book meets the guidelines for permanence and durability of the Committee on Production Guidelines for Book Longevity of the Council on Library Resources, Inc.

1 2 3 4 5 6 7 8 9 10

A TEXAS FRONTIER

THE CLEAR FORK COUNTRY AND FORT GRIFFIN, 1849–1887

For Peggy

CONTENTS

ILLUSTRATIONS

MAPS

PREFACE

W̲HEN TEXANS from the western part of the state travel to
other places, and someone asks, "Where are you from?" they will
normally say, "West Texas," with the same conviction as that of
a person from any state or even larger province within the country.
These people see themselves as members of a distinct society,
separated from the rest of Texas by a unique land and experience.
Much of that identity can be traced back to the region's formative
development. Around Abilene, San Angelo, and Amarillo local
citizens embrace the heritage of life as it existed when villages such
as Fort Griffin, Saint Angela, and Mobeetie were the flourishing
centers of West Texas. Ties with the past still survive in the
inhabitants' art, music, language, and dress as well as their attitudes,
economy, and patterns of living.

A significant part of that frontier experience was influenced
by events that occurred in the "Clear Fork country," a relatively
small territory where this Brazos River tributary cuts a path from
the Cross Timbers into the Rolling Plains of West Texas. The Clear
Fork provided Anglos and their dependents a main artery into the
unfamiliar land beyond the prairies. Explorers, military personnel,
and adventurers found the edge of the plains a natural entrepôt for
their activities. As they came and went, "cow hunters" quietly
gained a permanence, and eventually townbuilders and others
followed. Until the railroad connected West Texas with the interior,
the Clear Fork country remained the anchor for development in
the far reaches of what was then known as Northwest Texas.

The popular perception of early history in this area is most
typically recalled in stories of Indian raids, cavalry campaigns, wild
"nights on the town," vigilante hangings, buffalo hunts, and cattle

drives. Such colorful chapters have overshadowed the mundane activities that also formed the regional experience. *A Texas Frontier* is an attempt to portray more completely the cultural ascension of this society, depicting the everyday life of some ordinary people alongside the more dramatic events and personages. I have tried to demonstrate how the adjustment to an unfamiliar environment, the development of a viable economic base, and the effort to imprint familiar patterns of life were the true driving forces of this local history. At the same time I have tried not to ignore the ecological and social costs associated with Anglo expansion. This context, I hope, will place the larger-than-life events in perspective.

In crafting this account I have focused on several prominent themes that have defined the history of the Clear Fork country. First, a ranching-based society of Southern descent emerged in the late 1850s, forming a social and economic foundation. Despite the unfamiliar and often harsh environment, stock raisers persisted through conflicts with Plains Indians, the Civil War, Reconstruction, outlawry, rapid settlement, and diversification. The process turned Southerners into Westerners. Where sources have allowed, I have also tried to show how others shaped the region's history, notably the ordinary men and women who immigrated to this area, American Indians who came into contact with the emerging culture, and African Americans.

The formative development of the land, however, was not an insular experience. Events that occurred and policies devised in places as far away as New York City, Washington, D.C., and Austin profoundly affected the lives of the people whose story is told here. As if in league with the fickle land itself, distant markets and decision makers were responsible for wild swings in the material fortunes of people in the Clear Fork country, resulting in a "boom and bust" economy. Much of the history in this area unfolded during cycles of dizzying prosperity and sobering depression, a characteristic that still marks life in the Clear Fork country and West Texas today. For this reason I have continued the story after the arrival of the hope-inspiring railroad in order to chronicle the true lesson of history that settled in, when the cycle turned downward and the land's harsher face reversed the tide of immigrants.

A strain of lawlessness and violence also coursed through the formative era of the Clear Fork country and touched almost every aspect of life. Plains Indians and their conquerors, of course, battled for the land itself; the random acts of outlaws and brigands and the calculated extralegal "justice" of vigilantes also left scars on the emerging society. Short-tempered soldiers and otherwise peaceable settlers as well as racially intolerant townspeople and transients acted on their emotions, too. Like many areas in the American West, this region has generated romantic images of gunslingers and a casual acceptance of almost sociopathic behavior. Yet while life was indeed punctuated by occasional violence, it did not unfold in the manner that prevails in the popular perception. Distortions of fact, moreover, have been the stock-in-trade of local folklore. In my effort to set the record straight I have no doubt presented violence out of proportion to the true experience of life in the Clear Fork country. At the same time, the popular preoccupation with western violence compelled me to try to present accurately the events and the environment in which these acts took place as well as the reactions of citizens, the measures taken by the legal community, and the consequences to society.

A final word regards my use of terms to describe people of various backgrounds. When I began this work, *African Americans* was just beginning to enter the mainstream of the popular lexicon, and I learned long ago that women do not necessarily consider being called *ladies* a compliment. Except in illustrative quotes, I have tried to shun common references that American Indians and other groups might find disparaging. I found it pretentious and indeed impossible, however, to remain "politically correct" at every turn, and I apologize for any unintended offense. Ironically, only one term proved truly nettlesome: *Anglo*. I flirted with *European American* and other expressions, but all proved unsatisfactory. So, to Joe Kuzell in Tex-Czech heaven, I can only throw up my shoulders and say, *Ale toŝ, Dedeĉku* ("Oh well, Grandfather").

I am humbly indebted to the many friends, advisors, and others
who have provided both material assistance and encouragement
in helping me to produce *A Texas Frontier*—first, to Jack Kilby
and Robert Noyce, developers of the integrated circuit! I am even
more grateful for the encouragement of many friends and
colleagues, notably Jim Avery, Kirk Bane, Brandon and Beth
Battles, Bob Chandler, Tom Hall, Margaret Patoski, Jeff Pilcher,
and Jim Wetzel. I especially thank my "best man" for thirty-eight
years, Buddy Hamm, for his fraternal loyalty and unfailing
confidence in me. Mildred Jenkins and Light Cummins, one a
teacher, the other a professor, both inspired me along the way.

George Norris Green, Kathleen Underwood, and the late Sandra
Myres, all of the University of Texas at Arlington, took an early
interest in my work and provided both sincere encouragement and
sound advice. I owe a tremendous debt of gratitude to others at
Texas Christian University. My former advisor, the avuncular Ben
Procter, labored tirelessly in editing the original dissertation
manuscript. Donald Worcester extended both his support and his
friendship. His long familiarity with West Texas, moreover, saved
me from an occasional factual blunder. Through his works, native
West Texan Jim Corder illuminated the historical facts for me by
giving his land a spiritual voice. Paul Boller provided a most
generous travel grant. I also thank Grady McWhiney, Bill Beezley,
Ken Stevens, Kathy McDorman, Clayton Brown, and department
chairman Spencer Tucker for their frank and helpful advice. My
colleagues at East Texas State University, notably Harry Wade and
long-time Texas historian Joe Fred Cox, have been very supportive
as well.

Many others also deserve special recognition. UT–San Antonio's
John Miller Morris provided many thorough and insightful
comments. In every case the many library staffs I encountered
offered their assistance unstintingly: Joyce Martindale, Nancy
Bruce, and Brenda Barnes of Texas Christian University; Mike
Meier at the National Archives in Washington, D.C.; Gerald Saxon
and staff at the University of Texas at Arlington's Jenkins Garrett
Collection; Ralph Elder and William Richter of the Center for

American History at the University of Texas at Austin; Jim Bradshaw at Midland's Nita Stewart Haley Memorial Library; David Murrah of the Southwest Collection at Texas Tech; John W. Anderson at the Texas State Library; and Sonia Walker at the Baird Public Library. Prolific Fort Belknap chronicler Barbara Ledbetter also gave her time and advice freely. Distinguished Professor Kenneth F. Neighbours, author of the thoroughly researched work on Indian Agent Robert Simpson Neighbors, pointed me to some long-neglected primary sources regarding the Clear Fork's antebellum period. Frances Wheeler and Cheri Hawkins at the Shackelford County clerk's office guided me through early-day court records and helped me understand the intricacies of other documents. Archivist Joan Farmer at Albany's Old Jail Art Center also provided photographs and opened all but a few files regarding African Americans and some other information that reflected unfavorably on local early-day pioneers. Ohioans Eleanor Phillips, Marjorie Kirkwood, and Ramona Thompson along with Arlene Rainey of Benton, Arkansas, helped me unravel the mystery surrounding James Brock. The charitable Mrs. Kirkwood, especially, provided assistance by combing through personal effects, uncovering some almost forgotten newspaper articles and pictures. To collector and friend Larry Jones, who so graciously allowed me to use many rare and valuable photographs, I am most grateful. In particular, his photographic record of the 1872 Texas Land and Copper expedition provided several priceless images. And the West Texas Historical Association, by providing in its yearbook a forum for so many historians and enthusiasts, formed a substantial foundation for my research. Distinguished local historians such as Rupert Richardson, Carl Coke Rister, W. C. Holden, J. R. Webb, Ben O. Grant, and many others exuded in their writings a deep love for West Texas and nurtured in me a respect for the land, people, and culture.

Most of all, I thank my family—my parents, Bob and Joann Cashion, my sister, Michelle Redwine, and my son Sam. Foremost, I acknowledge the faith, love, and encouragement of my wife Peggy, to whom I have dedicated this work.

A TEXAS FRONTIER

THE CLEAR FORK COUNTRY AND FORT GRIFFIN, 1849–1887

INTRODUCTION
MARLBORO COUNTRY

JUST AS THEY HAD FOR YEARS, folks from nearly every part of West Texas recently gathered on the courthouse lawn in Albany to celebrate their frontier heritage with an annual barbecue and parade. The town's merchants, who had grown used to the sluggish business climate, welcomed the throng and even tolerated the temporary booths where peddlers hawked their homemade crafts and wares. A light breeze carried the aroma of smoldering mesquite and blackening meat to every corner of town from a massive smoker, where sweaty cowboys tended briskets. Some comely young women nearby, apparently unperturbed by the dry summer heat, served tea to hungry visitors lined up at the chuckwagon. A couple of blocks away a calliope began puffing a lively tune, prompting everyone to grab their plates and elbow for a good spot on the main street. The monstrous instrument soon came into view at the head of Old West characters and floats depicting scenes of frontier life. Rows of whooping cowboys, saber-wielding cavalrymen, side-saddle–riding women, painted warriors, and settlers in carriages waved to delighted children and admiring adults; on trailers, "Indian" children sat cross-legged, a blacksmith shod a horse, and some dance-hall girls entertained gamblers. As the last sheriff's posses, flag bearers, and antique cars disappeared behind the old stone courthouse, the crowd melted away. Many visitors, their sense of nostalgia still unsated, idled about town and waited until dusk to see the local folks' musical history pageant, the Fort Griffin Fandangle.[1]

The Fandangle parade. (Photo by author)

For more than a century picnics and community gatherings have
typified life in the Clear Fork country, yet anyone who knows this
place only casually associates the name "Fort Griffin" with its
wilder and sometimes violent side. The town always stands ready
with a shootout, brawl, or some other event to enliven a romantic
narrative. In his text *Lone Star*, T. R. Fehrenbach painted a distorted
picture of the village as a "typical western hell-town," where
raucous trail drivers and buffalo hunters—"a rough, bearded, dirty,
violent band of men"—camped in the shadow of the army post.
Here, he asserted, red-haired poker queen Lottie Deno ran her
game, "cold-eyed gunmen all around." Almost forty years ago a
Doc Holliday biographer described how the phlegmatic dentist
eviscerated a fellow gambler and escaped when his moll, Big Nose
Kate, set a building on fire to divert a lynch mob. Although the
episode never occurred, Ian Frazier was still passing it off as fact
in his otherwise absorbing *Great Plains*, published in 1989. Even
stories based on fact have grown almost unrecognizable over the

years. Typical was an incident involving diminutive Jewish merchant "Cheap John," whom a bully supposedly killed for his boots. The author neglected to mention that the provocation was actually a debt owed the accused murderer, who sweated for his life before a jury decided that evidence for a conviction was lacking. And after a saloon shootout where two bystanders fell dead, people went about their business—until the next day, when townspeople circulated a petition expressing their disgust and remorse over the senseless tragedy.[2]

The readiness of both writers and readers to believe images of gratuitous violence and a society out of control have formed an important part of the self-perception that West Texans hold dear. Their forebears certainly suffered violence and endured a longer and more tumultuous period of formative development than did most pioneers, yet the ordinary experiences of westering also shaped their identity. Many local people who know their history—and many do—will tell you that men, women, and children had been trying to gain a foothold on the edge of Comanchería for more than two decades before the buffalo hunters ever arrived at the Clear Fork of the Brazos.

After the U.S. Army had built, occupied, and abandoned the dismal Fort Phantom Hill following the Mexican War, Lieutenant Colonel Robert E. Lee helped establish its short-lived successor, Camp Cooper, where he patrolled for renegade Comanches. On an adjoining reservation the Indians' docile and defeated kinsmen struggled to survive until settlers ran them *and* the federal troops off just before the Civil War. For a decade afterward, the reinvigorated tribe, joined by hostile Kiowas, tried desperately to push the interlopers off their former home and hunting grounds.

To the Anglos, nature seemed to have conspired with the Indian raiders, at times withholding rain and otherwise generally frustrating them. But Texans eventually learned how to adapt to this unfamiliar and unyielding land. It is this conquest of the Plains Indians and the tenuous subjugation of nature that Clear Fork country people celebrate in their Fandangle. The brief and fleeting heyday of Fort Griffin is an important and colorful part of the production, but their history is much larger in scope—a home-grown version of Manifest Destiny affected by the tenacity of the conquerors and their resilience in the face of many setbacks.

In few places is the continuity between past and present more obvious than in the Clear Fork country. It is readily evident in the land, in many places reclaiming what it grudgingly conceded: here, patches of an old highway with weeds breaking through; there, a weathered farmhouse half toppled over. Except for the stone remains of the combination Masonic lodge and schoolhouse, the town of Fort Griffin is gone entirely.

The business climate also presents an unbroken story in cycles of prosperity and ruin. The same economic forces that felled old Griffin have taken Albany on a fiscal roller-coaster ride of railroad booms, cotton booms, oil booms, highway booms—and a bust for every one. Even society has clung to many of the values that guided it more than a century ago. The Old South, from which many first-comers pushed their cattle right up to the edge of the plains, reaches deep into the largely Anglo population. The people are conservative in politics and fundamentalist in religion, yet also characterized by a casual informality. More forward-looking than self-searching, they are realists out of necessity and dreamers from seeing once poor neighbors become wealthy off everything from harvesting buffalo bones to finding oil.

Today, along the road from the county seat at Albany to the ruins of Fort Griffin, the countryside beyond the barbed wire and cattle guards looks much the same as it did to Fort Worth editor B. B. Paddock, who traveled through the Clear Fork country in 1879. Observing the "rugged steeps and verdure clad ridges," he proclaimed that "Shackelford County will long remain the home of the cowboy." And indeed it has. On one of the same scenic overlooks that the newspaperman lauded, Marlboro posed a slicker-clad cowboy cupping his hands against the wind to light a cigarette. The man and the place are fitting counterparts, raw, austere, and somewhat tortured looking. The image the company portrays is that of a "man's land," a place magnificent in its immensity, with a sky that composes as much of the scenery as the rolling plains and mesas.[3]

If visitors wonder whether native West Texans are being sarcastic when they call this harsh place "God's Country," they need only be here in the spring to see a tornado threaten to dip from the greenish black clouds, or on an early summer evening when lightning illuminates the countryside, or on a winter day when a bracing blue norther sweeps in from the treeless plains. Such spectacles reassure religious-minded men and women who is really in charge.

The Clear Fork country is indeed a land of extremes. In 1978 Albany set the Texas record for the most rain in a single day: over twenty-nine inches. The land periodically suffers droughts, too, sometimes receiving hardly any rain at all. In years when nature smiles, crops grow high and cattle, hogs, and sheep grow fat. Rusting farm implements, weed-filled cowpens, and the remnants of feebly turning windmills attest that occasionally nature turns its back as well.[4]

The inhabitants' love-hate affair with the land has inspired both efforts to change it and efforts to protect it, but most, ever mindful of nature's sovereignty, are happy just to make a living. The same man who has preserved the stone and picket homes of first-comers and tucks his pump jacks behind the hills to keep from disturbing the natural setting occasionally hangs dead coyotes to bare-branched trees as if they were Christmas ornaments. He sees nothing duplicitous about his actions; he is a rancher and his animals cannot coexist with the predators. Bison, bears, mustangs, and other wildlife were not as resilient as the coyotes and long ago vanished before the advance of the determined and industrious people who accompanied the rancher's forebears.

The stingy land, however, turned back more pioneers than it accommodated. Men and women who quit the land and returned to the interior would have thought it inconceivable that near the ruins of old Fort Phantom Hill, abandoned by the army for lack of water and timber, a reservoir bearing the fort's name would help supply over a hundred thousand people in Abilene. The land nevertheless at times reminds the present occupants of their limits. At a recent soldiers' reenactment at Fort Griffin, a man lost a horse and almost drowned while crossing the swollen Clear Fork. Doing things the old way, he learned, still carries old-fashioned risks.

The tenuous hold on the country is never more apparent than when prairie fires race across the landscape. In 1988 a particularly fierce conflagration swept toward Albany from more than twenty miles away, fortunately playing out before reaching town. Businesswoman Stacy Dees, flying back to Dallas from Midland-Odessa, remarked how insignificant the town looked, "as if it could have been erased like writing on a chalkboard." A similar blaze once stirred a man on the ground to compare the sound of a prairie fire to "the beating of a heavy surf on a rock-bound coast." An "irresistible billow of fire" could ascend "fifty or more feet into the air," he exclaimed, and travel "at a rate of twenty miles an hour." Such events were more frequent in earlier times when the prairie grass grew unchecked; the on-site description, in fact, was written by cavalryman H. H. McConnell just after the Civil War.[5]

Just as the fickle land beckoned and then turned back many hopeful immigrants, the capricious economy has made and broken the fortunes of countless others. Most of the people who settled here were impelled westward by decision makers in places far removed from West Texas. When men in a New York boardroom signed papers, an overland mail company and passenger service set up a relay station at the Clear Fork crossing to assist stage coaches traveling back and forth between Saint Louis and California; when generals in Washington, D.C., placed pins in maps, forts began popping up along the western frontier of Texas a hundred miles beyond the line of settlement; and when legislators in Austin pounded a gavel, colonists from as far away as the Ohio Valley rolled their wagons right up to the edge of the plains to claim free lands. Even lately, when Middle Easterners embargoed oil, crews of "doodlebuggers"—seismic explorers—combed the land to find reserves that earlier oilmen had missed.

Yet every time, pockets ran empty or the unforeseen hands of progress dashed the plans of businesspeople. A trip through the Clear Fork country provides a historical tour of erstwhile business cycles. Most recently a trend toward consolidation is evinced in

Leftover from busts and changing times: wooden oil rig. (Photo by author)

the bolted doors of the empty telephone company building in Albany. The efficiency of computers and a dispassionate "bottom line" left little to justify that personal touch of keeping a presence in the small towns. And the nearby Ford dealership sells only used cars these days; it cannot compete with lots in larger towns. A generation earlier the Aztec Theater closed when television and improved roads provided quick access into Abilene. Down the street the faded words "Albany Ice House" on another vacant building attest to the technological progress of an even earlier era. Booms and busts in the oil patch have characterized the times, too. On the edge of town a historical marker tells the story of a steel drilling rig that shoots skyward as if awaiting the return of roughnecks from a break. A few miles farther down the road is a much older rig, lying prostrate, its cables awry and wooden frame rotting where its crew abandoned it a half-century ago.

Also left to nature are several derelict farmhouses that survived the Great Depression but did not quite make it into the bed-and-breakfast era. And the majestic Shackelford County courthouse—*1883* carved over its limestone archways—has grown comfortably worn since the day when townspeople dedicated their new depot, heralding the arrival of the railroad. Beside the Cisco highway the trackless roadbed appears suddenly in places and vanishes in others; granite and concrete supports that once buttressed bridges suggest that promoters thought the railroad would be a permanent fixture. Traces of the Western Trail and the Butterfield stage and military roads are more evident from the air. At old Fort Griffin a few crumbling stone structures line the edge of the parade ground; upriver nothing is left of Camp Cooper except a springhouse and a residence that a local gunman fashioned from the abandoned officers' quarters. The picket cabin of a pioneer who settled here before the Civil War was dismantled and reassembled at an Albany park; a rusting iron salt vat that he used to refine the precious mineral rests beside it. Except for arrowheads that turn up every so often, the Clear Fork country's first inhabitants left nary a vestige of their centuries-long occupancy.

Ironically, the physical evidence of business and personal failures that so poignantly communicates the region's heritage has provided Albany's latest economic revival. Part of its charm is this state of arrested development, complemented by rejuvenated structures that townspeople have lovingly rescued from the elements. Some local businessmen, for example, have recently given the Aztec another chance and are finding alternative uses for other downtown buildings.

Nothing, however, evokes nostalgia more than Fort Griffin, the least typical but the most easily recognizable spot on the former Northwest Texas frontier. Twice a year people gather at the fort to reenact skirmishes. The state maintains the grounds and also keeps a herd of longhorns in an adjoining park. Although ambitious plans to reconstruct the town fell through during the Great Depression, the Fandangle nevertheless preserves its memory. A restaurateur purchased one of the village's last establishments, a false-fronted merchandising store, and moved it to Albany, where it now sits next to an apocryphal re-creation of the notorious Bee Hive Saloon.

Other attractions at the county seat, such as the Old Jail Art Center, antique and crafts stores, a Texana and Western book shop, and bed and breakfasts, keep visitors occupied. Many come just to enjoy the slow pace of life and to walk around town and see the distinctly western homes as well as business houses that suggest town fathers once aspired to greater ambitions.

The focus on their heritage is no recent phenomenon, however; Clear Fork people have staged the Fort Griffin Fandangle since 1938, often at great personal sacrifice. The stirring musical production, performed on an expansive outdoor stage overlooking Albany, expresses the local people's self-perception of conquest and settlement at the edge of the plains. Residents from infants to the elderly take part; even some nonresident members of old-time families return once a year to participate. The pageant is utilitarian history that engenders a love of land and culture. Steeped in myth and admittedly shaped by the rose-colored reminiscences of old-timers, it underscores the triumphs of Anglo stockraising families, town builders, and other settlers against the Indians, outlaws, and elements. Like an old man whose grandchildren have gathered around his feet to hear him spin yarns about his youth, the play tells an idyllic story that winnows out any hurtful details that might bring shame or discomfort to its listeners.[6]

During a recent Fandangle production, mounted cowboys sang their usual song of the open range amid a small collection of longhorns borrowed from the Fort Griffin State Park. And as usual they afterward shooed away the herd for the square dance number. Only this time, the troupe bounded onto the stage to face an imposing meadow muffin left by one of the animals in the middle of the arena. The dancers did not dare remove it; they could, however, avoid the unpleasant obstacle—and they did, for a while. They stepped gingerly around it, the crowd focusing on the dropping, wondering if a sudden whirl would send a billowing skirt spinning over it. But the seasoned hoofers, their pattern upset, tolerated only a few awkward do-si-dos before damning the stool with that "indomitable western spirit," and then proceeded aggressively with their routine. By the time the number was over, the pattie was trampled into the ground and embedded into the boots of the dancers. It was still there; the smell, in fact, reached several rows into the stands. But it was out of sight and soon forgotten.

For many Anglos, a similarly nettlesome problem has plopped down on the stage of history. As a racially sensitive society has emerged in the past generation or so, the traditional interpretation of Anglo hegemony in the West has come under fire. Historians have irrevocably broadened the story of convergence among Anglos, Native Americans, Hispanics, African Americans, and other groups to encompass the experiences of the conquered and subordinated peoples and to restore to them a measure of dignity. Anglos have reacted to the multicultural backlash by retreating behind the aegis of myth, arguing that because it defines *their* ethos, distortions of fact are perfectly acceptable. Yet stepping around this volatile issue has become increasingly awkward.

The history of the Anglos' ascension at the expense of other races, however, should not be judged by late-twentieth-century values. Just as scholars have looked objectively at the Comanches' reduction of the people who occupied this land before them, so too should scholars be able to look dispassionately at the succeeding conquest. Late-nineteenth-century notions of "frontiering," Manifest Destiny, and white superiority do not excuse, but do largely explain, the formative development of the West. A sense of closure certainly lends perspective to the experience, separating the participants from their descendants. On the other hand, addressing the legacy of conquest is very complex, because race and attitude undeniably connect the people who fought over the land and the people who inhabit the land today.

In the century following the Anglo expansion into the Clear Fork country, the victors' attitudes changed little. With the memory of stolen stock, burned-out homes and fields, and women and children carried into captivity still fresh in 1876, real estate developers at a village near Albany triumphantly advertised that "city lots are staked for sale Above Old Indian graves."[7]

Ninety-four years later, in 1970, a local stock raiser dedicated a historical marker for a ranch house with a speech extolling the triumph of "the people of the open range." Reaffirming the attitude of the frontier land agents, he proclaimed: "I personally am glad the Comanches are not still running buffalo here—I am glad WE are here."

Lately, however, the "WE" has become clouded. Certainly he was referring to white ranchers who followed their stock onto the grasslands. But what about the handful of former slaves who came West and settled among them? A few died at the hands of Indian raiders while supporting the Anglo expansion. African American buffalo soldiers of the U.S. Army, many who stayed and made the Clear Fork country their home, also helped. Even "Yankee" troops who rotated in and out of various companies assigned to Fort Griffin were part of the conquest. Nor can the role of the Tonkawa Indians be ignored. Mortal enemies of the Comanches, their scouts rode with soldiers and settlers alike. And women, their presence so easily subordinated in this "man's land," helped sustain the expansion. Figuring out just who "WE" were is not so easy anymore.

Since that 1970 speech, Anglos in the Clear Fork country— including the proud rancher himself—have demonstrated more social progressiveness than in the previous hundred years. Cultural chauvinism still exists, of course, but probably in no greater proportion than in any region where the inhabitants are pre-dominantly of one ethnicity. The outlook and activities of many residents, however, suggest that attitudes are changing. Curators at the Old Jail Art Center have lately showcased the work of African Americans. And even though one of the Fandangle's singing cowboys still glibly brags, "I dusted off a few redskins," writers have at least edited from the script a drunken Tonkawa woman who had provided comic relief by stumbling in and out of scenes attempting to beg or steal drinks. During the 1993 parade that preceded the pageant, two "buffalo soldiers" represented Fort Griffin's black troops for the first time—accompanied by an

occasional ripple of respectful applause. Clearly, the insular leanings
of the dominant culture have been breached by the same magazines,
periodicals, cable television, and educational enlightenment that
affect the rest of the nation.

As in any distinctive region, people in the Clear Fork country
and West Texas in general are products of both tradition and a
society in perpetual transition. A strong identity with the frontier
era still bridges their world view and life-styles in music, dress,
language, and art; the sense of continuity also persists in the boom
and bust economy and the hardships of living in a harsh land. At
the same time, the enhanced cultural awareness suggests that
residents here are beginning to acknowledge the closure that marks
the region's formative development. But, as the Fandangle
illustrates, they are still somewhat unwilling to let go of their
romantic and Anglocentric past.

This particular story encompasses the same years as the annual
pageant but takes a more comprehensive and objective look at the
history of this region. Like the meadow muffin that briefly upset
the square dancers, the facts may appear at times unpleasant. Some
local people may well greet with a measure of indignation passages
regarding their forebears' reduction of American Indian peoples—
allies as well as enemies—along with such shameful episodes as
the Clear Fork's vigilante movement. Knowing fully, however, the
costs of cultural imperialism, or Anglo hegemony, and the roles
of all the participants can only make their story of conquest and
cultural ascension more interesting and meaningful.

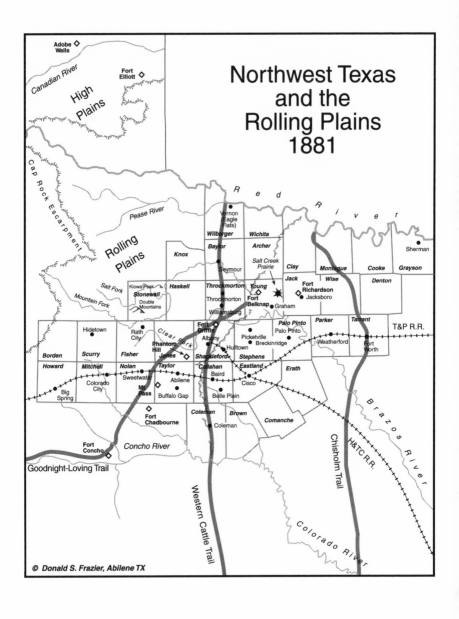

Northwest Texas and the Rolling Plains 1881

Adobe Walls

Canadian River

Fort Elliott

High Plains

Cap Rock Escarpment

Rolling Plains

Pease River

Red River

Sherman

Vernon (Eagle Flats)

Wilbarger   Wichita

Baylor   Archer   Clay   Montague   Cooke   Grayson

Knox   Salt Creek Prairie   Jack   Wise   Denton

Salt Fork   Seymour

Kiowa Peak   Haskell   Throckmorton   Young   Fort Richardson   Jacksboro

Mountain Fork   Stonewall   Throckmorton   Fort Belknap   Graham

Double Mountains   Williamsburg

Fort Griffin   Palo Pinto   Parker   Tarrant

Hidetown   Clear Fork   Albany   Picketville   Breckinridge   Palo Pinto   Weatherford   Fort Worth   T&P R.R.

Rath City   Phantom Hill   Hulltown

Borden   Scurry   Fisher   Jones   Shackleford   Stephens

Howard   Mitchell   Nolan   Taylor   Callahan   Eastland   Erath

Colorado City   Sweetwater   Baird   Cisco

Big Spring   Abilene   Belle Plain

Mt. Pass   Buffalo Gap

Coleman   Brown   Comanche

Fort Chadbourne   Coleman

Fort Concho   Concho River

Goodnight-Loving Trail

Western Cattle Trail

Chisholm Trail

H&TC.R.R.

Brazos River

Colorado River

© Donald S. Frazier, Abilene TX

CHAPTER ONE
MIGHT MAKES RIGHT, 1849–1859

T HE LAND BEYOND the Texas prairies had piqued the curiosity of Anglos long before they took an interest in occupying it. For many years Indian scouts, Chihuahuan traders, hunters, travelers, and adventurers painted vague images of a wondrous region alternately blessed and cursed by nature. Then, after 1849, when U.S. Army soldier-explorer Randolph B. Marcy led an expedition through West Texas, any number of accounts seemed all at once to popularide this unfamiliar country. New York newspaperman William B. Parker, who returned with Marcy on a follow-up expedition, remarked, "Why is it that no one returns from the plains disappointed? It is because their anticipations have been doubly realized."[1]

Parker described a magical land of contrasts and contradictions: a place "oppresively hot" yet cooled by a "delicious breeze"; where rivers and creeks existed in abundance and "not one in fifty having any water in it;" where "large slabs of sandstone . . . poised upon pencils of red clay," resembling "the ruins of the Parthenon," mercifully broke the dull monotony of the flat plains; where one day he might enjoy a fresh, dripping spring and the next despair over "some rainwater in a hole filled with snakes and green scum."[2]

On one particular evening that found the expedition marching to escape the scorching heat of the day, Parker described being caught between a prairie fire and a thunderstorm. "On one side a pillar of fire—on the other a pillar of cloud—and the wilderness in between," he commented dramatically. Later inhabitants might have found Parker's entry a fitting analogy for the alluring but perilous land itself. The same wonders of nature that overawed the newspaperman overwhelmed hopeful settlers. Few, in fact, would realize their anticipations as Parker promised. If the land was sometimes generous and at other times miserly, it always possessed an abundance of disappointment.[3]

When westward-moving Anglos first cast their eyes toward Northwest Texas, the native people were already in retreat. Scarcely three decades of contact with these Texans had upset patterns of living that the Penateka, or Southern, Comanches had enjoyed for well over a century. Their extended tribal alliance, stretching into Indian Territory and Kansas, was beginning to fragment. Alcoholism and other social pressures as well as disease and the destruction of their game provoked a cultural upheaval. Many of the destitute survivors surrendered both morally and spiritually. The more willful either pledged to take up farming or tried to reassert their dominance by steeling themselves against the interlopers' advance. But as the Comanches plummeted along both courses toward a cultural perigee, the vanguard of strangers to this land determined to brush them aside. Like the fickle land, the original inhabitants exacted a much larger price than the conquerors had envisioned.

Not even four decades earlier, when in the 1820s American immigrants first gained a foothold in Texas, the Comanches had been the undisputed rulers of the Southern Plains—the lower third of the great American grasslands that stretched into Canada. But these Indians had only arrived at the beginning of the eighteenth century to challenge the Apaches. During the 1720s Comanche warriors won the first of many battles between the two tribes. By the early years of the next century they had all but evicted the Apaches from the vast buffalo range and served notice to the Spaniards as well. As the "Lords of the Plains" rolled both enemies steadily southward—beyond the Red River, the Brazos, and even the Colorado—"Comanchería," in the graceful script of cartographers, burgeoned over wider swaths of parchment.[4]

The Comanches, their life-style well suited to the plains, were also well situated. For more than a century their consonance with the land helped them to resist the encroachments of Spaniards,

French, Mexicans, and Anglos. But more importantly, even before the Europeans' challenge, the Comanches' ascendancy over this immense and largely treeless land left them strategically located. For a people who measured their wealth in horses and their prestige in the honors of war, none grew richer or more distinguished than the Comanches. They raided Spanish corrals on one side and traded with the French for guns on the other. Material goods certainly begat power, but the "low utility" of the land equally deflected their white rivals and prolonged the tribe's predominance.[5]

Until mid-century, Anglo efforts to remove the Comanches lacked a singleness of purpose, largely because the expanding culture had expressed little interest in the unfamiliar country beyond the treeline. The landscape changed imperceptibly as families pushed outward from Fort Worth and the Grand Prairie through the Western Cross Timbers. Immigrants encountered less water, fewer trees, and lighter ground cover the farther west they came, until finally they reached the Rolling Plains on the Southern Plains' lower edge—an immense and almost treeless mosaic of grassy seas, broken here by undulating hills, there by rocky mesas, and everywhere scarred by dry river beds, crags, and canyons. A Southern woman, long accustomed to mornings filled with the "sound of axes and the merry songs of the colored race," remarked that on the edge of the plains "there was no sound to greet my ears but the howling of wolves and other kindred animals." She learned quickly that the habits and routines of life in this country contrasted sharply with those to which she was accustomed.[6]

When Randolph B. Marcy established a trail into the plains in 1849, he made note of this geographical and institutional fault. East of the Cross Timbers, he reported, are "numerous spring brooks, with a great abundance of good timber, and a productive soil." On the other side, however, were "but few feeble streams . . . and these are generally absorbed a short distance from their sources."[7]

An important exception was the Clear Fork of the Brazos, "a bold clear stream of sweet water" with a valley that in places stretched over two miles in width. Beyond its well-timbered banks, Marcy crowed, was a rolling prairie covered by "a luxuriant growth of grass." He also praised the "brilliant yellow hue" of sunflowers that spread over the entire country as well as the "cool fresh water springbrooks" that fed the river. Such sights inspired the explorer to pen an immigrants' guide, *The Prairie Traveler*, designed to impel settlers to the edge of the plains. But this land that Marcy found so inviting could show a harsher face. Another army officer would attest shortly afterward that "the Clear Fork no longer deserves its title, but is converted into fetid stagnant pools." Hopeful settlers who counted on a plentiful water supply upon reading the explorer's exhortations learned the hard way that 1849 had been a wet year.[8]

The Penateka Comanches, who made their home below the Red River, did not share the Anglos' bewilderment with the land. As long as game was plentiful and they could supplement their subsistence by stealing from the Texans, the line between the plains and the prairie made little difference to them. And they, too, found the Clear Fork country a favorite spot. Throughout the valley, in fact, Captain Marcy had found "numerous remains of old Comanche camps."[9]

Those of Buffalo Hump, a chief of the most bellicose Penatekas at the time of Marcy's arrival, were no doubt among the ones that the explorer observed. Truly a son of the Clear Fork, the warlord had entertained emissaries of Texas President Sam Houston along its banks and ventured from there to take part in numerous treaty councils with the former republic. In his native language he was Porchanaquaheap, "Buffalo Penis." The Anglos' sense of propriety, however, neutered the "strong medicine" of the chief's proud name, leaving him the innocuous and inoffensive sobriquet. In an earlier era Buffalo Hump might have taken his place among the great Comanche war chiefs, but he was a product of his times, and the forces of change overwhelmed him. During the days of the Texas Republic he had demonstrated wisdom in council, shrewdness in action, and ferocity in battle. As Anglo expansion claimed more and more of Comanchería, and the ruinous effects of contact took their toll, he grew increasingly desperate and rash, taking expediencies that no doubt caused him some shame.[10]

In that earlier time, German scientist Ferdinand Roemer had visited the Penateka camp of Buffalo Hump. He noted that others wore the regalia of the white man, but this chief "scorned European clothes." A buffalo robe around his waist provided his only protection against the sun. His hair, long and black, hung straight down, perhaps coated with the "dusky reddish clay" of the Rolling Plains or the fat of a buffalo. He adorned his arms with brass rings and wore a string of beads around his neck. "Buffalo Hump," remarked the scientist, "was the genuine picture of the North American Indian."[11]

It was in 1844 at Tehuacana Creek, near present-day Mexia, that Buffalo Hump first demonstrated his diplomatic savvy. Sam Houston had called a great council to repair the damage of the Lamar years, when genocide against the Indians was the prevailing policy. The Texans even offered to set a permanent frontier line and establish trading posts to supply the Indians. Buffalo Hump, however, discerned the significance of Houston's proposals even more clearly than did the older chiefs who had allowed him to join the assembly. He knew every village along the Anglo vanguard and understood that if the tribe allowed the Texans to establish posts beyond them, settlers would follow and new towns would surely arise. He pledged to respect the fragile peace, but he asserted the right of his people to inhabit the land. Buffalo Hump rejected the line that Houston proposed, complaining that it cut too deeply into the buffalo range. He reluctantly accepted the trading posts, however, knowing fully how dependent on the white man's goods the Penatekas had grown.[12]

This treaty, like almost every other agreement, demonstrated why the two races could never cement better relations. Cultural differences in executive decision making led each side to sense treachery in the proposals of the other. Each side also demanded more concessions than it could possibly expect, and the result was an almost constant state of warfare. The Comanches, moreover, certainly did not understand the vicissitudes that attended changes in Indian policy between the administrations of presidents Sam Houston and Mirabeau B. Lamar. On the other hand, Anglo settlers failed to appreciate the loose political structure that failed to bind all the Comanches to the promises made by a particular band. Perhaps neither side took seriously the treaties made by their signatories, but the Indians enjoyed receiving presents, and the Texans invited the hollow concessions that served as a pretext for seizing new land.[13]

While both sides enjoyed periods of relative calm, a permanent peace, of course, was illusory. The Plains Indians who attended councils like the one at Tehuacana Creek rarely represented all of the Penateka bands, much less the more hostile Northern Comanches. White traders dealing in stolen horses easily pandered to impetuous warriors on both sides of the Red River. The young native men, hoping to gain a reputation, recruited kinsmen in Texas camps, flouting the warnings of conciliatory chiefs such as Old Owl and Santa Anna. Those beyond the Red River had little reason to halt raids along the frontier; it was their supply line on the road to Mexico. Even Buffalo Hump enjoyed an occasional foray across the Rio Grande, often pausing to secure provisions, and sometimes scalps, from Texan settlers.[14]

For pioneers living along the expanding western border of Texas, Indian depredations were not just fodder for campfire tales but also an ever-present danger. Vivid accounts of babies dragged behind horses through prickly pears, of old women raped and scalped and pinned to the ground, and of men emasculated and disemboweled kept settlers on constant alert. Even though few families experienced death or captivity, even fewer remained entirely untouched by rapine. Many endured thefts, others survived skirmishes, and everyone, it seemed, knew someone who could tell firsthand of a gruesome killing. Such a precarious life stunted the growth of a land already disadvantaged by nature.

The fear of Indian atrocities had bedeviled Texans long before they had won their independence, prompting a succession of leaders to address the issue of frontier defense. Stephen F. Austin had commissioned the first mounted rangers in 1823, and although the organization grew with the task at hand, the new Republic clearly needed a more formidable first line of defense. The prohibitive cost for a series of forts inspired politicians to promote schemes for some sort of buffer colony. After rejecting a plan to place eight thousand French settlers along the hinterland, a more realistic proposal—the Peters Colony—captured legislators' attention in 1841.[15]

Many envisioned the Peters Colony as a panacea that would soften expansion into the Indian lands, protect the interior settlements, and raise land values. A grant of vast proportions, it stretched from east of Dallas to near present-day Abilene. By design, only settlers from outside of Texas—largely from the Ohio Valley—would receive land, but the intrigues of politicians, speculators, and squatters opened much of the colony to anyone brave enough to challenge the Indians and the elements.[16]

The Peters Colony affected the development of North Texas profoundly, but its influence faded at the western border of the grant. In 1850, for example, colonists comprised 75 percent of the population in Tarrant County, but only one man, Englishman Thomas Lambshead, had dared test the edge of the plains. The colony nevertheless propelled the first pioneers right up to the treeline years before the area would otherwise have attracted the attention of prospective settlers. Men and women who ventured into this country in the 1850s demonstrated the liabilities of underestimating the land and its inhabitants. While Captain Marcy had lauded the well-watered and "verdant herbage" of the Clear Fork country, hopeful farmers quickly learned that it was no Eden. And the Comanches, as another observer described, may have appeared "ugly, crooked-legged . . . squalid and dirty," but they would not be pushed to Indian Territory on a "trail of tears."[17]

As the frontier line creeped ever westward during the 1840s, Buffalo Hump and other warriors grew increasingly intractable. The chief remonstrated against the casual trespass of the Comanchería, venting his frustration by occasionally raiding exposed pioneers who, he could claim, had violated territorial agreements. When the United States assumed responsibility for arbitrating the clash between the races, Buffalo Hump rejected an overture to go to Washington with elder Penateka chief Santa Anna and a delegation from other tribes. Upon returning, the leaders held a grand intertribal meeting to distribute the presents they had received. Buffalo Hump, however, showed his confederates that he was capable of collecting his own booty. Rather than appearing at the council, he staged a raid on Mexico that netted prisoners, plunder, and over a thousand horses.[18]

Such actions led other chiefs to suspect Buffalo Hump's judgment, but his perspicuity remained as sharp as ever. After Texas joined the United States, he niggled with federal Indian agents just as he had parlayed with representatives of the former republic. Always he remained aloof and defiant. Referring to previous agreements with the Texans, he complained to U.S. Indian agent Robert S. Neighbors about the continual trespassing into and wanton disregard for the Comanchería. "The commissioners of our great father," he reminded Neighbors, "promised to keep these people out of our country." He alleged that the white men now refused to draw a permanent frontier line because they planned to build towns and settle on Comanche land.[19]

Everywhere the chief saw evidence of such designs. Forty-niners heading for California disregarded the tribe's sovereignty as well as their own safety. They crossed the plains on well-marked trails and no trails at all. From San Antonio, the Santa Fe Trail, and places in between they moved westward, living off the land. Indians from dislocated eastern tribes came, too. Some old Texas neighbors such as the Wichitas, Wacos, Tawakonis, Tonkawas, and Lipan Apaches took advantage of the chaos to repay ancient grievances against the Comanches. They wandered across the Rolling Plains, indiscriminately slaughtering the game on which the Penatekas subsisted. Frequently they raided settlers' stock, blaming the thefts on the Comanches. Other, more "civilized" tribes—Delawares, Shawnees, Seminoles, Cherokees, Kickapoos, and various Caddoan remnants—wandered in and out of West Texas from lands set aside for them. Well-armed with the best European weapons and tutored by the Anglos in double-dealing and Indian fighting, these native people proved more than a match for the Southern Comanches. They also delighted in keeping the plains bands in a constant state of near paranoia by passing them wild rumors of "imminent" Anglo treachery.[20]

The effete influences of these foreign cultures also broke down Comanche traditions. Captain Marcy, in fact, commented in 1849 that the Penatekas had grown familiar with the "customs and habits of the white man," but that "they unfortunately only see fit to adopt such as are detrimental to them." Adversaries that the Panatekas could not battle—smallpox and cholera as well as alcoholism and tribal fragmentation—proved even more formidable than their flesh-and-blood enemies.[21]

These devastating troubles were compounded by a decade-long hiatus when the bison disappeared from the Southern Plains. Anglo expansion beyond the Arkansas River along with drought and the introduction of livestock diseases had disrupted the animals' migration patterns, but to the Penatekas it seemed as if nature were punishing them for straying onto the "white man's path." After the bison deserted their southern range sometime between the Mexican War and the Civil War, the Texas Comanches had to subsist on lesser game such as antelope and deer—elusive targets for the limited range of bowmen. Hunger broke down their independence, driving the Penatekas to seek peace with the white interlopers. Even Buffalo Hump grew conciliatory. Shortly after Marcy's first entrada into the Rolling Plains, the chief guided an expedition to El Paso in return for gifts. A passionate medicine song, designed to impress the guests in his camp, only bemused them. Former Ranger Captain "Rip" Ford wrote that the performance "stirred up recollections of boyhood—the calling of hogs, the plaintive notes of a solitary bull frog, the bellowing of a small bull."[22]

In 1851 the advance that Buffalo Hump had feared became an alarming reality when the U.S. Army set up a new line of forts that penetrated the Rolling Plains. The new configuration leap-frogged a hundred miles beyond Fort Worth, which the army had established just two years earlier. The federal government had assumed the Texans' responsibility for protecting the frontier, and with the end of the Mexican War a general feeling prevailed that battle-seasoned troops would arrive to support the Anglo expansion.

The line of forts going up that year seemed imposing. Stretching northeasterly from just above Eagle Pass on the Rio Grande to a site near present-day Abilene, Texas, they included Forts Clark, Terrett, McKavett, Mason, Chadbourne, and Phantom Hill. Fort Belknap, between Phantom Hill and Fort Worth, bolstered the ambitious cordon.[23]

The ill-fated Fort Phantom Hill lay far beyond what was then the natural boundary of settlement. Even General William G. Belknap reported that "it is not probable that white settlements will be made [there] for a century to come, if ever." A young lieutenant, Clinton Lear, wrote to his wife Mary of the land's natural beauty, "alive with deer, turkey & bear," but grieved, "It is a pity that so pretty a position should be destitute of the other requisite advantages." Less than a week on this "barren waste" convinced him that this land was singularly unsuitable as the location for a new post. He complained that in five days his detachment had been unable to gather enough timber to erect even a small log hut. And the situation grew worse. Numerous hardships—isolation, monotony, and brackish water—tormented the troops incessantly.[24]

On sight, Phantom Hill certainly failed to intimidate the Comanches and other tribes who occasionally visited this plains bastion. Between 150 and 200 infantrymen occupied the bleak outpost, which lay naked before the searing summer heat and arctic blasts of winter. The garrison included mostly untrained recruits, although a few "old soldiers" filled out the ranks. Most of the largely foot-bound troops, many dressed in ill-fitted overalls and jackets, carried only percussion muskets. W. G. Freeman, who inspected the line of defenses, noted that "upwards of fifty recruits appeared on parade *without arms.*" He also remarked that "no post . . . except Fort Ewell"—surrounded by a salt marsh in the South Texas desert—"provided fewer attractions." Although he found both officers and enlisted men living in dilapidated "pole huts," the troops eventually managed to erect a handful of structures from native limestone. Several miles from Phantom Hill an intermittent stream and a "black jack thicket" provided the fort's only water and fuel. About the only thing the men enjoyed in abundance was an ample supply of provisions. On hand was fifty thousand pounds of salted meat—more than that at any of the other posts—and "an equal quantity of beef on the hoof." Weighing all considerations, Freeman concluded that if another site nearby could be found without upsetting the line, "it would really be a charity to remove the garrison to it."[25]

Despite the army's incursion, relations between white man and Indian actually seemed promising in 1851, when poor health forced Jesse Stem to abandon his Ohio law practice and sound out his friends for opportunities in the West. His influential clique included future president Rutherford B. Hayes. Another powerful associate secured for Stem the authority to establish an "Agency for the Indians of Texas." Such appointments were notorious for enriching their holders, a fact that Stem grasped fully. "I intend to get some of Uncle Sams [sic] bounty," he wrote Hayes. He originally coveted a post in California for the "privileges" in a land then seized with gold fever. Although the position of Indian agent at this lonely outpost was no political plum, he crowed to his friends about the promise of imminent settlement and of his chances for gaining wealth and prestige.[26]

Stem had every reason to believe that the land would soon be occupied. Speculative fever was then beckoning pioneers to places throughout the West. The year he arrived on the Texas frontier, an Indiana editor, in a phrase later popularized by a more eminent peer, exhorted: "Go West young man, go West!" Many young men—and women—responded. The Oregon Trail became a busy highway. The Mexican Cession lands drew many settlers as well. The prevailing wisdom held that "rain follows the plow," and promoters' talk made places such as Kansas and Nebraska seem appealing. Settlers in Northwest Texas were pushing far beyond Fort Worth. Many Peters colonists obtained patents for large tracts as far west as the unorganized counties of Throckmorton and Shackelford. In Stem's estimation nothing stood in the way of westward movement. "The land investment," he trumpeted to Hayes, "is past all doubt."[27]

Early in 1852, Stem devised a plan for his agency, reading the situation carefully but in the context of how he could best realize his personal goals. He viewed with ambivalence the line of federal military posts strung along the length of the Texas frontier, assessing correctly the impotence of infantry in such a wide-open country. Confident that a change in strategy would "open all the intermediate country [between Forts Belknap and Phantom Hill] for location and settlement," he attempted to bridge relations between the military and the "wild tribes." Stem immediately established a farm that functioned as a sort of goodwill mission. As he envisioned it, the operation would buy peace with the natives and supply frontier troops with goods. The Indians, in fact, did not even have to settle at the reservation; Stem demonstrated his trust—or perhaps naïveté—by posting no soldiers.[28]

The natives peoples, especially the Comanches, seemed hardly an obstacle to the new Indian agent. He viewed the southern bands in his charge as representative of the tribe in general. Noticing evidence of alcoholism, malnutrition, and disease, Stem informed his wife that he expected to "have a good sized party of Indians hanging around me, anxious to be fed and clothed." He naturally scoffed at reports of atrocities, calling them exaggerations designed to further the interests of pioneers. "It would amuse you vastly," he wrote his friend Hayes, "to hear one of the knowing ones spin yarns about the Comanches." In 1852, after meeting some of his future charges on a trip to Fort Graham, above Waco, he professed to know as much about the Indians "as any Texan . . . and a leetle [sic] more."[29]

But Stem never saw the angry side of Buffalo Hump, much less the Northern Comanches who menaced life and property all along the Texas frontier. Raiding parties, passing through the agency, continued to appeal to their southern kinsmen to join them. Chief Ketumse, like Old Owl and Santa Anna before him, strived to prevail upon his villagers to resist such overtures, warning that the whites would "hold them to a strict accounting for any atrocities they may commit."[30]

Stem seemed more aroused by the prospect of scouting for desirable land than by the danger of recovering stolen horses. Perhaps he grew accustomed to the false alarms that sent the frontier into a panic during 1852. One of them, thoroughly unfounded, alleged that soldiers on the Clear Fork had been surrounded and killed. No wonder Stem dismissed a newspaper report of fifteen hundred warriors as being closer to sixty. "It is marvelous," he remarked incredulously, "how they lie about the Indians here."[31]

The same God who watches over children and fools crowned Stem's efforts with both peace and a bumper crop in 1852. The Southern Comanches seemed pleased, looking at the reservation as a kind of embassy. They received goods as intended and even saw the agent as a conduit for their grievances with the army for locating Fort Phantom Hill on the buffalo plains. Stem and a few of the Comanches even joined forces to recover some horses stolen by a band of Waco Indians. The next year the agent harvested another good crop and enjoyed another year of peaceful coexistence with the Penatekas.[32]

A sudden run of bad luck, however, erased Stem's quixotic designs in 1853. The Democrats, back in power with the election of Franklin Pierce, threatened to sweep out Fillmore's appointments. Stem's days as Indian agent were probably marked anyway. He wrote that he was ready to "resign in disgust" over poor relations with fellow frontier officials. More tragically, he became party to an incident that violated the precarious trust he had established with his charges. Ironically, renegade Wacos and Wichitas, rather than the normally volatile Comanches, provoked the affair.[33]

Early that winter the Indians had stolen horses from a dragoon company at Fort Croghan, northwest of Austin. Major Henry Hopkins Sibley pursued the thieves northward, but rather than remain on their trail, he made a beeline for Phantom Hill and then to the agency. Stem, whom he had befriended when the Ohioan was new to the frontier, sent runners to the Wichita village with Sibley's demands that the horses be returned and the thieves punished. Chief Koweaka and a band of Wichitas responded by trailing a small herd of worthless mounts to the agency. On a bearskin rug spread upon the ground, the chief bargained with the major to no avail. An outfit of dragoons, on Sibley's signal, emerged from a nearby thicket and seized the entire Indian delegation. After unsuccessfully entreating Sibley to let him return home and negotiate with the renegades, Koweaka decided to play the martyr. He awaited nightfall, then stabbed his compliant wife and son through their hearts and left them lying in their tent, safe from the imagined reprisals of their captors. He then sacrificed his own life in order that his men could escape.[34]

Stem returned briefly to Ohio in the wake of this affair, scheming to return and resume speculating and farming. Less than a year after the fatal incident, however, some nonreservation Indians bludgeoned him and a companion to death outside of Fort Belknap. A drought, moreover, ended the agricultural experiment, and the Northern Comanches renewed their raids across the Red River. Thus ended the sanguine chapter of bringing Anglo civilization to the edge of the plains. While Stem expected his trading post to anchor westward migration into the Clear Fork country, others approached more cautiously. They were dubious of peace and felt that two years of relative calm was but a brief respite in their protracted and checkered relationship with the Comanches.[35]

In 1853 the army's effort to maintain Fort Phantom Hill failed as well. Scarcely three years after it was founded, troops had endured enough of life at this untenable site and retreated farther up the Clear Fork. The last to leave reportedly set fire to the buildings in order to assure that they would not have to return. Northern Comanches presumed that their threat to the post commander—to "come and whip him . . . as soon as the grass greened for their horses"—prompted the abandonment. The military, however, had no intention of surrendering the land, nor did they have a choice.[36]

The Texans, upon entering the union, had forced a dilemma upon the federal government, bringing Indian policy to an impasse. Settlers had exploited the new frontier line, encroaching upon territory that officials at almost every level acknowledged belonged to various native tribes. Federal laws bound the army to protect both settlers and Indians. Texas, however, retained ownership of all its public lands, and after decades of fighting Mexicans on one

side and Indians on the other, citizens of the state were determined
to expand. If this meant that the army would have to erect forts
to protect them, then fine; if it meant that the U.S. government
would have to remove the native peoples altogether, then that was
fine, too. Either way, the state thrust the onus onto the federal
government. The United States thus became an unwilling accomplice in eradicating the Indians from Texas.

The policy that resulted from conflicting agendas was
predictably confusing. Officials in Washington and Austin seldom
sustained a coordinated plan; the mission of various departments
at every level seemed at times as if it were conducted in a vacuum.
The federal military command for the Department of Texas changed
frequently. Even though such strong-willed men as Albert Sidney
Johnston and Robert E. Lee eventually held the position, the War
Department in Washington had its own opinions regarding problems
on the frontier. At the same time, Texas often conducted its program
independently of the capricious federal government. Local
companies of minutemen, moreover, often composed of vengeful
firebrands, acted autonomously, damaging fragile relations between
the races. Even Indian agents, representing both the United States
and Texas, ranged from sympathizing activists to apathetic desk
jockeys. Appointees changed as often as the military, each seemingly
with a different view of his responsibility. Rather than easing frontier
tensions, these organizational layers actually exacerbated them.[37]

Nevertheless, when Jefferson Davis became secretary of war
in 1853, the federal policy designed late that year appeared as if
it would finally provide the leadership and resoluteness to solve
the problem once and for all. At the insistence of Robert S.
Neighbors, the federal government leased from Texas land for two
reservations; one just above the site of Stem's farm for the Southern
Comanches and the other downriver from Fort Belknap for the
semisedentary tribes. At the same time, he recruited a formidable
group of officers to complement the reservation policy. Among them
would be sixteen future Civil War generals. Their ranks included
the brilliant tactician William Joseph Hardee, who would earn fame
at Shiloh; Edmund Kirby Smith, who would surrender the last

rebel-held territory at the war's end; John Bell Hood, who would lead his men to disaster at Franklin, Tennessee; George Thomas, who would earn the nickname "Rock of Chickamauga"; and Albert Sidney Johnston and Robert E. Lee, who would command entire armies. Secretary Davis obviously selected the best men available; he appointed Johnston to lead the 750-man 2d Cavalry Regiment.[38]

In 1856 Johnston divided his strength. Among several adjustments, Camp Cooper—within the confines of the upper reservation—filled the void that Phantom Hill had left. Lieutenant Colonel Robert E. Lee took command of four cavalry companies there, doubling the strength of infantrymen already on hand. In contrast to the rag-tag dragoons, Lee's men were well armed and equipped. Each of his Camp Cooper companies consisted of men entirely from the same state. Even their horses were selected by color: Alabamans riding grays, Missourians on sorrels, Kentuckians astride bays, and Ohioans atop roans.[39]

This new federal strategy placed settlers, soldiers, and Indians side-by-side. Many of the native people at the lower reservation near Fort Belknap—remnants from East Texas and tribes of the South—welcomed the protection of troops. On the other hand, they feared marauding Plains Indians as well as settlers who might blame them for Comanche and Kiowa depredations. They also worried that the trickle of Anglo pioneers would become a flood like that which had already swept them this far. The former East Texas Indians kept the peace and tilled the soil, hopeful that the troops would protect them against encroachments on their reservation. And once again, the Southern Comanches acquiesced, this time pledging to settle down and adapt to an agricultural life.[40]

About one-fourth of the Penatekas—broken wraiths of the warriors who had terrorized the frontier—gathered at the Comanche reservation. The miserable bands that Jesse Stem had found in poor condition by now had lost any vestige of their fearsome attributes. About twelve hundred of the once horse-rich band rode into the reservation on a motley collection of spindly and rheumy-eyed nags. Their shabby clothing, a combination of traditional dress and articles acquired from Anglos, lent a quality of pathos to their appearance.

Some chiefs shaded themselves with umbrellas; a few warriors carried looking glasses. And they were starving. Everyone—women, children, warriors, and chiefs—begged unabashedly. For a quart of whiskey, even their leaders were willing to part with almost all their possessions. Before long the little village, about a hundred tipis scattered up and down the river, became littered with bones and refuse; swarms of flies hovered everywhere. Lethargy seized the people, too. About the only active inhabitants were small groups of malnourished children playing near the camp.[41]

Even Buffalo Hump would probably have arrived if not for an unfortunate rumor that induced the Penatekas to panic. Many of his people, along with those of the more tractable Chief Sanaco, were already on the reservation, and just as the two chiefs were preparing to lead others to the banks of the Clear Fork, an Indian trader at Fort Chadbourne confided to a warrior that "the white people were making plans to attack them and kill them all." At the chiefs' behest, scores of their followers, both those at the reservation and those on the way, fled for the open prairies. That winter they suffered terribly. Sanaco's band, some naked and almost all without arms, took refuge along the Red River and were reduced to eating their dogs and horses.[42]

Buffalo Hump retreated as well but at least kept in contact with the Indian agents. Once so inimical to the trappings of white men, he grew increasingly jaded and pathetic, accepting presents in return for promises to settle down, only to skulk off and launch feeble raids. The chief capped his ignominy when he appeared at a Caddoan village, threatening to attack unless their warriors agreed to cease scouting for the whites. Anadarko chief José María saw through the bluff and backed him down.[43]

At length Buffalo Hump crossed the Red River for good, but for those who remained, reservation life almost completed the destruction of the Penatekas that alcohol and forced assimilation had set in motion. The Comanches—like all Indians—had adopted European animals, weapons, and ways. But the gradual adaptation of things that improved the quality of their life was no different than the process that forced Anglos to adjust to life on the plains.

Borrowing from other cultures, in fact, was a universal tradition. In time the Penatekas might have resembled the Indians at the lower reservation, who possessed a longer record of contact. Changes thrust upon the band, however, stripped from them their identity, breaking traditions that had been adopted gradually.[44]

The troops and a few unscrupulous settlers routinely invited the Indians' corruption. Soldiers often supplied them whiskey, and others were more than willing to sell it to them. Briefly, during 1856, a man named Terry operated a trading post five miles from the reservation. There he dispensed liquor until one of Neighbors's subagents destroyed his supply, declaring the shop within a federal "intercourse boundary." The next year, too, agents put a man out of business after noticing that reservation Comanches coming from the direction of his shop seemed always to be drunk.[45]

Despite tribal decline and a general resistance to assimilation, many Penatekas made an earnest effort to adjust. By the autumn of 1856 the reserve's population had climbed to 557 after ebbing at 277, and a few had adopted Anglo clothing and had begun constructing crude cabins. Over the next two years they even tried to police themselves and develop a government suitable to their new life-style. Several children, moreover, even showed promise as students in a school run first by a D. Stimson and later by one Richard Sloan. The reservation Comanches had also gathered a herd of about three hundred cattle and had put two hundred acres in cultivation. Despite grasshoppers and drought, they harvested crops, however meager. In a letter to the commissioner of Indian affairs, Neighbors reported that "every old settler who has visited the reserve has remarked the improved condition of the Indians."[46]

Many of the settlers in the area who became familiar with the reservation Comanches considered them friends, even if the troops held them in contempt. On one occasion a drunken cavalryman rode through the reservation trying to trample an Indian; when later he died after falling over a cliff, soldiers accused the Indians of murdering him. Another time someone in Comanche disguise shot at a Lieutenant Biggs while he was lying in his bunk. Soldiers on the trail of the culprit headed directly for the Penateka village, paying little regard to the women and children scrambling to get out of the way. When a soldier actually did turn up dead, reservation Comanches again took the blame, even though evidence suggested the man was "beastly drunk and probably killed himself."[47]

The Indian village adjoining Camp Cooper was hardly an irritant to soldiers and settlers, much less the fountain of destruction that detractors claimed. Still, under Subagent Robert Baylor's direction, young warriors came and went as they pleased, arousing suspicions that they were wandering off to raid distant settlements. Non-reservation Indians also passed through the Clear Fork village, stealing horses, recruiting young warriors, and throwing blame on their innocent kinsmen. As if these troubles were not enough, unfamiliarity with a sedentary life presented its own problems. Impatient Indians plucked melons and ears of corn long before they were ripe. Others, contemptuous of farming, turned their horses loose in the fields. Partly as a result, malnutrition was a constant companion; venereal diseases, typhoid, and pneumonia visited frequently as well.[48]

When the Interior Department in 1855 assembled its staff to reappraise the reservation policy in Texas, Secretary of the Interior Robert McClelland could not have appointed anyone more qualified than Robert S. Neighbors as supervising agent over the Texas Indians. On the other hand, he could have found no one more disruptive than the subagent selected to manage the Comanche reservation, John R. Baylor. The former state legislator was a natural leader of men. Six foot two and sandy-haired, he possessed a beguiling demeanor and penetrating, steel-blue eyes. He inherited the vision that Jesse Stem had worked so diligently to achieve, viewing the Southern Comanches as a welcome mat at the doorstep of government largess and private riches. But where Stem hoped that his reward would result from efficient service, Baylor seemed less concerned with the job than with the benefits it provided. For a while he was popular with his charges, giving them carte blanche to hunt and camp wherever they pleased. He even accompanied them on occasional buffalo hunts. When Baylor, however, tried to rein in the Penatekas for continually taking advantage of his loose stewardship, their rapport degenerated into a test of wills. Ignoring regulations as well as failing to balance his accounts soon cost the free-wheeling agent his job. The Interior Department replaced Baylor with Matthew Leeper in March 1857.[49]

Baylor was outraged at being dismissed and blamed Neighbors. With a vengeance he turned on his former boss, trying to destroy him by undermining the thing most precious to him: his beloved Indians. Baylor, whom followers found jovial, humorous, and a thoughtful friend, proved he could be equally opinionated, vindictive, and ruthless. He was a shrewd man as well, and when he preyed on the fears and prejudices of settlers, many followed him eagerly. From his new home in Jack County he copublished a "hate rag," *The White Man*, that transformed the legitimate grievances of settlers into unreasoned hysteria.[50]

In Baylor's wake the military confronted the bedlam he unleashed. Lieutenant Colonel Robert E. Lee harbored no doubts that the reservation Indians were capable of horrifying depredations, despite their pitiable condition. He also noted that about a thousand Comanches, able and more hostile, made their home in Indian Territory. Determined to display a show of force, he conducted an exhausting eight-hundred-mile patrol from Camp Cooper. Four renegades and a "squaw," however, were all the colonel netted from the campaign.[51]

Lee never won any decisive battles against the Comanches, but after he departed for San Antonio in 1858, the federal and state governments finally concerted to punish Indians found away from the reservations. Both the state Rangers and the U.S. 2d Cavalry won significant engagements that year. In May, Rip Ford's mounted Texans, accompanied by Tonkawa scouts, surprised a band three hundred strong on the Washita River in western Indian Territory. The leading war chief, Iron Jacket, so called for the mail armor bequeathed to him from some long-dead Spaniard, was a revered medicine man who professed the ability to blow arrows from their aim. But Ford's men wielded long rifles and six-shooters. When the confident and "gorgeously caparisoned" chief charged them, two volleys rang out; the first allegedly sent Iron Jacket's horse "six feet into the air," and the second betrayed his pretensions of invincibility. The seven-hour fight ended with a third of the Comanches killed or captured.

Near Wichita Village, Indian Territory, Captain Earl Van Dorn commanded the U.S. Army's signal accomplishment in the pre–Civil War Indian campaigns. On October 1 he surprised a camp of about five hundred Comanches and Kiowas, killing fifty-six but allowing tired old Buffalo Hump to slip away. Both engagements together cost the white troops only seven men.[52]

Not content with this campaign and others against the Comanches, Baylorites manipulated racial tensions to a climax in what became known as the Reservation War. Late in 1858, Erath County man Peter Garland learned that "Choctaw Tom" and a small party of families from the lower reservation had accepted the invitation of some settlers to hunt with them in Palo Pinto County. Garland led a massacre on the Indian group, all but wiping them out as they lay sleeping in their tents. Stoking panic over the likelihood of retribution from the aggrieved natives, Baylor agitated so strongly in favor of driving away or continuing the massacre of the peaceful tribes that Texas Governor Hardin Runnels refused to enforce an order that would have clapped the attackers into irons.

Official inaction emboldened the former Indian agent to divide five hundred men between himself and Garland to march on the two reservations. Baylor was to take the Brazos Agency, his confederate the Comanche reserve. The plan, however, collapsed. Warriors near Belknap dogged Baylor's mob, killing seven of the whites after one of them murdered and scalped an old Indian man in plain sight of his own people. Garland's force failed to outrace the news of their campaign and simply melted away when the forewarned and prepared garrison at Camp Cooper challenged them.[53]

The faction nevertheless persisted in exciting settlers' fears, all but forcing the government finally to remove the Indians at Neighbors's recommendation in the summer of 1859. The 384 Comanches who fled the upper reservation left behind almost fifteen thousand dollars worth of livestock in addition to their ancestral lands, which, by the time of their exodus, had contracted to the four leagues along the Clear Fork of the Brazos.[54]

Thus ended any chance that the two races would coexist peacefully. Men such as Robert S. Neighbors held lofty ideals that blinded them to the futility of trying to reconcile the Indian and the white man. The association of the two cultures was a long record of broken treaties, land grabs, and raids. The final opportunity for a peaceful settlement died on the streets of Belknap in September 1859. Neighbors had stopped at the village to settle his accounts after escorting the reservation Indians beyond the Red River. While one man accosted the agent from the front, another walked up behind him and fired a shotgun into his back from almost point-blank range. Eight months later a posse finally dispatched the murderer, Edward Cornett, who had fled into the hills after killing another man.[55]

CHAPTER TWO

IN THE EYE OF A STORM, 1856–1861

Driving the reservation Indians from Texas invited unexpectedly fierce reprisals. Not long after the native peoples' flight, hostile raiding parties returned to their late homeland, ripping through the frontier settlements. The Cross Timbers became the target of particularly fierce forays, the first violent spasms in a pattern that persisted for more than a decade.

While the Clear Fork country suffered far fewer depredations, it did not escape the Indians' wrath entirely. A hostile band passing through Throckmorton County in April 1860 killed fifteen-year-old James Hamby, who worked for Thomas Lambshead on his farm abutting the former Comanche reservation. Two months later, a war party attacked two young cow hunters, Josephus and Frank Browning, in the river bottoms near the mouth of Hubbard Creek. They quickly killed the younger boy, Josephus, then turned on his brother. They felled Frank, too, but he returned their fire, forcing the Indians to withdraw. His riderless horse, with arrows protruding from it, wandered back to the ranch, alerting the boys' father, who hastened to the scene. He found his youngest son dead and scalped and the other barely alive and bleeding from more than a dozen wounds—two from shafts that passed completely through his body.[1]

John R. Baylor had assured his neighbors that tranquility would follow the Indians' ouster, and they had believed him. Rather than losing heart, the frontier folk rallied around the well-liked Browning family and elected Baylor to lead a retaliatory raid. The men set out immediately, and above Camp Cooper they were enraged at discovering the Browning boy's scalp that some careless warrior had dropped. Baylor's band feverishly pressed onward and quickly caught up with the casually retreating war party at Paint Creek, where they attacked and slaughtered the Indians in a short skirmish. On their triumphant return the group brandished the forelocks of several Indians and flaunted a small herd of horses they had recovered. Settlers held several celebrations to honor the victors; some of them even mimicked their enemies by dancing around the Indians' scalps. Baylor, sensing that the hand of providence had guided him, proclaimed that all his men were "hard-shell Baptists," adding that "God Almighty went with their sort."[2]

Early in September Browning vented his hatred personally. When he and a group of cow hunters spotted smoke rising from a small thicket, they investigated and surprised "Louis," the son of Comanche Chief Toshahua, who was cooking a "polecat" for his supper. They kept him prisoner for several days before extracting a confession that he had come to Texas to steal horses. "The citizens," according to Baylor's *White Man*, "turned the Indian loose, and gave Mr. Browning the first shot, which was all that was necessary, as it killed our red friend."[3]

If God saw hypocrisy in Baylor's affairs, families in Northwest Texas paid for his sins. Donning horned headdresses, war bonnets, and body paint, the former inhabitants of the land cut a bloody swath through the middle Brazos country and the Cross Timbers in 1860. Just after Thanksgiving, Comanche and Kiowa warriors surprised a home in Jack County, killing or leaving for dead at least five women and children—one a baby, whom they tossed repeatedly into the air. They beat one woman over the head with rocks and ran several arrows into her, but she lived. Two teenage girls were raped and left naked. A party also burst into the rural Palo Pinto County home of Ezra Sherman while his family was seated at the dinner table. Several mounted Indians drove them toward a neighbor's house, then suddenly a few of the Comanches grabbed Mrs. Sherman by the hair and dragged the woman to a spot where they raped and scalped her and stabbed her with arrows. She lingered in unbearable pain for three days, continually reliving her ordeal in tortured babbles. North of Mineral Wells about sixty

Indians "dressed for war" passed right by the home of Joe Stephens. That they left him unmolested was no oversight; this raid was calculated retribution to repay the treachery and broken promises that had uprooted the tribes. Stephens, quite simply, was not marked for revenge. At the grave of a recently deceased settler, raiders left smoking pipes as a tribute to a white friend who had decried the hysteria that swept up his neighbors.[4]

The startling and unforeseen reprisals elicited mixed emotions. Some settlers were terror-striken. "The road is lined with movers," reported the *White Man*, "who have at last determined to quit the country." Many more, however, reacted with rage and indignation. Anglos along the frontier believed this land was theirs by right and might. To them, these were the same coarse savages who had camped along the Brazos; their invasion seemed more like insolence than an act of war. People responded with confidence, reasoning that a quick and severe chastening would end the violent protestations. After Baylor exhorted his fellow frontiersmen to cross the Red River with him and attack their enemies where they lived, almost every able-bodied man took up arms. The troops at Camp Cooper, sure to clean up any mess the settlers could not handle, strengthened the firebrands' resolve.[5]

Before anyone could lead a citizens' expedition, recently elected Governor Sam Houston assembled a Ranger force that performed admirably, dampening the most ardent of the rabble. The Indians had won a Pyhrric victory against the mounted Texans in the fall of 1859, but despite laying an ambuscade and enjoying a five-fold advantage in manpower, they still lost several warriors. A momentous battle a hundred miles north of Camp Cooper in December 1860 left the settlers convinced that peace on their own terms was at hand. Captain Sul Ross, who commanded the troops, remarked that the "war which had been waged for more than thirty years was now virtually at an end." In the "Battle of the Pease River," Ross and a detachment of the U.S. 2d Cavalry surprised and routed an entire Comanche village. Those who were not killed immediately became caught in a pincers movement upon fleeing. The troops allowed most of the women and children to escape;

some of the warriors fled along with them, leaving behind 450 horses and their stock of winter food. Upon his triumph Ross declared—prematurely— that the "great Comanche confederation [is] . . . forever broken."[6]

Hopeful settlers viewed these chaotic times as a prelude to unopposed expansion into the Clear Fork region. They had seen the Indians who inhabited the reservations and were sure the ragged legacy of the "Lords of the Plains" was in the last desperate throes of defiance. People familiar with this frontier believed that Fort Phantom Hill, Stem's farm, and especially Camp Cooper would have been magnets for families and businesses had these irritants from beyond the Red River not frightened the weak of heart. Even Buffalo Hump had taken for granted that when the posts came, townbuilding would be inevitable. Only one ingredient had been missing—people.[7]

Before the Civil War, the effective limits of settlement ended at Fort Belknap in the middle Brazos country. The U.S. Army, of course, had planted it at the same time as Fort Phantom Hill, which lay seventy miles west of the interior post. Belknap enjoyed many advantages that its sister on the plains did not possess. Much closer to the settled areas eastward, it provided a natural extension for the Anglo advance. The verdant land, with cedars and post oaks overlooking fertile river valleys, was also more inviting. Many Peters Colony immigrants established farms in the region and tried their hands at a variety of occupations; they and other pioneers also ran hogs and cattle. A thriving community soon grew up around the fort. In 1858, when the Southern Overland Mail began its service through the little town of Belknap, about 150 people lived there or close by. The community included a number of residential dwellings anchored by a small business district composed of a post office, several stores, a hotel, and a billiard saloon.[8]

Pioneers who settled along the Clear Fork of the Brazos between Belknap and Phantom Hill hoped that soon they, too, would enjoy the advantages due first-comers in a new land. Despite the threat of Indians, they believed the edge of the plains was the natural limit for settlement. Phin Reynolds, whose family came to Gonzales

Creek near present-day Breckenridge in 1859, remarked that before the Civil War people just presumed that families would never inhabit the arid barrens beyond the treeline "on account of the lack of wood and water." Land on the edge of settlement, therefore, would soon be hot property; everyone anticipated that civilization was merely pausing at Belknap while the advance gathered momentum before crowding the rim.[9]

The decision that might have set an irreversibly progressive course for the Clear Fork region was determined, like so many others, at places distant from the Texas frontier. In 1857 the postmaster general entertained several bids to deliver mail and carry passengers between Saint Louis and San Francisco. He awarded the coveted prize to the Southern Overland Mail, headed by an upstate New York firm under John Butterfield. Well grounded in finance and communications, Butterfield had been the driving force in consolidating his interests with those of Henry Wells and William G. Fargo to form the American Express Company. His acquaintances included newly elected President James Buchanan, whose political leanings toward the South no doubt influenced the selection of a route favorable to that bloc. The path of the stage road was of paramount importance; most politicians believed that it would presage a Pacific railway.[10]

Many perceived a potential windfall in locating along the route. When Grayson County businessmen learned that the stage would be crossing the Red River at the tiny community of Preston, they built a new road, inducing the stage line to shift its course through the more populous town of Sherman. From there to Belknap, each county followed Grayson's lead, continuing the road, making improvements, and even building bridges. The effects were significant. Not only did the new road save forty miles on this stretch, but it diverted traffic from the old California emigrants' trail, roughly paralleling it to the north. Towns along the route benefited from the improvements and increased usage; some grew 50 percent or more during the life of the route.[11]

Others anticipating the coming of the Butterfield settled along the proposed roadway. James M. Franz, a Peters Colony immigrant,

moved his family to a lonely spot along a barren stretch between
Fort Belknap and Camp Cooper, where he built a log and stone
house for his wife Frances and their seven children. The two-room
dwelling was spartan, but travelers welcomed the stop as a "safe
house," for rumors persisted that Indians "frequently took scalps"
in the area. Franz also constructed a log stable and a corral made
of cedar pickets and stacked rocks. Stock tenders, whom the
company hired, slept in the stable with the mules but ate their meals
with the Franz family and their guests. The stage might arrive at
any hour of the day or night, whereupon Frances would prepare
a meal over an open fireplace. Henry Bates, who supervised the
station, occasionally called on James Franz; the two passed many
evenings smoking and chatting by the fireplace while Frances knitted
in the light of a single tallow candle.[12]

About thirteen miles beyond Franz's, the Butterfield crossed
the Clear Fork. *New York Herald* correspondent W. L. Ormsby
documented the first run and commented on the stretch that passed
into this unsettled region. Although civilization seemed to end at
Belknap, the forty-mile leg was not without an occasional dwelling
built by one of the few stock raisers who were beginning to take
advantage of the open prairies. Ormsby indeed made note of
untended cattle herds in his report. He also remarked that settlers
at Belknap were abuzz over the recent rash of depredations.
Townspeople placed the blame squarely on the former reservation
Indians, subjecting the correspondent to "terrible tales . . . of
stealing stock and taking the scalps of straggling travelers." Ormsby
seemed almost disappointed that he spotted but one Comanche—
a woman "riding straddle."[13]

At least a handful of pioneers did not share the negative
sentiments regarding the reservation Indians. The few who lived
near the Penateka land in the days preceding the Reservation War
believed that the Southern Comanches had become docile and
trustworthy, even if their visiting kinsmen occasionally provoked
unrest. Long familiar with these Indians, Thomas Lambshead and
a brother felt safe enough to accept jobs as station masters at
Mountain Pass and Valley Creek, well beyond the Clear Fork. In

1858, when local station agents located a crossing at the river, they, too, anticipated little trouble. Company officials, in fact, placed the stage stop on the far side of Camp Cooper, with the agency between them. Across the entire length of the route, Indians seldom attacked the stages. Complaints of marauding seemed to emanate largely from settlers beyond the vicinity of the reservation. Raids on Maxwell's farm and the Givens ranch, both in close proximity to Camp Cooper, were attributed to Comanches, but some believed that a gang of white outlaws committed the acts. Both times the raiders drove away many horses, some belonging to the reservation Indians themselves. The Butterfield, even though it lost no passengers in Northwest Texas to raiding parties, still blamed Comanches for taking almost 250 horses and mules during the winter that Ormsby made his trip.[14]

If "The Butterfield" or "Southern Overland Mail" conjured up any romantic visions, the sight of the stage all but betrayed its euphonious names. The coaches bore little resemblance to the familiar ones of the postwar era. A later vehicle, the mud wagon, copied Butterfield's design. Boxy and low-slung with small wheels, the celerity was light and fast, able to withstand the rocky trails between Texas and California. Despite its ungraceful design, the stage nevertheless boasted cushions and side curtains of russet leather; damask appointments and fringes adorned the interior. The coaches, varnished red or bottle green, rode atop straw-colored carriages striped in black or brown. Paintings graced many panel doors, but dirt and dust no doubt obscured them. Stocky and sure-footed mules, moreover, replaced the swifter teams of horses once the stage broke through the Cross Timbers. One item did remain consistent with the image. "The stage driver," according to first-comer John Chadbourne Irwin, "was the cussing, whip-cracking fellow the story books picture him."[15]

When *Herald* correspondent Ormsby visited the Clear Fork station, the scene that greeted him contrasted starkly with the colorless countryside that passed before his window on the road from Belknap. Up and down the river, activity fostered the impression that a town was about to flower at this isolated spot.

The company was erecting a log hut and a corral yard on the east
bank. On the other side would be a facility for keeping a coach
and team ready in case the river might suddenly rise. The Butterfield
also provided jobs, boosting the civilian population. Besides the
station keeper, the company employed several "stage masters" to
handle the fractious mules and the increasing number of runs. Most
were Hispanic men who brought their families; at least fourteen
of them eventually resided among the otherwise Anglo settlement.[16]

Like the Butterfield, Camp Cooper nurtured the emerging
community in several ways. Farmers on the Clear Fork at last had
a market; their only problem now was raising a surplus. Other
civilians moved here to supply the goods and services that troops
required. Herder John G. Irwin, John Chadbourne's father, secured
a contract—signed by Lieutenant Colonel Robert E. Lee himself—to
supply beef. He even dropped roots, building a house close to the
river where he had found a large spring. Tennessee farmer Hugh
Harper, lured west by a Peters Colony grant, abandoned his plow
for a job as post sutler at Cooper. Such a position was potentially
lucrative; sutlers not only outfitted the soldiers, but also were
prepared to supply westering pioneers as the area grew. Harper's
business, if not brisk, nevertheless enabled him to hire a clerk—a
Polish man—with whom he shared his residence. The families of
a few officers were also among his customers. The women, besides
lending an air of domesticity to the garrison, added a measure of
diversity to this male-dominated society.[17]

Life on the Clear Fork, however, was unceasingly austere and
often harsh. In an 1856 letter to his wife, Lee complained that the
atmosphere was "like the blast from a hot-air furnace," adding that
"our hopes for a few cabbage-plants and roasting ears have passed
away." The next year he reported that the temperature had climbed
to 112 degrees "in the Hospital Tent, the coolest place we have."[18]

Lee nevertheless believed that this place held a unique promise
for future settlers. Perhaps he also realized the high price in human
lives that would ensue from imprinting an Anglo society at this
place. Twice he officiated at funeral services for the young sons
of his men, victims of heatstroke. Of one, a sergeant's year-old boy,

Lee reflected: "I was admiring his appearance the day before he was taken ill."[19]

The return of Cynthia Ann Parker, an Anglo woman whom the Comanches had taken captive in 1836, proved equally poignant. At the Battle of the Pease River she was again taken against her will—this time by the whites. Long assimilated into the tribe, Cynthia Ann had even married Chief Peta Nocona and had borne him two sons. The woman clutched their third child, a baby girl, to her side and fled as the troops ran their horses through the Comanches' camp. The soldier who captured her noticed that she had blue eyes. Speculating that she might be the long-lost Cynthia Ann Parker, Sul Ross sent her to Camp Cooper, where he knew the officers' wives would provide her comfort. There she sat crying most of the time for her husband and sons, while troops sent for her uncle, Isaac Parker. B. F. Gholson, who had fought with Ross, remembered that when her uncle mentioned her name, the woman seemed rejuvenated. Leaping up from the box, she patted herself on the breast, exclaiming, "Me! Me! Cynthia Ann."[20]

Despite the harsh conditions, an embryonic society was emerging in which happier events also transpired. James and Frances Franz, who moved their children to the Butterfield station, soon surrendered a daughter to one of the Clear Fork's eligible young men. Another couple married at Camp Cooper but left to make their home in Brown County, a day's ride to the south. By 1860 several families resided along the river, an inviting oasis in an otherwise desolate environment. If the military post provided peace of mind, the stage provided a link with the world outside, bringing mail and news. The passengers who disembarked while the stage changed relays included a rich assortment. Prosaic travelers comprised the bulk, but young Irwin remembered that "prospectors, gamblers, cowmen, and unassorted adventurers" also stopped for a look around. The "marginal types" gave little thought to staying—there was no action here.[21]

At last a town appeared forthcoming, and it possessed every reason to succeed. In 1858 the state had appointed a small group headed by Thomas Lambshead to organize the new county of

Throckmorton. To the east-west route of the stage the military added a north-south road, making this place a potentially important crossroads. Distant sources of capital, needing desperately to nurture markets at this isolated spot, provided funds for both the Southern Overland Mail and Camp Cooper. The Butterfield, especially, desired to stimulate the local economy; it was adding runs. Trade for aspiring hotel owners, blacksmiths, and merchants seemed certain to arise. In other places, even as close as Belknap, the stage line prompted a flurry of building contracts. The price of town lots there had increased 200 percent. New Yorker A. J. Mackay sensed the same potential on the upper Clear Fork. He was worth twenty thousand dollars and came to this spot to invest his fortune in land. Camp Cooper was taking on the appearance of permanence as well. Where once Lieutenant Colonel Lee had pitched a tent, an officers' quarters and barracks arose. By 1860 other merchants had joined sutler Hugh Harper. They were hopeful that settlers would populate the countryside. Already a trickle had spread along the creek banks and watersheds of the Clear Fork.[22]

Along with the conscientious pioneers came others who made a living by trading in stolen horses and livestock. And not all of them were rootless outlaws; among the cabal were leading citizens and otherwise forthright settlers. The network extended across the length of the Texas frontier and even into Indian Territory and Kansas. Just after the Reservation War, soldiers at Camp Cooper found the corpse of a man who had seemingly run afoul of the gang. A letter on the body verified what many had long suspected. It revealed that Anglos had been responsible for at least part of the depredations plaguing frontier settlers. They had diverted blame to the native inhabitants by disguising themselves as raiders and encouraging their "friend at the *White Man* . . . to keep up the Indian excitement." Some of the gang living in the Clear Fork country had even burned their own stables and sacrificed stock to cover their complicity and earn compensation from the government. About the same time that they began having trouble concealing their wide-ranging activities, the *White Man*'s editors lashed out at the administration of Governor Sam Houston for "spreading rumors" about the illicit theft ring "and not backing it up with facts." Before the state could gather enough evidence to call the challenge, the larger events of secession intervened.[23]

Part of the gang's subterfuge to cover their misdeeds was apparently a vigilante movement known as the Old Law Mob, or O.L.M. A couple of times the group's initials turned up on the bodies of dead men supposedly killed for criminal activity. The accusations, however, were normally transparent, and the abuses of the movement led to its quick demise. Belknap attorney M. B. King, for example, was hanged by the mob after reportedly trying to obtain a divorce for a woman whose husband objected to his meddling. Post sutler Hugh Harper, along with two other local men, had painted King as an abolitionist and had accused him of trying to poison one of them. King's friends decried the allegations and asserted that his only crime was "that he was too weak to defend himself." A correspondent reported that some cow hunters found his "half devoured body" in the Clear Fork, adding that "every tree within several hundred yards was filled with buzzards."

The O.L.M. ambushed and killed another man, L. F. Collins, whom they labeled a horse thief, near Camp Cooper. But, like King, Collins had friends who swore to his innocence. Collins was supposedly carrying about eight thousand dollars in cash, notes, and drafts at the time of his "execution." When shocked citizens, including cow hunters John Snyder, William Hittson, and Joe Matthews, drafted a letter denouncing the mob, the O.L.M. afterward grew silent.[24]

The outlaw gang no doubt found this part of Northwest Texas an ideal spot for accumulating their stolen horses and cattle before herding them northward. This particular land at the edge of the plains, while treeless except along the watercourses, still harbored fine valleys in the hilly brakes. Vast and arid—yet inviting when droughts were not prevailing—it dictated how the first permanent settlers would use it. Passing from the Salt Fork to the Clear Fork of the Brazos on one of his explorations, Captain Marcy called the change in the land "almost magical." In a day's ride he found "all that is rude, barren, and uninteresting in nature, in close proximity to that which is most pleasing and beautiful." Rainfall in this section normally sufficed to sustain cattle. It also did not evaporate so quickly as in areas farther west, so streams flowed longer and the tall gramma and buffalo grasses grew more lushly. The region's nearness to places such as Weatherford and Fort Worth appealed to immigrants who saw the potential for stock raising.[25]

The first to pursue this endeavor was an unlikely rancher, a Hoosier with no background to prepare him for herding on the open range. Newton Curd Givens, of the U.S. 2d Dragoons, served at each of the three antebellum frontier posts in Northwest Texas. Commissioned a lieutenant in the Mexican War, he was among the first federal officers sent to the Texas frontier and was the last commander at old Phantom Hill. Later, at Belknap and at Camp Cooper, he used his West Point connections to make the most of an otherwise unpromising situation. He became familiar with the land, and like that of Jesse Stem, his opportunist's eye saw the potential of this region.[26]

Givens seemingly attended to everything but duty. An ardent sportsman, he bred dogs to hunt the jack rabbits, wolves, and panthers that ranged the unsettled countryside. William B. Parker, traveling with Marcy, remarked that they were "the finest pack of hounds . . . on the continent." Parker accompanied Givens on a hunt in which mounted riflemen followed the dogs until they cornered a big cat. One of the hounds suffered a crushed skull and another had a leg torn open, "but it was a right royal hunt." The frolic reportedly ended with Givens shooting the quarry through the eye—just as it was crouching to spring. Such élan ingratiated the lieutenant with his superiors. At Belknap, they allowed him to join a coterie of senior officers who bent regulations by purchasing land around the post and along the river bottoms. Among his neighbors in this venture were Albert Sidney Johnston and Majors George Thomas and Henry Hopkins Sibley.[27]

When the army sent Givens to Camp Cooper, he executed a grander design. In 1855 he had purchased land along Walnut Creek, which flowed into the Clear Fork about seven miles west of the military encampment. Within three years, along the picturesque banks of this intermittent stream, arose his Stone Ranch, consisting of a house, an auxiliary building, a five-foot-tall fence enclosing about half an acre, another three-foot-tall corral, and a spring house—all built of native stone. The "dog-run" style of the unusually high-walled main house—that is, two units separated by a hallway with a roof over both—belied its majesty for such a desolate place. All the stone was finely masoned, and double doors enclosed the open hallway in the winter. On Army freight wagons came materials that detailed the house on every side: large windows north and south, chimneys east and west, and a transom over every door. Even the outbuilding was finer than any other structure within a day's ride.[28]

Something of a mystery has surrounded the origins of the Stone Ranch. Later inhabitants insisted that the officer built the complex during or before 1856 at his own expense. More likely, however, it either came into existence in 1858 as the temporarily relocated Camp Cooper, or else Givens at that time diverted the Army's resources. If he really did dupe the government, his commanding presence, as well as the garrison's brief tenure at the new post, at least led local folk to believe that he alone was responsible for building it. Correspondence identifying the post site as Paint Creek and the later discovery of a Stone Ranch cornerstone dated 1856 no doubt added to the confusion.[29]

Walnut Creek, however, better matched descriptions of Camp Cooper's temporary location; in fact, Indian Agent Matthew Leeper placed the post at "Capt. Givens' Rancho six or seven miles distant from the agency." The marker might have signified merely the date that the officer arrived to take possession of his ranch. In any event, such easily impressed travelers as Parker or Marcy would have mentioned the Stone Ranch in their journals. Cooper commander Robert E. Lee, moreover, was living under canvas in 1856 while Givens was supposedly building his grand estate. That the lieutenant colonel would have tolerated the sight of luxury-laden wagons making their way to the ranch of a subordinate while his own fatigue parties were busy scouring the countryside for "logs, pickets, and loose stone" for the original Camp Cooper is unlikely.[30]

More believable is that Givens, after Lee left the post in 1858, used the distractions of the Reservation War to manipulate the government into improving his prospects for retirement. In June of that year U.S. Senator Sam Houston delivered a bitter speech condemning the army for removing Camp Cooper to the private property of an officer "with the understanding that all the improvements made there were [eventually] to revert to the owner of the ranch." Contractors, Houston commented, had hauled timber "some twenty miles to consummate that handsome establishment." He also speculated that the owner—presumably Givens—would have grounds to file a claim against the government of $150,000 for "spoilization upon his property."[31]

Whether through his own funds or as a result of clever scheming, the Stone Ranch was a tribute to Givens's megalomania. Shortly after the garrison reoccupied the original site, he stocked the spread with about three hundred cattle and a flock of sheep. Later he began trading meat and supplies, apparently without official authority. When Buck Barry led a party of state Rangers onto the plains, he stopped at Givens's ranch—the last dwelling between Camp Cooper and New Mexico—where he obtained some pack mules and saddles in exchange for his wagons.[32]

Givens lived on the edge of probity, and his pursuit of personal aggrandizement progressively led him down a destructive path. In 1855 he reportedly wrote some letters, published by the *Austin State Times*, criticizing the frontier policy of the Military Department of Texas. For that indiscretion General Persifor Smith brought him before a court martial. Givens, by then a captain, was acquitted for lack of evidence, but he did not go entirely unpunished. The army reassigned him to "topographical duty" in 1857, again at Camp Cooper, just as the Reservation War was about to erupt. Joining forces with the Baylor faction, he became embroiled in the violent disagreements over reservation policy. For the flamboyant Givens, the conflict—and his ambitions—ended with his death in 1859 while he was on leave in San Antonio.[33]

Death spared Givens disappointment, just as it had Jesse Stem. The land would not allow the type of ranching that the captain envisioned any more than it would sustain traditional farming. The sophistication and planning that went into his operation were impressive but of little practical use in this environment. Here, only open-range herding was viable. And for this, Givens's fenced pastures and sporting dogs were of little use. If he had survived his fatal trip to San Antonio, the late captain would have either changed his methods or failed.[34]

Herding folk who knew how to take advantage of open country were advancing to this frontier even as Givens's grandiose scheme cratered upon its shaky foundation. At last someone would discover a use for the land. And the military, if it had been able to keep Plains Indians north of the Red River, would have solved the pioneers' other great problem. Within a few months after Ormsby's journey, the reservation Indians were gone, and with them, settlers hoped, most of the petty raids. Comanche depredations came unanticipated, but the military was stepping up its pressure, and the belief that such episodes would end no doubt encouraged recently arrived prairie families.[35]

But about 1860—at the apogee of hope—the dreams of frontier folk collapsed. The Indian depredations that everyone expected to die down continued and in fact grew more intense. Despite Sul Ross's declaration that his campaign on the Pease River had broken the Comanche confederation, the state failed to follow up his victory. The Indians soon recovered and raided anew. The federal line of posts, moreover, disappeared when the Union foundered, and the larger conflict of civil war sucked up the manpower necessary to fill the vacuum.[36]

The sedentary tribes, so troublesome before their removal, remained north of the Red River, but the once destitute Comanches, joined by the Kiowas, arose phoenixlike, almost intoxicated with bloodlust. Even during the reservation years the northern bands, joined occasionally by renegades from the agency, had never ceased to probe the soft underbelly of the Anglo advance. They badgered settlers too far removed from the interior to arouse more than sympathy from men and women comfortably behind the vanguard. The marauders had always seemed to know just how far they could push. They ran a balance between satisfying their warriors' ambitions and risking a level of retribution that might bring grief to their poorer cousins concentrated in the shadows of the army posts. With nothing to lose, they exhibited a pitiless barbarity that the Spaniards and Mexicans had known all too well.

Most important, a dramatic sign played to Comanche superstitions: the bison had returned to the Southern Plains. Countless times in recent years warriors had faced the skulls of old bulls toward their camps, futilely beckoning the animals' resurrection. At last the bison seemed to materialize as if by magic, blanketing their old range where each migrating season for more than a decade the Penatekas' hope for their return had sunk into despair. If the ignominy of being pushed from their ancestral lands had not proved sufficient to bestir the tribe, nature itself seemed to exhort them to reassert their ascendancy over the plains.[37]

Settlers took notice of the bisons' reappearance as well. From his father's ranch house on the edge of Camp Cooper, young John Chadbourne Irwin witnessed their seemingly endless procession, passing in their migration "both north and south . . . for a week at a time." The indelible impression of bison "as far as the eye could reach," staggered the Reynolds family when they breached the treeline upon occupying the recently vacated Stone Ranch. "Hills, plains and valleys," exclaimed their youngest daughter, "were simply covered with them."[38]

The return of the bison completed a precipitous succession of events. The Reservation War, Indian retribution, and campaigns conducted by federal soldiers and state militia completely destabilized the social landscape of the Texas frontier as the Civil War approached. Texans realized that compelling their enemies to come to terms would become difficult without a significant military presence supported by a resolute policy.[39]

Because the Indians had refused to accept subjugation, the question of secession weighed especially heavy on frontier folk. The prospect of facing hostile raiding parties with little or no assistance inspired sober reflection when the time came to choose between union or dissolution. Peters Colony settlers, dubious of the Southern cause, diluted the vote in much of North Texas. In fact, a ten-county area along the two northern- and westernmost tiers of organized counties cast one-fourth of the antisecessionist vote, despite comprising only a tenth of the state's population. But the Peters Colony influence waned and all but disappeared at the plain's edge. In Shackelford, Throckmorton, and Buchanan counties, almost nine-tenths of American-born males over age twenty-one hailed from a future Confederate state or from Kentucky or Missouri. Surely they weighed the certainty of losing federal troops and the uncertainty of living under a preoccupied and loosely bound confederation. Nevertheless, among 349 votes cast in Palo Pinto, Young, and Jack counties, to which the three unorganized Clear Fork country counties were attached, only 45 men affirmed the Union. Buchanan County, moreover, was soon renamed Stephens County in honor of the new Confederate vice-president. Ardent sectionalism probably inspired the change, but no doubt the thought of beguiling the dispensers of frontier protection also crossed the settlers' minds.[40]

When Texas seceded on February 2, 1861, approximately 1,500 federal troops manned the line of posts along the state's frontier. Captain Stephen Decatur Carpenter commanded the 250-man garrison at Camp Cooper. The air was already charged with tension over uncertain loyalties at distant outposts; questions over who possessed decision making authority added to the chaos. The secession convention that thrust Texas into the Confederacy had empowered Colonel Henry E. McCulloch to take possession of Forts Colorado and Chadbourne as well as Camp Cooper. He accepted the peaceful surrender of the two lower forts, allowing the soldiers to leave. But before he could reach the Clear Fork, some "hotheads" from Parker County, led by H. A. Hamner—John R. Baylor's partner at the *White Man*—had besieged Camp Cooper. The group demanded its surrender even before the secession vote became known. Carpenter resolved to defend his post against this rabble, but he was probably relieved when McCulloch's representative arrived to accept a formal surrender.[41]

Captain Carpenter knew the folly of such a standoff, and he was no doubt thankful to cut his losses and send the troops home.

A spontaneous skirmish on this barren plain would have drawn
little popular notice, even though a similar situation would arise
two months later at Fort Sumter. By the time Washington and
Richmond would have been able to sort through rumor and fact,
a battle here would have been no more meaningful than encounters
already plaguing Kansas and Missouri. This war would begin by
the intrigues and machinations attending the calculated moves of
generals and presidents, not by the indiscretions of citizen soldiers
and minor officers in the isolated backwashes of Texas.[42]

After Cooper lay sacked and abandoned, pioneers along the
upper Clear Fork faced Indians, outlaws, and deserters with little
help. In a land where the future had once appeared so promising,
plans for town building and settling the Clear Fork country
foundered completely. D. S. Howell, an enlistee with a group of
state Rangers, happened upon a poignant reminder while patrolling
near old Camp Cooper late in 1864. Near the spot where the
Butterfield station lay abandoned, he encountered thirteen men
convened for the purpose of organizing Throckmorton County.
Howell did not name any of them; the brief mention in his
reminiscences is the only record of their endeavor. But that day—
six years after the state endorsed the county's petition—their effort
again miscarried. Fifteen more years would pass before their
successors finally prevailed.[43]

CHAPTER THREE

A HOME ON THE RANGE, 1860-1865

LATER GENERATIONS OF TEXANS would look back at the Civil War era and the early years of Reconstruction and exclaim that the frontier had receded 100 to 150 miles. They were surely correct if they judged the advance by how far the antebellum military posts had extended. They were right again if the disappearance of the Butterfield and the abandonment of the civilian settlement at Belknap were the criteria. Everywhere charred chimneys and empty houses emphatically supported their claims. But not only did herding families remain in the Clear Fork country throughout the war, but their numbers also actually increased, and their activities and patterns of settlement expanded and intensified as well.[1]

At the same time that businessmen and families envisioned towns and farms alongside Camp Cooper and the Comanche Reservation, stockmen were quietly probing the near reaches of the valleys and creek banks. By 1860 thirty cattlemen headed households in the Clear Fork country. Most of them brought large families and were normally accompanied by one or more single men who hoped to gather herds of their own. By the end of the decade their numbers had almost tripled. Farmers, on the other hand, all but disappeared; only three remained in 1870, where ten years earlier a score of agrarians had tilled the capricious land. Most of the aspiring town builders at Cooper were also gone. The mixture of people on the eve of disunion, in fact, looked more eclectic than it would a decade later. And even though lacking diversity, the population of the Clear Fork region doubled during the war decade, while that of neighboring counties to the east retrenched dramatically.[2]

Even in the darkest of these unpropitious times settlers
established a social and economic foundation. The South provided
the parent culture; ranching was its midwife. Southerners learned
quickly that their cattle adapted well to the open grassland just as
they had thrived in the pine barrens and coastal savannas along
the paths of migration. Despite living in dread of Indian raids, herder
folk implanted a palpable culture, drawing on the older patterns
and traditions. Their confrontation with the native peoples of the
plains as well as with the unfamiliar environment, however, was
a uniquely western experience. Adverse conditions broke up many
families, but herder folk stubbornly persisted, even in the face of
the cruelest forces of man and nature. A generation later, when
this frontier joined the interior, the society would reflect a tortured
maturity distorted by a protracted period of development and marked
by the vicissitudes of war and social dislocation.

The complex origins of open-range ranching, which characterized life in this region, were nevertheless simple in many respects.
For all the pretensions of the civilization that propelled them into
this land, Southern ranchers at first shared some common
characteristics with the Plains Indians. They followed their cattle
herds just as Comanches and Kiowas followed the bison. Scouting
for good grass and water, stockmen erected crude shelters, then
moved on when their animals exhausted the natural fodder. As the
grass regrew behind them, their abandoned shacks became
headquarters for some new outfit. They owned no land; the range
belonged to the cattle, the bison, and anyone who could occupy
and hold it.[3]

Even the imposing Stone Ranch, the last house between Camp
Cooper and New Mexico, changed hands several times during the
war years. After Newton C. Givens died in 1859, two businessmen,
Knox and Gardiner, brought a large herd to the surrounding range.
When Gardiner for some reason was apprehended and taken to a
Houston prison, Knox, thinking they might return, buried their
personal effects and then vacated the place. After them others came
and departed of their own volition. In 1866, Barber Watkins
Reynolds located his family there even though Indian raids were

at their worst. But the imposing stone structure, magnificent for
the place and time, was nothing more than a shelter to them. When
the grass played out, they moved on just as they had moved from
picket cabins elsewhere. Afterward, other cow hunters either lived
or wintered there without attempting to obtain ownership. Not until
1880, in fact, did J. A. Matthews bother to approach the owners
of Givens's estate about acquiring it.[4]

Familiarity with herding ways proved far more important than
strength of resources. Men more practical than Givens—men with
a long tradition of herding—were already advancing toward the open
grasslands even as his plans went awry. The first families to sink
permanent roots in the valleys whose watershed flowed into the
upper Clear Fork were part of a steady migration possessing a
heritage of Old South and Celtic cattle raising traditions. Between
the buffalo plains and Fort Worth, some of the most prominent
cattle barons of the postwar generation were seeding the bends of
the Brazos River in Young and Palo Pinto counties. Among them
were Oliver Loving, Reverend George W. Slaughter, and Jesse
Hittson. Well beyond their ranges, the first cattlemen moved into
the Clear Fork country. As early as 1859, John G. Irwin arrived
from Fort Chadbourne to supply Camp Cooper with beef. Not long
afterward, John Hittson, who had herded with his father Jesse,
settled briefly at old Camp Cooper before moving to the open range
that ran through the lower part of Shackelford into unorganized
Callahan County. Joseph Beck Matthews and Barber Watkins
Reynolds pioneered ranges that straddled the Clear Fork in
Shackelford and Throckmorton counties, and John C. Lynch made
his home about nine miles southeast of present-day Albany.[5]

Genealogically and culturally, these ranchers—the vanguard of
Great Plains cattlemen—owed a tremendous debt to herding
traditions that spread through colonial South Carolina from the
Celtic Highlands country. From the Atlantic colony the open-range
cattle industry expanded along two paths, eventually reaching the
Great Plains. One route spread through the Piedmont and Appala-
chians into the Ohio Valley and the Midwest, where cattle readily
adapted to the tall-grass prairies. Finally, through Missouri, they

reached Northeast Texas. The other path wended through Georgia, the Florida Panhandle, Alabama, Mississippi, and Louisiana before reaching deep East Texas.[6]

As the herding culture spread westward from the Atlantic coast, regional environments and local customs influenced the older traditions. Along the upper route herders developed methods to fatten livestock by penning and feeding them, but the Scotch-Irish in the back countries kept something akin to the open-range Carolina traditions intact. Celtic peoples also lined the southern channels, upholding the older customs, while Spanish, Creole French, and English herders added practices unique to their own traditions.[7]

Scores of migratory cattlemen filed into Texas along these two routes in the decades following independence from Mexico. During the Republic era the Blackland Prairie in Northeast Texas and the Pineywoods region adjoining Louisiana were the farthest limits of penetration. Settlers from the Ohio Valley—mostly upper Southerners—dominated ranching in Northeast Texas. Impenetrable thickets lining the open prairies provided natural enclosures for cowpenning and roundups. This upper Southern yeoman tradition not only shunned black cowboys but also resisted Spanish customs as well. The other cradle of Great Plains ranching that emanated from the Old South and pine forests of East Texas drew on a variety of methods. Since the land along the Gulf rim did not vary significantly, migrants found each new place much like the ones they had left behind. These stock raisers were more inclined to employ African Americans and to use dogs and whips in managing their herds. They also looked to New Orleans as their primary market.[8]

As the Civil War approached, herders from both paths reached the edge of the Rolling Plains; increasingly the two methods became one, shaped by the environment and close association. Newton C. Givens might have been familiar with the Corn Belt operations of his native Indiana, but he certainly had not been seasoned by ranching in East Texas. Ohio Valley families who moved into the Western Cross Timbers before the Civil War—including many Peters Colony immigrants—outnumbered those from the Old South. But they flagged upon reaching the unfamiliar terrain at the edge of the Rolling Plains. By the end of the 1860s, herding families from the lower tier who reached the Clear Fork had caught up with them in number, and the Ohio Valley people who remained, as well as recent arrivals, scrapped much of their penning and feeding operations and altered their methods of managing range cattle. On the other hand, Old South herder families came to depend more on single white men and less on their former slaves. In 1870 less than a third of African Americans residing in the Clear Fork country worked cattle.[9]

The migration of the Barber Watkins Reynolds family, chronicled by daughter Sallie Matthews, reflected the influences of westering on the rich Southern and Celtic heritage. The patriarch, born in Georgia, traced his roots to England and Wales. He migrated to Florida before advancing to Alabama; there, he married a Gaelic-speaking South Carolinian whose family had risen to the planter class. The newlyweds moved across the Louisiana border into East Texas, where they learned of the open grasslands west of Fort Worth. In 1860 the couple moved their growing family into Palo Pinto County, but other ranchers—many former neighbors from East Texas—had already appropriated the best land. After acquiring a herd from John R. Baylor in return for a young slave girl and an unspecified sum of gold, they made it as far as Buchanan County in the year before the war.[10]

Not many Southerners left written records, for they were more inclined to oral tradition, but census takers who canvassed Shackelford, Throckmorton, and Buchanan counties in 1860 noted the same steady movement that Sallie Matthews outlined. While a few herders such as J. A. Whitten and John Snyder hailed from the South Atlantic coast, the birthplaces listed by most others revealed that the migration had begun earlier. The fathers of future Texas stockmen hailed largely from Tennessee, Georgia, Kentucky, Alabama, Illinois, Mississippi, Missouri, and Arkansas. The birthplaces of their wives normally demonstrated the stockmen's first westward steps beyond their places of origin. The census, noting the states where their children were born, detailed the march;

typically, the last few were native Texans. And the upper Clear Fork was not without its links to the rich herding traditions of Ireland. John Maxfield, John G. Irwin, J. C. Lynch, John Maxwell, and John Shirley—all born of Erin—were raising stock on the upper Clear Fork when war broke out.[11]

These ranching families and others were perched at the precipice of the vast, treeless plains on the eve of disunion. They encountered problems that settlers even a day's ride to the east did not face. Many pioneers came as farmers, and a few stayed but adapted to stock raising out of necessity. The thin soil and constant drought in these years frustrated them. The effective limits of normal farming practices soon became evident. In Palo Pinto County, where the Peters Colony influence was strong, more than half the population in 1860 grew wheat, corn, and other produce. The Clear Fork country conceded little to settlers; many of them kept kitchen gardens but consumed everything they grew. Fencing was particularly difficult, for the thick stands of post oaks dwindled into prairies in the Clear Fork country. If settlers wanted a pen for separating stock, they stacked flat rocks one upon the other to make walls. Fencing the land was beyond their ability; cattlemen could not possibly enclose enough land to pasture and water their stock adequately. Even if the land and weather had cooperated, they did not possess the resources to grow feed crops. The only option left to them was open-range ranching.[12]

Unlike Lambshead, Stem, and Givens, the rootless Southern ranchers did not bother to purchase their land; that was a pointless expense. Besides, the tradition of Southern laws protected them. Almost everyone recognized the right of stockmen to allow their animals free ranging. Just to enclose their property, Southern landowners typically had to acquire the right by special county elections. This "local option" system continued in Texas until after World War II. People in Shackelford County did not even consider fencing until 1878, when some angry farmers petitioned the county court to compel stockmen to restrain their hogs. This practice assured ranchers that even if another man owned the range, their livestock could still roam freely. On the plains more than anywhere else, the land seemed as if it possessed no use outside of grazing.[13]

The methods that ranchers applied were well suited to the open range. They called their endeavor "cow hunting," a very Southern but misleading term. Granted, they did have to find the animals in an open country, but most of the time they knew where to look. The long-established practices that Southerners had come to take for granted piqued the interest of Connecticut boy Sam Newcomb, who mentioned some of them in his diary. Among the typically Southern practices, herders used cow whips that could reach sixteen feet in length. They also marked and branded their stock, transferred them to seasonal pastures, and used a labor force beyond their immediate families. Most of them erected pens for young calves, not only to protect them but also to keep the mother cows from straying.[14]

Herders also used salt to control the movement of their cattle. At a remote, "snow white" spot about twenty-five miles below Camp Cooper, W. H. Ledbetter set up an operation to extract this precious commodity in 1862. From Jefferson, Texas, near the Louisiana border he hauled a large furnace and some massive kettles in which he refined the mineral. Merchants and the Confederate Army were among his customers; some came in freight wagons from a distance of two hundred miles. Ranchers, however, bought the greatest portion. Open-range herders knew what a European traveler had long ago noted: "salt makes up for the lack of fences."[15]

Complicating the management of cattle was their bad temper. A wounded bull, like an angry bear, might tree a man and even attack a mounted rider. Only killing the animal would assure a cow hunter's safety. As beef cattle, the herds in North Texas were superior to the more plentiful longhorns below San Antonio. Celebrated rancher Charles Goodnight called the upstate breed "Texas cattle" to distinguish them from the typical South Texas stock. He believed them to be a hybrid of Spanish and Southern cattle—"dark, line-backed, mealy-nosed, round-barreled, and well-built." And they were wild, their horns "set forward to kill 'like those of the buffalo.' " About the time of the Civil War these feral animals wandered onto the Rolling Plains as if it were their natural environment.[16]

The herders' dogs, however, did not cower before these beasts. Cow hunters along every path of migration had found the dogs as indispensable as salt or even horses in managing cattle. The British, particularly the Celts, had been using shepherd dogs as far back as the fifteenth century. The animals that ranchers brought to the Clear Fork country were fair-sized, often mottled or brindle-coated. Known as "Catahoulas," "leopard dogs," or "Tennessee brindles," not only were they capable of cutting cattle from a herd, but they also could "bulldog" a running cow or hog, dragging it down by the nose or snout. A dog belonging to Clear Fork herder Phin Reynolds found great sport in taking down buffalo cows by snapping at their hamstrings; it "had no luck" with the big bulls, however. Still, no other dogs could consistently perform this feat, certainly not the dogs that Givens had bred for sporting. The wide-ranging herds, which could wander more than a day's ride by horseback, eventually diminished the importance of the dogs on the Great Plains. Stockmen continued to use them, however, out of habit and fondness.[17]

The only thing for which the Southern background did not prepare the Clear Fork herders was their conflict with Plains Indians. From 1861 until long after the Civil War ended, raiding parties hit settlers in the Clear Fork country. Even though confrontations occurred infrequently, the constant dread of Indian depredations kept settlers ever vigilant for the rare occasion when chance brought them face to face. In 1863, W. C. McGough and some cow hunters in the lower part of the region narrowly avoided an ambush by knowing better than to pursue blindly three Indians whom they caught driving away some cattle. As the herders followed, about nine more Indians appeared; the men's caution afforded them the distance to avert a calamity.[18]

An almost comic episode involving two youths and a Comanche warrior demonstrated the peril of relaxing guard. Hol and James Clark mistook an Indian for a friend whom they had invited to hunt turkeys. Calling to the figure silhouetted against the dim skylight, they approached quite close before realizing their mistake. One of the frightened brothers shot the Indian's horse from under him, but as they fled for their cabin, the boys somehow crossed paths with the equally terrified Comanche. Leaning against a tree, "screaming with almost every breath," the warrior finally alerted several comrades on horseback, who rescued him.[19]

Pioneer rancher T. E. Jackson and his wife learned just how swift and irrevocably life-changing these confrontations could be. One moment their young son Henry was playing with his whip at the family's cowpen; the next instant an Indian who had burst from a thick motte was standing on the boy's neck, steadying his tiny head for the scalping knife. Jackson and some ranch hands rushed to save Henry, but arrived too late. As they chased after the raider, the little boy, bleeding and disoriented, picked up his whip and started for the house.[20]

Frontier settlers received only patchwork assistance against the terror of living so vulnerably and had to rely mainly on themselves to hold the land. Counties raised militias, and both the state and the Confederacy maintained a presence part of the time, but manpower was short, and the commitment to frontier protection was weak. Settlers and their unreliable protectors nevertheless gave a good accounting, besting Plains Indians in most encounters, but only infrequently did troops and the home guard engage them. The Indians' continual raids frustrated the thinly distributed troops and demoralized pioneers. Many settlers moved behind the tenuous frontier to await more tranquil times.[21]

Clear Fork herders were lucky; they spent more time worrying about Indians than fighting them. Their neighbors in the Cross Timbers, however, were less fortunate. The middle Brazos country lay directly below the Comanche reservation and presented a more inviting target than the sparse westernmost region. Perhaps, too, the marauders harbored more antipathy toward the Cross Timbers settlers for their role in the Reservation War. In any event, the Comanches and Kiowas saved their most savage raids for families in Young, Parker, and Palo Pinto counties. Small bands normally struck without warning, fighting only as long as they held an advantage. Punishing the Texans added to the warriors' laurels, but looting their stock and possessions was undoubtedly the reason for the raids.

During most of the Civil War era, settlers resolutely resisted encroachments. The usually small size of raiding parties meant that encounters were hazardous for both sides. The Indians were normally at a disadvantage regarding firearms, and with ranging companies and local militia frequently patrolling the frontier, warrior bands sustained many casualties. Living in unbroken anxiety discouraged many settlers, yet others saw little advantage in returning to the war-torn East and remained on the frontier.

In the fall of 1864 perceptions changed when the desperate Indians turned to massive attempts to drive the whites away. Just north and west of Belknap over five hundred Comanches and Kiowas—some reports claimed a thousand—besieged settlers along Elm Creek and the middle Brazos. Men and women living in the weakly protected valleys above the abandoned fort had never seen warriors in such numbers. Little Buffalo, who led the raid, could not have chosen a better time. Ironically, most of the Rangers assigned to this area were on a scouting mission seeking these very Indians. A large group of settlers who had congregated at civilian post "Fort Murrah" were unaware at first that the raiders had skirted them to attack the more exposed pioneers. Several men who could have defended their families had left for milling and supplies, and still others were cow hunting.[22]

At midmorning a smoke signal drifting above the hills alerted the warriors to launch their surprise raid. The protracted assault ended only with nightfall. Several settlers caught unprotected in their fields and homes met with horrible deaths. From the safety of Fort Murrah, Franz Peveler watched through his telescope as Indians killed two neighbors, Isaac McCoy and his son. Peveler later stated: "I never had a more horrible and helpless moment." At another home, warriors prodded a Mrs. Fitzpatrick with a spear, forcing her to watch them scalp and split open her daughter's skull. At the same home they raped and scalped another young woman and killed a baby by slamming it against a wall. When some nearby men spotted a group of Indians on the other side of the Brazos, they secreted their families in a cave, then tried unsuccessfully to draw the raiders away. The barking of some dogs that had joined the women and children betrayed the refuge, but the Indians remained cautious. They called—in clear English—for everyone to come out, that they were friends of the whites. Arrows protruding from the frightened dogs, however, made clear their true intentions. At the home of George Bragg, a picket structure with only cutouts for doors and windows, "hundreds" of Indians besieged five men— one of them an eighteen-year-old black youth—and over twenty women and children. Most of them survived only because a nearby skirmish distracted the attackers. Covering the settlers' retreat, several Rangers and pioneers sacrificed their lives.[23]

The fight was not all one-sided, however. Even Joseph Myers, whom the settlers found scalped, disemboweled, and quartered, had exacted a price for his hideous death. At the Bragg house the occupants were well armed, and the men—"expert shots"—kept up a constant fire as the women loaded and fed them fresh guns. Twice the sharpshooters rebuffed desperate charges on the cabin. With a volley of shots ringing out from cracks in the pickets, the men cleared the yard; soon the flagstone doorway became too slippery with blood for the Indians to enter it.

Rangers put up the fiercest resistance. They engaged the marauders in the open field, killing seven or eight before retreating toward Fort Murrah, where the Indians laid another brief siege. That night the uneasy settlers watched the silhouettes of their attackers against the backdrop of campfires; when dawn came, they were relieved to find the Indians had departed.[24]

When the raid was over, the warriors headed back toward the Red River with loot and captives. Some estimated the loss in cattle at between five thousand and ten thousand head in Young County alone. All the way to the Red River, the territory was virtually denuded of beeves. The Comanches and Kiowas had driven off many horses as well. More devastating was the capture and captivity of almost a dozen women and children. A final act of barbarity punctuated the ferocity of the attack. When hard riding proved too much for one little boy, his captors placed him on a pile of brush and set it afire as his mother watched helplessly. Had it not been for the foresight of those who erected Fort Murrah, the loss of life would have been compounded.[25]

The aggressive nature of the Comanche-Kiowa offensive and the extremes by which they savaged their victims overshadowed the greatest significance of the Elm Creek raid. The Indians had failed. By all reports more of their number were left in the field than those of their enemy. Death was just as final for a warrior felled by gunfire as it was for the disfigured corpse of a white child. However harsh they may have treated their victims, life was equally precious to the Comanches and Kiowas—especially at a time when their population was declining at an alarming rate. Their territory was contracting as well, and the killing and looting on this raid were of little comfort as long as their enemies remained entrenched. Along with the spoils of war, they carried away the realization that their best effort had fallen short of intimidating the settlers into a full retreat. Never again would this frontier see Indians in such numbers descend across the border to attack the well-armed, tenacious Texans.

News of the terror spread quickly, impelling the Clear Fork settlers to reappraise their situation. Before Elm Creek they felt relatively equal to the Indians' challenge. Small raiding parties had been ill-suited to wholesale marauding. Open confrontations against the herders' superior weaponry had usually proved foolhardy, and the wide-open range did not afford the Plains tribes many opportunities to lay ambuscades. On one occasion, typical of their methods, Indians lured some cowmen to a creek bank with an old horse. Although no lives were lost, the herders, through long familiarity with such ruses, should have known better. As long as families remained near their homes and cow hunters stayed in groups, their security was largely assured.[26]

But now, the prospect that Indians in overwhelming numbers might descend upon them at any moment provoked a drastic response. On New Year's Day, 1865, Sam Newcomb wrote in his diary that "a great many of the old settlers have left the frontier . . . to older settled counties where Indian depredations are unknown." Only to this degree had the massive attack been

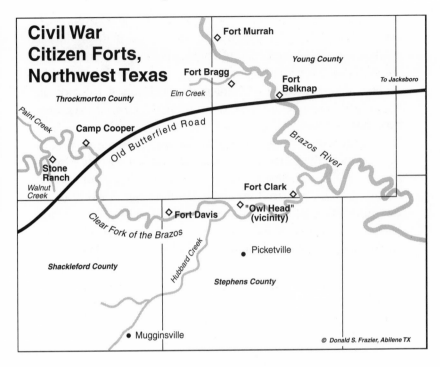

Civil War Citizen Forts, Northwest Texas

Fort Murrah

Young County

Fort Bragg

Throckmorton County

Elm Creek

Fort Belknap

To Jacksboro

Paint Creek

Camp Cooper

Old Butterfield Road

Brazos River

Stone Ranch

Walnut Creek

Fort Clark

"Owl Head" (vicinity)

Clear Fork of the Brazos

Fort Davis

Hubbard Creek

Picketville

Shackleford County

Stephens County

Mugginsville

© Donald S. Frazier, Abilene TX

successful. Those who refused to leave followed the example of Fort Murrah and congregated for protection. All along the Texas frontier settlers "forted up" in neighborhood bulwarks. In the upper Clear Fork region they came together at several places. Downriver from Camp Cooper, just inside Stephens County, pioneers took refuge at Fort Davis. East of that post were Forts Owl Head and Clark. South of them families clustered around Fort Hubbard and the tiny village of Picketville. Even farther south, they assembled at Mugginsville, near present-day Moran.[27]

Any of these places could have provided the seed for a permanent settlement, but few inhabitants were inclined to stay. These people were mostly cow hunters, pioneers of an independent nature, Southerners with no predilection for town building. In other regions, crossroads towns would have emerged as supply points or as centers where farmers could bring produce and buyers could congregate. But in this country, herders trailed their product to market. Their goal was self-sufficiency. Besides, the countryside was too sparsely settled to support such a crossroads community without the stimulus of something akin to Camp Cooper or the Butterfield. Even before the Civil War ended, most of the citizen forts had dissolved.

These "forts" varied in size and layout. Hubbard was really nothing more than a ranching operation belonging to J. C. Lynch and C. C. Cooper. Fort Clark, in Newcomb's estimation poorly defended, was "scattered up and down the bank of the river for two hundred yards." Picketville, resembling a true community, had become a collection of small, ramshackle homes around a school, which provided a communal focus; in 1861 the state had designated it the temporary county seat. Several families remained even into the 1870s, attracted to the school and the picturesque valley where large pecan trees lined the creek banks. Still, it possessed no business district and was never more than a collection of shacks.[28]

The largest, best-planned, and in some ways the most "un-Southern" of the citizen posts was Fort Davis, where approximately 125 people assembled, including twenty-five families. The community, named in honor of the Confederate President, was reminiscent of an orderly New England town. Sam Newcomb, the only true "Yankee" in the entire area, may have been responsible for helping plan the 300-foot by 325-foot compound. He was certainly a respected member of the community; his neighbors, in fact, seemed to have overlooked his northern background. The fort, divided into sixteen seventy-five-square-foot lots, was laid out with streets and alleys. The settlers constructed all but one house from pickets daubed with mud. The exception, a stone building, provided greater security. The crowning achievement was to be a palisade, but the settlers never completed it. This defect did not matter; Indians never attacked the post, although after a dance men once found moccasin prints where warriors had jigged to fiddle music before stealing the horses of the invited guests.[29]

Life at Fort Davis was probably typical of that at all the citizen defenses. Despite privation and a sense of mortal danger, the experience grew bittersweet with the benefit of hindsight. Many developed a sense of community that outlasted their association at the little forts. They normally lived far apart and only infrequently gathered for social events. For the women and children, especially, the daily contact with others filled a void. Cow hunting and other activities regularly brought the men together, but seldom did their families enjoy the ordinary social intercourse that community living afforded.[30]

Despite that banding together, the want for normal conventions of civilization persisted. A few children reached adulthood on the frontier before ever hearing a sermon. An ardent suitor once rode all the way to Palo Pinto just to obtain a marriage license. Part of the adjustment to frontier life was simply learning how to remain alive. When "Uncle Billie" Sutherlin fell ill, he refused to allow anyone to traverse the Indian-plagued frontier to bring a doctor. Someone finally rode to a settlement sixty miles away only to return empty-handed, but it did not matter; Sutherlin's neighbors had already buried him.[31]

Davis, more than any of the other places, possessed the earmarks of a nascent town. Settlers raised several homes and other buildings, such as smokehouses, a school, and a blacksmithing operation. Just before the fort broke up, William G. Hoover had attempted to establish a store, but he was robbed and killed while returning from New Orleans, where he had trailed a herd of cattle. Sam Newcomb was the schoolmaster and initiated a regular fourteen-week term. At his first session he counted nineteen "scholars," who were obviously not the sort that he was accustomed to teaching in New England. They were, Newcomb wrote, "rude and wild, [and] unacquainted with school discipline."[32]

The one establishment that would have made Fort Davis a true community was a church, but this frontier in the mid-1860s did not begrudge such a blessing. Organized spiritual contact would remain almost nonexistent in this country for another decade. When settlers in Buchanan County could not sustain a Methodist meeting house before the war, the nearest church was at Palo Pinto, a prohibitive ride for Sunday worshipers. People observed the Sabbath as a day of rest, but with no service, it was normally long and boring except for those who played marbles or ball or found other diversions. Forting up nevertheless provided a ready-made congregation that attracted an occasional visit by itinerant clergymen. Newcomb logged the occasion of the first Sunday school at Fort Davis, noting that "old father Clark" started by reading a chapter from the Bible; Parson George W. Slaughter later delivered the first sermon. Newcomb wrote that some "persons in this place . . . are grown, married, and are the parents of children and have never been to a religious meeting."[33]

The memories of old-timers winnowed out hard feelings as well as the sometimes vindictive nature of inhabitants living in such small settlements. But as the diary of Sam Newcomb testified, all was not idyllic. On a visit from Owl Head, Joe Matthews brought news that it "may be breaking up." One-half year after coming together, the little post indeed dissolved. The same feeling existed at Fort Clark as well. Perhaps a tinge of jealousy accompanied the seeming success of Fort Davis. When the people there invited everyone in the surrounding country to attend a formal dedication of their orderly and well-built little stronghold, all but a few ignored their hospitality. Such offers did not normally go unanswered.[34]

Several times Newcomb logged in his diary incidents concerning the fort's inhabitants that illustrated the pressures of the confining isolation. Hol Clark and Mitch Anderson, for example, engaged in a two-year feud over their dogs. They shot each others' animals and got into fistfights, prompting Susan Newcomb to fear that it would end with one of them dead. Even the women were not immune to emotional outbursts. The matriarchs of the Musgraves and Clark families became involved in a "small but disgraceful" fight over their children. A more lethal disagreement ended in two deaths at Mugginsville, where a man named Mayhare killed stock raiser J. A. Whitten. A party of citizens, circumventing the uncertain legal system, quickly settled the matter by executing the suspected murderer.[35]

Gaiety broke the monotony of life more often than ill will. Several times Davis settlers held dances that neighbors did attend; young people traveled to Camp Cooper for picnics, and some even enjoyed a little rough fun at the expense of their neighbors. Once, someone ran an unusually large bison through the fort, scattering screaming women and children. About forty large, fierce dogs immediately set upon it, killing the beast in a matter of minutes. The formal ceremony at Fort Davis that settlers from the other posts ignored—no doubt because they viewed it as pretentious—was "the hoisting of the flag." At noon the men formed a company under arms, while a train of women, joined by a band, marched to the front of the line and presented the soldiers with the flag. Sam Newcomb received it, and in the name of his fellow settlers he led a procession through all of the streets of the fort. At the flagpole they raised the banner "amidst three loud and long cheers for Fort Davis." After firing eleven salutes, the soldiers dispersed. The ceremony, however, was not without incident; a cartridge burst, slightly wounding Mr. Sutherlin. Lightning later destroyed the flagpole, and the settlers never replaced it.[36]

A favorite diversion for the men was buffalo hunting. During the winter of 1865, a party of hunters took two wagons on such an expedition and made camp, spreading their blankets on the cold, wet, ground. The men ate and "spun a few yarns," Sam Newcomb recalled, then turned in with "no other canopy . . . except a dampt cloudy sky." The next day some boys in the group caught a couple of bison with their dogs. They killed one with a knife after their animals dragged it down. A few miles farther on the hunters made another camp on Ranger Creek, then split into several groups. One killed four or five bison; another, despite locating some great herds, experienced a run of bad luck because they positioned themselves upwind of the beasts. The other groups fared better. Sam Newcomb wrote that a Mr. Musgraves charged one old buffalo that was "so poor it could not get up and killed it by stabbing it and knocking it in the head with rocks."[37]

The herder folk did not allow the threat of Indian depredations to keep them from the plains, but occasionally a scare conjured

Alice Reynolds, *Flag Ceremony, Fort Davis,* 1941, oil on canvas. (Robert Nail Foundation Archives, supported by the Old Jail Art Center, Albany, Texas)

up images of Elm Creek. Almost any "Indian sign" could trigger terror. During the spring of 1865 some cow hunters alarmed the people at Fort Davis when they returned with a yearling calf that

had an arrow in its side. When four or five warriors who had
ventured within three miles of the fort gave Press McCarty a close
race to safety, all was confusion. Women gathered up children,
some of them tearfully voiced distress about husbands and sons
away from the fort, and others ran amok "like they had lost all
reason." Several men saddled horses and gave chase but returned
in the evening without a fight. Everywhere, Newcomb reported,
the pursuers saw evidence of Indians.[38]

After stories of the Elm Creek raid had spread, anything seemed
possible. Occasional incidents reinforced rumors, lending an air
of credibility to the wildest speculation. If the Indians were not
enough of a threat, settlers feared that the Civil War itself would
reach the frontier. "Every one in this whole country," wrote
Newcomb, believed that "the Indians and Kansas Jayhawkers will
come down on us in the Spring in numbers heretofore unknown."
Returning from Decatur early in 1865, John G. Irwin brought news
of a "glorious victory won by the Confederate army at Richmond."
Eventually, however, the sad truth of the defeat reached them. They
also heard that Union forces had captured and were about to execute
Jeff Davis and his cabinet, who were "apprehended in possession
of $16 million." As the war was winding down the startling news
that the French had drawn a reunited United States into a war over
Mexico filtered into the frontier. Soon, the rumor "proved true."
American troops, they mistakenly learned, had engaged the French
twice, splitting victories with them below the Rio Grande.[39]

As rumors such as the "new war" proved unfounded, more
and more people felt secure enough to return to their accustomed
life-style. Herders John and Bill Hittson moved into the old officers'
headquarters at Camp Cooper. A Mr. Hightower and the McCarty
and Browning families settled there as well. The Reynolds family,
along with the Newcombs, appropriated the Stone Ranch. Just as
the prewar advance had brought them this far, other herding families
were considering a postwar move to the Colorado, Concho, and
San Saba countries to the west and south.[40]

As the forts broke up and herding families returned to their
independent ways, women readjusted to a different kind of life than

that confronting men. Isolation and monotony replaced the feminine contact enjoyed daily at the little citizen posts. In a land where men did manly things together, women often faced solitude. Their youth, moreover, succumbed early to pioneer life and a multitude of suitors longing for companions.[41]

Sam Newcomb's wife, Susan, provided a case in point. She followed her husband's lead, recording thoughts in her own diary. Feelings of loneliness and hardship pervaded her writing. After the war ended and the Newcombs had moved into the Stone Ranch, Susan appraised her life on this frontier, where Indians had "captured many little children" and "killed and scalped many a one of our poor countrymen." She lamented over the long stretches of time that Sam spent away from home driving cattle and the fact that she was "eighteen miles from a living being." But she felt thankful to "see the little birds warbling their sweet songs," the vast herds of cattle, and, in the autumn, the bison, which "blacken the valleys and hill sides." But never, she wrote, could she go to church or visit a friend. Deprivation and loneliness had been constant companions for this woman in the four years since she had been married—this woman of eighteen years.[42]

With social contact generally lacking, pioneer women took full advantage of the rare occasions that brought them together. Weddings and dances were especially welcome events. Late in 1862, when the Connecticut youth Sam Newcomb had married his Susan, news of their wedding spread by word of mouth; everyone, of course, was welcome to attend. Women prepared for days, looking forward to the big event, baking, roasting, and barbecuing, and making do without ingredients that war had denied them. Neighbors were quite gracious, pooling their scarcest items, such as eggs and butter. The festivities included candy pulling and dancing; frontier folk would use any excuse to dance. Three years later Susan's brother George married Elizabeth Matthews at Picketville. A large part of the upper Clear Fork population attended this affair as well, filtering into the village over three days, some riding seventy-five miles. Again, women planned the festivities and prepared the food. They made sure that everyone had plenty of cake and provided a washtub full of hot coffee to keep them dancing to the fiddles that played until daybreak.[43]

Women saw to it that the festivities possessed all the proper trappings for such merry occasions, and this was no small feat. They had to improvise for the simplest items, even in everyday life. When men wore out their shirts, the discards provided good material for bed sheets and children's clothing. The forelocks from bison made comfortable mattresses. From deer and antelope skins women fashioned suedelike suits for the boys; their only defect was that after they became wet "the buckskin would stretch and become stiff and hard." At times even the basic necessities were wanting. Anne Reynolds, matriarch of the extended herder family, recalled a four-year stretch when she did not even taste coffee. Parched sweet potatoes and okra, however, would pass for this staple if the memory were short and the imagination strong. Bolts of cloth were unknown as well; pioneer women had to spin their own yarn and weave their own cloth. But as the cattle-rich reputation of this frontier spread during the war, Fort Davis attracted a Waco trader named Wilson, who brought a wagon filled with items seldom seen by the pioneers. This windfall threw the homemakers "into a fever" as they fingered through gingham and calico cloth, tobacco, hats, pins, needles, buttons, hooks and eyes, sewing thread, knives and forks, teaspoons, matches, gun caps, combs, shoes, and pencils. Wilson drove a hard bargain, but the women would not let him leave with any item unsold.[44]

Even though social and material conventions were lacking, frontier standards for "acceptable behavior" differed little from those of anywhere else. When a young woman "from a respectable family" bore a stillborn baby out of wedlock, she got nothing but sympathy from Sam Newcomb. He wrote in his diary that the man responsible had used every means in his power to win her "affection and confidence." Sam believed that she would have done almost anything for the man—even to let him "rob her of her virtue." In Sam's opinion this philanderer was "guilty of the most heinous, blackest crime that a man can commit." The women were not so forgiving. Before the year was out another unmarried girl found herself in the same condition. She had somehow managed to conceal the pregnancy, although her neighbors had grown suspicious. When the time came for her to deliver, she stole down to the creek and disappeared long enough to prompt a search party. When the group found the young woman, she claimed that "something burst inside her" while she was climbing the creek bank, causing her to hemorrhage. The gossip finally caught up with her when someone found a baby in the stream. The next day, the young woman tried to commit suicide.[45]

For women more "deserving," only another woman knew how to comfort a kindred soul suffering the burdens of giving life and facing death. Doctors were scarce on the frontier, and at most birthings women helped each other. When Anne Reynolds was distressed over the burden of parturition at forty-five years of age, a neighbor lady knew just what to tell her. "This little girl," she vowed, "would prove God's blessing in her old age." Several years later Mrs. Reynolds returned the kindness when an old Fort Davis neighbor, a Mrs. Selman, fell mortally ill. The sick woman sent word to her friend that she wanted to see her before she died. Despite her age, Mrs. Reynolds set off for the old citizen post, riding sidesaddle at a gallop. "She felt repaid," her daughter later wrote, "when her dying friend held her hand and whispered a fervent, 'God bless you.' "[46]

Such tender mercies sprang from the same expectations as raising children or keeping the homestead. Still, frontier conditions often enlarged women's roles. Many helped their mates when extra hands were scarce. When husbands died or deserted, wives sometimes assumed their burdens. Five years after the slaying of J. A. Whitten, his wife, Sarah, still tended their herd. And she was not the only female raising stock in the Clear Fork country. Several women headed households, and sadly, Susan Newcomb joined their ranks. After Sam died during a measles epidemic in 1869, she made ends meet by taking in boarders before remarrying ten years later.[47]

Assuming the responsibilities of men was uncommon, however; even in the rare instances of Indian attacks, women fulfilled the feminine roles expected of them. Support was such a duty. On one occasion a woman went to tell her husband, who was among a group about to pursue some raiders, to lay back in case of a fight. But as she approached, so many men were gathered within earshot that "her heart failed." And women generally did not defend—they were defended. Given the opportunity, raiders killed men, women, and children indiscriminately, but only women and children suffered the horrors of prolonged captivity. This fear provoked different reactions from two women during a raid at the Ledbetter Salt Works just after the war. One panicked, running senselessly through a vicious crossfire; the other coolly loaded guns for the men.[48]

Few women came to this land expecting encounters with Indians. Even fewer possessed the choice of remaining behind if their husbands were set on westering. Like all pioneers, however, they no doubt anticipated arduous conditions. They were comforted by the thought that the vanguard of this new land would be due the rewards of persistence. This no doubt sustained first-comers through incredible hardships. Sallie Matthews remarked that her parents had come here "for the sake of . . . preparing an easier road for their children." They expected "civilization" to grow up around them—and it did. For a scant handful of settlers, the rewards would be even greater than they had envisioned, but enduring the transformation would also prove more difficult than they had imagined. Imprinting their civilization, moreover, was long in coming.[49]

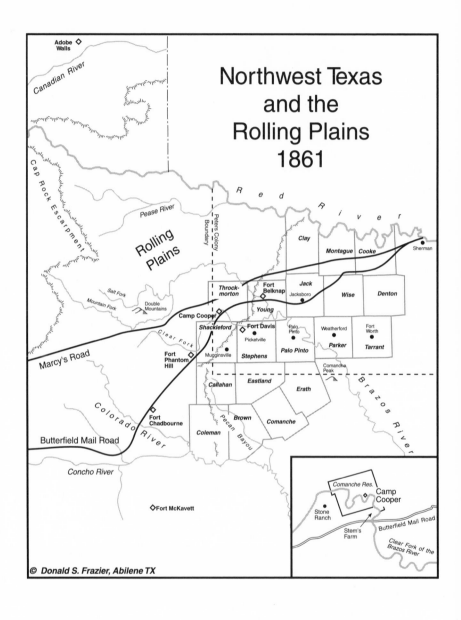

Northwest Texas
and the
Rolling Plains
1861

Adobe Walls

Canadian River

Cap Rock Escarpment

Pease River

Rolling Plains

Peters Colony Boundary

Red River

Clay

Montague   Cooke

Sherman

Salt Fork

Mountain Fork

Double Mountains

Throckmorton

Camp Cooper

Shackleford

Fort Belknap

Jack

Jacksboro

Young

Wise   Denton

Fort Davis

Picketville

Palo Pinto

Weatherford

Fort Worth

Clear Fork

Marcy's Road

Fort Phantom Hill

Mugginsville

Stephens

Palo Pinto

Parker   Tarrant

Callahan

Eastland

Erath

Comanche Peak

Brazos River

Colorado River

Fort Chadbourne

Brown

Comanche

Pecan Bayou

Butterfield Mail Road

Coleman

Concho River

Fort McKavett

Comanche Res.

Camp Cooper

Stone Ranch

Stem's Farm

Butterfield Mail Road

Clear Fork of the Brazos River

© Donald S. Frazier, Abilene TX

CHAPTER FOUR
KIND'A LIKE OLD TIMES, 1863–1874

FRONTIER HERDING FOLK demonstrated their hardiness and persistence during the Civil War years. They welcomed help from the parade of ranging companies that had replaced the federal garrisons, yet even when a military presence was lacking, the cow hunters held tenaciously to the land. Stockmen even tested the near reaches of the plains, withstanding both Indian raids and thefts by a growing body of rustlers. Many abandoned the frontier entirely, but others took their places, joining first-comers. They erected dwellings along the length of the state's western border from the Red River, near present-day Wichita Falls, to south of old Fort Chadbourne. Despite new challenges, the remaining cattlemen were poised to conquer the greatest grassland on the continent as the Civil War wound to a close.[1]

Early in the summer of 1865, Sam Newcomb wrote in his diary that the situation on the Clear Fork was "getting a little like old fashioned times." But at first glance, if he saw the end of the war as a return to normal, he was soon disappointed. The South had been vanquished, and the Texas government writhed in confusion. The troops that remained on the frontier became demoralized and shortly returned to their homes, leaving the backcountry unprotected. The population between Fort Davis and the interior had thinned considerably, and the future for settlers in the region grew increasingly uncertain. During the war an undercurrent of deserters and criminals arose; they did not come to settle, but to take advantage of social instability. Above all, the imminence of Indian raids hung over the region like a dark pall.[2]

Settlers along the Texas frontier suffered terribly just after the war, and none were more exposed than the herder folk on the edge of the plains. Late in the summer of 1867, Governor J. W. Throckmorton wrote to Secretary of War Edwin Stanton that since Appomattox, Indians had killed 162 Texans and wounded or carried off many more. He estimated that they had also stolen thirty-one thousand cattle and almost three thousand horses. Clear Fork settlers during the war had remained on constant alert for the rare but ever threatening encounters with Indians. Now, without troops to help check the onslaught, they felt even more vulnerable to the large-scale raids that had so frequently plagued their neighbors in the Cross Timbers.[3]

Scarcely a month after Newcomb's optimistic entry, Indians hit the Clear Fork country in the first of three raids that confirmed the settlers' worst fears. Phil Reynolds, a single man unrelated to the herder family, had departed from the Ledbetter Salt Works for a load of wood when some Indians ambushed his wagon and killed him about ten miles from the mine. Reynolds's oxen wandered off the road and into a tree, knocking his lifeless body from the driver's seat. Some men later came upon him and found the team lodged in the branches of another tree about a mile away.[4]

About the same time, near old Camp Cooper, two dozen or so warriors attacked seven cow hunters who had left Fort Davis to set up a residence closer to their herds. One of the stockmen, Press McCarty, fled to the post to warn their families. J. A. Browning also made it back, but everyone feared the worst when the others failed to return by nightfall. Their apprehensions were surely justified. John Hittson had been wounded in the hip; an arrow had pinned his brother William to his saddle. They still managed to lead the others to the shelter of a ledge on nearby Tecumseh Creek. Freeman Ward, a black youth with the group, never reached safety, however. The fatal mistake of stopping to retrieve his hat allowed the raiders time to overtake him; as Ward resumed flight, they ran his horse into some boulders and then "slaughtered him," according to a chronicler. At the creek bank the war party tried to dislodge the besieged men by rolling rocks upon them, but after an hour they settled for the herders' horses and departed. Phin Reynolds recalled hearing that as the men and women at Camp Cooper braced themselves for a follow-up assault, all but Ward appeared—on foot—as welcome as "dead would be from the grave."[5]

"Uncle Johnny" Eubanks, who settled his family near the source of Hubbard Creek, endured a more heart-wrenching experience. Nine days after a roundup on Pecan Bayou, south of Shackelford County, he learned that his son Thomas had failed to appear. A search party scoured the countryside southeast of Mugginsville, where they found two dead horses. They discovered an Indian buried close by with Thomas's powder horn and belt along with two shields, some silver plates, and other belongings. Fearing the raiders had taken his son captive, Eubanks traveled to Fort Cobb, Indian Territory, where several white boys were presented to him, but Thomas was not among them. About three years later some men found the boy's skull and some personal effects in a dense motte near the spot where the dead horses had been discovered.[6]

These encounters represented the sum of recorded depredations in the Clear Fork country during the three years following the war; thus, conditions were not as dire as the mood indicated. That settlers refused to surrender the range is not surprising. The threat of atrocities, however, unsettled them as tales of raids and captivity filtered in from the Cross Timbers and elsewhere. Many again recoiled to the safety of the citizen posts, but others, at their peril, remained exposed. In 1867, for example, a war party attacked the Stone Ranch, where the Reynoldses had taken residence. The family was fortunate that two travelers had stopped there and were able to help defend the place in the absence of the men, who were cow hunting.[7]

No doubt settlers found the redoubled intensity of raids over the length of the frontier disturbing. But the backcountry had never been as peaceable as Sam Newcomb remembered—and not solely on account of Indians. The immediacy of present conditions had perhaps caused him to forget about the Old Law Mob and the gang of horse and cattle thieves that had worked the frontier before the war. While earnest settlers had forted up, outlaws and opportunists had strengthened their operations, and by 1863 countless deserters had begun to join their ranks. Even before the end of the war they had burgeoned into a noticeable menace, threatening the tenuous stability that herder folk had brought to the range. North Texas, especially, had seethed with criminals and deserters, who drained manpower from Indian patrols. As the war wound to a close, units such as Colonel James Bourland's Border Battalion had scattered the renegades into the sparsely peopled hinterland of West Texas, from the Wichita River to the Concho River. Other lawless men were already there. General Henry E. McCulloch, pressed to divert his frontier troops to eastern theaters, responded that if his command left, "this country would, in some places, be at [the deserters'] mercy." Above the Clear Fork country, in 1864, a large group of Unionists assembled, many with families, to depart for California. According to one Ranger, hardened "fugitives and renegades" flocked to the émigrés with plans to remain and plunder the poorly guarded frontier. They even grew so bold as to enter homes demanding arms.[8]

Billy McGough, a second lieutenant with a divided regiment that patrolled between the Clear Fork and Stephenville, remembered the confusion of a country "overrun by bad characters of all kinds, both colored and white." Major George B. Erath had ordered him to arrest all deserters and compel any "loose men" to account for themselves and "hang all of those who were robbing and stealing." But McGough commanded only a tiny band normally outmatched by gangs of deserters, and his effectiveness—like that of other undermanned patrols of his kind—proved minimal.[9]

Often men abandoned their units or evaded conscription. Many were Unionists and resisted compulsory service in the Confederate army. A large number were concerned simply with protecting their families and crops. Still others had merely provoked the enmity of their commanders. Rip Ford pointed out that "an officer when prejudiced against a private can give him a lively foretaste of hell." So, instead of submitting to harsh military discipline, soldiers— such as Fort Davis boy John Selman—often would desert then rejoin another short-handed group that would welcome them. Troops, in fact, arrested Selman at the citizen post in April 1865, but scarcely a month later he was back in the service of another unit guarding the frontier south of Waco.[10]

Yet another motive compelled deserters and draft evaders to flee to the unsettled regions. Indians, Comancheros, and even Union purchasing agents had cultivated a lively market with outlaws, bartering for stolen horses and cattle. Toward the end of the war, frontier troops concentrated more on uprooting these opportunists than on patrolling for Indians. Significantly, when McCulloch ordered Bourland's unit to the frontier late in 1864, the two men most familiar with the country were sitting in a Gainesville prison. Enlistee D. S. Howell claimed that the pair earlier had attempted to kill Bourland to avoid having to serve the Confederacy. The commander nevertheless commissioned them to guide a patrol to Camp Colorado, about sixty miles south of old Camp Cooper, where they had discovered a nest of "deserters and various renegades." One of the deserters saw the soldiers approach, Howell remarked, and upon the outlaw's warning, "Men streamed forth from the houses and ran away like rats from a burning barn." The sight amused the trooper, who numbered them at fifty-four, although he added: "I'm sure I did not count them all."[11]

Patrols, despite the limits of their abilities, made the frontier perilous for anyone not connected with the military. Early in 1864, Sam Newcomb and George Reynolds, among a group scouting for good rangeland, had intercepted some Indians trailing a herd of stolen horses between the Colorado and Concho rivers. They engaged the raiders, who fled bareback on the swiftest mounts. The men noticed blood on the saddle of one jettisoned animal, leading them to speculate the circumstances of its capture. Before the Clear Fork cow hunters could return the horses to their owners, rumors reached state Rangers that they had stolen the herd from the Confederacy. Soldiers confined the stockmen to an old cabin at Camp San Saba until they were able to satisfy the ranking officer of their good intentions.[12]

By the summer of 1865 conditions on the Texas frontier had worsened considerably. Although the militia continued to patrol the backcountry, anarchy reigned in certain areas of the state during the brief interlude before federal occupation forces arrived. Rapacious mobs, upon realizing that the Confederacy was doomed, looted entire towns and arsenals, even sacking the State Treasury in Austin. After their arrival on June 19, Union troops added to the bedlam, badgering civilians and plundering the interior. In turn, Texans on frontier duty, with their pay in arrears and former comrades returning to civilian life, gradually abandoned their posts.[13]

More than a year elapsed before Governor Throckmorton took office in September 1866; he strove valiantly to provide relief to the beleaguered frontier, but his administration met resistance at every turn. Having commanded the state's First Frontier District during 1864 and part of 1865, Throckmorton knew intimately the settlers' desperate situation, but Reconstruction and the federal occupation distracted those who might have responded to his appeals for relief. Among his first actions, the governor attempted to recruit a new frontier regiment; U.S. Army District Commander Philip Sheridan, however, forbade the former rebels to organize troops. Throckmorton thereafter tried to accommodate Union officers, reasoning that a pacific interior would release men for frontier duty. At the same time, he deluged federal officials at every level, importuning them to address the crisis. He even telegraphed the grisly details of recent Indian raids to President Andrew Johnson and implored him to assure some means of assistance.[14]

While the U.S. Army staged campaigns against the Plains Indians north of the Canadian and Red rivers between 1866 and the end of the decade, it all but ignored the threat to life and Anglo expansion south of Indian Territory. The Department of the Missouri, encompassing most of the Great Plains, did not extend its jurisdiction into Texas, which remained coupled with Louisiana under the same administrative umbrella until 1871. Thus, at the same time that the army was spending millions harassing Indians from Oklahoma to Montana, Comanches and Kiowas who raided Texas farms and ranches almost unchecked, enjoyed a lucrative trade with New Mexican Comancheros. Throughout the former

Confederacy, the military focus remained on occupation. General Sheridan demonstrated how little he knew about the pioneers' situation when he marveled that "over a white man killed by Indians on an extensive frontier the greatest excitement will take place," while Texans voiced little concern over "the killing of many freedmen in the settlements."[15]

By 1867 many pioneers had come to depend upon their own resources for protection. In April some of the Clear Fork herders exacted revenge against the Comanches for recent raids. T. E. Jackson, John and Mitch Anderson, Silas Hough, George and William Reynolds, and several others pursued a party of warriors to the Double Mountain Fork of the Brazos near the Haskell-Stonewall County line, where they noticed a large cloud of dust kicked up by running buffalo. A closer look revealed seven Indians—actually, five Comanches, accompanied by a Hispanic man and an African American in Indian clothing—slaughtering one of the beasts. Abandoning their quarry, the warriors charged the cow hunters. One "Indian" all but emptied two six-shooters in the direction of George Reynolds, who had separated from the others. The herder dropped the warrior from his horse, however, and later killed him by breaking his neck. Another of the Comanches shot Reynolds with an arrow, its iron spike lodging in his back, where it was to remain for several years. The cattlemen soon forced the warriors into a full retreat, with Silas Hough hotly chasing the one who had wounded his friend. He soon returned with several trophies, including the Indian's scalp. In all, they had lifted the hair from five corpses and left another adversary mortally wounded.[16]

The Double Mountain fight was a rare exception to encounters between herders and Plains Indians. Raiders most often would strike and disappear into the ocean of grass before the cow hunters could assemble a pursuit party. Even when they overtook the warrior bands, stockmen might "get the worst of it," as one group readily admitted after an unsuccessful confrontation.[17]

During the middle 1860s, cattle, rather than horses, became the chief targets of Indian raiders. Herder folk soon realized the reason. Distant population centers, their resources drained by war, needed beef desperately. The Waco man whose load of goods so excited the Fort Davis women in the spring of 1865 readily accepted steers as barter. Shortly afterward, men from Dallas and other places arrived, offering ten dollars a head for good stock. As people came to regard the animals as cash on the hoof, herders not only had to guard against Indians, but also against rustlers and con men, too. John Hittson, upon returning from Palo Pinto, warned his neighbors to beware of men issuing worthless quartermaster receipts for beef steers.[18]

In 1865, cow hunters began probing for markets, trailing herds to distant locations over familiar paths and also blazing new ones. Early in the summer, a Dr. West and T. L. Stockton gathered beef steers from the Clear Fork range and headed for Shreveport and New Orleans, favorite outlets for East Texas ranchers even before the days of the Republic. Others followed, such as Charles Neuhaus and William G. Hoover, but turbulent social conditions soon closed that avenue. That autumn, George Reynolds, Silas Hough, and Riley St. John drove 125 head to Santa Fe. Taking a southwesterly course through Taylor County, they crossed each of the Concho's three forks before braving a dry and unforgiving stretch of desert to Horsehead Crossing on the Pecos. From there they followed the river north into New Mexico. A few months later Cross Timbers stockmen Charles Goodnight and Oliver Loving—for whom the route was named—picked up this course after pushing a herd through the Clear Fork country bound for Fort Sumner, New Mexico. Visionary businessman Joseph G. McCoy opened the floodgates for all Texas cattlemen in 1867, when he convinced promoters to establish a railhead at Abilene, Kansas. Within a few years local ranchers were driving cattle to places as far away as the gold fields of California and the open plains of the Dakotas.[19]

W. H. Boyd, the youngest member of an outfit that took the Goodnight-Loving Trail in the spring of 1867, recorded witnessing a momentous development on his trip. Pushing over eight hundred head from Gainesville, the drovers followed the old Butterfield road through Jacksboro; continuing westward, through the prairies and the Cross Timbers, they periodically came upon vacant homes and fallow fields. Fort Belknap and Camp Cooper, as they expected, were abandoned as well. But shortly after leading the cattle from Robert E. Lee's old post, they ran into an unanticipated but most welcomed sight. In the Clear Fork river bottoms, soldiers of the 6th U.S. Cavalry had established a temporary camp; soon they would be moving to a nearby hill, where they would erect a permanent post, Fort Griffin. From the interim location, Camp Wilson, a sergeant and six privates—all Irishmen, "a good bunch"—escorted them to the Middle Concho, where a second column, setting up another post, took over.[20]

After relentlessly showering the federal command structure with letters and petitions, Governor Throckmorton had finally prevailed upon the War Department to provide relief for the Texas frontier. The very scale of Comanche and Kiowa raids had created disbelief. General Sheridan still suspected that settlers and prospective businessmen were exaggerating reports in the hope of attracting frontier posts that would provide markets to seed their economies. He also believed that Throckmorton was using stories of depredations as a pretext to rebuild the state's military. But General Grant, impressed by the governor's evidence, ordered Sheridan to investigate and even divert interior troops, if necessary, to assist the settlers. As a result, eleven cavalry companies rode to Jacksboro despite Sheridan's persisting doubts regarding the gravity of the problem.[21]

Sheridan and Fifth Military District commander General Charles Griffin had launched a stopgap plan late in 1866 that presaged the placement of the troops that the young drover Boyd had encountered the following spring. From their makeshift base at Jacksboro the 6th Cavalry was to guard the frontier line as far as old Camp Cooper; the 4th Cavalry was assigned the area from the Colorado River to the Mexican border. Federal officers recognized almost immediately the futility of patrolling this immense frontier from their ill-placed camps—especially with a policy of passive reaction to Indian assaults. The army, even though failing to reassess its tactics, at least adjusted the post locations on schedule, approximating the antebellum configuration. On July 31, 1867, Brevet Colonel Samuel Sturgis led his men from the swampy Clear Fork bottoms to the more strategically located site atop the nearby hill. In September, after a terrible yellow fever epidemic on the Gulf Coast claimed the life of General Charles Griffin, the army honored the commander by naming the new installation for him. Fort Griffin replaced Camp Cooper just as Fort Concho replaced Chadbourne farther down the line. Along with Fort Richardson, near the 6th's temporary headquarters, these defenses loosely guarded the postwar frontier of Northwest Texas.[22]

The smartly dressed federal troops, with their shiny brass buttons and gleaming bayonets, cut an imposing spectacle to the homespun-clad herder folk. And the soldiers' self-assured march into the Clear Fork country might have seemed "as a breeze from another world," as Sallie Matthews remembered, but she was only six years old at the time. While most of the pioneers welcomed any help they could get, many among them no doubt received the troops with bated enthusiasm. After all, this force had occupied the state for two years without visiting the frontier, and only a few months earlier they had been harassing "honest white folk" in the interior. Texans also remembered that U.S. troops had maintained a presence before the Civil War, endeavoring for more than a dozen years to pacify the backcountry. When those troops surrendered their garrisons to the rebels in 1861, however, the Indians were even more of a menace than when the army had arrived.[23]

Even though Colonel Sturgis led fresh troops to the Clear Fork, he brought with him the same old policies of waiting and reacting; pioneers had no reason to expect anything other than the same old results. Clear Fork rancher Emmett Roberts claimed that Union soldiers did little to stop Comanche and Kiowa depredations. On several occasions, in fact, warriors approached the fort itself, once venturing as close as two hundred yards. Even several years later, a Griffin commander reported that a war party had taken stock within a mile of the guardhouse, admitting also that afterward they "cleaned the valley of the Clear Fork and left for the Plains." Roberts maintained that seldom did patrols recover stolen horses and cattle.

"The General would always say that he would send out his men at once," commented the rancher, "but he usually did so two or three days after the Indians had disappeared." Although Roberts may have been harsh in his assessment, encounters between Indians and Griffin's troopers were few. Many times patrols stayed on the main trails in order to keep their cumbersome supply wagons within easy reach. Such methods assured an abysmal record.[24]

As Roberts suggested, small bands of Comanche and Kiowa raiders continued their minatory thrusts into the Clear Fork country. And, as before, contests between herder folk and their adversaries remained few, short, and about equal. When some cow hunters in 1869 ran twenty horseless Indians into a depression, the two sides exchanged fire; on this occasion, the raiders forced the stockmen to withdraw.[25]

More fatal was an encounter near Picketville that same year. Some herders who happened upon six Comanches slaughtering a cow gave chase, cornering one of the Indians in a ravine. The brief siege ended when a knife-wielding stockman charged and killed the warrior, but not before two of the Clear Fork men fell wounded—one fatally.[26]

About the same time, in the southern part of Stephens County, several Indians surprised some teamsters after their army escort abandoned them to hunt deer. The freighters bolted from the wagon and luckily escaped across a divide. Fourteen-year-old George Bishop was not as fortunate. East of Picketville, some marauders suddenly appeared, forcing him and his horse into a fallen tree. They dragged Bishop into a thicket, stuffed grass into his mouth to prevent him from calling for help, and then riddled him with arrows.[27]

Although home-bound pioneers had long known that moonlit nights were a particularly perilous time, cow hunters on the range could never predict when warriors might suddenly strike. Constant vigilance provided the only assurance of securing their persons and property. Routinely they hobbled their horses in different locations around camp to cut the chances of losing them all. Cow hunters never left or entered camp during the daytime, and seldom did they even remain in one location long enough to carve a path from their camps to the range. Men normally joined their herds early in the morning and did not return until after sunset, "no matter how tired we were," Roberts noted, "so that the Indians watching us could not follow." One outfit, he recalled, hid their camp so well that a raiding party almost ran a herd of horses right over the sleeping men, not realizing they were there.[28]

In part because the cow hunters were so cautious, Indians seized any advantage that chance allowed. One moonlit evening in July 1872, John Hittson and eleven others were camped near present-day Ballinger. Someone awoke to discover that Indians had spirited away many of their mounts. Gathering their few remaining horses, the men headed for their headquarters, just below Shackelford County. Before noon the next day, about seventy-five Comanches attacked the herders after feigning to offer a truce. Except for the cook, who fled for his life, the party took cover behind the chuck wagon, where they resisted a day-long siege punctuated by the desperate charges of screaming warriors. Only with nightfall did the men manage to escape.[29]

The casualties suffered by each side attested to the reluctance of both stockmen and Indians to engage each other in pitched battles. Despite escaping with their lives, one of the herders eventually died from his wounds. The dozen or so dead and wounded warriors bought their comrades neither territory nor stock.

Although Indians continued to plague herder folk, even Emmett Roberts conceded that the federal presence discouraged large-scale invasions. The growing roll of ranchers testified that the post provided a significant measure of comfort. Soon after Fort Griffin was established, B. W. Reynolds moved his wife and children to a river bend about a mile above the post because he felt that his family would be safe there. When Captain Wirt Davis toured the Clear Fork country in 1869, attempting to organize a local defense, he noted that eight or ten families still resided at Fort Davis; twelve more comprised the community of Picketville; and, eight miles west, another tiny settlement, Sand Creek, had arisen. Ranches radiated to the south and east from the Clear Fork of the Brazos, thinning at the hinters of Callahan, Taylor, and Eastland counties. Captain Davis enrolled sixty-one men and estimated that he had visited about three-fifths of the people in the immediate area. If sectional antipathy remained, it was overshadowed by the recognition that the troops had come as a relief force rather than an army of occupation.[30]

Such a large area, inhabited by a hundred or so cow hunters, their families, and people who worked for them, might have seemed insignificant to an unknowing observer. A year before Captain Davis conducted his enlistment tour, another officer reported: "No crops, what few residents there are here are stock raisers." Considering the environment, however, and the manner in which its inhabitants were using the land, the population was feeling out the limits of the area's resources. The society and economy had become increasingly one-dimensional: rural, cattle-based, Southern, and about 90 percent white. By 1870 all but a handful of civilians in this region were directly involved in ranching. Fort Griffin kept a few men and women busy, but most of the others, whether butcher, teacher, blacksmith, or salt maker, to some degree owed their livelihood to herder folk.[31]

A hidden wealth belied the cow hunters' humble appearance. Personal worth had swelled with the exponential growth of their herds during the Civil War years and the high price that cattle were bringing in distant markets. By 1865, in Nebraska, Iowa, Illinois, and Wisconsin as well as the Utah and Wyoming territories, cattle sold for $25 a head. In Kansas and Missouri they normally brought $20. The animals that the Clear Fork men trailed to Santa Fe commanded $60 apiece. Even though local herders delivered thousands of cattle to market, the average stock raiser on the plain's edge had listed the value of his personal property at about $125 in 1860. Stockmen typically underreported their holdings to lower tax valuations. William Hittson, whom Phin Reynolds called "the wealthiest man in the country," listed his net worth at $2,500 in 1860. Joe Matthews and John G. Irwin both estimated their worth at about $5,000 each. With a Texas cow appraised at four dollars, the figures suggest that Clear Fork cattlemen ran, on the average, only about one thousand head apiece. But when Indians raked off that very number in one raid, Sam Newcomb mentioned the theft in his diary with the same stolid commentary that accompanied the report of a plum hunt that took a group of young people down to the river banks.[32]

By 1870, families who had persisted against the elements, Indians, and rustlers had reaped a tremendous windfall. First-comers typically reported a fivefold growth in personal wealth over the decade; no doubt they based the price of their still underreported holdings on the Texas price of beef. Matthews admitted to twenty-five thousand dollars in personal property. Even at four dollars a head this translated to 6,250 animals. Valuated at the northern Great Plains rates, his holdings had increased more than thirty times since the war began. Perhaps the ranchers themselves did not know their true net worth; between the free-running animals and wide-ranging thieves, an accurate count proved difficult. The prolific growth of the herds, however, was beyond doubt. The men at Camp Cooper, for example, who in 1865 had suffered the Indian attack that claimed the life of Freeman Ward, were reportedly tending 25,000 animals.[33]

Despite accumulating small fortunes, ranching families continued to live simple, austere lives in the postwar period. Even with their operations growing to meet the size of their herds, and with others beginning to crowd them, few cattlemen bothered to purchase the land on which their livestock grazed. This de facto subsidy kept their capital outlays low. The Clear Fork's largest landholder possessed only $2,250 worth of real estate in 1870—twice as much as the second largest holder. Unlike the nouveau riche in other regions during the Gilded Age, herding folk did not build palatial mansions to herald their new-found prominence.[34]

Outwardly they remained as unpretentious as their mud-chinked picket cabins. In this land where no center for social and economic activities existed, people were not likely to be impressed with extravagances. Townbuilders, until almost the mid-1870s, ignored this edge of civilization, scrambling instead to refurbish older centers to the east such as Weatherford, Palo Pinto, and Jacksboro. People on the sparsely settled border of the Southern Plains found the distant centers sufficient, however inconvenient, for their limited trade and administrative necessities. "In the spring," Emmett Roberts recalled, "the boys would take a wagon, and at Fort Worth load twelve or fifteen hundred pounds of flour, canned good, etc." The low profile, coupled with the meager population, masked the cattlemen's social and economic dominance over the vast region.[35]

Cattle, pushed to the edge of the Great Plains by earnest stockmen during the Civil War, now pulled others into this country. A few, such as Roberts, had long been engaged in the business. They were simply westering in the well-established herding tradition. Many came solely for adventure or to better themselves with no intention of becoming rich. Others, expectant capitalists, possessed a larger vision. The opportunity of a "resource rush" lured men such as Ohioan James A. Brock, who brought with him no background in ranching. Still a few others, such as a handsome young drifter named John Larn, lusted for instant wealth and prestige, using any means necessary to achieve their objectives.[36]

Indians and the harsh environment suppressed the ranchers' migration even into the 1870s; yet other forces pushed westward some stockmen who sensed those obstacles as less of a threat than social conditions that disrupted the interior. Several from the Cross Timbers approached the plains undaunted. Despite being exposed to depredations, they suffered fewer losses at the hands of raiders and rustlers than from neighbors—well-intentioned and otherwise. As ranchers in the bountifully stocked ranges to the east prepared for long drives, foreign animals invariably coursed through the herds; cattle encountered along the trail also fell into line.

The state, with checkered success, erected a bureaucracy designed to limit such losses. Beginning in 1866, the Texas Legislature required cattlemen to file bills of sale and register brands at their courthouses before trailing a herd to market. Then, in 1871, Governor E. J. Davis appointed agents in every county to regulate passing herds. Rustlers naturally found the system disruptive, but even cattlemen, upon finding that many inspectors were dishonest, became inimical to this practice and resisted the state's efforts. Owners normally agreed by mutual consent to keep brand records and settle accounts after driving cattle to market. Left to their own word, however, many hedged. Some even evaded men to whom they were indebted. Even though cattle inspectors recorded the "tallies," obligations expired after two years, and many unfortunate cattlemen went unpaid.[37]

In 1873, Emmett Roberts and Mode Johnson, surfeited with conditions in Palo Pinto County, moved their headquarters well beyond the treeline to a site a few miles above old Fort Phantom Hill—then the farthest point on the range. Indians, they knew, would challenge them, but they did not expect the bald-faced expropriation of their herd by men with whom they shared the range. Roberts and Johnson, who had joined several cow hunters on a roundup, confronted a group in the act of "branding over" and leading away their cattle. Roberts recognized several of his animals, some of them milk cows that he handled daily. One of the interlopers directed him to their leader, John Larn, who treated him cordially yet firmly. After sharing a meal, the two rode to join the other cattlemen. The audacious Larn, who had intruded on this range, insisted that the other ranchers could reclaim only the animals that they roped, threw, and proved were freshly branded. According to Roberts, Larn's men outnumbered his group, yet despite flagging support he accused the dishonest stockman of the obvious and insisted upon reclaiming his animals. The impasse was broken when some Belknap-area ranchers arrived for the same purpose—"that is, to get some of their cattle," which Larn had "branded and was driving away."[38]

In one brief anecdote, Roberts imparted to Larn the qualities that propelled the aspiring stockman from the ranks of prosaic criminals into the caste of eminent ranchers. The beguiling and enigmatic young man, not yet twenty-five years old, was the polished successor of antebellum and Civil War stock thieves who rivaled first-comers for control of the range. An Alabaman by birth, he fit well into the largely Southern population; a man of action, he possessed a strength of spirit that naturally attracted a following. A contemporary newspaper described Larn as "fine looking, of good address, good nerve and a splendid marksman." He arrived on the Clear Fork by way of Trinidad, Colorado, followed by rumors that he had fled that town on a horse whose owner he had killed. Although the hearsay was unlikely—Larn openly trailed a herd through Trinidad soon after his departure—his quickness to favor expediency over principle invited such stories. Few times, in fact, did solid evidence betray his facade of virtues. When Joe Matthews's daughter Mary became enraptured with Larn, the widely respected herder reluctantly accepted the union. The influential relation cemented the young man's thrust into prominence.[39]

Henry Comstock, a Wisconsin farm boy newly arrived in Texas, described a cattle drive marked by the particularly opprobrious behavior of the drovers, notably their foreman, John Larn. The outfit, in the autumn of 1872, had contracted to trail the herd to Colorado for local stockman Bill Hayes. Although the owner tallied and registered his animals, the manner in which Larn became "lost" near Fort Concho, only to pick up the trail on the other side, left Comstock to speculate that Hayes had simply "gone through the motions." Not long afterward, a detachment of cavalry from the fort, "about twelve of them, all darkies, fine young men in the prime of youth," followed the drovers, ostensibly to compel them to return the herd for inspection. When the corporal in charge discerned that Larn had prepared his men to resist, the soldiers relented.[40]

Comstock had anticipated that riding for a living "would be like life in a rocking chair." The rough nucleus of the crew, however, disabused him of any romantic visions of frontier life. The young cowboy described how one of the men, Bill Bush, boasted about his pretensions of becoming "a desperado and dying with his boots on." Comstock claimed that along the trail Bush murdered at least three men, one a drunken comrade who had insulted and threatened him with a knife. Most of the drovers, in fact, feuded and fought; friends even turned on one another. Together the men bullied through any strangers they encountered. Hispanics especially shouldered the drovers' violence. Comstock declared that when a well-dressed pair crossed the herd's path at the Pecos River, Larn and Bush "fed them to the catfish." He also maintained that once the outfit reached New Mexico, the two again murdered a Hispanic

sheepherder for no apparent reason. Drover Tom Atwell, attending
a dance at the trail's end, reportedly killed yet another.[41]

Even if all of Comstock's wild tale were true, reports of
lawlessness in the Clear Fork country had diminished between the
troops' arrival in 1867 and the early years of the new decade. Most
Civil War deserters had either returned home or found other areas
more inviting. But as rootless men rediscovered the western edge
of settlement, rustling became a grave concern. During 1872 and
throughout the next year, post commander G. P. Buell believed
that rustlers had made horse and cattle theft "an established business
in this part of the country." Many of them raided "Indian fashion"
to throw blame onto the Comanches and Kiowas. The ruse, however,
fooled no one. By 1873, professed the colonel, "I became satisfied
that white men were behind most of the thieving."[42]

Buell was as anxious as the ranchers to stem the incipient crime
wave, but his well-intentioned response unwittingly nurtured a
vigilante movement. Almost since the troops arrived at Fort Griffin,
soldiers and stockmen had patrolled for Indians side-by-side. Stock
thieves were no less an economic threat than Indian war parties;
and with the Clear Fork's law enforcement and civil court—based
in Palo Pinto—incapable of capturing and punishing guilty men,
joining forces against them seemed a logical step. Buell viewed
the situation as "simply a question of power as to who should control
this country, the thieves or good citizens." Unfortunately, men such
as Larn were among the "good citizens."[43]

Superficially, an intensive campaign against the network of
rustlers carried all the earmarks of success. Lieutenant E. P. Turner
and a detachment of "buffalo soldiers"—the black troops of the
10th Cavalry—teamed with a citizen patrol to apprehend at least
twenty outlaws. Later, Turner and an unnamed "constable" pursued
others into East Texas.[44]

Buell's report no doubt convinced officials in Austin and San
Antonio that the effort had dealt a severe blow to criminals operating
in the Clear Fork country. Perhaps the colonel even believed it
himself. John Larn had nevertheless played him for a fool in order
to settle a personal dispute with his former boss, Bill Hayes. The

old cattleman had lost the herd that Larn had trailed to Colorado when the market collapsed during the Panic of 1873. In an effort to wrest control of Hayes's interests, Larn swore out a warrant for him when Hayes attempted to trail another herd to Fort Sill. At Boggy Creek, a few miles above Bushnob in Throckmorton County, Lieutenant Turner reported that Hayes's outfit had fired on his party. The soldiers and citizens killed two of the drovers instantly as well as two more who tried to escape upon being captured. After taking four prisoners that afternoon, the party camped at Bushnob Creek. Turner contended that sometime during the night these captives also tried to escape, forcing the sentinels to kill them all. Despite official reports, many citizens believed that Larn's men had simply executed their prisoners. Bill Bush, among the fallen, realized the aspiration he reputedly confided to Comstock—he "died with his boots on."[45]

Neither army officers nor stockmen recognized that the changing social conditions necessitated civil rather than military solutions. As new cattlemen, earnest settlers, and outlaws began pouring into the Clear Fork country during the mid-1870s, stock thefts multiplied. The fiasco at Bushnob, rather than raising a red flag, instead set an unfortunate precedent. The well-intentioned cooperation between the army and settlers degenerated into one of the bloodiest vigilante movements in the state's history.

CHAPTER FIVE
A BLOODY CONQUEST, 1867–1875

I F TEXANS LIVING on the northwestern frontier greeted U.S. Army troops with mixed emotions, the bluecoats' inability to end the Indian depredations validated the settlers' doubts. But the army faced many handicaps. Lessons learned from the Civil War did not prepare troops for Plains Indian warfare. The long and bloody sectional struggle, moreover, had left the country jaded, and most Americans were unwilling to rally around another armed cause. On the other hand, religious groups, pacifists, and Indian rights advocates still possessed a fighting spirit, and they directed it at generals, politicians, businessmen, and pioneers who advocated force to restrain the native peoples. And even though the army had established a presence in Texas, neither government officials nor influential citizens had any sympathy for the former rebels. Many, in fact, believed that the Texans had brought on their own troubles. Finally, shrinking budgets, reductions in manpower, and an ill-suited military strategy compounded the problems of defending the seemingly infinite frontier line.[1]

The Plains Indians, too, were less than awed by government efforts to protect the settlers. Despite the new cordon of posts, Comanche and Kiowa raiding parties easily slipped through the porous gantlet during the winter of 1867–1868. They viewed the renewed military presence as a challenge and were contemptuous of the bewildered soldiers whom they so easily eluded. The Department of the Interior, which directed the Bureau of Indian Affairs, also earned their wrath. The most northern and bellicose Comanche bands had spurned the 1867 Medicine Lodge Treaty that offered them a reservation in return for promises of peace; many of them nevertheless decided to inspect the land on which their more amenable tribesmen had settled. The warriors, expecting food and presents, found instead that Wichitas and other sedentary Indians had appropriated parts of the reservation. Soon the Comanches, joined by their Kiowa allies, began a series of raids on the peaceful tribes in defiance of their "benefactors." And upon returning from forays below the Red River, warriors brazenly flaunted the scalps of white settlers before federal Indian agents and even bragged of their exploits.[2]

The Plains Indians who swept across the Texas border country in the postwar years bore little resemblance to the destitute Penateka Comanches. The Quahadies, a northern band of the tribe—joined by various other Comanches as well as Kiowas and Kiowa-Apaches—had for years crossed Texas to raid Mexico but had had little contact with the Texans. They regarded the whites with no more respect than old Buffalo Hump had shown for the Mexicans. They pitched their tipis north of the Red River almost exclusively, venturing south only to steal cattle and horses. The Quahadies and their allies raided for livestock in small parties, but did not pass up opportunities to take scalps or captives. The raids were reminiscent of the Penatekas' before they had been weakened and pushed out of Texas.[3]

Major W. H. Wood, one of several Fort Griffin commanders, laid a plan of defense that looked equal to the challenge—at least on paper. The 6th Cavalry, primarily responsible for patrolling the vast area under his jurisdiction, would use infantry, Tonkawa Indian scouts, and a line of subposts for strategic support. The major wrote enthusiastically that Griffin was best situated among the new forts for defending the Texas frontier. It "embraces within its limits the counties of Haskell, Jones, Taylor, Throckmorton, Shackelford, Callahan, Stephens, Eastland, Comanche, [and] Erath," and parts of Knox, Baylor, Young, and Palo Pinto counties.[4]

Although the area was immense, Wood believed that the small and concentrated population made it easier to defend. He felt confident that with sufficient manpower he could safeguard the ranches scattered along the Brazos and its tributaries, because "the rest of the country is uninhabited." Only three towns, Palo Pinto, Comanche, and Stephenville, lay within these limits, and each, with about three hundred people, was on the extreme eastern front.[5]

To protect the westernmost country the army established subposts on the road to Fort Concho. At full strength, a company of infantry, five mounted cavalrymen, and two Tonkawa Indian scouts garrisoned old Fort Phantom Hill, thirty-three miles southwest of Fort Griffin. These troops furnished a small detachment for another bulwark at Mountain Pass, thirty-five miles closer to Fort Concho. From these small fortifications soldiers patrolled for Indians and provided escorts for the mail, travelers, and emigrants.[6]

Despite the military presence, settlers in the immediate area surrounding Fort Griffin remained guardedly watchful for their adversaries. By 1870, Stephens and Shackelford counties had become home to 785 people, largely situated along the Clear Fork of the Brazos and its tributaries; still others lived along the same fertile ribbon in Throckmorton County, which census takers failed to canvas that year. Although Indian depredations in the Clear Fork country were more an irritant than a mortal threat to the emerging Anglo population, trouble in other areas kept them seeing an Indian behind every tree.[7]

Pioneers who "saw Indian sign" near the center of Shackelford County in 1867 believed that raiders were responsible for the disappearance of the Ledbetters' youngest son. The homesick boy, attending school at the Hubbard Creek ranch of J. C. Lynch, reportedly attempted to hazard the fifteen perilous miles to the salt works not long before a heavy rain. After the storm passed, W. H. Ledbetter and some cowboys scoured the countryside, but "the calls of the searchers," remarked a chronicler, "floated away and died on the dark night air."[8]

The next year Clear Fork settlers were alarmed over news that two hundred warriors had swept through the North Texas counties of Wise, Denton, and Montague. This followed a smaller raid— but one much closer to the plains—in which Indians abducted a

woman and her baby. The infant's incessant crying provoked one
of the captors to dash its brains out against a tree.[9]

Wood admittedly harbored no illusions that his well-placed
defense would end the Indians' forays. Warriors raided all year
around, he noted, but "ordinarily at the time of the new moon,
in small parties, and for the purpose of stealing stock." The
Comanches and their allies knew the land so well, and were so
adept at concealing themselves, that they could enter the country
at will. Mobile camps and a nomadic life-style burdened the Indians
with few of the encumbrances of permanency; their homes and
few possessions could be easily replaced. For the army to dispatch
units to search for Indian camps or to await raiding parties at
predictable trails meant leaving some other area exposed. And the
raiders struck with lightning quickness. "Even old men, women,
and children can mount and disappear before scouting parties can
arrive," Wood reported in 1872. Packing skins of water and departing
with fresh mounts stolen from settlers, he added, they "are soon
beyond pursuit."[10]

Raiding parties seldom passed up a chance to kill an unwary
settler whom they found alone, but Comanche and Kiowa warriors
generally continued to avoid pitched battles if possible. They were
more concerned with plunder. Late in the eighteenth century,
Spaniards west of Comanchería had informally established an outlet
for the tribe's contraband. The New Mexican traders—Comancheros—nurtured their commercial ties, asking few questions about
the source of Indian barter goods. When the Civil War opened the
Texas frontier to wholesale depredations, the traders welcomed the
increased traffic. In return for Texas cattle and horses, they provided
the Comanches and their allies with guns and ammunition, when
available, as well as such "luxuries" as whiskey, tobacco, coffee,
and sugar. Trails leading from the edge of the plains into the
Panhandle and New Mexico became well worn. According to John
Hittson, Indians spirited off one hundred thousand head of Texas
cattle between the Civil War and 1873.[11]

In an effort to constrict the flourishing trade, commanders at
Fort Griffin invited local settlers to join forces with the army. Even

before federal occupation troops allowed the Texas Legislature to
raise "minute man" companies in 1871, stockmen in the Clear Fork
country were riding with soldiers. In January 1869, Colonel S. B.
Hayman complained to the Adjutant General's Office that his usable
cavalry force had dwindled to twelve, and he requested permission
to raise a hundred local volunteers. He punctuated the appeal by
warning that "unless some measure is speedily adopted . . . the
hostile Indians . . . will lay waste every vestige of civilization in
this country." His urgency no doubt sprang in part from the fact
that a month earlier he had authorized Sam Newcomb to enroll
the exact number that he now requested. His superiors in Austin
fortunately acquiesced, and before autumn sixty-one settlers had
"enrolled their names willingly and appeared anxious to organize
and participate in all movements for the protection of the frontier."[12]

The army also enlisted the ill-fated Tonkawa Indians as scouts.
The nomadic little tribe, native to the Texas heartland, had
endeavored to occupy a place between their traditional enemies,
the Comanches, and the aggressive, expanding Anglos. When forced
to choose sides, the Tonkawas entrusted their destiny to the Texans.
Ever afterward their culture, overshadowed by their guardians'
ascension, was marked by a steady decline. On the eve of the Civil
War the tribe had fled to Indian Territory with the other American
Indian groups evicted from the Lower Brazos Reservation. Once
more the Tonkawas became ensnared by conflicting loyalties, this
time between the warring whites. In 1862, in the southwestern
corner of the territory, several tribes from among their late neighbors
seized the opportunity to exact revenge for long-standing grievances,
all but exterminating the beleaguered Tonkawas.[13]

State and federal officials believed that military supervision
would provide the only hope for rejuvenating the demoralized tribe.
On August 4, 1868, 143 destitute survivors, poorly armed and on
foot, arrived at Fort Griffin. Since the massacre they had been
camping near the towns, begging for food and whiskey and annoying
settlers. In a letter to the governor, Agent John L. Lovejoy wrote,
"Their conduct has been so bad that I have determined to let them
shift for themselves." Governor Throckmorton, through the federal

command post at Austin, arranged for them to be moved to the frontier. The army agreed to provide the Indians refuge in return for their services as scouts.[14]

For many Tonkawas, the opportunity renewed their sense of purpose. Soon, twenty-five armed enlistees in blue uniform jackets sat proudly astride government-issued horses. The army even allotted them full rations and a private's allowance. Such treatment heartened the men, who viewed their new-found importance as a symbol of status among their tribesmen. And the Tonkawas performed admirably. When their enlistments expired the following year, Captain John Lee prevailed upon the army to retain them.[15]

When raiders struck the Clear Fork country one inclement spring day in 1868, the full might of the combined forces— stockmen, soldiers, and Indian scouts—enjoyed the singular occasion of a complete rout. A group of herders was the first to encounter the war party. At a roundup near Battle Creek, just south of Shackelford County, one of the stockmen raised his head into the cold, stiff wind and blowing sand and spotted a Comanche. He quickly rallied a force to scout the area, and at a nearby rise cowboys and Indians came face-to-face. The well-armed herders soon outgunned the bows and arrows of their more numerous adversaries, forcing the war party from the field. After the skirmish the stockmen combed the countryside; in a small grove of live oaks they found George Hazelwood lying dead with more than a dozen shells and several curious-looking black arrows scattered around his body. Gone were his Spencer rifle, pistol, and horse. On further investigation the men found a dead warrior and evidence that Hazelwood had wounded at least two others.[16]

The chastened Comanches then retreated northwestward, drawing the attention of settlers near Mugginsville. The next morning they besieged several men, women, and children at the Ledbetter Salt Works. A Hispanic trader who had ventured from San Antonio for salt had also contracted with the mine owner for a load of bison hides. The sight of about a thousand rotting carcasses littering the surrounding prairie no doubt strengthened the warriors' resolve. The deadly accuracy of the defenders' rifles, however, once more proved superior to bows and arrows. As the repulsed raiders fled, Ledbetter rammed the king bolt from a wagon into a small cannon and delivered a parting shot.[17]

After the aborted attack, two of the defenders walked twenty-five miles to Fort Griffin, where they reported the incident to Captain Adna R. Chaffee. The troops, accompanied by their Tonkawa scouts and a party of stockmen, immediately pursued the ragged war party. The scouts had no trouble tracking the Comanches, who were burdened by three wounded warriors dragged on litters behind their horses. Between the forks of Paint Creek, about eight miles south of present-day Haskell, the Tonkawas discovered the enemy camp. The pursuit party spent a miserable night without fires or sleep, waiting anxiously to surprise the Comanches at first light.[18]

The dawn attack on March 6, 1868, was short and one-sided. The Tonkawas particularly relished the initial assault, savaging their rivals with guns, knives, and clubs. The whites briefly suspended the action to question the survivors, who explained that they had fashioned the black arrows found near Hazelwood's body to honor their war chief—an African American whom the settlers had killed the previous day. The troopers believed that he was Cato, an occasional resident of Fort Concho. After learning this curious revelation, the soldiers unleashed the Tonkawas to complete the massacre. A tall, broad-shouldered scout named Johnson reportedly "came out of the fight with seven scalps dangling at his belt."[19]

The Comanches' total defeat contrasted starkly with their more successful visits to Northwest Texas. Yet the three-day affair demonstrated that many of the same attributes that made the Plains Indians consummate thieves also limited their martial abilities. Even though their surprise raids consistently frustrated the settlers, they lacked the military discipline and weaponry to concert their efforts and gain more impressive victories. And while nomadic customs made the warriors elusive and resilient, an unstable life-style and the inability to cultivate dependable forage offset their advantages. Most important, the Indians did not understand the monolithic forces of expansion that threatened their domain, and they were unable to comprehend an enemy with unlimited stores and manpower.[20]

For its part, the U.S. government was slow in adopting policies suited to ending the Indian wars. Its plans were ill-conceived and characterized by patchwork strategies within military divisions and tugs-of-war between personalities and federal departments. None of the army's top generals—Grant, Pope, Sherman, and Sheridan—advocated annihilation, yet they all agreed that aggressive action was absolutely necessary to pacify the Indians and confine them to reservations. Disagreements over strategy nevertheless divided the generals until 1871. Public pressure also constricted their freedom to take the offensive, and Congress was reluctant to support costly military campaigns. As a result, the most insurmountable obstacle to peace on the army's terms was not dealing the Indians a physical defeat; instead, it was reconciling the conflicting aims of the Departments of War and the Interior. Reformers, refusing to believe reports of Indian atrocities, assembled a potent lobby in Washington that fostered an unnavigable current of resistance to military solutions. Their efforts resulted in President Grant's Quaker Indian Policy, which reformers naïvely believed would concentrate, Christianize, and civilize the "wild" tribes without first subduing them by force. This moribund policy languished from 1869 until 1872, when it collapsed in the wake of Republican scandals and continued Indian depredations.[21]

The Comanches and Kiowas took full advantage of the environment manufactured by Grant's Indian policy. Paying lip service to their agents, war parties dipped across the Red River and then returned to the safe haven of the reservation, where troops were forbidden. Into the spring of 1871 the raids waxed in both numbers and cruelty. The worsening situation was in part a response to the overtures of a peace commission that entertained a delegation of Plains chiefs in Washington, D.C. Just as Buffalo Hump in 1845 had registered his condemnation of a similar gesture by executing a crushing raid on Mexico, his progeny now vented their wrath on Texas. Hardest hit were settlers between Forts Griffin and Richardson, due south of the raiders' reservation near Fort Sill, Indian Territory. In Young County the Indians killed four African Americans, including Britt Johnson, a "hero of the Elm Creek raid."

After scalping, emasculating, and disemboweling him, they stuffed his pet dog into his abdomen. Not far from that place they attacked another man and scalped him alive. Emboldened warriors twice attacked settlers within gunshot range of Fort Richardson, and by the fifth month of 1871, Indians had killed fourteen pioneers.[22]

The desperate outcry had already grown to numbing proportions, prompting General William T. Sherman to make an inspection tour of the Texas frontier. He landed in Galveston in April 1871 accompanied by the old explorer, Randolph B. Marcy, now inspector general of the army. Proceeding to San Antonio, the men skirted the frontier line from Fredericksburg to Fort McKavett. So confident was the commander that reports of Indian atrocities had been exaggerated, that he traveled in a cumbersome army ambulance escorted by only fifteen buffalo soldiers of the 10th Cavalry. Passing through Fort Concho and the picket outposts, Chadbourne, Mountain Pass, and Phantom Hill, the contingent arrived at Fort Griffin on May 14 without so much as sighting any Indians. Following the Butterfield road, the party reached Fort Belknap two days later. A picket squad manned it like the other subposts, but the cynical general did not accept the fact that this once populous site now stood deserted for reasons other than a lack of water. Sherman, in fact, could not understand why families remained exposed "as though they were safe in Illinois," if indeed the accounts of Indian depredations were accurate. "Actions are more significant than words," he concluded, all but dismissing as wild tales the reports that brought him to Texas.[23]

As Sherman and his escort headed toward Fort Richardson, ten Griffin-bound wagons belonging to Henry Warren and partners crossed their path just two hours behind them at Salt Creek Prairie. A hundred warriors, mainly Kiowas, impatiently observed the two unwitting parties from a solitary rise overlooking the uneven meadow. At the insistence of medicine man Owl Prophet, the warriors allowed the first group to continue its journey, unaware that the stern-looking man in the ambulance commanded all the troops of their enemies. As the Indians remained hidden, foreboding charcoal-colored clouds began to form in the midafternoon sky.

By the time the wagons emerged from the woods, the dark and roiling canopy had lowered, lending a surrealistic quality to the scene. When the train reached the middle of the open prairie, the blast of a faraway bugle pierced the stillness. The horrified teamsters looked up to see the huge Kiowa war party charging from about a half mile away. Hastily they circled the wagons. Four of the defenders fell immediately as the Indians rushed pell mell at the makeshift corral. But five whites—three of them suffering wounds—somehow reached the safety of the treeline, where the mounted warriors broke off their pursuit. As the shocked and disoriented survivors groped their way toward Fort Richardson, a torrential rain began to fall.[24]

Sherman's party reached the post at sunset; that evening he received groups of officers and citizens. He listened intently, if skeptically, to the complaints of one local delegation who presented him with a petition outlining a long and woeful record of deaths, tortures, and captivities. Then, about midnight, the first of the five survivors of the attack, Thomas Brazeal, hobbled into the fort. Sentries carried the man, who was bleeding from a bullet wound, to the infirmary, where Sherman and post commander Ranald Mackenzie listened to his shocking account. When the other teamsters arrived, confirming Brazeal's story, Sherman realized that he had narrowly escaped the same fate. At once he ordered Colonel Mackenzie to assemble a unit to gather details and pursue the war party.[25]

The detachment arrived at Salt Creek Prairie the next morning "in a perfect deluge of rain." The men were unable to discern the scene clearly until they came right upon the bloated corpses lying in several inches of water. The debris of the fight was scattered everywhere—"here and there a hat, an Indian gewgaw, and a plentiful supply of arrows." A soldier who observed the fallen teamsters remarked that they resembled porcupines. All of them had been "stripped, scalped, and mutilated." Some were beheaded, their brains "scooped out"; fingers, toes, and genitals of others protruded from their mouths. Those who survived the initial onslaught lived only to endure live coals heaped upon their exposed abdomens. The worst horror befell one of the men whom the soldiers found chained between two wagon wheels and "burnt to a crisp," his limbs drawn and contorted from being roasted alive. The dispatch that Mackenzie sent Sherman convinced the general that more than a half dozen years of reports pouring out of Texas were not, as he suspected, the fanciful exaggerations of grasping frontiersmen anxious to tap the federal dole.[26]

Even before this shocking incident, the swelling role of dead and captured settlers had convinced Quaker Agent Lawrie Tatum to adopt a sterner position. He wanted his Kiowa and Comanche charges held accountable for their deeds in the same civil courts that tried white men. Upon learning about the brief and bloody rout at Salt Creek Prairie, he summoned the principal chiefs to the agency. Satanta, confusing the government's faction-ridden policy with connivance between agents and Indians, readily boasted to Tatum that he had led the raid himself. The confession quickly earned charges of murder for Satanta and confederates Big Tree and Satank. On their way to stand trial before a cowboy jury at Jacksboro, Satank made a break for freedom, forcing soldiers to kill him.[27]

Despite death sentences for the two surviving chiefs, the affair ended unsatisfactorily for frontierspeople. First, the Interior Department failed to act on Tatum's recommendations for a more aggressive policy. His only recourse was to withhold rations, which provoked warriors to obtain goods and supplies by more violent means. More disquieting, carpetbagger Governor E. J. Davis of Texas believed that commuting the sentences of Satanta and Big Tree to life imprisonment would ingratiate him with President Grant. But his outrageous action only shocked the sensibilities of everyone on the Texas frontier. For a while the trial caused the Comanches and Kiowas to suspended their raids; before long, however, warriors redoubled their vicious plunges into the sparse backcountry.[28]

Settlers along the Clear Fork of the Brazos had long escaped the most sanguinary raids, but finally they suffered an incident comparable to the nightmares endured by pioneers inhabiting the Cross Timbers. Emerging from the banks of the swollen river, a party of Comanches crept silently toward the John Lee home east of Fort Griffin as the unsuspecting family was enjoying a Sunday respite. The warriors shot the patriarch as he sat on the porch, alerting the others inside. A young suitor visiting Lee's daughter Susan bolted from the house and disappeared into a corn patch, followed by a younger daughter, Cordelia. The young girl did not reach safety, however, nor did Mrs. Lee. After killing the woman and abducting Susan and the family's two remaining children, the Indians headed northward. The water, rising ever higher, prevented neighbors from crossing the river; all they could do was view the carnage from the opposite bank and speculate as to who had been killed.[29]

Depredations in the Clear Fork country peaked between 1871 and 1873. In Stephens, Shackelford, and Throckmorton counties, Indians killed at least four other people besides the Lees. Herders and other pioneers engaged raiding parties in no less than six other incidents. As usual, the mortal confrontations were stark and sudden. In another dawn attack near Ledbetter's Salt Works, four raiders lanced to death an unarmed hunter who had wandered away from camp. When warriors shot a teacher outside of Picketville, some cowhands alerted by the gunfire froze in place and only later dared venture to the scene. In another part of Stephens County, men found Ben Peobles, scalped and pinned to the ground by arrows, near his home. Most poignantly, a patrol on the Salt Fork of the Brazos discovered a young girl hanged from a chinaberry tree, her calico dress ripped open in front. The soldiers found a lock of auburn hair near the spot where warriors had scalped her from just above the eyebrows to the nape of the neck.[30]

The Indians' assaults had grown more desperate in the face of new pressures that threatened their way of life. Yet in view of the bloody raids, citizens in the Clear Fork country probably failed to appreciate that events in faraway places were bringing the racial contest to an end. In Washington and Austin politicians were clearing the way for more effective military policies. And Anglo expansion in the Central Great Plains continued to bring disease upon the native peoples and limit their ability to hold the land.

Technological and economic events, too, were making bison hides a valuable commodity. Together, these forces would all but spell an end to Indian depredations in Texas and open the Rolling Plains to Anglo exploitation.

The most telling change was a more aggressive military policy that began to take shape following Sherman's 1871 tour of the Texas frontier. If the power of decision had been left to the general, the army would have invaded the plains forthwith, compelling the Comanches and Kiowas to choose between annihilation and surrender. While the War Department failed to get carte blanche for conducting all-out war, it was nevertheless able to scrap the primarily defensive strategy. At long last Sherman won a consensus for staging winter campaigns. The conditions, though arduous for both sides, still favored the better-equipped U.S. Army.[31]

Another effective measure was combining the contiguous military departments of Texas and the Missouri. The results, however, were mixed. From old Camp Cooper in October 1871, Colonel Ranald Mackenzie led a large column of troops atop the Cap Rock, where he twice suffered the ignominy of absorbing a Comanche anabasis. The Indians' first strategic withdrawal, on October 11, netted the warriors about seventy army mounts; a little over a week later, as a blue norther whipped across the plains and canyons, the Indians created a welter of confusion in a nighttime strike that allowed their families to escape. Despite the setbacks, Mackenzie learned from his mistakes. The next year he surprised the Comanche camp of Chief Shaking Hand near the mouth of Blanco Canyon, killing more than a score of Indians—including several women and children—taking 120 captives, and burning the lodges. With their winter stores destroyed and many of their families held under guard at Fort Concho, the first Quahadie bands surrendered at the Comanche reservation late in 1872.[32]

In the meantime a fountain of Indians' grievances arose from civilian encroachments on the plains. Railroad crews, guarded by companies of troops, wandered over the land between Texas and Kansas scouting for potential routes. Even on the farthest reaches of the grasslands, surveyors peered over the tops of tripods, alarming the Indians, who knew the consequences of such activity. Far more dismaying, the work of buffalo hunters provoked both fear and rage. In June 1872, at an aborted peace conference near old Fort Cobb, Indian Territory, Plains Indians condemned the slaughter then taking place in Kansas. They also complained bitterly of being confined to reservations so their enemies would be safe in the tribes' former homeland. Ten Bears wryly suggested that since the government had so little success in moving the Indians, perhaps it should try "moving the Texans."[33]

The Texans, however, had no intention of retrenching. After Reconstruction ended, the state was finally allowed to place effective troops in the field. In 1871 the Texas Legislature authorized a score of small ranging companies, but the plan proved too costly for the state's finances. Two years later, when several companies finally assembled, the War Department refused to muster them into service, fearing that the volatile frontiersmen would surely worsen racial relations. But finally, in the spring of 1874, the legislature created the Frontier Battalion, composed of Texas Rangers. Its services, combined with those of federal troops and a small army of buffalo hunters, placed irresistible pressure on the Comanches and Kiowas. Just before the force took the field, war parties had roamed the Clear Fork country seemingly at will. In February they had stolen stock within a mile of Fort Griffin and had stripped the horses from settlers attending a revival at Picketville. By the end of the year, however, Indian depredations had all but ceased, and the Texas Rangers claimed no small part in the improved conditions. Their patrols among the settlements and the frontier line had allowed U.S. soldiers to concentrate fully on their "Red River campaign" in the Texas Panhandle. Ranger successes continued, and after 1874 even the report of sighting a hostile Indian in the Clear Fork country was rare.[34]

The great bison slaughter in Kansas and Colorado helped complete the "pacification" of the Plains Indians. Although the animal provided many native peoples with food, clothing, and shelter, it meant little to Anglos—materially at least—before 1870. A small market for cumbersome buffalo robes as well as carpets and other accouterments made from hides, horns, and hooves had provided Indians with a barter good since time immemorial. To white hunters the animal was good only for sport and food. During the 1860s a few outfits sold meat to the army, railroad crews, and settlements as far east as they could transport the perishable commodity. The rest of the animal, considered worthless, was often discarded. Hunters knew that tanners could not fashion serviceable leather from the thick, porous hides, and even the tallow was almost useless. And despite the bison's sapid meat, ranchers found domesticating the stupid and refractory animals impossible. Literally, the nature of the beast barred commercial exploitation.[35]

Then, shortly after 1870, technology transformed the bison into a valuable commercial resource. According to Kansas hunter J. Wright Mooar, an English firm hoping to develop a practical tanning process had requisitioned five hundred bison hides for its experiment. The plainsman proposed to a partner, Jim White, that they consign their own samples to his brother John Mooar in New York City. The perplexed commission firm that received the hides forwarded them to a storage facility amid much fanfare; as the noisome shipment plied through a curious crowd on Broadway, two venturesome Philadelphia tanners intercepted the hides. On both sides of the Atlantic leather workers soon conducted successful experiments; shortly afterward several firms announced they would purchase the commodity in volume. The big hunt had hardly begun when New England gunmakers facilitated the slaughter by providing hunters with a large-caliber rifle, the Sharps "Big 50." Out of its long, octagon-shaped barrel the twelve-to-sixteen pound gun hurled a .50-caliber lead slug from brass shells containing 110 grains of powder. A competent marksman, Mooar asserted, could fell stands of bison from "incredible distances."[36]

News of the new market ignited an immediate and irreversible resource rush. Before 1873 was over the rush had all but run its course on the central Great Plains. Colonel Richard Irving Dodge had observed late in 1872 that the numbers of bison in Kansas appeared limitless. The next autumn he noted that "where there were myriads of buffalo the year before, there were now myriads of carcasses." The stench from rotting animals sickened him, as did the sight of the surrounding country, which he described as a "dead, solitary, putrid desert." Dodge estimated that in the three seasons preceding the first large-scale harvest in Texas, hunters on the Central Plains killed over four million bison.[37]

As herds on the great middle range neared extinction, hunters looked for new fields. The most promising territory lay beyond the No Man's Land that formed the Oklahoma Panhandle, but the Medicine Lodge Treaty of 1867 had designated it off limits to whites. But according to Mooar, he and another man in July 1873 crossed "the neutral strip" into the Texas Panhandle, where they encountered "a solid herd as far as we could see." All day "they opened up before us and came together again behind us." Although excited over the discovery, Kansas hunters remained apprehensive, fearing that soldiers at Fort Dodge might confiscate their teams for violating the treaty. But when Mooar, at the head of a small delegation, met with Colonel Dodge, the commander reportedly satisfied their queries by declaring, "Boys, if I were a buffalo hunter, I would hunt buffalo where the buffalo are." Texas, never a party to the Medicine Lodge Treaty, extended its blessings to the Kansans with alacrity. By the end of the year hunters and skinners were hard at work on the Southern High Plains of West Texas, creeping ever closer to the Clear Fork country.[38]

Plains Indians looked upon the slaughter with horror and resolved to turn back the whites. During the middle of 1874, however, General Philip Sheridan received authority from the Department of the Interior to "punish these Indians wherever they might be found, even to following them upon their reservations." The new policy followed the moral bankruptcy of the Grant administration. No longer could Secretary of the Interior Columbus Delano sustain his peace policy against the incessant hue and cry of settlers in Texas and other states and territories contending with hostile Indians.[39]

When President Grant permitted the War Department to resume the offensive, the army executed its Red River campaign. The fatal, four-pronged thrust converged on the Texas Panhandle in separate

Comanche survivors of the Red River campaign languish at a Florida prison. In 1877, Chief Nigger Horse (first row, second from the right) would return to the Rolling Plains and make war on buffalo hunters. (Lawrence T. Jones III Collection)

columns from Fort Sill, Indian Territory; Fort Dodge, Kansas; Fort Bascom, New Mexico; and Fort Griffin. The climax of the relentless campaign occurred in September at Tule Canyon. Colonel Mackenzie, having captured over a thousand horses, had no means of transporting the animals, so he ordered his troops to drive them over a cliff. The destruction of their "treasury" broke the spirits of the defeated warriors; being herded to the reservation on foot added mightily to their discouragement. In the winter of 1875, Mackenzie and the other commanders completed the campaign, ingloriously ending two and one-half centuries of Comanche sovereignty on the Southern Plains.[40]

In this group of Florida prisoners, Chief Nigger Horse sits at the far right.
(Lawrence T. Jones III Collection)

CHAPTER SIX
A NEW ORDER, 1867-1872

SCARCELY TWO YEARS after Appomattox, the conditions of antebellum days had seemingly returned to the Clear Fork country. A new federal post, Fort Griffin, arose downriver from the ruins of Camp Cooper. Beside it, Tonkawa Indians erected a squalid village reminiscent of the old Penateka community. Other Indians— hostile plains bands—filtered through the tenuous defenses just as in earlier times. Settlers again cautiously approached the plains, still unsure of the land beyond the treeline but confident at least that the grasslands were suitable for grazing.

The situation had nevertheless changed dramatically, if subtly. Soldiers, Indians, and civilians, while again living side-by-side on the banks of the Clear Fork, looked at the future more warily than did their pre–Civil War counterparts. Townsmen forsook the edge of the plains for Cross Timbers communities. A cross-country stage line, a southern railroad route, and a patchwork of farms beside the river seemed like dreams miscast. In the place of visionaries such as Jessie Stem and those who had worked for John Butterfield, a handful of squatters eked out a living in the shadow of Fort Griffin.

The soldiers who manned the new post contrasted sharply with local herder folk. For the most part they were Northerners, but their places of origin also included countries as diverse as Prussia, the West Indies, and New Brunswick. More typically, however, men of foreign birth hailed from Ireland, England, and Germany, and most were in their twenties. The young men of the garrison, numbering about three hundred, brought with them an outlook shaped by the knowledge, if not the actual experience, of the Civil

War. Mounted soldiers and infantrymen—black as well as white—
rotated in and out of the frontier post. Some stayed only a few weeks
or months; others, such as the 4th Cavalry and the 11th Infantry,
remained for several years.[1]

Hardly any of the post–Civil War soldiers knew anything about
fighting Plains Indians. While many were veterans of the late war,
others had recently enlisted, and neither group was enthusiastic
about defending former Confederates. Englishman Jacob Howarth,
who expressed no particular purpose for joining the army,
experienced a typical term of enlistment. Recruiting officers in New
York City, where he had signed up in the fall of 1871, herded him
aboard a steamer with other enlistees and sent him to New Orleans.
At the Crescent City he boarded another ship that took him to
Indianola, Texas, where his squad caught a train to Victoria. On
Christmas day they marched toward San Antonio, arriving there
as the year ended. Advancing beyond Fredericksburg into the
seemingly endless expanse of West Texas, Howarth felt as if he
had "left civilization behind." He marveled at the sight of thousands
of bison between Fort Concho and the subpost Fort Chadbourne
as well as at seeing his first Indian, a Tonkawa. At last his outfit
reached Fort Griffin, a collection of ill-finished, rough-hewn, and
run-down shanties and tents.[2]

In five years at that miserable post he escorted mail, prisoners,
and parties of surveyors; he also took part in scouting expeditions,
but he never saw an enemy in battle. In 1874 and 1875 Howarth
witnessed what he called "the great roundup of Indians," helping
support Colonel Ranald Mackenzie's cavalry by "fetching up
supplies." At the fort he endured countless drills and idle hours,
and he saw the little town in the river bottom grow from about
fifty wretched civilians to a bustling frontier center. When his term
of enlistment expired in 1876, Howarth returned to his native
England a "seasoned veteran" of the great American Indian wars.[3]

When Howarth arrived at Griffin in 1872, the post was already
five years old. He might have been amused to learn that the men
who started work on the fort in 1867 launched their project with
great expectations. Within weeks of moving from the malarial

river bottoms, soldiers had erected a sawmill on a timbered creek and had begun hauling lumber to the hilltop. The commander believed that facilities constructed from the freshly cut boards would prove adequate until the army allocated funds for more permanent structures. Not bothering to wait for masons, men gathered native limestone and fashioned a magazine and a bakery. The quartermaster, anticipating the construction of a permanent post, ordered a hundred thousand shingles.[4]

A succession of senior officers afterward strove vainly to obtain funds for building permanent structures. The cost of stone, milled lumber, frames, and all the appurtenances for a first-rate post sufficient for six companies came to an estimated one hundred thousand dollars. In 1873, Secretary of War Belknap submitted to the House of Representatives a request for the appropriation, attaching assenting endorsements from seven levels of command. A stream of correspondence relating to estimates, plans, and sketches poured through official channels. Two years later, however, the topic remained under debate as bureaucrats waited to see whether a southern railroad would locate a right-of-way near the fort. In the meantime, troops had herded the last of the hostile Plains tribes onto reservations in Indian Territory, virtually negating any reason to rehabilitate Fort Griffin.[5]

While Forts Concho and Richardson flourished, this mid-distant post received only the barest improvements. In fact, Fort Griffin remained an eyesore until the government abandoned it in 1881. Among its fifty-two buildings the quarters of the commanding officer was the only other stone structure erected after the initial construction. Chief Quartermaster Holabird, conducting an inspection in 1872, reported that every building was "of the most temporary character." By the time he arrived, pickets had replaced lumber as the choice construction material. And of the new buildings, several were "upon the point of falling in as much as it requires propping along the sides and ends." Not one of the soldiers' barracks, he noted, provided adequate shelter. Several companies shared tiny quarters constructed of logs and pickets, four men to a hut, with chimneys that wasted enough wood for

Officers' quarters and cannons at Fort Griffin, 1872, reflect a spartan but orderly appearance. (Lawrence T. Jones III Collection)

a room six times the size. Some troops and even officers' families, he noted, "are under canvas." The tents at times caught the high winds and blew away. Fires, of course, were forbidden in such quarters, and the occupants, Holabird admitted, "have no means of keeping warm during the winter months."[6]

Conditions never improved. The dilapidated and unpainted structures added a bleak touch to the austere surroundings. Any number of small shanties, from chicken coops to outhouses, littered the unenclosed grounds. The ramshackle dwellings crowning the hill cut the sky starkly with hardly a tree to provide shade. Not only had the original lumber proved of poor quality, but also builders had miscalculated that the arid climate would dry it sufficiently to prevent it from warping. Cold wind and rain in the winter, and sand and dust in the summer, blew through cracks in every building. Flies and vermin—even in the kitchen and hospital—entered just as freely, contributing to unsanitary conditions. A hospital ward

for officers was the only place on the hill properly enclosed; patients were thankful that at least muslin covered the windows of the dispensary. The cleanest quarters in the entire complex was, ironically, the "dead room" where the surgeon conducted postmortems.[7]

Conditions outside were no better. A thicket of mesquite brush on the northeast slope of the hill provided any number of places where soldiers on duty defecated rather than walk an extra hundred yards to the privy. When the stench became unbearable, Colonel Wood ordered the men to clear away the growth. Anything for which troopers no longer had a use was casually discarded; prisoners, they knew, were always on hand to clean up after them. One such group emptied the contents of the hospital sink at the rear of the building instead of dumping it with other waste matter. Even the post surgeon admitted throwing out a decomposing human brain that he found in a bucket while policing the storeroom. He cleaned and reused the bucket. About once a month prisoners loaded the offal that accumulated at the post into wagons. Normally they dumped it about a mile downriver, where eventually the water would rise and carry it away. On one occasion a spiteful detachment deposited a load upriver at a time when a steady northwesterly breeze was prevailing. The garrison withstood the "assault" until the offal dried, and then they set it afire, which, according to the post surgeon, only partially "improved the evil."[8]

By 1875 little could be done to mask the dilapidated condition of the post. (Prints and Photographs Collection, The Center for American History, The University of Texas at Austin [CN05183])

Despite the lack of hygiene, a seasonal lack of potable water, a chronically poor diet, and the concentration of so many men on such a small patch of land, serious medical problems seldom incapacitated soldiers. The most common ailment, amoebic affliction, might have seemed epidemic considering that the surgeon reported 263 cases in the first three and one-half years. But even that number, spread over so many men, represented less than one attack per person for the period. During that time the post physician treated minor cases such as contusions or boils less than once a week. Scurvy was more dire, but fortunately rare; he reported only twenty-one cases. And even though rattlesnakes were ubiquitous hazards, the doctor treated only one bite. Malaria spread through the camp in 1869, but less than twenty men fell ill.[9]

Diseases caused by slack moral habits, such as syphilis and gonorrhea, also remained few. Yet unlike other maladies, time and treatment did not cure these afflictions. The post physician reported less than forty venereal cases when he compiled statistics for the years 1867 through 1871. Still, the percentage of infected soldiers was alarming, considering that troops spread the disease readily. But the "wild life" of the fledgling settlement contributed little to the epidemic—at least at first. Several of the thirty-nine men who contracted venereal diseases had just arrived from San Antonio;

that others had been afflicted before they reached Fort Griffin was certainly likely.[10]

Drunkenness, too, disrupted the troops' routine. In fact, only the lack of money and idle time stood between soldiers and unbroken revelry. Nevertheless, relatively few men became incorrigible alcoholics. A report of men interred in the post cemetery in 1873 did note that among the thirty-four graves were cases of alcohol poisoning and "asleep of the liver." Yet despite the free flow of "rotgut" whiskey, the doctor admitted only four men for alcohol poisoning and logged but a single case of delirium tremens in four years. The military routine assured that soldiers would have free time for only brief binges.[11]

The greatest source of disease was the intolerably foul condition of the guardhouse. Filthy and overrun with lice, fleas, and rats, the room was unventilated and never allowed to air out even though refuse under the flooring created an unbearable stench. The post surgeon noted in 1872 that "more than one fourth of the cases of sickness occurred amongst the inmates of this dungeon." He used a case in point to illustrate the problem. Private Martin McDonough had landed there in "good health" despite being charged with habitual drunkenness. Five months of confinement had brought on a "severe attack of scurvy and Chronic Rheumatism." His condition continued to deteriorate until he was finally discharged and released to the post hospital.[12]

Many of the prisoners, confined for offenses ranging from insolence and drunkenness to fighting and theft, no doubt deserved punishment. They generally policed the grounds or performed other menial tasks. Yet penalties were often more severe than their misconduct merited. At other Texas forts soldiers were tied up by the wrists, thrown into icy ponds, and confined in sweatboxes. Punishments at Fort Griffin were no less severe; mere detention in the post guardhouse could be inhumanly cruel. Other than confinement, discipline included such measures as walking a beat with a heavy log thrust over the shoulders. When a sergeant prescribed that very punishment for James Henderson, the recruit balked, vowing: "I'll be damned if I do. . . . When I get my gun,

I'll fix you." The experience, however, gave the chastised private second thoughts.[13]

A state militiaman, A. J. Sowell, once observed a man who did act on such an impulse. Arriving at Fort Griffin on a day when sleet and a cold north wind cut through the post, he beheld a soldier marching endlessly around a pole to which he was restrained. Reportedly, the man had shot to death an officer who had slapped him across the face with the flat of a saber. The trooper, Sowell later heard, "died chained to the post where we saw him."[14]

Harsh punishment and the unspeakable conditions of the guardhouse compelled the post surgeon to engage Colonel Wood in a test of wills—the former concerned over preserving the men's health, the latter concerned with maintaining discipline. Even with an average occupancy of eight during 1869, the post surgeon considered the guardhouse overcrowded. The next year, the average occupancy swelled to twenty. After Thanksgiving day 1871, when fifty-six men were jammed into the dark, warrenlike cell, the physician filed a report with the assistant adjutant general. He requested that the officer conduct an inspection "owing to the danger of some dangerous epidemic such as typhus breaking out." The commander, enraged over the request, accused the physician of insubordination and ordered the report expurgated of remarks that he considered offensive. A new post surgeon shortly replaced the refractory doctor. Conditions remained deplorable until 1875, when a new guardhouse, constructed of stone at a price of three thousand dollars, finally replaced the abysmal hell-hole.[15]

Such an austere environment was more than some soldiers could endure. Strict military discipline and a near-despotic routine attended almost every activity. Drills, inspections, and tedious duties filled the days between rigorous patrols, prompting many to desert. Almost to the man, those who were caught insisted that their intolerable situation and cutbacks in pay and clothing allowances drove them to risk jail and a dishonorable discharge. Food was seldom satisfactory. Bread, often made from the poorest flour, was tough and doughy. Even beef, although plentiful, became monotonous when served at almost every meal. The quartermaster contracted for vegetables when they came into season; local farms, however, failed to produce the bulk necessary to sustain such a large number of people. Farmers from the interior could bring only items such as sweet potatoes and onions, which did not perish quickly, and the limited stock of the post trader seemed always exhausted. There were few places for the men to spend their pay, but saving money proved impossible because the soldiers could not trust one another. A depository for their pay did not even exist, and even the commander admitted that sending it by mail or carrying it on their persons only invited theft.[16]

For officers—especially the handful who brought their families to Fort Griffin—life was somewhat better. Their meals included a wider assortment: spices to make the beef more palatable, jam to spread on their bread, even oysters and pork for variety. "Domestic servants" eased the burden for their wives and children, while single officers regularly retained "grooms." The company of local herder families often eased the monotony of social life, as officers and their wives frequently visited homes in the countryside. Sallie Matthews remarked that pioneer women "as a rule" shunned the newcomers out of sectional prejudice and the fear that they "would be snubbed" by the more polished Northerners. Yet social deprivation quickly bridged bonds of friendship. The wives of Colonel Chaffee and Lieutenant Kendall, for example, reciprocated kindnesses by entertaining local women and their children at the post. Herder folk received occasional invitations to attend dances and receptions as well.[17]

The two societies also joined to provide their children an education. Herder folk in the Clear Fork country had long emphasized schooling, and with the coming of the post, opportunities improved. Fort Griffin was scarcely a year old when about forty children from the post and the surrounding neighborhood attended classes together on Government Hill. Major Samuel Starr, at Fort Richardson, temporarily transferred Private Benjamin F. Stockhouse to serve as teacher, and the "tall, handsome man" soon attracted close to twenty additional pupils. Amid stacks of supplies, he conducted classes in the commissary building, opening each

Sergeant James W. Foley and wife, Rachel. (Robert Nail Foundation Archives, supported by the Old Jail Art Center, Albany, Texas)

morning with songs and a prayer. Pleased with the situation, the commander at Fort Griffin requested that Stockhouse be permanently assigned to the post.[18]

But after two terms, Stockhouse deserted—reportedly with a large sum of the government's money. He stopped at the Shaw residence at Picketville, where student Sallie Matthews claimed that he sent back the message: "A swift team, a good buggy with

"Baby Foley." (Robert Nail Foundation Archives, supported by the Old Jail Art Center, Albany, Texas)

wheels well greased; catch me if you can." The affair no doubt set back the process of education. Not until several years later did Colonel Buell advertise in the *San Antonio Express* for a teacher to establish a school for soldiers' children—both white and "perhaps colored," and "possibly some Indian children as well."[19]

In the hope of exposing adults to scholarship, good intentions again fell short. In 1869 post surgeon Carlos Carvallo seeded a post library with fifty-six volumes. But if the literate men and women of the area expected to borrow popular works by Charles Dickens or Sir Walter Scott, they were sadly disappointed. At Forts Richardson and Concho, soldiers and others could find such volumes, along with newspapers and popular magazines of the day such as *Harper's Weekly* and *Leslie's Pleasant Hours*. Selections at Fort Griffin, however, included only such colorless titles as *Treatise on Diseases of the Ear*. The books that Carvallo had bequeathed covered the fields of science and medicine, physics, chemistry, and pharmacology. By comparison, the lone manual for disciplining soldiers and another book covering army regulations probably seemed like lively reading. As the libraries at Griffin's sister posts multiplied to between one and two thousand volumes, the "athenaeum" on the Clear Fork distended to about a hundred crumbling texts.[20]

The poverty of activities, along with the cheerless and unforgiving frontier life, proved a great leveler between enlisted men and officers and their families. Particularly sobering, acute dysentery claimed the life of Mrs. Kendall while the lieutenant was on patrol. All the officers present, accompanied by their wives, followed the young woman's body to the soldiers' cemetery, where she was buried in a Roman Catholic service. When the lieutenant returned, he had her body disinterred and moved to the couple's home in LaPorte, Indiana. Drunkenness, so common among regulars, occasionally became a problem among officers as well. And at least one, Lieutenant C. N. Garringe, turned to drugs. While in an opium fit, he tried to shoot his black servant, James F. Irwin, point-blank, but the gun misfired. The verbal and physical assault that followed attracted a group of enlisted men who finally restrained Garringe.[21]

Such instances of officers disgracing their rank were few. Most of them remained impervious to the temptations that frequently ensnared enlisted men. The army constantly lost property to soldiers, but the want of necessities was more often responsible for petty thefts than a larcenous character. The cookhouse was a favorite target, and items such as blankets frequently disappeared from other buildings. Hospital steward Richard Lincoln once sneaked a bottle of morphine from the dispensary and sold it to Molly McCabe, a notorious prostitute at the Flat. On the frontier the going rate for a heavy army coat, according to cowboy Rollie Burns, was a bottle of whiskey. Of the trail hands in his outfit, Henry Comstock remarked: "I think every man had a cavalryman's overcoat with a cape over the shoulders." Deserters naturally absconded with horses, clothing, and arms. The extent to which civilians aided soldiers fleeing with government property alarmed Colonel Buell. In 1873 he complained that some men had recently stolen twelve guns. Emmett Roberts alleged that even the Indians "had good Spencer rifles like the ones we got from the government at Fort Griffin." Three times in 1871 soldiers received sentences for trafficking in army horses and guns; one was even convicted for stealing nuts and bolts from the post blacksmith's shop. Soldiers occasionally apprehended local thieves and turned them over to civil authorities; seldom, however, did courts prosecute them.[22]

If officers recorded the slightest peccadilloes in their records of "Charges and Specifications," then certainly violence among soldiers did not go unreported. Minutes detailing any number of confrontations peppered official reports, often in colorful language and with graphic descriptions. Yet spread over a decade the incidents paled in significance, considering the composition of the military community: about three hundred young, single, ill-fed, poorly sheltered, and sometimes idle men of various ethnic backgrounds, under arms and often drunk, with only enough women present to underscore the dearth of femininity in their midst!

Tensions attributable to distinctions between officers and enlisted men provoked a number of physical confrontations. For example, when a Lieutenant Taylor issued an order that a private found offensive, the young man seized the officer by the neck and threw him to the ground. Placing a pistol to his temple, the soldier vowed: "Damn you I'll blow your head off!" The lieutenant deflected the gun just as it fired, but the shot nevertheless mangled his ear.[23]

Fortunately, murder in that instance was averted, and while an infrequent killing on patrol or at the Flat may have occurred, only two cases of manslaughter among the troops ever reached official army reports. Gottfried Schuler, a sergeant in the 11th Infantry, was the first victim. A soldier—likely the very man that Ranger Sowell had observed chained and marching around the pole—fatally shot Schuler just before Christmas in 1870. Such cases proved so rare that the sergeant's name became a catchword. A trooper, confined for drunkenness on duty, tried to escape and threatened his pursuer with: "I will make Schuler out of you."[24]

Alcohol, which fueled that incident, predictably accounted for the largest share of violence. Private Michael Finnell, for example, once became inebriated while visiting the quarters of another company. After he challenged any of them to a fight, a sergeant ordered his arrest. Finnell resisted, and before striking one of the men, he proclaimed that "no son-of-a-bitch in 'D' troop can take me to the guard house."[25]

The presence of African American troops at Fort Griffin added another dimension to violence. When a razor-wielding buffalo soldier bloodied an Irish sergeant during a drunken brawl at the civilian settlement, the official report noted that "grossly abusive language provoked the assault." Like most explanations, this one did not mention whether the harangue included racial epithets. Yet animosities between whites and blacks were no different in the army than in civilian life. Anglos in the service generally believed that African Americans made poor soldiers; some of them even feared that white women at military posts were unsafe as long as the government allowed black troops in the army.[26]

While segregation kept racial violence somewhat under control, confinement at the small post made contact inevitable. For some unreported reason, Edward Kitrell, a black musician in the 24th Infantry, became so enraged that he attacked a white soldier with a knife. After a sergeant secured the weapon, Kitrell wrested it from him and renewed the attack.[27]

Even the white officers who commanded black troops were not always sensitive to their precarious relationship. One black cavalryman, wearied by the bullying of his commander, chased the man with an axe and actually hacked him before someone managed to end the assault. Even though ill feelings between the races certainly prevailed, instances of violence were nevertheless uncommon; in fact, six assaults topped official records for that category in 1875.[28]

Threats of violence occurred more often than physical confrontations. Reports and reminiscences, as well as mere insolence, fostered the mistaken impression that violence was common. In just one of many cases, a soldier stopped a potentially fatal confrontation between two privates on garden detail just as one of the men swung a pickax at the other. Another time, an enlisted man attempted to unnerve an adversary by continually pointing his carbine at the man's head and snapping the hammer. More innocuously, when a sergeant ordered Private John Hammin to his quarters, Hammin regaled the "son-of-a-bitch" with any number of "opprobrious names," pulled down his pants, and exposed his buttocks.[29]

Accidents, in fact, caused more deaths and serious injuries than violence among soldiers. Men froze to death, suffered frostbite, and allowed minor wounds to fester into gangrene. Even the daily routine resulted in tragedy. Several times men drowned fording streams that had swollen deceptively from near-dry beds to wide, swift-flowing rivers. The current once upended a wagon on its way to Phantom Hill, sending a soldier to his death; another time a carriage accident almost killed the post surgeon, who suffered a concussion along with numbness and impaired sight and hearing. Despite the large number of men under arms, cases of unintentionally inflicted wounds were few. "For the second time in two months," the post surgeon once noted, "an accidental shooting death occurred." That report proved an exception.[30]

Accidents, especially those involving deaths, must have been particularly poignant in such a bleak setting. Life at the little outpost, as austere as the surroundings, offered few diversions. Playing billiards at the post sutler's store and gambling were regular pastimes. Music provided an agreeable diversion as well; the 11th Infantry assembled a band, and at other times banjos and violins broke the stillness. But marching to the music or dancing with other men diminished the pleasure. Occasionally, soldiers picnicked at the river. Emmett Roberts said that the men at the subpost Phantom Hill regularly camped and fished and killed time drinking. Drinking, in fact, seemed to be the choice pastime of most troopers. Just before 1872 the arrival of bootleggers at the Flat provided the soldiers an irresistible temptation. The post surgeon, writing about that time, complained that drunkenness "prevails to quite an extent." Only a year earlier he had commented that alcohol posed few problems except on pay day. But with the little village flourishing, even Colonel Wood admitted that the men wasted their pay. "They just gamble it away," he said, "and spend it on whiskey and women."[31]

In 1868, almost a year to the day after federal troops pitched their tents on the Clear Fork, Lieutenant Colonel S. B. Hayman noted that an unruly little community was beginning to arise in the bottoms below Fort Griffin. "I found some twenty settlers near the Post who are nearly all engaged to some extent in the traffic of liquor," he wrote the adjutant general. Hayman expressed an inability to prevent the unwelcomed trade unless authorized "to make a forcible examination of premises where [alcohol] is likely to be found." The commander requested that the area be considered "Indian Territory"; failing that, he wanted to establish a military reservation of "fourteen miles square" and enforce martial law within it. This, he reasoned, would afford "better protection to the deserving."[32]

The army evidently acted on Hayman's recommendations. Texas' ownership of its public lands, of course, prohibited even the occupying forces from appropriating any tracts unclaimed by private citizens. But officials did examine land records to determine who owned the property on which the government had already expended almost sixty-eight thousand dollars. The proposed reservation, they soon learned, straddled parts of three 320-acre half-sections patented by the Texas Emigration and Land Company—the old Peters Colony. Quartermaster General J. G. C. Lee reported that "without doubt, the land has been occupied without authority or lease." Somewhat anxiously he expressed hope that the owners, recognizing the advantages imparted by Fort Griffin, might donate the land.[33]

The seemingly innocuous oversight of failing to obtain permission to use the land proved to be a monumental headache that plagued every commander afterward assigned to the post. A measuring error regarding the original survey in 1854 had entitled the Peters Colony to receive several large tracts equivalent to the shortage. The State of Texas divided the land among sixty-eight shareholders of the Texas Emigration and Land Company, largely in unsettled counties, including Shackelford, Throckmorton, and Stephens. One of the stockholders, D. M. Dowell of Louisville, Kentucky, fortuitously acquired ten very important shares. Not only did his "Survey No. 478," beside the Clear Fork of the Brazos, happen to be where the U.S. Army constructed its military complex, but most of the future townsite of the Flat rested on this plot as well. Dowell indeed eventually recognized the benefits of proximity, but not in the manner that the army had envisioned.[34]

For four years, from 1867 to 1871, the military tried to coexist peaceably beside the benighted collection of hovels scattered along the river bottom. Some sort of civilian population was indispensable for the post's day-to-day maintenance. Citizens prized federal contracts in the weak Reconstruction economy. Joe McCombs, a seventeen-year-old unemployed cow hunter, could find no work in Weatherford or around Stephenville, so he drifted to Fort Griffin in 1871. The fifteen-dollar-a-month wages that "Uncle Joe" Matthews paid him to tend cattle failed to satisfy his financial needs, so he bid for and won a government job "running the wood yard" at the post. Several ranchers held beef contracts, among them Matthews and Irishman Dennis Murphy. Murphy also sold the army two milk cows, which no doubt ingratiated him with the officers. The most coveted job at the fort was that of post sutler. W. B. Hicks ran the first "government store"; reportedly he was unable to keep a satisfactory inventory. Local men such as Dutch Nance and

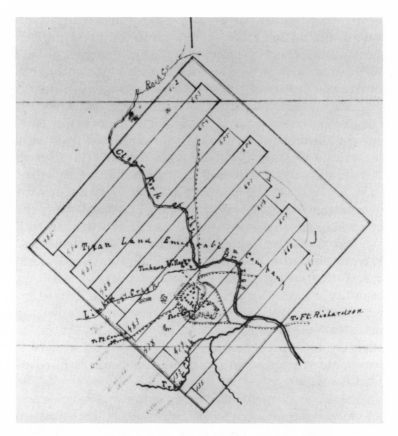

Fort Griffin Reserve (1871) includes a layout of fateful "Survey No. 478." (National Archives)

T. E. Jackson opened private stores, hoping to fill the business Hicks could not meet. About 1870, however, Frank E. Conrad left the sutler's job at Fort McKavett and established a successful operation on Government Hill. Providing capable management, he bridged the military and civilian communities and opened an outlet for a wide range of commercial and financial activities.[35]

Both isolation and a paucity of local production, however, left the government wanting for a nearby source of market goods. Post

Trader Henry Warren, part owner of the freighting outfit that met with disaster at Salt Creek Prairie, did not even reside at Fort Griffin. Provisioning in Austin and San Antonio, he circulated little of his money locally. With the exception of the beef contractors, Warren was typical of big suppliers who won their awards at Jacksboro. Gathering there once or twice a year, hopeful suppliers competed for contracts to provide such commodities as fuel, corn, hay, flour, and transportation. The large numbers of government horses and mules at Fort Griffin required great stores of provender that this arid and capricious land could not produce reliably. About 1874, two local boys, William Poe and John C. Jacobs, raised a good crop of corn to maturity, only to see it devoured by a swarm of grasshoppers so immense that it "darkened the sun." Even if they had succeeded, they could not have produced enough feed to corner the market. At the height of the Indian wars in 1874, when Fort Griffin became a primary rendezvous for the Red River campaign, a single shipment of corn totaled 100 tons. In 1869 one hay contract alone called for 475 tons. The supplier, a Belknap man, made deliveries almost daily. Fort Griffin, in fact, had to rely on contractors as distant as Denison—almost 175 miles away— for some of its needs, while many men and women at the Flat lived hand-to-mouth.[36]

The only true "need" filled by any number of loathsome post towns was to provide an outlet for restive soldiers. The perception of the parasitic settlements as centers for wholesale debauchery and casual violence, however, was somewhat exaggerated. Among them, the Flat, Saint Angela, and Scabtown—leeches that attached themselves to Forts Griffin, Concho, and McKavett, respectively— did pander to the worst nature of the troops. Remarkably representative was the little village below Fort Griffin that in 1872 was composed of less than a hundred men and women. The settlement never boasted more than three saloons until the days when buffalo hunting and trailing cattle eclipsed the post as the town's economic focus. In 1870 the post surgeon at Fort Concho complained bitterly that free-flowing liquor and an absence of civil authority had fostered unbridled lawlessness at Saint Angela, across the river. During his residency, the medical officer asserted: "Over one hundred murders have taken place within a radius of ten miles . . . in a population which has never . . . exceeded two hundred and fifty." Although a rash of murders had indeed occurred, such wild exaggerations fueled the reputations of the little villages as "rough towns." Another chronicler reported that "a visit to Scabtown was . . . as dangerous as an Indian campaign." His statement was true, but neither actually proved especially fatal. Of the several battles involving troops at McKavett, seldom did soldiers fail to return safely; a trip to town was no more hazardous.[37]

Each of these settlements, isolated and possessing little economic stimulus outside of soldiers' pay, remained rowdy but small and inconsequential while the Indian wars raged. The Flat, for a while, and Saint Angela survived their sometimes violent infancies, eventually blossoming into regional centers. Scabtown, however, all but disappeared as the garrison at Fort McKavett dwindled and the military campaigns wound to a close.

None of the little shanty towns was the equal of Jacksboro. Many settlers who had populated the area before the war returned when federal troops arrived. Throngs of newcomers—many of them rootless opportunists—also came. The population swelled to between 650 and 800 by 1871. New homes, a courthouse, and a public school reflected the promise of a stable community, while one-half mile away the "ten company post," Fort Richardson, represented an economic beacon. Between the town and the fort any number of tents and hastily erected shelters with names such as "Mollie McCabe's Palace of Beautiful Sin" and "The Last Chance" lined the road. Paymasters, disbursing thousands of dollars to the troops, unleashed an orgy of drinking, gambling, and prostitution at the twenty-seven saloons the lusty hamlet supported. Many visitors also sampled their offerings. Not only was Jacksboro the center for bidding on contracts, but it also hosted periodic auctions to dispose of condemned wagons, horses, clothes, and other items for which the government no longer had a use. The town bloated to over a thousand persons on these occasions, benefitting hotels, businesses, bars, and brothels. A bartender at the Wichita

Saloon swore that after one particularly busy evening he could have walked on the backs of soldiers "from the square to the creek and never touched the ground."[38]

The landscape of memory, viewed through a romantic prism, certainly distorted life's peaks and valleys. Occasional confrontations, like the wildness that seemed pervasive, provided anecdotes to enhance the fond reminiscences of old timers. Most of them recalled the post towns as wild, sporting, and often casually violent. Reflecting on conditions at Jacksboro, Captain Henry Strong remarked in his memoirs: "I think [it] was one of the toughest towns in the United States, for its size." Yet the old soldier also remembered that Marshal William C. Gilson had little trouble keeping order. "Very few wished to try old Bill," he wrote. While the "crack of the six-shooter" in the hands of the town's revelers could be heard throughout the night, men rarely turned their revolvers on each other. Even fistfights were seldom reported.[39]

While Jacksboro prospered during the first two or three years of the 1870s, only a handful of gamblers, prostitutes, and "toughs" blighted the Flat's lone street. The village became boisterous, however, when thirsty troopers, survey crews, and other parties of men hit town. Susan Newcomb, visiting the village with her children for the first time, called on D. A. Nance at his store and found the place so full of people—mostly drunks—that they went on to his house for an early supper with his family. Although Newcomb returned to shop and have a picture made at a little gallery, she seldom came back to the Flat.[40]

Miner Kellogg, an artist who camped within earshot of the village one summer evening, noted in his journal: "Whiskey very noisy tonight as he always is near towns & plays the Devil with order & progress." The nightmarish quality that attended a "night on the town" kept the cultured gentleman at a distance. The saloon—whether tent, lean-to, or shanty—was likely unadorned, tiny, and dimly lit, with a low ceiling and dirt floor. Unwashed and foul-smelling soldiers, sometimes with a month's pay in their pockets, crowded shoulder-to-shoulder to consume the cheap liquor that barkeeps unfailingly watered down. They gambled in games

D. A. "Dutch" Nance poses beside his picket-cabin store at the Flat while a Tonkawa Indian peers around the corner. (Robert Nail Foundation Archives, supported by the Old Jail Art Center, Albany, Texas)

that were often rigged and fornicated with women whose lack of hygiene rivaled their own. Any soldier who descended into this hellish environment risked the loss of his meager wages, flirted with a variety of social diseases, and chanced confinement in the guardhouse.[41]

Army officers increasingly perceived the village as a threat to maintaining discipline and good relations with the general civilian population. Squatters had hardly begun to collect below the post in 1868 when soldier Ben Mixon became responsible for the Flat's first killings. An officer noted that one of the two civilians whom he shot with his Enfield rifle was a "colored man" named Hector; the provocation for the killing went unreported. Others were punished for lesser offenses against townspeople. During one month in 1869, a trooper slapped a civilian, another beat a man severely, and yet another shot at a Mrs. Dodson. Despite the odds, however, a few locals were undaunted by the soldiers. Twice in the same month one James Parker tried to kill Sergeant George Thompson. After the second incident, soldiers held Parker in the post guardhouse while Major Wood appealed to civil authorities at Palo Pinto to issue a warrant for the man's arrest. But the sheriff refused to cooperate, expressing doubt that the magistrate would even try the case. Wood complained bitterly that civilians in these situations "almost invariably escape punishment."[42]

The lack of cooperation soon ran both ways. Military authorities became reluctant to respond to trouble at the Flat not involving enlisted men. The army ignored an incident in which a cowboy, attempting to prevent a fight, fell dead between two gunmen. Even the most spectacular murder of the few that occurred at the Flat met with indifference. The affair involved a saloon owner, Joe Bowers, who engaged a disgruntled patron named J. B. Cockrell in a running feud during the spring of 1872. It began at Bower's bar, where Cockrell supposedly accused a gambler of cheating him. The disagreement grew into a skirmish as parties supporting both men spilled onto the dirt road outside the building. Cockrell, who took cover behind a pile of post oaks, received gunshot wounds that landed him in the army hospital. Upon recovering, he began frequenting a neighboring dive, where Bowers, fearing reprisal, reportedly burst through the doorway and discharged a shotgun blast into him from close range. For several days the murderer openly went about his business, even visiting Fort Griffin, yet Colonel Buell stolidly held to his policy of distancing himself from local crimes involving only civilians.[43]

Another violent incident in 1872 finally stirred Major Wood to attack the problem at its source. A clerk at the post, George Henrie, had ventured into the Flat, where for some unknown reason he killed two privates—one an escort for a Texas and Pacific Railroad survey crew and the other traveling with Colonel Ranald Mackenzie. The deaths of two soldiers unattached to Fort Griffin greatly embarrassed the commander. He no doubt feared that superiors would question whether he had lost control over the little village below the fort. To Wood's disgust, the judge at Palo Pinto charged Henrie with only second degree murder and released him on bail. Not surprisingly, the killer immediately fled.[44]

The army responded harshly and decisively. As 1872 ended, Colonel Buell declared the Flat a part of the government reservation. Confident that the War Department would be able to negotiate with Kentucky businessman Dowell for a lease, he sent troops to clear all civilians from the area. The post surgeon commented that "the whiskey dens closed, the gamblers disappeared and murders ceased" for a while. The Flat did not reemerge for about two years, although a few men and women took refuge on the adjoining property of resident owner T. E. Jackson and remained on the fort side of the Clear Fork. A family man and store owner, Jackson brooked neither disruption nor competition from the men and women who had provoked the army's wrath. Buell nevertheless considered him a "squatter" along with the others. Suggesting that they, too, should leave, the commander arrogantly recommended razing their "improvements," which were "of no value to the Government except for fuel."[45]

Between the predominantly white military and civilian societies, African Americans formed an almost unnoticed subculture. Colonel Hayman, when ordered to assess their conditions in 1868, reported:

"I know of no freedmen in my district except those connected with this post and therefore do not think the troops are necessary to protect freedmen." Yet they were there, and in significant numbers. They did not comprise a single, separate community, but instead represented a subordinate class beside each body of Anglos. The buffalo soldiers, the most visible group, were only temporary residents. They closed ranks within their respective companies, of course, and no doubt fraternized with black civilians. A number of them remained in the Clear Fork country after their enlistments expired. Former buffalo soldiers and others, in fact, established a small enclave among their white neighbors at the base of Government Hill. Other black persons resided at the post or were scattered throughout the countryside. Their lack of a community focus obscured the fact that in 1870 nearly a hundred African Americans lived in the Clear Fork country—and this was before the first buffalo soldier had arrived.[46]

The occupations of African Americans varied. Officers' families at Fort Griffin employed black and mulatto women exclusively as domestic servants. Some worked for single officers, too, but more often unmarried men of rank hired grooms. This "domestic" class, along with their children, were normally listed as members of their employers' households. The census taker also noted that black men typically listed "laborer" as their occupation. They performed tasks such as hauling wood, helping contractors, and working for anyone who would pay them wages. A few developed specialties. John Carter became a butcher and Milton Sutton a carpenter, and young Tennessean James Romey founded a school for black children. Others, such as Floyd King and Alfred Smaldin, raised stock and planted gardens in the countryside, and about a dozen worked for cow hunters. Like most Anglo herder folk, the rural blacks hailed from the South exclusively.[47]

As elsewhere in Texas, African Americans endured the prejudice and humiliation of second-class citizenship. Colonel Buell, who was sensitive to racial animosities, was apprehensive about committing his black troopers to patrol for white outlaws. Before the Bushnob incident he had feared that some of them would be

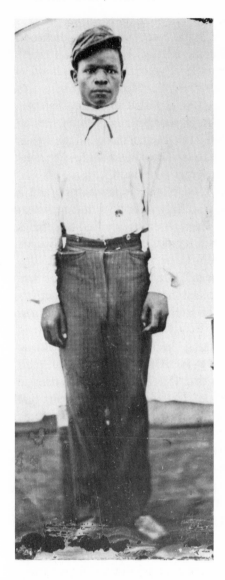

Unidentified buffalo soldier. (Robert Nail Foundation Archives, supported by the Old Jail Art Center, Albany, Texas)

killed, "for a Texas cattle or horse thief hates a colored soldier." The scarce and scattered numbers of African Americans, however, did not invite the extreme forms of protest that carpetbaggers,

scalawags, and soldiers in the interior encouraged. Anglo settlers
nevertheless remained on guard in the event that black soldiers and
civilians should unite and become unruly. An occasional crime
reinforced their suspicions, as in 1873, when a buffalo soldier was
apprehended for stealing sixty-five dollars from T. E. Jackson's
store. Another man in the same unit accosted an officer who was
escorting two women from a church service; after striking him on
the head with a stone, the assailant fled into a patch of high weeds
and fired several errant shots at them. Once black soldiers became
civilians, however, their aggressions were few.[48]

A third community, composed of the Tonkawa tribe and a
handful of Lipan Apaches, lived in tiny river-bottom camps next
to the fort. The Tonkawas, never prosperous, showed the effects
of steady decline. When Captain Randolph B. Marcy had visited
them in 1854, he disdained the tribe as "the most ragged, filthy,
and destitute Indians I have seen." Many subsequent observers
echoed his conviction. Upon receiving them at Fort Richardson
in 1867, Major Samuel Starr—himself described as "captious and
cranky"—called the Tonkawas a "lazy, vagabond race." If they could
get enough to eat without hunting, he asserted, they would do
nothing. When the tribe moved to Fort Griffin the next year, their
rag-tag survivors numbered less than 150. The post surgeon decried
the "frightful hygienic condition" of their village, reporting that
"nothing is done for its proper policing." Befitting their nomadic
traditions, they simply moved camp whenever it became too filthy
for habitation. Their intemperance also alarmed the physician.
"Indians, both men and women, in a state of beastly intoxication,"
he claimed, were a common sight. Noting that the men had "bowie
knives and fire-arms about them," he declared it unsafe for a person
to descend into the Flat without protection.[49]

Anyone familiar with the tribe would have considered ludicrous
the suggestion that a Tonkawa might assault an Anglo. In fact,
anyone who passed quick judgment on these Indians did not know
them intimately. Yet the Tonkawas' own fatalistic self-perception
advanced such casual assessments and even contributed to their
decline. The Wolf Dance—a sacred creation rite—was the

provenance for their guiding principles. The secret and mystical ceremony, predating European contact, commemorated the tribe's belief that the first Tonkawas emerged from the earth through the agency of wolves. Major Robert S. Neighbors, highly esteemed by these Indians, was likely the only white man ever to witness the ceremony. Secreted in the corner of a "dance-lodge," he observed about fifty warriors, covered with wolf skins "from head to feet," enter on all fours, single file. They circled the lodge, howling, growling, and sniffing the ground and air. At length a shrill cry signaled them to paw the earth at a single spot. The major was astonished to see a Tonkawa rise naked from the ground as the participants feigned "delight and curiosity." The "progenitor" lamented his summons from the spirit world where he had been "contented and happy." He entreated the pack to return him, fretting: "I know not what I shall do for subsistence and clothing." A council of the "sage old wolves" refused his plea. Placing a bow and arrows in his hands, they advised this new species of man to live like the wolf. "Rob, kill, and steal," they commanded, and wander about the land.[50]

A conflict between culture and condition naturally arose as the Tonkawas strove to reconcile their traditions with the assault on their way of living. Warriors satisfied their predatory habits largely through military service, using the aegis of the army to prey upon the Comanches and Kiowas. Occasionally, however, they purloined stock from distant ranchers. One cowman claimed that if caught holding stolen animals, Tonkawa scouts would contend that they had "just now" recovered them from the Comanches. Many times they did gain the honors of war by reclaiming stolen horses. Tonkawas patrolling with the troops trailed strings of ponies into Fort Griffin from as far away as San Saba and the Colorado country. Such admirable service helped soften the tribe's subservience to the dominant culture. And despite exhibiting an almost childlike loyalty to anyone who exuded an air of authority, they resisted the army's efforts to Anglicize them. Tradition forbade a Tonkawa to till the soil or build a permanent dwelling. "If he did," said the wolf legend, "he would surely die." According to an old army veteran, when a colonel asked "Charley" why his people did not acquire some land, plant corn, build houses, and live the like white man, the Indian responded by asking, "Why don't you plant corn, Colonel?" When the officer replied that he was a soldier and was "not supposed to work," Charley slapped his breast and proclaimed: "You soldier, you no work; me warrior, me no work."[51]

While warriors such as Charley idled away their time, Tonkawa women remained very busy. They preserved the only semblance of community enjoyed by the tribe. With the blessings of their hungry men, women planted gardens near camp. They also tanned buffalo and deer hides and collected "rags of blankets" to cover the tipis they alone built. A traveler who observed the matrons sitting proudly inside their "wigwams" found the domiciles "picturesque." Tonkawa women paid no less attention to their own appearance. Fond of brightly colored calico, they fashioned poncho-style garments from the material to cover their knee-length skirts. The top "trailed the ground in back," remembered Sallie Matthews, "and when the wind blew . . . it floated out behind like a sail." The women also made and wore beaded moccasins. Their handi-craft, in fact, gained a reputation for painstaking neatness. A local Anglo woman recalled that "a squaw," upon admiring her infant son, exclaimed: "Heap pretty papoose, me make him moccasins." In a few days "she brought them, all beaded and a perfect fit." Leather dolls that Tonkawa women presented to local children were also considered treasures. Mostly, though, the women peddled their curios to anyone who ventured near their river-bottom village. With their children, they crowded around parties of travelers in hope of receiving presents.[52]

Although prevented by order of the commander from leaving the post, the Tonkawas moved freely within their limited range and became acquainted with townspeople and herder folk. Those who forgave their sloth and habitual drunkenness viewed them sympathetically. A rancher's wife wrote that "they were a kindly, inoffensive people." Their long association with Anglos enabled most of them to communicate in at least a tortured form of English. Local people, who considered the Tonkawas childlike in nature,

Tonkawa wigwams in the flats below Fort Griffin. (Lawrence T. Jones III Collection)

found their choppy and ill-constructed grammar endearing. And when they spoke to strangers, they talked "scarce a word above a breath." These Indians were not shy, however, and often visited their Anglo neighbors. D. A. Nance, whose family had lived near the lower Brazos Reservation, knew many of them from boyhood. Groups frequented his store at the Flat almost daily to purchase raisins and admire bolts of calico and other goods. Hardly ever did they bother to knock on a door. In a land where raids were a constant dread, the unexpected appearance of a silent Indian could be startling. The phrase, "He comes in like a Tonk," became a colloquialism in the Clear Fork country. Their routine "visits" to the mess house and kitchen finally stirred Colonel Buell to issue an order prohibiting them from entering government buildings as they pleased.[53]

Most members of the tribe lived a mundane existence. Army regulations and their predilection for adopting the worst aspects

Two Tonkawa boys. (Lawrence T. Jones III Collection)

"Jenny and Tansy," two young Tonkawa women. (Lawrence T. Jones III Collection)

of Anglo culture, moreover, sapped their vitality. Even so, martial celebrations occasionally allowed them to revel in their past and display flashes of their former glory. Nance remembered that before one expedition the Indians paraded through the streets of the fort and civilian settlement stripped and painted for war. When scouts returned with Comanche scalps, the tribe celebrated throughout the night. The eerie glow of two bonfires illuminated both men and women dancing triumphantly before the grisly prizes mounted on poles. Along the river bottom, crowds of soldiers and civilians marveled at the spectacle.[54]

Like the Plains Indians, the Tonkawas believed that mutilating the corpses of their enemies would scar them in the next life; but unlike the other tribes, they also engaged in ritual cannibalism, sampling bites from the bravest of their dead adversaries. Once, in a frenzy of rage and grief, they mangled the body of a dead Comanche who had fallen alongside a Tonkawa warrior within earshot of their village. A local man, J. J. Bragg, approached the Indian encampment to learn the cause of the shouting and gunfire that had attended the skirmish. He reported that a warrior, heading to the fort to present his trophies to a respected sergeant, had suspended the heart of the dead Comanche on one side of his horse and the severed and scalped head on the other. Tonkawa women quartered the remains and burned the torso over a fire. Bragg also observed the old chief, Campo, dressing the scalp. The Comanche's hair, "nicely plaited" and "profusely set with silver ornaments," fell four to five feet in length. Campo, laying a hand over his own heart, told Bragg, "all sick here," adding that they would mourn their dead warrior for ten days, "then heap big war dance."[55]

Old-timers who characterized Tonkawa life as idyllic failed to mention that "caging the wolf" had set the Indians' culture on an irreversible decline. Despite laws and supervision, many of the Tonkawas could not resist alcohol. When their war chief, Johnson, was not patrolling with the troops, he passed much of his time courting a local Anglo girl, Ida Creaton, and drinking to console himself for her rebuffs. A young woman at the Flat told how he once stumbled in a drunken stupor toward the Creaton home—a place where he was otherwise welcome—and pulled a knife on the family's son John. The Indian, a huge man, reacted with such deliberate sluggishness that young Creaton had little trouble disarming him.[56]

Captain Richard Henry Pratt tried earnestly to rehabilitate another chief, Castille, an elder of the tribe; the captain's harsh and insensitive measures, however, only humiliated the former warrior and the rest of his people as well. The sight of their respected patriarch pushing a wheelbarrow full of garbage collected at gunpoint aroused universal indignation. A succession of aggrieved elders and wailing women could not persuade Pratt to rescind his order. Later the officer felt vindicated when the chief helped break up a ring of bootleggers who had been peddling whiskey to the Indians. The drinking did not end, however; the tribe's malaise had become too well ingrained.[57]

Insensitive treatment at the hands of their guardians constantly reminded the Tonkawas of their subordinate caste. An observer complained about the disgraceful situation in which the government liberally fed and clothed the Comanches and Kiowas while the Tonkawas, "always friendly Indians," received no support, save for their scouts. Colonel Wood, during his tenure as commander, openly disdained his Indian charges. He tried unsuccessfully to have the Tonkawas reassigned to Fort Concho, then he offered their services to anyone who would take them away from Fort Griffin. When no one accepted his invitation, Wood took consolation in their declining population, noting that soon they would "become extinct and no longer be a burden to the government." The tribe endured such unwarranted indignities time and again. Once, Colonel Mackenzie, who had posted twenty Tonkawas to guard a herd of horses, berated them for retreating before a hundred Comanches. Even when they were commended for "rendering good service" during the campaigns of 1873, the army "rewarded" them by cutting their rations and replacing the scouts' repeating rifles with single-shot Sharps carbines. Only when Chief Castile proposed that his men buy Winchesters did the army allow the Indians to keep the superior arms.[58]

Castile, Tonkawa war chief. (Lawrence T. Jones III Collection)

Ida Creaton and "Johnson." (Lawrence T. Jones III Collection)

During the last days of 1872 a particular injustice involving the probable murder of a scout cut at the heart of the tribe. The Indian William was part of a detachment assigned to escort a survey crew to El Paso. No one disputed the fact that he became drunk and suffered the condign punishment of confinement. But when he died the next day, the other Tonkawas arduously disputed the official explanation. Captain E. M. Heyl, the officer in charge, reported that Sergeant Ainright had detained William forcibly after he resisted arrest. The scout, he alleged, escaped during the night and was later seen in an El Paso saloon, again drunk. The next day William accompanied a patrol to a local landmark, Hueco Tanks. Exposure to the bitter cold, coupled with his condition, Heyl asserted, resulted in the Indian's death. The other scouts insisted that the sergeant had kicked William several times in the head and body, breaking his ribs and breast bone. Dragging William about seventy-five yards at the end of a chain, Ainright then bound his wrists and left him tied to a tree in the snow. Late at night some soldiers mercifully cut him down. William, the Indian scouts complained, was certainly in no condition to make the trip to Hueco Tanks. Colonel Buell declared the incident "a great outrage" and forced a civil court to press charges against the sergeant. But to the Tonkawas' great sorrow, the jury acquitted him.[59]

The sullen Indians had little choice but to accept the decision, and they went about their lives with a renewed sense of fatalism. From their little villages along the Clear Fork they witnessed many changes over the next few years. After the soldiers completed their campaigns against the Plains Indians, the garrison dwindled and the town grew. Within a few years the countryside began filling up, and men and women with no memory of the struggle for the land would have little use for either the Indian scouts or the soldiers who campaigned with them.

CHAPTER SEVEN
WHITE TIDE RISING, 1872–1879

During the last half of the 1870s Texans finally burst beyond the treeline. As the great bison slaughter and trail driving intersected with the advance of westering pioneers, a transformation of breathtaking swiftness unfolded. The Comanches and Kiowas, demoralized and impoverished by the bison's destruction, made only one last, desperate effort to challenge their conquerors. And with both the Indians and their commissary out of the way, stock raisers quickly moved their cattle onto the lush grasslands. A sprinkling of farm families also established homesites along creek banks and river bottoms well beyond the treeline even before the hunters' guns fell silent. At the same time, trail drivers, taking advantage of the unfenced and undeveloped land, cut new trails to railheads in western Kansas. This same land that had once discouraged town builders now demanded new centers to provision the wide-ranging activities. At the Clear Fork, more than any other place, the door to the Rolling Plains and the land beyond it yawned widely.

Although thoroughly explored, West Texas before the great bison slaughter remained largely unknown to most settlers. Men as well as women who found themselves on the plains in the early 1870s marveled at many unfamiliar sights. The immensity of the land, the suddenness of weather changes, and all sorts of strange animals shaped their impressions. Artist Miner Kellogg, who accompanied a copper prospecting expedition, beheld a full palette in the scenery: bull thistle, brilliantly purple, "like candelabra of many lights," as well as extensive plains of sunflowers, withered green carpets of mesquite grass, and masses of white-topped milkweed. Prairie fires also presented scenes of "terrific grandeur," as one witness proclaimed, but they were also dangerous. A hunter told how he had once disemboweled a bison and crawled inside the wet carcass to escape the terrific heat and suffocating smoke of a quickly moving wall of fire. Another time a surveying party riding toward such a blaze one evening misjudged its distance and speed, and it almost overtook them. Other nighttime visions—falling stars and the roseate Aurora Borealis—provided meditative sights. Daylight also revealed exceptional scenes. Kellogg described a mirage as "a long blue belt of forest suspended in air close to the horizon." Real, and more ghostly, were "white forests" that covered the plains half a day's ride northwest of Fort Griffin. Composed of dead mesquite trees, many large and well preserved, these victims of some long-forgotten drought presented an eerie sight to pioneers. Phin Reynolds noted that "there was hardly a living mesquite tree or bush in all that section." Even trash, so out of place in a seemingly uninhabited land, prompted comments. One diarist mentioned a campsite littered with "old bottles, boxes, envelopes & ashes." A hunter who stumbled upon a hastily abandoned Indian village noted everything from tin cups to brass kettles strewn for half a mile along a creek.[1]

The natural abundance of wildlife overawed observers, yet men thought nothing of shooting animals indiscriminately. Common descriptions told of a country filled with turkey, deer, and antelope. Mustangs in herds of forty or fifty also ran free, and occasionally domestic horses fell in with them and shortly became just as wild. Jack Elgin, surveying for the Houston Central Railroad, told how a blue norther once forced him into a thick growth of post oaks where he spotted "turkeys as thick as they could stand" covering a "ten or twelve acre" clearing. On Christmas Day 1872, his party enjoyed a feast that included fourteen varieties of meat; they could have had sixteen, he boasted, "but our cook drew the line at rattlesnakes and polecats." Men shot these last two on sight, along with such animals as bears, panthers, wolves, coyotes, and bobcats. Prairie dogs, considered a nuisance for the hazardous holes they burrowed and the rattlers they attracted, made good targets as well.[2]

The following five photographs, taken on the Texas Land and Copper expedition, graphically depict changes in the land as the group moved from the prairies and post oak belt to the Rolling Plains. (Lawrence T. Jones III Collection)

Top right: Valley of the west fork of the Trinity River. *Middle left:* Farther up the Trinity's west fork. *Middle right:* "White forest" of dead mesquite, Archer County. *Bottom left:* Kiowa Peak. *Bottom right:* Copper gulch.

Because of its numbers, habits, and majestic appearance, no other animal inspired more comments than the bison. In 1870 Pennsylvania teenager John Creaton, along with his mother and sister, hitched a ride from San Antonio to Fort Griffin with a teamster. They "were stunned," he said, to see a large herd of buffalo "wild and running." Creaton recalled that "for two hours they pushed on and the earth seemed full of them." Surveyor Elgin endured a more harrowing experience one afternoon. Crossing a gap between two canyons, he paused in bewilderment at a thundering noise. Suddenly an enormous herd of running bison seemingly materialized, sending him barreling for a narrow crevice in the canyon wall. For several hours, he recalled, the animals passed so close that "I could have put my hands on any of them." They soon wore away Elgin's shelter, forcing him to dig into the wall until he had formed a platform nearly level with their backs. Wondering how long his trial would last, he remembered old Indian fighter Sul Ross telling him that his soldiers had once waited three days for such a herd to pass.[3]

The wanton destruction of these animals that so amazed travelers began long before the great slaughter. In 1872, Kellogg noted that members of his expedition killed far more than they needed for food, "as every man must have his shot." That same year the sight of acre upon acre littered with carcasses "festering in the sun's heat" sickened Henry Comstock, who was driving a herd of cattle across the Goodnight-Loving Trail. "One great monarch . . . had fought death hard," he noted. With his forelegs "braced wide apart," the animal eventually sank to its knees; his "shaggy head dropped down between them with his nose just touching the ground." In this pose the "sportsmen" had left him—"and so we found him," remarked the herder. Cow hunters, whose herds competed with the bison, seldom registered such feelings. Rancher Emmett Roberts commented that range hands lassoed the pugnacious beasts to improve their roping skills. "We shot them down," he said, "when we were through with our fun."[4]

This alien land, so full of natural wonders, inspired tales of minerals, occasionally luring prospectors beyond the treeline. In

1873 Colonel Buell reported finding a vein of "pure burning" coal within fifteen miles of the post. On his orders a group of soldiers extracted chunks one to three feet square and eight inches thick. Pioneers came across evidence of mining potential as well. They not only found what they believed were the remains of Spanish mines, but also claimed that "wagon loads" of copper lay on the ground. Many expeditions—such as the Texas Land and Copper Association that Kellogg accompanied—exhausted fortunes only to learn that the cost of refining the greenish rocks far exceeded their value. One such group, after losing their oxen in a bison stampede in 1873, returned the next year to recoup their losses by harvesting the very beasts that had cost them their initial "grubstake." They also carried a camera and captured on film the beginning of the first truly great West Texas resource rush—the bison slaughter.[5]

Inroads by the army, cattlemen, hunters, surveyors, and prospectors represented the latest vanguard of the Anglo advance. The confluence of these activities attracted men such as Cornelius K. Stribling and George A. Kirkland, who became land agents and helped shape the development of the region. Stribling, induced by glowing promises of opportunity, left his Palo Pinto law practice in 1872 to settle near the fort; Kirkland, a South Carolinian driven west by tuberculosis, joined him two years later. Their partnership grew to encompass any number of activities that promoted expansion. Among their many endeavors, they surveyed, engaged in land speculation and brokering, lobbied government officials to extend a legal framework to the frontier, and conducted business for absentee owners.[6]

The threat of Indian depredations gave Stribling second thoughts when he first arrived. Twice in 1873, raiding parties stole his horse—once within half a mile of the post. When a prospective client that year asked him to arrange the purchase of twenty-three hundred acres in Jones County, Stribling advised the man to abandon his plans. The land, he noted, lay well beyond the treeline—"30 to 40 miles from any Settlement." He also informed the hopeful speculator that he would not even accompany him to the site without an armed guard of soldiers.[7]

The dangers and hardships so immediate to men and women living on the edge of the Rolling Plains must have looked less imposing from a distance. As the months passed, the volume of mail addressed to Stribling and Kirkland swelled with inquiries about the land and local conditions. The threat of Indian raids did not concern speculators who had no plans to take possession of their purchases. The army's campaign was progressing successfully, and farsighted capitalists realized that the land would "settle up" soon enough. At the same time, the Texas treasury lay prostrate, and the legislature started releasing land from the public domain to settle its financial problems and also to satisfy hopeful immigrants clamoring for cheap land.

Men and women who reached the edge of the treeline before 1874 found only the fort and a vast, sparsely populated country awaiting them. A generation of Indian warfare, unfamiliarity with the land, the independent nature of Southern herder folk, and the setback of the Civil War and its aftermath had left this frontier without a civilian commercial center. Services, with few exceptions, did not exist. Whatever supplies westering pioneers needed—including liquor—they could obtain from the post sutler, Frank Conrad, or from T. E. Jackson, who operated his little store below the post. Those seeking more prurient entertainment had to cross the Clear Fork, where they found only a shadow of the small group of gamblers and prostitutes that the army had cleared from the Flat two years earlier. Until almost 1875 the military post overlooking the river remained the region's only significant focal point. The Jackson family; Stribling and Kirkland; jack-of-all trades Hank Smith and his capable wife Elizabeth, or "Aunt Hank"; and a few others remained on the edge of the government reservation, but their aggregation hardly resembled a community. Colonel Buell described them as "very poor people, struggling for a foothold in this country." The citizen post Fort Davis had long since disbanded, but a few families remained at Picketville and in other isolated pockets; most of these were also inclined to break up once the Indian menace subsided.[8]

Despite such conditions, most of the men and women residing within sight of the post believed that opportunity would eventually

A wagon makes its way across the Clear Fork just below the Flat. (Lawrence T. Jones III Collection)

overtake them. A few hopeful merchants, and no doubt some whiskey peddlers and riffraff, had pleaded with Jackson to sell them land, but the old pioneer stubbornly refused. He enjoyed the business monopoly that he shared with Conrad and looked forward to better times as immigration revived. Stribling, having seen the Cross Timbers rapidly resettled, also poised himself for the expected advance. With the fort anchoring the region's livelihood, he and Kirkland felt that this spot leading onto the Rolling Plains possessed bountiful potential as a commercial center.[9]

The break for which the aspiring saloon owners and town builders awaited arrived in the spring of 1874. Through the quartermaster in his hometown of Louisville, Kentucky, D. M. Dowell finally learned that the army had built Fort Griffin on part of the old Peters Colony land that he had purchased in 1858. The post actually straddled three surveys running from Government Hill to the river. Jackson, of course, resided on one edge, and Stribling's old law partner, W. G. Veale, held the other corner absentee. Both men were content with the money they received from leasing the land to the government. But the tract on which sat the post and the former site of the Flat belonged to Dowell. The Kentucky businessman seized the opportunity to recoup his investment that had lain dormant for sixteen years. He had a spurious lease for the land invalidated and retained the services of a delighted Stribling and Kirkland to promote his interests. Over the howling protests of post commanders and Conrad and Jackson, Dowell announced that he would resurrect the Flat as the "Town of Fort Griffin."[10]

The situation in May 1874 seemed ripe. Kirkland wrote Dowell that a demand for town lots already existed and that he and Stribling would begin surveying and dividing the tract at once. They were confident that formally establishing a community would assure them the county seat when residents of Shackelford County voted in November. Stockmen had nominated an unpopulated spot eighteen miles south of the post near the center of the county; but this new development, along with the imposing presence of Fort Griffin, presented a formidable challenge. Dowell and his representatives looked forward to consolidating both the administrative and economic control of the surrounding country. By October 1874 they had sold eleven lots, and once again shanty bars began springing up on the river bottom.[11]

Colonels Buell and Schwann reacted angrily. As long as Conrad and Jackson controlled the liquor trade, the army could maintain order among the troops and even a measure of control over civilians. The officers felt betrayed by Stribling and Kirkland and sabotaged their efforts to establish the town and secure the county seat. Buell even contacted Dowell, painting the land agents as unreliable opportunists. To the adjutant general he wrote that "Mr. Stribling has not the confidence of the substantial people of this country," adding also that he "seldom fails to injure any one who has dealings of trust with him." When post trader W. B. Hicks produced a lease

purportedly signed by the Kentucky businessman, the commanders
threatened to remove settlers from the land and prevent the erection
of new buildings until Dowell or his agents demonstrated they had
full legal authority.[12]

Questions over clear title threw the budding village into turmoil
and swayed the election into the camp of those who supported a
location in the center of the county. While Dowell and Jackson
vied for the privilege of donating land for a public square, a handful
of residents declared they would simply "squat" on the river bottom
until the land agents and the army settled their feud. Then, just
before the November election, a detachment of soldiers removed
at gunpoint everyone who had settled on the Dowell survey. The
unseemly episode no doubt influenced many undecided voters, yet
the election was close. John Chadbourne Irwin claimed that the
victory for the center of the county swung on the ballots of some
"discharged Negro soldiers" whom some local men had registered
illegally.[13]

However dubiously attained, the plebiscite affirmed the political
sovereignty of first-comers. Conservative stockmen did not want
the county seat at a spot controlled by an unstable element that
represented values and interests so different from their own. The
accumulation of seedy hangouts that attracted rootless and transient
men and women was inconsistent with the vision they possessed.
Certainly the coup of winning the county seat assured stockmen
a strong voice at a time when the economy and social conditions
were about to change drastically. Although the town of Fort Griffin
would control the commerce of the Rolling Plains, the administration of justice and the development of more than a dozen
unorganized counties would be controlled from the new town of
Albany at the center of Shackelford County.

By the summer of 1875, Dowell and Colonel Buell had worked
out a lease agreement. Post commanders afterward tried to keep
contact between troops and the raucous townspeople to a minimum.
Buell quickly issued a circular forbidding soldiers to descend into
the village and placed the fort off-limits to tavern keepers. The
boundary of the government reservation, he declared, would be

the base of the hill. In at least two instances, when the owners of
saloons tested his resolve, the colonel forcibly removed them. "I,"
he dryly reported, furnished "the fatigue party and transportation."
Generally, the army distanced itself from the village's unseemly
characters. Infantryman Jacob Howarth commented, "We did not
bother the civilians and they did not bother us." But occasionally
troopers and townspeople mingled freely, and at times violence
resulted.[14]

As Griffinites busily carved a foothold at the Clear Fork of the
Brazos, their reluctant leaders joined ranchers and other settlers
in launching a community at the county seat. The name Albany,
after the Georgia hometown of future sheriff William C. Cruger,
proved acceptable to the largely Southern population. The roots
of the new village spread slowly, but town fathers assured they would
run deep. Organizers at once attended to matters regarding taxes,
a means of assessing public lands, plans for electing officers, and
even allotments for ordering desks, office supplies, and books for
record keeping. County affairs were administered at Griffin
temporarily, while in January 1875 Kirkland and Henry Jacobs
surveyed the Albany townsite and marked off lots for a public
auction. In March, Shackelford County applied to the state for four
leagues of school land to help finance public works. One of the
primary orders of business was an ambitious road building program.
The first road would join the county seat and the fort; others would
assure that both Albany and Fort Griffin would have access to
established centers to the east as well as to Phantom Hill and the
Colorado River country on the way to Fort Concho. County officials
also authorized eight hundred dollars for building a one-story picket
and stone courthouse. The first resident, T. H. Barre, erected a
tent-and-dugout home but soon replaced it with a hotel—the Barre
House. By autumn all the county officers resided at Albany, and
a handful of others had joined them.[15]

Griffinites, meanwhile, had not given up their earlier ambitions.
In December they petitioned the court to relocate the county seat
at the Clear Fork. "Captain" George W. Robson, editor of Jacksboro's *Frontier Echo*, wrote that "the inconveniences and annoyances

of court week have sounded the death knell of Albany." The town, he stated, "is fifteen miles distant from where two thirds of the population resides and four fifths of the business of the county is transacted." Robson's prediction, however, did not come to pass. On the last day of the year the *Echo* reported that advocates for the county's center had again defeated their rivals.[16]

Even before Shackelford County residents wrangled over the seat, Griffin received visitors who perceived the significance of the fledgling community beside the Clear Fork. Buffalo hunters Jim White and Mike O'Brien arrived in 1874 looking for an avenue leading to the herds that had drifted south from the Central Plains. For several weeks they scouted the country and reported to their associates at Dodge City, Kansas, that the prospects looked good, but that five hundred miles lay between the heart of the Texas range and the nearest railroad terminal at Denison, Texas. An intermediate point for depositing hides, outfitting hunters, and coordinating the activities of buyers, freighters, and others would be imperative. The visitors recognized that this site, on the edge of the plains and protected by the fort, would make an ideal spot.[17]

That winter several hunting outfits probed the Rolling Plains helter-skelter from various points in western Texas. The Causey brothers, veterans of the Central Plains, broke the tree line beyond Brownwood before ending up more than a hundred miles northwest of Fort Griffin. Other parties from Brownwood and the town of Comanche ventured just far enough onto the plains to gather meat and a few hides. Inexperience, cold weather, and the fear of Indians, however, limited their success. Even at the most extreme southern edge of the plains, crews from Menard hunted on the North Concho. Significantly, several outfits rendezvoused on the flats below Fort Griffin. Among them, a local outfit composed of Joe McCombs, John Jacobs, and Joe Poe organized two hunts that netted two thousand hides. The perspicacious sutler Frank Conrad purchased them for $1.50 to $2.00 apiece; he had learned their value from the sprinkling of Kansas hunters who had stopped at the nascent village to camp and secure some last-chance supplies.[18]

Over the next season, during the winter of 1875–76, Griffin
became the primary entrepôt for the great Texas range. This spot,
of course, had long been a popular jumping-off point for westward-
bound explorers and army personnel, and freighters also found the
well-traveled military roads and the old Butterfield trail a convenient
artery to rail centers in the interior. And if the suddenness of the
resource rush had caught merchants unprepared the previous season,
Conrad, Jackson, and a handful of recent arrivals had in the interim
stocked massive stores of lead, powder, and supplies. Other
businesspeople anticipated the boom, too. Saloon owners, gamblers,
and prostitutes, whom the post commanders found so loathsome,
provided alluring attractions to hunters starved for human contact.
With such advantages, Griffin became the principal base for the
experienced outfits out of Kansas and Colorado.

Among the first Central Plains hunters to stage an expedition
from Fort Griffin was J. Wright Mooar, who had been instrumental
in helping eastern tanners realize the market for bison hides. Just
as he had played a significant role in cultivating the trade in Kansas,
he became a key figure in Texas as well. Only twenty-three years
old when he arrived in West Texas at the head of a dozen wagons,
the seasoned veteran assembled a crew and set up camp near the
present-day town of Weinert in Haskell County. Pooling a three-
month's kill with White, O'Brien, and a few other experienced
hunters, Mooar sent his brother John to test the market at Denison.
The load of four thousand hides required eighteen teams of six yokes
of oxen, pulling three wagons apiece. News of the great train drew
onlookers all along the route. The overpowering odor sent normally
aggressive dogs scurrying under porches, while their owners reacted
to the sight with stunned amazement or animated excitement. Even
before the train reached the Red River depot, prospective buyers
rode out to meet John Mooar and inspect his cargo. The Denison
merchants, uncertain about the value of the hides but cocksure that
the hunters would know even less, conspired to offer low bids. The
experienced hide trader, however, rebuffed their pretentious
overtures and headed for a telegraph office, where he quickly nego-
tiated an acceptable price with W. C. Lobenstein of Leavenworth,

Kansas. The transaction convinced the hide buyer to locate a branch office at Fort Griffin. Soon other agents, as well as men and women hoping to benefit in some way from the resource rush, reached the flourishing village arising on the Clear Fork bottoms.[19]

At the same time that buffalo hunters were redirecting their attention to the southern range, cattle trailers were also looking westward. Not long after the first herds reached Kansas following the Civil War, the Chisholm Trail—from South Texas through Fort Worth and Indian Territory—had commanded the majority of traffic. Changing conditions, however, began to affect the trail adversely by the middle of the decade. In North Texas the farms of recent immigrants had begun to obstruct the herds' movements. Beyond the Red River, once menacing Indians who had earlier forced drovers to pass through the reservations of less bellicose tribes to the east now softened as the bison population dwindled. New Kansas railheads farther west also beckoned drovers farther afield and added extra miles to the old route. The fear of "Texas fever," which infected domestic cattle, prompted the Kansas legislature to impose legal barriers. In 1876 lawmakers set a quarantine line at the eastern boundary of Foard County. Dodge City, the county seat and the state's western terminus for the Atchison, Topeka, and Santa Fe Railroad, already had eclipsed its competitors, and it soon became the unrivaled destination for Texas longhorns. While the Chisholm Trail remained the preferred route for northbound herds until 1878, drovers looked increasingly to the Western, or Fort Griffin and Dodge City, Trail. The route ran roughly on a line between the two cow towns, skirting the western edge of the plains and brushing the villages of Albany and Griffin.[20]

The new trail did not emerge with the suddenness of the great bison slaughter, nor did it burn with the same economic intensity. Its impact on the local economy was nevertheless considerable and longer lasting. South Texas trailing contractor John T. Lytle actually organized the first drive over the new trail before buffalo hunters ever conducted an expedition from the eastern approach to the Southern Plains. In 1874 he had contracted to deliver a herd to the Red Cloud Agency in northwestern Nebraska and decided to test a direct route following the edge of the plains. Early that spring he gathered about three thousand head of cattle below San Antonio and started north over the new route. Toward the end of April the outfit reached Fort Griffin, where it bought supplies and rested for a few days before resuming its trek. At least one other South Texas outfit reportedly used the trail in 1874, but other contractors were not as venturesome. Merchants, preoccupied with the bison slaughter, paid scant attention to the still meager numbers of cattle crossing the Clear Fork the next year. In 1876, however, the new trail had intercepted about a fourth of the Kansas-bound traffic, stirring excitement among local businessmen. Newspapers in Jacksboro and Fort Worth reported that by the end of July between 73,000 and 108,000 cattle had passed through Shackelford County.[21]

During these years newspapers reported that prodigious numbers of immigrants were also making trails into western Texas, although the middle 1870s seemed a most unlikely time for a settlers' boom. The Panic of 1873—the country's most severe to date—had just turned the American economy upside down. For more than five years the nation's business activity stagnated. Railroad building ground to a virtual halt, and hopes for extending lines evaporated. The Texas and Pacific, which in 1873 had laid tracks within twenty-six miles of Fort Worth, did not complete the leg until 1876. At the same time, self-serving "hard money" men contracted the supply of currency to paralyzing levels. No segment of society suffered as badly as farmers on the Central and Northern Great Plains. Many had bought and improved their holdings when prices were high, and the economic debacle triggered their near collapse. Compounding the farmers' anguish, the worst grasshopper plague in the nation's history darkened the skies from Canada to Texas in 1874. Among the losses were "1,500 acres of corn" that Colonel Buell noticed growing close to Fort Griffin in May. A drought provided the capstone to the farmers' nightmare. Soon, western migration to the upper plains states declined by half.[22]

In western Texas, however, booming activity betrayed neither economic lethargy nor a shortage of money. Fort Griffin, gaining a reputation as the "metropolis of the Texas frontier," proved just as alluring to pioneer settlers as it did to hunters and drovers. A resident who had returned from Bryan, north of Houston, exclaimed that money was more plentiful in Griffin than anywhere else he had been. In July 1875, Jacksboro's *Frontier Echo* published the first of many columns extolling the "inducements" and "attractions" of western Texas. The overenthusiastic Captain Robson announced that the unorganized counties west of Jack, including Clay, Young, and Throckmorton, were still partly unsettled but "are filling up rapidly." The following February he noted that "hardly a day has passed for the last two months but we see on our streets emigrant wagons, one, three, five and ten at a time." Wisconsin man J. M. Herron and his family occupied one of the wagons that Robson observed. They had learned from a former neighbor that land in West Texas was virtually free and well suited to raising stock. Upon auctioning their farm, the Herrons fled the economic depression and settled in Shackelford County.[23]

Although the land was not free, westering pioneers nevertheless found conditions most inviting. In 1874 the state legislature began endowing counties, charities, and special interests with huge tracts of land to fund their concerns. Speculators acquired much of it, but competition kept prices within reason. J. L. Sellers, trustee for a fifty-thousand-acre grant bestowed upon the Baylands Orphan Asylum, wrote Stribling and Kirkland in May 1875, wanting "all information possible" concerning the land. The next year he contacted them again with news that he was accepting an offer of one dollar per acre from a New York man. Despite such a seemingly low bid, the orphans probably got the better deal; they let the new owner divide it, advertise it, arrange financing, and collect payments. Undeveloped land, depending on its attributes, normally ranged from fifty cents to four dollars an acre. At ten percent down, an ambitious immigrant could take possession of a thousand-acre tract of grazing or farming land in West Texas for as little as fifty dollars. Two years after the state began issuing these massive grants, Governor Richard Bennett Hubbard boasted that Texas still possessed seventy-five million acres of unappropriated land.[24]

The sudden interest in West Texas thrust Stribling and Kirkland into prominence. Their growing list of clients included many absentee owners who enlisted the firm's aid in maintaining tax payments, collecting debts, dispossessing squatters, and staying apprised of the real estate market. Houstonian W. R. Baker, who acquired "sight unseen" the land on which Phantom Hill sat, retained Stribling and Kirkland to resell it. Prospective settlers also wrote, asking the agents to describe the land and to estimate its value; others wanted to know whether it was sheep, farming, or cattle country. Occasionally someone would question them regarding the reliability of land companies, railroads, and individuals offering acreage for sale. A faithful response to the hundreds of nonclient letters pouring into their office rapidly established the agents' reputation as credible boosters. With official blessings, the firm routinely appraised lands, conducted surveys, and assured patents. In 1875 they successfully lobbied the state to release the former Comanche Reservation to settlement.[25]

At the peak of the hunters' boom and the advent of heavy traffic over the Western Trail, the frontier country opened its arms to westering pioneers. Like Griffin and Albany, other communities just short of the plains arose—a few only briefly—between 1876 and the end of the decade. Breckenridge arose a few miles from Old Picketville. On a line north of Fort Griffin, settlers founded Throckmorton; Williamsburg; Oregon City, later renamed Seymour; and Eagle Flats, which became Vernon. South of Albany were Callahan City, Belle Plain, and Coleman. Patterns of immigration remained largely the same as before the Civil War, although several groups of northern colonists arrived en masse. Most men and women hailed from former Confederate states and the Ohio Valley, settling first in the interior of Texas before reaching the frontier. Officials estimated that four hundred thousand people entered Texas in 1876; forth-three thousand reportedly passed through Denison alone in the last eight months that year. During that time the governor reported that "not less than 20,000 people live and camp on the prairies of Texas." Many of them were westward bound; Captain Robson claimed that in a three-month period toward the end of 1877 that "ten thousand new settlers have been added to Coleman, Brown, Shackelford and Comanche counties." The following spring, four hundred German families from Indiana took possession of one hundred thousand acres in Baylor County; another four hundred Pennsylvania farmers briefly occupied a tract about half that size in Throckmorton County. Immigration was even beginning to spill over the treeline. In 1878, Stribling and Kirkland wrote a client that Taylor County "is fast settling up," and they predicted that it would be organized within a year. Already the hunters' supply camp of Buffalo Gap had grown into a village. Jones County, west of Shackelford, was also beginning to attract settlers.[26]

Pioneers arriving in large numbers as well as an increasing familiarity with West Texas fostered a feeling of security during the middle and late seventies. Material progress also lent a sense of permanence. In the summer of 1875 telegraph service connected Fort Griffin with the outside world. At Jacksboro the *Frontier Echo* trumpeted itself as a "home paper devoted to the interests of the frontier." That autumn mail service to Fort Griffin increased to twice weekly, and stagemaster Charles Bain replaced his "hacks" with more comfortable coaches for his regular passenger service throughout Northwest Texas. The next year he coordinated his timetables to complement the arrival of the Texas and Pacific, which had finally reached Fort Worth. As excited residents in Weatherford held "railroad meetings" to beckon the line farther west, the Texas Central ordered a survey to explore a possible route between Waco and Belknap. In August 1876, the state legislature designated Shackelford County as the administrative and judicial arm for ten unorganized counties then crawling with buffalo hunters and the first of the region's ranchers.[27]

Although hostile Indians and outlaws remained a threat to life and property, real progress was also being achieved toward "pacifying" the frontier. In April 1876, Major John B. Jones, who commanded the Texas Rangers' Frontier Battalion, issued a report describing the success of his troops. In the first six months after their June 1874 enlistment, Rangers engaged fourteen of some forty-odd Indian raiding parties that had ventured into Texas. Only one—in which ranch hand Lute McCabe suffered a leg wound—occurred in the Clear Fork country, and it was the area's last reported encounter. Incursions afterward dwindled steadily until the commander reported that not one hostile party had visited the frontier from the Nueces River to the Red since September 1875. Nor did they return the next year. In September 1876 the *Fort Worth Democrat* reported that "no depredations by Indians are known to have been committed on our northwestern border within the past twelve months." Criminals also received the Rangers' attention. Jones reported that his troops arrested over a hundred fugitives, returned about twenty thousand dollars' worth of cattle and horses to their owners, and "broke up several organizations of outlaws." Reflecting on his two years of service, he noted that eleven former frontier provinces had been organized and that he now considered Palo Pinto, Coleman, Parker, and Jack "interior" counties. For the first time, he proclaimed, residents of Young could "ride the county without need of an army." Conditions had grown so tranquil by 1876 that the U.S. Army diverted several companies from Forts Richardson and Griffin to the more troubled Dakota Territory. Two years later the military abandoned its post at Jacksboro, and concern that Fort Griffin would soon suffer the same fate persisted until rumor became fact in 1881.[28]

Fort Griffin's rapid ascension spectacularly evinced the impact of three booms, one atop the other. From a collection of "squatters," as Colonel Buell called the Flat's inhabitants in 1873, the town had become the unrivaled center of the Texas frontier scarcely three years later. John Chadbourne Irwin, who had seen Camp Cooper come and go, asserted that Fort Griffin hit its peak between 1876 and 1877. "There was buffalo hunters, hide money, trail herd money, and soldier money," he recalled, and "it was the provisioning point for settlers going west and north." Just after the turn of the century, Don Biggers nostalgically recalled a brief visit to Griffin in 1877. The lively scene that his nine-year-old eyes beheld included "buffalo hunters, bull whackers, soldiers, cowpunchers, Indians, gamblers, toughs, refined business men and fallen women mingling in one

common herd." Biggers's description, however, fell short of fully
capturing the town's profile. The "refined business men" he noticed
might have included the town's half-dozen attorneys and physicians.
Others, less visible to the impressionable youth, included people
who owned or worked in the various hardware, grocery, and general
merchandising stores. The proprietors of the four hotels and
boarding houses employed others who provided a nondescript
backdrop for the more colorful characters that young Biggers
remembered. Butchers, barbers, druggists, tailors, bakers, blacksmiths, livery stablers, wheelwrights, hide dressers, carpenters,
and builders also competed for Fort Griffin's trade. A fruit dealer,
confectioner, saddle maker, shoemaker, dressmaker, gunsmith,
watchmaker, and photographer offered goods and services to fellow
townspeople and transients as well.[29]

The rough-and-tumble town itself presented an appropriate-
looking eyesore to match the hastily established enterprises that
dominated the frontier economy. Just after the new year in 1877,
Fort Worth Democrat correspondent Bill Akers wrote: "There is
nothing very attractively beautiful to gaze on. Nothing save a few
dobie and picket houses, corrals, and immense stacks of buffalo
hides." Even though the town had been surveyed and platted, Griffin
Avenue remained about the only definable street. On both sides,
businesses and houses lined its length from the base of Government
Hill to the riverbank. Pockets of residential dwellings accumulated
haphazardly. The largest collection arose west of town on Collins
Creek; another significant enclave, huddled below the western slope
of the hill southwest of Fort Griffin, represented most of the
community's black population. Smaller groups clustered east of
town and across the river. T. E. Jackson had erected an imposing
two-story stone house, but most of the homes and business buildings
were rudely constructed two- and three-room structures. Some,
however, were nothing more than lean-tos; a few boasted rough-
cut stone and boards planed on one side. Not until the summer
of 1878 did citizens erect the first all-stone building—a combination
Masonic lodge and schoolhouse.[30]

Of all the endeavors that brought men and women to Fort Griffin, buffalo hunting was most responsible for the town's meteoric rise. The cyclical business lasted only five seasons, primarily during the winter months from 1874–75 through 1878–79. Veterans of the Central Plains comprised most of the outfits the first year, and when the herds moved north, they followed. As the next season approached, during the fall of 1875, a throng of people—new hunting outfits and freighters, entrepreneurs and laborers, gamblers and prostitutes, and an assortment of adventurers—flocked to Fort Griffin in anticipation of the imminent resource rush. An old-timer recalled that by spring, rows of hides, "tier upon tier," stacked on the edge of town, "resembled a lumber yard." People on the road to the interior, who earlier stood agog watching the Mooar brothers' first load of hides make its way to Denison, no longer regarded the trains as a novelty. As the season wound to a close, as many as a hundred wagons a day made their way past these same homes.[31]

The handful of businessmen who profited most from the boom possessed ample capital reserves, a head for management, and an eye for new opportunities. A successful buffalo hunter, especially, had to possess considerable skills as both a marksman and a businessman. Outfitting, organizing, and winning the respect of a crew of independent frontiersmen and negotiating for the sale of the tediously prepared hides required tremendous savvy. Still, those who fueled the boom, rather than the hunters themselves, actually dominated the local economy. Hunter W. S. Glenn remembered Frank Conrad telling how he became alerted to the business potential at hand. A long-bearded plainsman "in a pair of old greasy overhauls" had stridden into Conrad's store and said, "Give me three kegs of powder and about four hundred pounds of lead." Conrad, Glenn remembered, exclaimed that "it nearly took my breath away." After learning from the man what was about to transpire, the sutler sent to Bridgeport, Connecticut, for twenty-five kegs of powder. Even before the shipment arrived, he declared, "There were men who would have taken twice as much." Conrad quickly adjusted. The *Fort Worth Democrat* reported in January 1877 that he posted a four-thousand dollar day, twenty-five hundred dollars of it in guns and ammunition. The balance went toward supplying some of the "forty or fifty wagons . . . waiting to be loaded." The next month the paper reported that "there has been more lead sold in Griffin in the last six months than in the state of Alabama in six years." After the season ended, Conrad traveled to Chicago, where he cultivated connections with eager suppliers. Offering to arrange for "anything" to be shipped to Fort Worth or Dallas, he wrote his associates to "attend to running the machine until I return."[32]

The "machine" to which Conrad referred contrasted sharply with the typical small-town Texas economies. In the wake of the Panic of 1873 the hard money that flowed so freely at Griffin provided opportunities that few places could match. During the decade the per capita wealth of the average Texan remained around $200.00, or roughly the value of 133 bison hides at $1.50 apiece. For common wage earners the prospect of easy money must have seemed irresistible. A farm hand could expect to earn less than $20.00 a month for working sunup to sundown; if he received board, his employer deducted almost $7.00. Cowboys were scarcely better off. Most of them, such as Frank Collinson, who helped blaze the Western Trail to Red Cloud in 1874, earned $30.00 a month plus board. By contrast, one "robe quality" buffalo hide could bring $3.00; even the "kip hides" of the smallest cows fetched at least $0.75. No wonder anyone with a gun or wagon seemingly flocked to the plains once the slaughter began in earnest. Freighters conducted a lucrative trade transporting hides to railheads and bringing back supplies. Some "old settlers" who sat for interviews in the 1930s asserted that Conrad once accumulated a pile of hides "higher than a man's head and covering ten acres." Perhaps the piles grew with the telling, and then again, perhaps not; in any event, freighters had difficulty keeping up with the kill. The partnership of Causey & West, while a proficient hunting outfit, found that hauling could be just as profitable. They employed fifteen drivers to guide their thirty wagons behind the power of more than a hundred oxen. Even men with almost no possessions or experience could earn top wages as skinners, drivers, camp tenders, or any number of jobs. Henry Herron, son of the Wisconsin farmer who had fled the depression, collected $200 skinning for Jacobs and Poe during one season. On his way to the buffalo range he encountered carpenter Bill Downtain returning to Griffin with a load of hides. Herron also met a young jobber from Tarrant County called "Big Ollie" who refused to reveal his real name because he did not want his father to find him.[33]

More handsome profits awaited buyers who possessed either the capital or business connections to move the staggering volume of hides. Both Frank Conrad and T. E. Jackson entered the market early. The fall season had barely begun in 1876 before Jackson had stockpiled two hundred thousand pounds of hides bound for Dallas. One of the most prominent buyers, a little Irishman named J. L. Hickey, represented Lobenstein of Leavenworth. He established the practice of venturing onto the range and negotiating with hunters in the field. Skinner John Cook, on his way to Fort Griffin for supplies, once found him at a neighboring camp inspecting a mountain of twelve thousand hides that several big outfits had stockpiled. When Cook told him that Dodge City buyers Rath & Wright had promised to purchase and transport hides taken by northern hunters, Hickey worked quickly to make the rounds of nearby camps. He was soon issuing checks on the spot for half the harvest and the promise of bearing half the cost of guarding the hides until he could arrange for freighting to Fort Griffin. At the end of the season he had a half million pounds of hides stacked along the Clear Fork.[34]

Although Fort Griffin remained the primary center for the Texas slaughter, other towns and supply camps competed for a share of the trade: San Angelo, in the shadow of Fort Concho; Hidetown, a hundred miles onto the plains; Buffalo Gap, about fifty miles southwest of Griffin; and Mobeetie, in the Texas Panhandle. Rath City, also called Camp Reynolds, arose near the Double Mountains and became Griffin's most immediate competitor. The brainchild of Dodge City hide dealer Charles Rath, the complex consisted of about half a dozen adobe and cedar buildings. In 1876 he had sent a train of supplies with lumber, nails, and tools along with some carpenters to build the village in the middle of the range. Another train of fifty wagons carried supplies and merchandise to stock his store. Rath counted on the loyalty of northern hunters and the north-south movement of the herds. Although Rath City cut into the Griffin trade, the size of the market left enough business for everyone. After a series of Indian raids in 1877, Rath and Conrad formed a partnership that lasted until the hunt subsided.[35]

The peak of the trade came during the winter of 1876–77. Hickey, passing through Jacksboro on his way back to Leavenworth in the summer of 1876, remarked that he expected "an immense business in hides the coming fall and winter." And he was right; over the next two seasons gangs of hunters all but exterminated the southern herd. In September 1876 a correspondent reported that "the range is full of hunters and more going out." By February 1877, the *Echo* reported: "It is estimated that 1,500 buffalo hunters are on the range west of Griffin." Probably less than half that number were competent hunters, yet counting skinners, freighters, and others, as many as 5,000 people swarmed beyond the treeline that year. Groups of men with no experience and owning only a gun and some ammunition rushed to the plains. They interfered with the big outfits, who often gave them their meat for the promise of leaving the herds undisturbed. Joe McCombs, who had seen "neither white man nor Indians" during his first hunt two years earlier, grew accustomed to hearing the steady sound of anonymous guns. The kill over the two peak seasons was staggering. J. Wright Mooar amassed 8,200 hides; McCombs' outfit tallied 7,200. A man "grubstaked" by Griffin merchant W. N. McKay claimed to have killed 9,352 bison in 1877 alone.[36]

The awesome destruction of the Texas herds horrified Comanches and Kiowas and other Plains tribes who had sullenly witnessed the disaster on the Central Plains. During the winter and spring of 1877 they staged a desperate and violent protest. War parties sacked several camps on the far reaches of the Rolling Plains, burning wagons and stealing or destroying supplies. Five men in one hunting outfit boldly pursued a large party to the raiders' lodges, but the Indians, after "firing their tipis" and fleeing, discovered

Buffalo hunters' camp on the plains. (Archives Division—Texas State Library)

Buffalo hunters' camp in the brush. (Archives Division—Texas State Library)

their attackers' meager strength and in turn set them to flight. Most of the hunters and skinners in the vicinity of Rath City, about three hundred in all, beat a hasty retreat to the makeshift village, where they compiled a list to account for those missing. Groups of men

Buffalo hunters gathering hides. (Archives Division—Texas State Library)

then ventured to likely crossroads, where they placed signs atop piles of bison skulls beckoning to safety anyone left on the plains. News soon reached Rath City that Marshall Sewall had been killed. Unbeknownst to the hunter, about fifty Comanche warriors had stealthily encircled him, waiting until he had spent his ammunition. Then they charged. Sewall's skinners watched helplessly from across a ravine as the warriors overwhelmed him. The men quickly retreated, barely outracing the war party to the cover of a brushy creek. A group that went to bury Sewall the next day found their friend mutilated and scalped. The warriors had broken off the points of the "rest stick" on which Sewall propped his gun and placed them in gashes in his temple and belly. With butcher knives Sewall's mourners "scalloped out" a shallow grave and buried him.[37]

Warriors continued to harry hunting outfits throughout the spring of 1877, but the raids, and especially Sewall's killing, stirred both hunters and soldiers to end the mortal nuisance once and for all. Parties of the dead man's outraged friends and acquaintances twice reacted before the soldiers launched their campaigns. The first band of hunters met some Indians in an inconclusive skirmish before regrouping at Rath City. Still early in the spring, a larger and better armed party started out for the tipi village of Comanche war chief Nigger Horse at Yellow House Canyon, just short of the Cap Rock. After locating the Indians, the overexcited hunters headed haphazardly up a draw and into a well-orchestrated defense. As many as three hundred Indians participated in the battle, a few charging, some shooting from a flank; the bulk, however, started a grass fire, which they used as a cover to approach their startled adversaries. The Indians' fierce resistance sent the chastened hunters into full retreat. The deadly accuracy of the buffalo guns and the haste by which the marksmen left the field, however, resulted in far more Indian than Anglo casualties.[38]

From Fort Griffin, Captain Lee staged a more successful assault. His squad of Tonkawa scouts and buffalo soldiers, accompanied by yet another group of hunters, captured all the women and children in the Indians' camp before defeating the warriors in a brief but fierce battle. Among the Indian dead was Nigger Horse.[39]

Hunters afterward returned cautiously to the plains, but in May, raiders resumed their forays. One party of about seventy-five Indians boldly hit Rath City one morning at dawn. Shrieking war cries and charging their mounts through the tiny village, they rounded up about a hundred horses, leaving the residents "flat-footed." Other parties hit camps as far east as the edge of the plains, prompting most hunters to head for Griffin. Another military expedition, though strategically unsuccessful, nevertheless convinced the renegade bands that the army would brook no resistance. This time the Indians retreated to their reservations, and afterward few warriors ever ventured onto their former hunting grounds.[40]

The 1877–78 season proceeded without incident, but the scarcity of bison soon become apparent. John Cook, enveloped amid a seemingly infinite herd during the first season, thought that "it would take the standing army of the United States years to exterminate them." As late as 1877 even conservative hunters, he claimed, believed they were killing only the natural increase. Henry Herron, traveling with the Poe and Jacobs outfit the next year, moved through continuous herds that casually parted for their wagon and closed in behind them. He remarked to his companions that "there would be plenty of buffalo as long as we lived." When he heard the next spring, 1879, that virtually all of them had been killed, he could hardly believe it.[41]

The waste accompanying the slaughter reached gigantic proportions. For every hide that reached the market, others were squandered. Killing grounds without fail presented scenes of prodigal waste. In many places carcasses stripped of the hide and a few choice cuts of meat lay rotting. At the peak of the kill, hunters camped at river crossings and water holes and opened fire when bison appeared. The animals, forced to bypass their regular watering spots, would eventually find another and rush into it "pell-mell, crowding, jamming, and trampling down both the weak and the strong," commented Cook. Many wounded animals wandered off to die in some unseen ravine or thicket; others, disoriented by the relentless pursuit, wandered into bogs and quicksand. Even skins awaiting market became ruined by "hidebugs." Hickey, the diminutive Irish buyer, decried the scale of the slaughter. "No regard whativer to economy!" he supposedly declared, adding a litany of products that could have been fashioned from the wasted horns, hoofs, and hair. Captain Robson calculated that in one season a particular hunter "actually threw away over *two and one-third million pounds* of as good meat as man ever ate." The "*Echo* man" concluded: "What better argument can be adduced for the necessity of a law to prevent the wholesale slaughter of these animals which are fast becoming exterminated."[42]

But government regulation was never forthcoming, and when the waves of amateurs joined in the slaughter, the bison's virtual destruction was assured. As the kill transpired, the Texas legislature considered a conservation act, but the impassioned speech of General Sheridan exhorting the hunters to "destroy the Indians' commisary" swayed state representatives and assured that the remaining bison would travel "through a hail of lead." Hunters expressed little remorse about exterminating the majestic beasts. Cook lamented the slaughter but took comfort in the knowledge that he had helped open the plains to white settlers. Still, when he graduated from skinner to shooter and beheld the "eighty-eight glassy-eyed carcasses" of his first stand, the scene haunted him years later. By contrast, J. Wright Mooar felt nothing but pride in his work. He dismissed the negative perception of both the hunters and the bison's extermination. "I resent their ignorance," he declared. "Any one of the many families killed . . . by the Indians would have been worth more to Texas . . . than all of the millions of buffalo that ever roamed from the Pecos . . . to the Platte."[43]

Economically and ecologically, the buffalo hunt was a disaster. The apparently infinite supply of animals dissipated within five years. Restraint could have sustained indefinitely a vibrant demand for robes, meat, hides, and any number of other products. As in any resource rush, a few became wealthy, but most of the participants had little to show for their high hopes. The hunt generally stimulated the regional economy, yet the effects were short-lived. During the last two seasons many outfits failed to make

enough money to cover their investments. Other hunters and
skinners squandered their money at the welcoming saloons and
brothels. Even the people who took their money did not fare well
in the long run. Many of them eventually went broke, although
a few farsighted bar owners and businessmen made timely moves
to other "hot spots." A handful of big merchants such as Conrad
and Jackson also profited, but even Conrad lost a fortune by
grubstaking men who had no intention of repaying him. Jackson
survived only to face bankruptcy when a clerk absconded with all
his capital. Most significantly, Fort Griffin itself—the center for
the great slaughter—gasped to a slow death, vainly pinning its
economic hopes on a succession of drovers, settlers, and railroads.[44]

Even before the annihilation had run its course, Griffin's
businessmen turned to supplying and entertaining cattle trailing
outfits to buoy their sagging fortunes. In March 1878, local
merchants complained that few buffalo hides were coming in from
the winter's kill; still, they expected a good season and counted
on trail herds to supplement their business. The good hunting season
failed to materialize. The Mooars netted fourteen hundred bison
but had to supplement their kill with the hides and fur of three
hundred deer, antelopes, wolves, and other animals. The Western
Trail, however, was showing signs of overtaking the Chisholm. By
October the *Frontier Echo* reported that "trail traffic is replacing
the buffalo trade." According to the *Fort Worth Democrat*, 150,000
cattle passed through Shackelford County in 1878, surpassing by
50,000 the number that had walked up the older trail. Perhaps as
many as a thousand cowboys had visited Griffin that year, raising
the spirits of merchants worried over the declining bison harvest.[45]

The long drive saved its greatest impact for railhead towns at
the end of the trail, where the cowboys were paid, and for owners
at the places of origin. Towns such as Griffin and Albany nevertheless enjoyed a lively trade with the passing herders. Cooks
restocked and bought parts to keep their chuckwagons rolling, while
trail herders replaced worn-out gear. An old Griffinite exclaimed
that stores there offered "everything a cow man could possibly
want." They stocked saddles, blankets, quirts, six-shooters, and

all articles of clothing—"from high heeled boots to $50 Stetson hats." Most of the drovers' spending, however, occurred in the bars and brothels. Brief "blowouts" relieved the stress and loneliness of eighteen-hour days on the trail.[46]

Conrad and Jackson, caught off guard by the bison hunting boom, worked with other Griffin merchants to develop trade with trail-driving outfits. Their efforts instigated a heated contest with Fort Worth. In 1877, Clear Fork businessmen, in league with their counterparts down the Western Trail at Coleman, sent boosters such as one "Major" Hinkle to South Texas. Intercepting the northbound herds, they boasted of the advantages of the western route while planting seeds of doubt regarding the Chisholm. Progress and use, they declared, had seen the old trail broken by farms and obstructed by fences; years of constant grazing, moreover, had reduced its forage. Such arguments helped Griffin merchants draw the majority of traffic in 1878, but Fort Worth businessmen beat the upstarts at their own game the next year.[47]

The competition grew into a war of words between Captain Robson, who had moved the *Echo* to Fort Griffin in January 1879, and B. B. Paddock of the *Democrat*. For two years the diminutive and "walrus mustachioed" Robson had nursed a grudge against his well-heeled rival. Deriding the folksy style of the *Echo*, Paddock once chided the frontier paper for borrowing from an almanac "its supply of knowledge and inspiration." Another time he chortled that his complaining counterpart had confused "impudence with enterprise" after the *Democrat* had "scooped" Robson in his own county. Now, however, Griffin appeared to have the upper hand over Fort Worth, and the "*Echo* Man" took full advantage of it. Waxing indignant over unfavorable comments regarding the Dodge City route, he parroted the litany of the Chisholm's negative attributes while championing the positive qualities of the new path. After the *Democrat* predicted that the established trail would capture all but "three or four" northbound herds that year, Robson trumpeted that "the *ECHO* is authorized to say that $500 or $1,000 will be . . . placed in a bank at Dallas or Fort Worth" to cover any bets against the Western Trail commanding the most traffic.

Two unnamed but confident Chisholm boosters not only raised the stakes to $2,500, but also bet that three-fourths of the cattle would use the older trail. As the race grew close during the summer months, the bettors declined to step forward. Had the gentlemen not given odds, they would have grown richer, for cowboys did drive a majority of cattle up the Chisholm Trail in 1879. But the next year the Western Trail overtook its competitor and afterward never relinquished its supremacy.[48]

Albany enjoyed Griffin's victory as well. In any other location, settlers and newspapers would have heralded the emergence of such an enterprising little town as Albany in an otherwise desolate setting. During their few years of coexistence, the county seat quietly grew into a prosperous community in the shadow of its rambunctious neighbor. In 1877 land agents advertising town lots promised "numerous streams and beautiful valleys of unsurpassed fertility." Their embellished sales pitch reflected as much community pride as exaggeration. "Albany," they proclaimed, has "several stores, comfortable county buildings, one church, two schools and numerous residences." For drovers and travelers the town also boasted three hotels, a saloon, and a public well on the square. Building continued, according to a resident who forwarded a letter to the *Echo* later that year. Several homes were either going up or were planned, and the county had authorized the construction of a new jail. T. E. Jackson had already established a branch store at Albany, and the Fort Griffin grocery firm of Palm & Wilhelm was considering a similar expansion. Such inducements swelled the local population. "Shackelford county is fast settling up," the letter-writer announced, adding that "immigrants arrive daily." The next year Captain Robson traveled there and called on attorneys J. N. Masterson and Peter Hart and merchant Sam Stinson, former Jacksboro residents who had relocated to Albany. The "*Echo* man" concluded that "citizens feel confident that the prospect is flattering for a large, thriving city."[49]

As the bison hunting boom withered and the frontier began showing evidence of becoming settled, the prospects for Albany appeared even brighter. Yet Griffin, suffering from the notoriety of its fading heyday, clung precariously to its commercial predominance. Cowboys from passing trail herds as well as transients still preferred the Flat's wide-open nightlife to the sedate atmosphere of the county seat, but the mere fact that such rootless people preferred the wild dives engendered misgivings. Too, the sight and activities of the ramshackle town no doubt repulsed many prospective families who could now choose among several small communities in the area. When the demand for town lots at Griffin ebbed at the end of the hunting and trailing season of 1878, Dowell wrote Stribling to express sorrow that "things in our town are so flat." Nevertheless, large merchants accustomed to quiet months in the seasonal trade still dominated the regional economy. The Kentucky speculator moaned that an acquaintance with a stock of goods had wanted to settle on the Clear Fork but had decided to move to Belle Plain because Griffin's competition would have prevented him from making much money.[50]

As the decade neared its end, Griffinites hoped their town would remain the regional center of commerce. Although the garrison had been trimmed and rumors persisted that the fort would soon close, uneasy contractors and businesspeople found solace in waking each day to see the United States flag still waving proudly from the top of Government Hill. And with the rising but cyclical trade of the Western Trail not even near its peak, local merchants expected no sudden turn of fortune. Robson even predicted that "when the buffalo hide trade is completely played out the town will, in our opinion, lose most of its 'hurrah' element, and settle down into a good frontier town." The arrival of a railroad, moreover, seemed imminent, and boosters felt confident of attracting at least one of two proposed lines through the county. Stribling and Kirkland issued a circular, crowing that "the completion to this point of either of these lines will inaugurate a new era of progress." A new era was indeed coming, but few at Fort Griffin would have predicted the fate that lay ahead.[51]

CHAPTER EIGHT
A WILD TIME IN THE
OLD TOWN TONIGHT, 1875–1879

O
NE SUMMER DAY IN 1877, Charles Bain's stage delivered the *Jacksboro Frontier Echo* to Fort Griffin. Between the headlines and the local news, the paper dedicated an entire page to a devastating railway strike that had left much of Pittsburgh "in ashes." Pennsylvania militiamen, on hand to preserve the peace, instead provoked a riot by turning their rifles and Gatling guns on an unsuspecting crowd of factory workers and curious spectators who had gathered at a railroad roundhouse. Later that day and throughout the night several thousand civilians responded by attacking the troops with any kind of weapon they could find. The mob pillaged the city and destroyed buildings, railroad cars, and other property. A month later the *Echo* reported that "forty persons killed and two-thousand six-hundred cars destroyed are among the fruits of the late strike at Pittsburgh."[1]

About the same time as the riot, news coming out of Northwest Texas created the impression that keeping order was beyond the ability of civil authorities at Fort Griffin as well. In December 1876 the *Fort Worth Democrat* reported that vigilantes in Shackelford County had just hanged almost a dozen horse thieves, adding: "Their bodies will make good food for the vultures." And only a month earlier the *Frontier Echo* vividly recounted the brutal slayings of two freighters by a pair of outlaws who had hired their team. After departing the village, the murderers marched the drivers into the brush; one of them shot his man point-blank in the head, the other pistol-whipped his victim to death. The *Dallas Daily Herald* covered an equally violent incident. This time it was a gunfight inside a Griffin saloon, where the sheriff and county attorney left one reckless cowboy dead and another wounded. Two bystanders had also been killed—one "with his brain oozing from the hole in his forehead."[2]

While the strikers at Pittsburgh erupted as one body protesting their intolerable conditions, Griffinites acted as individuals, seemingly resorting to violence in the normal course of their affairs. Compared with other frontier communities, Fort Griffin was a bloody boomtown, but the sensational reports emanating from the little outpost did not always paint an accurate picture. Such incidents were infrequent but widely reported, giving the impression of lawlessness out of proportion to daily life. Travelers, in fact, frequently expressed surprise at finding Fort Griffin so peaceable. Editor Robson wrote tongue-in-cheek that a number of itinerant prospectors thought they would "see nearly every citizen a walking arsenal"; they also expected to "hear of at least one man being killed here regularly each day in the week and several killed on Sunday." Wildness was nevertheless ever present in the whiskey houses and brothels lining Griffin Avenue, and the volatile environment indeed invited occasional violence.[3]

Griffin's "heyday" began about 1875, shortly after D. M. Dowell reopened the Flat to settlement. The socially deprived enlisted men welcomed the development, and despite the efforts of everyone concerned with maintaining military discipline, the army had little success keeping the soldiers away from the rough-and-tumble little town. The fort's medical officer noted that "the habits of the men might be materially improved by the removal of a number of lewd women living in the vicinity of the post." He also complained that recently a soldier had been wounded by a "pistol ball" in one of Griffin's "drunken haunts." Inspector General N. H. Davis resigned himself to accepting the "nuisance under the bluff," remarking that "this kind of evil . . . will follow the troops to any locality they may go."[4]

Colonel Buell did not surrender so easily; in February 1875 he ordered his men to stay out of the Flat. The enlisted men openly flouted him, however, and several of them even erected shacks in the village. To the colonel's consternation, the situation further degenerated. In October a dispute over sectional differences resulted in a bloody row between drunken soldiers and civilians. When the troops threatened to burn the settlement, the townsmen vowed they would march on the fort. A few weeks later the colonel removed one of the worst offenders, a man named Krause, even though he held a legal lease for what Buell described as a "grog shop and gambling hole." Ill feelings lingered, and in January an infantryman on sentinel duty fired a round into the Flat, mortally wounding a civilian.[5]

When the first session of the district court met in recently organized Shackelford County during June 1875, Judge J. P. Osterhout dealt severely with lawbreakers. In thirty-seven cases during the five-day session he found a dozen men guilty of gambling and selling liquor illegally, and although the fines ranged from only $10 to $15, some of the accused faced multiple counts. Many of the same men who sold illegal spirits were also pandering prostitutes, a more serious crime that cost the guilty parties between $100 and $150. In many instances attorneys for the defendants got cases discharged or transferred to the more lenient county court. The signal was nevertheless unmistakable: the legal community would hold miscreants accountable for their actions. Many petty delinquents such as those listed on the court docket as Banjo Bob, Curley, Smokey Joe, and Frenchy skipped town rather than face Judge Osterhout. Among them was Doc Holliday, whose single crime at Fort Griffin resulted in a gambling and liquor charge.[6]

Osterhout also presided over more serious cases. He issued warrants for two suspected murderers who fled Fort Griffin before Sheriff Henry Jacobs could apprehend them. Several men facing assault charges also eluded the court. W. L. Browning was not as lucky. He was convicted of trying to murder an acquaintance, John Jackson. According to the testimony of Jackson's sister, the two men were sharing a watermelon outside a picket residence when they suddenly began arguing. As Browning pulled a gun, Jackson hit his arm with a shovel and then bolted indoors to get a shotgun. The defendant also ran to the house and began shooting through a crack in the wall, firing so close to the witness that she suffered powder burns. Browning, by then outgunned, retreated across the river. The Court of Appeals in Austin upheld Osterhout's verdict after the defendant contested the decision of the local jury.[7]

Despite its earnest efforts, the court could not stem the proliferation of vice and violence at Fort Griffin. As the activity in saloons, gambling dens, dance halls, variety theaters, and brothels grew with the great bison hunt and cattle trail traffic, increasingly prosperous merchants and businessmen convinced officers of the court to wink at the "victimless" crimes. A more tolerant climate indeed existed when citizens in Northwest Texas elected J. R. Fleming to the district court bench in 1876. A resident of the frontier town of Comanche, eighty miles southeast of Fort Griffin, he understood loose social conditions. Judge Fleming concentrated on controlling violence and let the justices of the peace work with local people to set community standards. During two terms that year he issued a lone indictment for "selling liquor without a license" and a single charge against one "Swayback Mag" for prostitution. Even into the 1880s visitors who remained within the wide latitude of acceptable behavior at the Flat could enjoy a spree without running afoul of the law. "Old Griffin had its night life," remarked one-time resident "Jet" Kenan; "everything went but murder, arson, and burglary."[8]

A ride down Griffin Avenue provided visitors an indelible impression of the little village. Smells, sounds, and sights assaulted the senses. The putrid odor from thousands of buffalo hides rotting in great stacks started many a horse to reeling. More pleasant was an impromptu concert that greeted a transient as he passed by York's store; there he saw a black man holding the reins for a mounted fiddler grinding out "Arkansas Traveler" to the delight of a crowd. Loitering cowboys occasionally passed around Jew's harps, and when stabler Pete Haverty got his organ, the music could be heard throughout the valley between the fort and the river. Rollie Burns described his first visit to Griffin in 1877, while on a cattle buying trip. On the main street were freighters, some unloading wagons, and others starting for Fort Worth with mountains of hides; trail outfits, too, were taking on supplies. "Alongside this busy element," he remembered, "was another, half drunk, boisterous, and bent on raising hell." One visitor recalled that the business district "was a Babel of boisterous talk, whoops, curses, laughter, songs and miserable music." The passing of time no doubt sweetened the memory. Cowboy Ken Cary more accurately declared that "Fort Griffin was more disgusting, after first glance, than alluringly picturesque."[9]

Inside the dives lining Griffin Avenue the coarse scene of filthy transients enjoying a visit to the Flat was even more primitive. "I've seen men and women dancing there in the dance halls without a bit of clothing on," remarked one visitor. Another man affirmed that indeed "the women were scarcely dressed"; they also danced with the patrons, and when the music stopped, "you bellied up to the bar, took a drink and paid fifty cents for it." Animating the drab adobe and picket hovels were women known only by names such as Polly Turnover, Slewfoot Jane, and Monkey-face Mag.[10]

Despite the wide-open conditions, not more than a handful of saloons ever opened their doors at the same time. Many tried to enter the lucrative trade, but the few proprietors lucky enough to gain a foothold connived with the legal community to limit competition. No one was above the law. Even Frank Conrad once had to climb out of a jury box to fight a charge of "selling spirituous liquors without a license." At the peak of the buffalo slaughter a Stribling and Kirkland circular advertised only five Griffin bars; Henry Herron later recalled that as many as five more operated for various periods. Among the lucky owners was Mike O'Brien, who came to hunt bison but quickly found serving drinks more profitable and infinitely more entertaining. Few of his former associates passed through town without stopping at the Hunters' Retreat; Charley Meyers's Cattle Exchange drew much of the drovers' trade. Under one sprawling roof "Uncle Billy" Wilson ran a beer and dance hall, variety show, restaurant, and lodge called

Local merchant "Dutch" Nance "turns dude" for a shot at a Griffin gallery. (Robert Nail Foundation Archives, supported by the Old Jail Art Center, Albany, Texas)

the Frontier House. A frequent patron commented that "a blueprint would have been interesting."[11]

None, however, was more popular than Donnely and Carroll's Bee Hive. The saloon gained notoriety as the scene of at least one fatal gunfight and one unprovoked murder. English drifter Jim Grahame, otherwise known as *Dallas Daily Herald* correspondent "Comanche Jim," claimed credit for naming the place. He also asserted that over the entrance he painted a "rough representation of a beehive" under which he scrawled a rhyme that had the drunken inhabitants beckoning visitors to "come in and try the flavor of our honey."[12]

The seasonal nature of hunting and trailing also drew professional gamblers who made Fort Griffin an important stop on their "circuit." Reportedly, a game could be found in the back room of any saloon. The weakly regulated activity invited the use of marked decks, loaded dice, and other aids. "The ordinary fellow did not have the ghost of a show," commented Henry Herron. "I saw a buffalo hunter come to town one day and market his season's kill for $1,500.00," he continued. "The next morning he had to borrow money for his breakfast. The gamblers had gotten all of it."[13]

Prostitutes also scrambled for the money of free-spending transients. In 1877 the *Dallas Daily Herald* reported that "Griffin, which has long been the roost of a large quantity of 'soiled doves,' can now boast of a larger flock than any other town on the frontier." According to Jet Kenan, "Fort Griffin would not have been Fort Griffin" without its "red light district." For about two blocks the brothels extended in a broken line down each side of the main street near the river. The women worked with the blessings of saloon keepers and merchants alike. During the day prostitutes "boldly and openly took their 'friends' around from bar to bar and store to store"; together with the shopkeepers, Kenan claimed, they would "bleed them of every possible dollar in every conceivable manner." At night women worked the saloons, "drinking, cursing, smoking, and contributing greatly to the loud hilarity."[14]

The prostitutes, who added so much color to the stories that men told, led anything but glamorous lives. Low pay and high expenses kept them in poverty. Their fondness for gaudy clothes, material possessions, and alcohol and drugs further drained their earnings. The degrading conditions of prostitution, moreover, elicited the most wretched of human qualities, producing hardened, cynical, grasping women. Among themselves, any number of negative forces—competition, suspicion, jealousy, and petty incidents—checked the bonds that mutual privation might have formed. And because their profession rested outside the law, they were at the mercy of the legal system. The justice of the peace set the rules for the illicit trade, and the women normally observed them. The local court, they knew, provided their only protection against the abuses of an uncaring and often hostile society. For example, Griffin's justice of the peace, who usually ignored petty crimes in the black community, came to the defense of some African American prostitutes harassed by a group of drunken black cowboys. He promptly had the men arrested for brandishing their weapons "in a private house" and fined each of them. Rarely did the county and district courts become involved in the prostitutes' affairs.[15]

The profiles and experiences of prostitutes along Griffin Avenue were neither flattering nor heartening. Although many were youthful, some stayed in the profession long after their looks had faded. Two of the nine women who listed their occupation as "courtesan" for the 1880 census were in their mid- to late thirties; others, who had been teenagers during the town's heyday, had reached their early twenties and looked forward to middle age with few prospects for improving their social condition. Some were married, such as Minnie Delno, who got the sobriquet "Hurricane Minnie" for her forced union with "Hurricane Bill" Martin. But marriage did not add stability to their lives; instead, it made them even more disreputable. A society that already frowned on the trade held a special contempt for a married prostitute. Their husbands, moreover, represented the dregs of society, assuring that the women would remain at the bottom of the social ladder. Bill Martin, for example, became legendary for his frequent brushes with the law. Few women escaped this miserable environment. Griffin resident George Newcomb claimed that a local man had once tried to marry a particularly striking young prostitute—"white and fair"—but authorities supposedly refused him a license because she "had some Negro blood." The sorry legacy of a broken life was often passed down to the children of prostitutes as well. In the same house that Sarah Dickinson operated, her twelve-year-old daughter also entered the profession.[16]

Beyond Griffin Avenue was a more conservative society that frowned on the dissolute life-styles of its neighbors. The occasional trial for adultery and the formation of a temperance union in 1875 demonstrated the rigid moral standards that governed the rest of the community. Only the economic force behind the vices of prostitution, gambling, and unbroken revelry kept the local dives in business. Early in 1876 the *Dallas Daily Herald* reported that some upset citizens chased several of the most disreputable prostitutes out of town, "this done on the principle that bad meat draws flies." In June, when several more arrived to take their places, townsmen threatened them, too. A prominently posted notice, signed "Vigilance," read: "Leave or you are doomed." Evidently merchants checked their zealous neighbors; in September, a docile Griffinite registered a complaint in the *Fort Worth Democrat*, feebly pleading with the sheriff to appoint a deputy to control the rampant vice. The "hard-visaged," part-Indian Kate Gamel was certainly not intimidated by hollow threats. At her cramped adobe brothel that Henry Herron called "a known rendezvous for criminals," officers laid an ambush one dark evening. The outlaws reportedly escaped by spurring their horses over the bluff and into the swollen Collins Creek.[17]

In this pitiable environment Charlotte Tompkins briefly enjoyed part control of a boarding house, the Gus, as well as a saloon. But even though she transcended the normal sphere of her gender, Tompkins could not escape the degrading consequences that attended a woman's entry into this male-dominated environment. More widely known as "the poker queen" Lottie Deno, she gained a reputation for her ladylike dress and the cool manner in which she relieved her rough patrons of their money. Yet just as men mistakenly attributed the raucous gaiety of prostitutes' lives for

insouciance, they also misinterpreted Tompkins's aloof demeanor.
She certainly shared the desperation of other women who worked
on Griffin Avenue. Whether by dint of business acumen or simply
because she had accumulated some working capital, Tompkins
managed outwardly to earn a more honorable living. But where
other saloon owners such as Hank Smith, Owen Donnely, and
Charley Meyers were accepted socially, Griffinites shunned
Charlotte Tompkins. On one occasion she registered her defiance
by staging a "masque ball" while other townspeople gathered at
a nearby hotel for a dance. Several old-timers nevertheless asserted
that such strength of character was only superficial.[18]

The tragic and impenetrable life of Tompkins invited
speculation. Former sheriff John Jacobs called her "unapproach-
able" and claimed that "she had nothing to do with the common
prostitutes." Just before she arrived at the Flat, however, a Jacksboro
court had fined her $100 and costs for running a brothel. Supposedly
she had worked other "fort towns" on the Texas frontier as well.
Her circumstances at Griffin began to sour about the same time
as the apparent murder of a tawdry young drifter, Johnnie Golden.
Henry Herron commented that Golden was a "nice looking boy,
had a little money to spend, and spent it freely." And although little
evidence supported his claim, Herron asserted that "Lottie fell for
him." Equally dubious was a rumor that she was the unwilling
paramour of saloon keeper Dick Shaughnessey. Old-timers nevertheless asserted that the whiskey peddler became jealous and paid
Constable Bill Gilson and an accomplice, Dan Draper, $250 to
kill his supposed rival. The circumstances of Golden's death
certainly implicated them. The pair claimed that they had served
him an arrest warrant and were taking him to the post guardhouse,
even though the local "calaboose" was only twenty yards away.
Gilson and Draper further maintained that Golden's death came
at the hands of "rescuers" who fired on them from a ravine; the
powder burns on the dead man's body, however, cast doubt on the
alibi. In any event, the citizens of Shackelford County "ran Gilson
off" after a brief inquest.[19]

Shortly afterward, Tompkins's business situation also deteriorated, forcing her hasty departure from Fort Griffin. For a woman to obtain a mortgage on a bar or brothel was really not so unusual, and neither were the consequences when she could not meet her financial obligations. Typically, courts in tolerant frontier towns overlooked illegal activities as long as participants squared their own affairs discreetly. But in January 1878, shortly after George Matthews brought suit against Tompkins for a $290 debt, she found herself fighting a second charge of "keeping a disorderly house." At first she refused to acknowledge the local court. Her stubbornness cost Owen Donnely and Charley Meyers five hundred dollars—the price of her forfeited bail. An arrest warrant soon compelled her to appear for trial, where a jury found her guilty on both counts. Tompkins appealed the pandering charge, but mounting attorneys' fees and the considerable sum that she still owed to her former confederates prompted her to take expedient measures. Rather than wait for the outcome of the new trial—which, ironically, cleared her—she simply fled.[20]

Stribling and Kirkland, representing George Matthews, later traced Tompkins to Bracketville, adjoining Fort Clark. Unknowing sympathizers believed that Tompkins, still grieving over Johnny Golden, had finally had enough of Fort Griffin. Although the sketchy details surrounding her life as Lottie Deno eventually grew to mythical proportions, her departure was no more mysterious than that of any number of men and women who left town owing money or evading the justice system.[21]

Just as the so-called "lady gambler" inspired exaggerations and even outright fabrications, other dubious tales circulated that probably had just enough basis in fact to seed Griffin's reputation for unequaled violence. Gunman Jeff Milton claimed that as he tried to break up a bar fight between two buffalo hunters, one of them shot the other, splattering Milton with "blood and brains." Jeff, according to his biographer, "learned right there the importance of tending to his own business." On another occasion, an inebriated "tough" supposedly killed a Tonkawa Indian and was simply thrown in the calaboose "until he sobered up." Another time a drunken Lipan Apache was said to have stumbled into a Griffin hotel, where a woman killed him for his disruptive behavior. And when a partially deaf man refused to acknowledge a deputy's order to halt, the lawman reportedly emptied his pistol into the man and then offered to bet that he could cover the bullet holes with a silver dollar. Soldiers also contributed to the list of unprovoked and uncorroborated killings: a post guard murdered a buffalo hunter; a lieutenant, who had lost all his poker money to an enlisted man, shot him in the back; and a recently discharged "Scotty" killed a soldier even as the victim's wife fell to her knees, begging him not to shoot. In each case nobody seemed particularly interested in bringing the killers to justice, nor did anyone mention that any of them ever served a day in jail.[22]

In contrast to these doubtful reports, the court strove assiduously—but seldom satisfactorily—to bring murderers to justice. Between 1875 and 1881 the 12th District Court, which included the counties administratively attached to Shackelford, issued eleven warrants for suspected killers. No case better illustrated the court's persistence than a bill against J. E. Kennedy, who was jailed at Fort Griffin for the 1877 killing of a man on the buffalo range. When he escaped, Texas Rangers recaptured him. After a mistrial, a new jury sentenced him to hang; upon appeal he won a new trial and a change of venue. Finally, after two years of legal maneuvering, he received a sentence of ninety-nine years.[23]

Some other cases, although ending badly, still merited the earnest attention of the court. When a man fired a shot through a saloon window, killing Thorndale man Andrew Brownlee, a coroner's inquest swiftly rounded up witnesses and conducted a thorough interrogation. Narrowing their list of suspects to drifter James Oglesby, a posse combed the town and surrounding area for him. Soon the pitch blackness of night ended the search, and Oglesby escaped, leaving a fugitive warrant on the docket along with an underlined notation left by the court's transcriber—MURDER![24]

Three years later the court was again unsuccessful when it tried Henry Cruger for killing quartermaster clerk June Leach. The case dragged on for more than a year before jurors finally issued a verdict of not guilty. The slaying evolved out of an argument at a billiard table when Leach accidentally stepped on Cruger, who rebuffed an apology with the admonition that he would "whip him" if it happened again. To the good fortune of the accused murderer, testimony conflicted about what happened next, but witnesses— subpoenaed from as far away as Mason County—agreed that after a brief fight Leach fell dead from Cruger's gunshot.[25]

Even after the Flat's heyday waned, the court still had trouble securing murder convictions. The shooting of Jewish merchant "Cheap John" Marks in 1879 nevertheless stirred the court to conduct a scrupulous investigation. The "pesky drummer," as editor Robson once called him, had left town for the Panhandle owing money to Griffinite Frank Schmidt. Special deputy William King, accompanied by the creditor, went after Marks, and upon apprehending him about fifty miles from town, camped for the night. Schmidt claimed that while King was hunting turkey for their dinner, Marks had somehow secured a gun. When Schmidt supposedly attempted to seize the weapon, it discharged, fatally wounding Cheap John in the back. Hearing the shot, King raced back to camp. Skeptical over Schmidt's story, he left him to care for the unconscious and dying man and then went on to Fort Griffin, where he notified Texas Rangers. After Marks died, four Griffin-bound waggoners happened upon the scene and helped bury him, then carried Schmidt with them. A jury—after hearing the testimony and cross-examination of both Schmidt and King, as well as the statements of the four travelers—returned the supposed murderer his $5,000 bail and set him free.[26]

Contrary to the perception of the Northwest Texas frontier as a place where violent acts were accepted casually, gratuitous killings were rare and violence was never taken lightly. For example, Griffinites held a public meeting in January 1877 to express sympathy to the families of two bystanders who were killed in a senseless crossfire. Several months later, at isolated Rath City, hunter Tom Lumpkins shot an unarmed man who had taken exception to his constant carping. As another man tried to subdue

Lumpkins, bartender "Limpy Jim" Smith ran up and jerked him aside and then shot Lumpkins point-blank. The surly hunter, still firing, stumbled backwards out of the saloon, followed by Smith, who reportedly kept a stream of bullets flying as he came. At the bartender's insistence a group of men accompanied him to Fort Griffin, where he surrendered himself to authorities. With the sympathetic testimony of the other hunters, a grand jury decided not to prosecute.[27]

While assiduously attempting to bring "deserving" killers to justice, local courts did not overlook the petty crimes that plagued the unstable frontier society. Many were the reports of minor thefts and the records of prosecutions. During the hot summer of 1875, for example, traveler Billy Smith, overcome by heat, awoke to discover that someone had gone through his pockets, robbing him of a lottery ticket, some tobacco, and his keys. County Clerk J. N. Masterson recounted another typical incident, complaining that a thief had broken into his office and stolen $4 in change. Another time a man named Christianson was arrested for breaking into the home of Mrs. Mary Mitchell and taking $165 in greenbacks and some silver. The court at all levels—justice of the peace, county, and district—prosecuted such indignities zealously. Thieves seemed always to be sitting in jails at Griffin and Albany or working on roads between the two towns. County Judge W. H. Ledbetter normally assessed sixty days to nine months for petty thefts. Judge Fleming was even harsher. In 1876 he sentenced one George Robinson to two years at hard labor in the state penitentiary for taking clothing valued at $49. The next year he meted out the same punishment to a man for stealing almost $500 and a butcher knife. Fleming prosecuted cases of swindling, forgery, and other non-violent crimes as well.[28]

Still, the legal community was sometimes frustrated. Hurricane Bill Martin, for example, was a one-man crime wave. He constantly sparred with the courts but was seldom held accountable for his many illicit activities. He reportedly loaded wagons with buffalo hides from stacks lining the river bottom, then rode into town and sold them to the very men whom he had "fleeced." He was also believed to have been the leader of a gang of horse thieves, and ironically he was the only one who survived a vigilante roundup. A deposition recorded that after Sam Stinson accused him of stealing a watch and chain, Martin pulled out his army Colt and "dropped it down on his [Stinson's] head saying, 'You can't give me any such game.' " Somehow Martin was again found innocent. Extenuating circumstances in another case forced the court to try him for "discharging a firearm" instead of attempted murder. In several other cases he was charged with assault, forfeiting bonds, and trying to enter the underworld of gambling, liquor, and prostitution.[29]

While the resolute efforts of the court faded in the minds of former Griffinites, memories of killings and the tales of men such as Hurricane Bill seemed to grow. One-time sheriff John Jacobs related to fellow officer Henry Herron that "conditions got so bad . . . he could not feel easy sleeping in the same place two nights in succession." Fort Griffin was "a veritable robber's hole," according to rancher Emmett Roberts. "They would throw a blanket over your head and take your money in a flash." A surveyor, C. U. Connellee, recalled that "of all the places I have ever been, that was the worst." Long familiar with the frontier, he asserted that "men who had committed crimes, and fleeing from the law often went as far as they could from civilization, and that was the end."[30]

Nothing did more to burn indelibly the image of Fort Griffin as a violent frontier town than a fatal gunfight at Donnely and Carroll's saloon. The "Shooting Bee," as the spontaneous incident came to be known, emanated from a poorly handled confrontation between Griffin authorities and local ranch hands Billy Bland and Charley Reed. Befitting the image of drunken cowboys, the pair raced their horses down Griffin Avenue, guns ablazing. Entering the Bee Hive, they interrupted dancers by trying to shoot out the lights. As Bland was taking aim on another fixture, Deputy Bill Cruger, accompanied by County Attorney Robert Jeffries, barged into the saloon and demanded that the revelers "put up their hands." The abrupt order provoked Bland into wheeling around and firing in the deputy's direction. When Cruger started shooting, both Jeffries and Reed joined the sharp firefight. The lawman and attorney sustained minor wounds; two bystanders were less fortunate. Newlywed Dan Barrow, shot through the forehead, died instantly. As a Lieutenant Myers tried to flee, he suffered a mortal wound in the back. As for the instigator, Billy Bland, a bullet passed completely through his body, leaving him writhing on the floor. Some men took him to the Occidental Hotel, where "Aunt Hank" Smith said "the poor fellow begged to be killed." According to Phin Reynolds, "Reed left the country that night."[31]

For such a wide-open town, the legal system generally executed its duties in a credible manner. Few times did peace officers experience such mortal tumults as did Deputy Cruger. In fact, a former Griffinite recalled that "no man ever became so bad but that he might land in the 'calaboose' if the marshal so decided." Zeno Hemphill, a would-be badman, might have agreed. In 1878 he and some other cowboys had reportedly planned to kill special deputies Henry Herron and Dave Barker for nothing more than the notoriety. The two officers, appointed to help keep order during a meeting of the Northwest Cattle Raisers' Association, learned of the plot and waited in a crowded saloon for their supposed executioners. When Hemphill knocked a woman backward with the intention of starting a brawl, Herron grabbed the man's six-shooter and "whacked him over the head." Barker then pulled his own gun and covered the crowd while Herron hustled Hemphill off to jail.[32]

Henry Herron, reflecting on his Griffin days, remarked that the calaboose was always occupied. "They were in there for every kind of offense, ranging from fighting to horse stealing and murder, but not many for murder." A jailer normally escorted prisoners to a blacksmith, who fit them for shackles; at night they were chained to the wall. If assaults were common, so were assault charges. The justice of the peace did not keep records, but the district court issued twenty-four warrants for such crimes between 1875 and 1880. Many of the accused simply fled town, and the legal community was probably satisfied to be rid of them. And while a few fought the charges and won, most lost and faced fifty-dollar to one-hundred-dollar fines. Still others earned jail time. Robert

Brown, for example, was sentenced to two years' hard labor at the state penitentiary for "assault with intent to kill."[33]

Despite a generally credible record, the law at times was ineffective. Vigilantes, composed of both court-appointed officials and respected citizens, ran amok during 1876, executing almost a score of suspected horse and cattle thieves. A succession of sheriffs, responsible for the entire county, did not often have the time nor the inclination to concentrate on controlling Griffin's transient revelers. Townspeople begged in vain for the court to appoint a deputy to control the gangs of raucous buffalo hunters and trail drivers, but finally had to hire a local officer at their own expense. Jet Kenan remarked that even then "a man had to act very, very badly to be molested by the 'marshal.' " Certainly the violent death of Johnny Golden undermined the reputation of the local legal community. His killers were never brought to trial. The elaborate story that Gilson and Draper told of a "lost" warrant and a three-o'clock-in-the-morning shootout kept the officers out of jail, but also made the court appear indifferent.[34]

Where African Americans were concerned, the law also broke down, but only because it reflected the attitude of the Anglo-dominated society. Joe McCombs claimed that a drunk hunter once burst into the mess hall at the post and fired over the heads of some buffalo soldiers, prompting them to flee. When troops cornered the hunter, Sheriff John Larn convinced the commander to release the man into his custody and afterward let him go. Another time, when a black soldier full of "tarantula juice" shot his gun in the street and declared that he could "smash any 'white descendant of a female canine' in town," officers allowed some irate townsmen to take care of the matter. In buoyant prose a correspondent for the *Fort Worth Daily Democrat* wrote that "by careful maneuvering he at length succeeded in acquiring a 'head' of gigantic dimensions, and was forced to make a retrograde movement on the Fort." The dispatch ended with the comment: "No arrests."[35]

Regarding violence that occurred entirely among African Americans, local authorities throughout Texas routinely turned their backs. Fort Griffin was no exception. For example, an exchange of gunfire between two black men at the Clear Fork crossing went unaddressed, even though one of them, Joe Brandt, was gravely wounded.[36]

Another racial incident, although it occurred after Griffin's wildest days had passed, demonstrated both the court's insistence on following "proper legal procedure" and its attitude toward African Americans. In 1879, Captain S. H. Lincoln, on the eve of his transfer to another post, shot and killed black infantryman Charles McCafferty. The private had escaped the guardhouse, where he had been confined for habitual drunkenness, and headed for town. He promptly became inebriated again, and upon spotting the captain at Conrad and Rath's, he unleashed a verbal assault that ended when the army officer physically removed him from the store. The drunken soldier—in front of everybody in town— then knocked the officer off the sidewalk with a roundhouse punch to the jaw. The ignominious blow prompted Lincoln to draw his pistol and shoot the impudent McCafferty, who died the next day. Despite being released on a two-thousand-dollar bond, the captain left Fort Griffin for his new assignment, forcing Texas Rangers to bring him in. A preliminary hearing bound him over for the "felonious" murder of Charles McCafferty, but in the civil trial Judge Fleming reminded the jury that murder was distinguished from manslaughter by "malice aforethought." The lesser charge, he advised, could also be mitigated by "provocation." In his own defense, Lincoln reportedly declared that his action was "the only dignified course to pursue." Evidently, the jury agreed and found the captain "not guilty."[37]

Certainly, violence and any number of petty crimes and vices underscored the instability of Fort Griffin's boomtown environment. Nevertheless, rough but otherwise unmenacing people and a lighter side of life also represented "wildness" in this frontier society. Buffalo hunters and cattle drivers, little concerned about manners and morals, descended in raucous packs upon Fort Griffin after long periods with little human contact. More frolicsome than reckless, they typically spent a few harmless days and nights of unbridled revelry before resuming their monotonous routines.

Skinners and nonprofessionals among the hunters and a handful of "maverick" drovers caused most of the trouble that gave the two groups their undeserved reputation for violence. Rootless opportunists, itinerant pioneers, and people from the interior who ached for a little excitement and some quick money also contributed to occasional lawlessness. Yet even among these largely anonymous men and women, very few came West intending to launch a career outside of the law.

Typical of many buffalo hunters was "Charlie," who traveled to Griffin at the head of his crew when the season ended in 1875. After cashing a large check at Conrad's store, he paid his men, and they camped with about thirty other outfits under the big pecan trees lining the Clear Fork. "I never intended to get drunk," he said, "but what could a fellow do?" According to a friend, Charlie "had a glorious spree"—twenty-one days long, in fact. Once, after he had passed out, some of his men set a stuffed panther over him. When the hunter awoke and saw the beast staring down at him, he lurched backward into the river and had to be "fished out."[38]

Cowboys had their fun, too. Frontiersman Jim Gordon recounted that a pretentious Englishman once arrived at Griffin and hired two men to escort him to the ranch of a countryman. Word reached some herders farther up the trail, who prepared a reception as the "lord" and his guides made camp for the evening. With whoops and gunshots, the cowboys pulled the Englishman's well-appointed wagon into a creek. Boldly he emerged in cap and gown, brandishing a small pistol, only to face a dozen gun-wielding "desperadoes" trying hard to suppress an explosion of laughter. After reaching his destination, the Englishman endured further indignities such as affectedly rough language and manners and the sight of the cook dishing out supper in a pair of the visitor's own kneepants. "He was mad as a hornet," Gordon recalled fondly. "Many were the tricks we played on him but eventually he came to be naturalized and proved a jolly good fellow."[39]

Such earthy amusements were typical in an environment where large numbers of unattached men did "manly" things together. Few places gained a greater reputation than Fort Griffin as an oasis

Cowboys at Fort Griffin. (Robert Nail Foundation Archives, supported by the Old Jail Art Center, Albany, Texas)

where frontiersmen could enjoy themselves unencumbered by conventional social pressures. And not all the fun was just drinking, gambling, and prostitution. Jet Kenan recalled that "many times

Anonymous visitor to Fort Griffin. (Robert Nail Foundation Archives, supported by the Old Jail Art Center, Albany, Texas)

Reynolds Company cowboys, frequent visitors at the Flat. (Robert Nail Foundation Archives, supported by the Old Jail Art Center, Albany, Texas)

saloons sent for me to participate in boxing matches . . . or to preside over a 'Kangaroo Court.' "[40]

Dancing and "varieties" were more common forms of entertainment. "Frank Smith & Co. have completed their music hall in Fort Griffin and have secured the services of ten or twelve well known *artistes*," the *Echo* reported in 1876. "They are performing nightly to crowded and delighted audiences."[41]

Concerning a prominent local merchant, Captain Robson chided: "We noticed Caleb Cupp one day this week amusing himself by holding two Tom-cats up by their tails, while the cats amused themselves by picking fur from each other." Pitting animals against each other was always a crowd pleaser. Another time the editor noted that "next Saturday there will be a fight at this place, between a young black bear and Hemphill's two bull dogs, for $50 a side." He did not follow up the report, but presumably the dogs won. A few weeks later the *Echo* reported that Mr. Chifflet, the local tanner, "has a bear skin robe which is a beauty."[42]

Another favorite diversion was horse racing. Stabler Pete Haverty often staged contests at a track across the river. Like many of his patrons, however, he was often in debt because of his losses. In the fall of 1876 the *Fort Worth Daily Democrat* reported that local tough John Selman and bootlegger Jack Greathouse had declared John Larn the winner in a close race—by precisely three inches. "Some dissatisfaction was manifested at the decision," reported the correspondent, adding that bettors were incredulous at the judges' "being endowed with vision of such mathematical nicety, as to be able to determine the exact number of inches the winning horse was ahead at the string."[43]

Like the cowboys who found sport in the Englishman's misery, men who idled countless hours at Fort Griffin found that a ruse or practical joke could provide an amusement that demanded repeated tellings long after the event. "Uncle Billy" Wilson seemed always to be working on a scheme. Jet Kenan claimed that Wilson once concocted a "wonder cement" that he matched against all comers—"Old Hickory, Spauldings, and others." He appeared to patch up some broken dishes with the competing glues and then dropped them all into boiling water. Soon every dish had come apart—except those mended with Uncle Billy's secret compound. According to Kenan the trick was that a friend of Wilson, an accomplished engraver, had etched matching lines on the top and bottom of some china that looked remarkably like cracks. Since few people washed china in boiling water, his scheme worked.[44]

On another occasion Edgar Rye, editor of the *Albany Tomahawk*, fell for a practical joke that Captain Robson could not resist reporting. Rye, upon learning that a woman from Fort Worth had just arrived in town searching for another woman's husband, wrote a few indignant lines, ending with the demand, "Explain!" A few days later the supposed out-of-towner confronted Rye, demanding that *he* explain. As the editor rose to offer an alibi, he looked up into the muzzle of a gun. Aghast, the floundering Rye lost his hat and glasses, then tripped over his stool. Rising to his knees, he begged her not to shoot. Suddenly the "woman" and a group of men standing at the window burst into laughter. His antagonist, it turned out, was a townsman "in drag."[45]

As Rye could attest, Fort Griffin was not the only Texas frontier town to see bawdy action, and neither did it have a corner on lawlessness. Pranksters at the county seat exploded a barber pole with gunpowder, to which Captain Robson lamented: "the old striped sign is seen no more in the land." And, as Albany began to intercept some of the trailing business in the spring of 1879, it also reaped some of the unpleasantries. "Every day or two," the *Echo* reported, fistfights had erupted. "Someone would appear on the streets with a black eye or banged up nose," but as in Fort Griffin the law swiftly put an end to it.[46]

Ironically, Frank Conrad's daughter had left the county before she became a crime victim. Between Fort Worth and Weatherford stage robbers relieved her of one hundred dollars. Virtually every edition of the *Echo*, the *Fort Worth Daily Democrat*, and the *Dallas Daily Herald* carried stories from around the state that comprised a woeful record of crime. Robson complained that Northerners viewed Texas as a "community of murderers and robbers." Blaming frontier conditions and the ubiquitous carrying of weapons, he admitted that his fellow citizens were a law-breaking people "to a fearful extent." B. B. Paddock of the *Democrat* was more defensive, asserting that Texas was not alone in experiencing violent acts. Economic times, he declared, had "thrown upon the country hundreds and thousands of men who, having no families or homes, become reckless and careless, and are wandering over the country depredating upon the rights of others and committing acts of violence."[47]

In the public perception, as in fact, Fort Griffin was nevertheless among the toughest spots on a tough frontier. To contemporaries, distance and unfamiliarity no doubt caused imaginations to magnify the image of lawlessness. The tunnel of memory likewise inflated the level of violence, the colorful descriptions, and fond reminiscences of an otherwise bleak and harsh environment. Fort Griffin in part earned its reputation; violence touched nearly every segment of society, and when trailers hit town, no one could avoid hearing hoots, hollers, and gunfire as they spurred their frenzied horses up and down Griffin Avenue. But revelers most often knew how far they could push local authorities, and more violent offenders knew that when they acted, consequences would surely follow.

CHAPTER NINE
BLOOD ON THEIR HANDS, 1876–1878

THE WAVES OF EARNEST SETTLERS, townspeople, buffalo hunters, and cowboys that transformed life in the Clear Fork country also pushed before them the dregs of society. While citizens at Fort Griffin dealt with miscreants and revelers, stockmen in the surrounding area contended with rustlers and horse thieves. During 1876 cattlemen staged an ill-fated vigilante campaign—the decade's bloodiest in a state that was racked with such movements. Then, for the next year and one-half, apprehensive members of the secret society worked to extricate themselves from the consequences. Most of the shocked vigilantes, whose only objective had been to stop the epidemic of stock thefts, found themselves saddled with a faction that had grown comfortable using its power and anonymity. Despite repeated admonitions, the renegades continued to further their personal interests illicitly. Intimidation, deceit, and dishonor were the price that many prominent citizens paid to disentangle themselves from their predicament and outwardly preserve their good reputations.[1]

The vigilante movement in the Clear Fork country arose, as did so many others, out of volatile conditions on the Texas frontier. Loosely tended stock on the edges of settlement attracted gangs of outlaws who thrived in the unstable social environment. Cedar brakes in the Hill Country, dense thickets in the Cross Timbers, and the vast empty spaces of Northwest Texas and the Rolling Plains provided any number of places to hide purloined cattle and horses. In Kansas, Indian Territory, and other places, opportunists found eager buyers who did not ask questions. As a result, the scale of

thefts was staggering. The *Houston Telegram* estimated that one
hundred thousand horses had disappeared from Texas homes, farms,
and ranches between 1875 and 1878. Frequent shootings and
hangings of criminals caught in the act became the outgrowth of
pioneers' frustrations and the inability of lawmen to solve the
problem.[2]

At least sixteen extralegal movements occurred in Texas during
the 1870s. Mob action in such frontier counties as Comanche,
Coryell, Erath, Llano, Burnet, and Montague provided a politically
expedient topic for the inaugural address of newly reelected
Governor Richard Coke in January 1876. His proposals reflected
the outrage of many citizens—mostly in the interior—over the
actions of vigilantes. The governor asserted that as "a rule of
evidence" law officers should be held accountable as accessories
for the murder or escape of prisoners in their charge. With the
exception of inmates forcibly removed from jails, Coke contended
that the actions of vigilantes had not resulted in a single casualty.
"Nor have I ever known," he continued, "a resolute resistance made
by a sheriff or a jailer to the demands of a mob, fail to be
successful."[3]

During the first week of April 1876, Clear Fork stockmen
responded to Coke's impassioned address by wiping out a gang
of outlaws about ninety miles west of Fort Griffin. In many respects
it was a repeat of the incident at Bushnob two years earlier. As
before, John Larn rode at the head of a citizen posse, and again
U.S. Army troops stamped his actions with legitimacy. This time
he possessed authority as the sheriff of Shackelford County as well.
The party of thirteen civilians and a Lieutenant Shipman, leading
twenty soldiers and two Tonkawa scouts, trailed the rustlers to their
hideout just beyond the Double Mountains. There the outlaws had
established two rendezvous camps, where they regularly
accumulated sizable herds of stock animals and then moved them
up the buffalo range to Kansas. The first of the bunch to meet
vigilante justice was "Larapie Dan" Moran, whom the posse
captured astride a stolen mount at the gang's lookout post. Civilians
and soldiers then surprised eight more outlaws who were tending

over a thousand cattle and horses. Shipman officially reported that after he and the Indian scouts rode ahead to search for other members of the gang, the posse rushed to him and declared that all of the rustlers had escaped. To Captain Richard Henry Pratt, however, the lieutenant intimated that Larn confessed to killing at least some of them. "The best way to end" stock thefts, the sheriff supposedly told Shipman, "was to end the thieves when caught."[4]

If Pratt felt that he had gained a confidence, it did not remain a secret for long. Shortly, "MOB LAW!" and "SWUNG TO A LIMB" jumped out from the columns of Texas newspapers. The *Echo* proclaimed that "the gang of horse and cattle thieves which have infested Shackelford County for some time has received a death blow at the hands of the cowmen of that section." Both soldiers and herder folk remained closemouthed, yet their reticence did not stop editors and correspondents from trumpeting the results. According to the *Echo*, only four members of the gang were actually killed. Ringleader Joe Watson and Charles McBride were hanged after being wounded. *Dallas Daily Herald* correspondent "Comanche Jim," who viewed the "blackened and hideous corpse" of McBride, wrote blithely that he "now hangs as they say here, a hard looking sight." Captain Robson added that frontierspeople were "rejoicing" over the affair "as the men were notorious desperadoes and the country is better off without them."[5]

Local citizens were still abuzz over the slayings when two more rustlers met the same fate. After someone wounded Houston Faught in the act of stealing a horse, he was taken to the post doctor for treatment and, according to the *Echo*, was remanded into the custody of "some of the best citizens of the place." A party of "armed and masked men," however, soon disarmed the guards and promptly hanged the man to a tree beside the Clear Fork. On his back they pinned a card that read "Horse thief No. 5." A rhetorical postscript added: "Shall horse thieves rule the country? He will have company soon." And he did; one "Reddy" joined Faught two weeks later. Authorities in neighboring Eastland County had captured the suspect and handed him over to some deputies charged with the task of transferring him to Albany. Without explanation the *Echo* reported: "Yesterday his body was found hanging to a tree three miles from here." In town, vigilantes underscored the killing by posting another placard—signed with a skull and crossbones— warning all rustlers to leave the country.[6]

Stockmen no doubt justified their actions. Through the Civil War and the early years of Reconstruction herder folk had banded together against hostile Indians while inertia seized every bureaucracy that controlled the avenues of relief. In the mid-1870s many cattlemen felt that the local legal community, the army, and the Texas Rangers had grown similarly incapable of addressing wholesale stock thefts. Just after the Vigilance Committee's decisive action, Captain Robson reported that "twenty six horses were recently stolen from one ranch alone." Thefts had become so widespread, he asserted, that citizens "could not purchase fresh stock fast enough to satisfy the demand of the horse thief." First-comers had taken the land from the native inhabitants, and now, goaded by other angry cattlemen, they were loath to tolerate depredations at the hands of their own people. Members of the secret society could arguably rationalize that they were only acting on a long-established tradition of self-preservation.[7]

But as the countryside developed, so had the legal community. In earlier times no framework for administering justice existed within a reasonable distance. In 1876, however, when the vigilantes first acted, the county had been organized for two years. On the payroll was a sheriff with the power to appoint deputies. Four local justices of the peace, a county court, and a district court also stood ready and capable of trying anyone brought before them. And if loose cannons such as Larn had not acted so rashly, the federal troops might have worked more closely with local herder folk. Texas Rangers, moreover, were active, even if at the time preoccupied with other matters.

A large part of the stockraisers' discontent lay in the verdicts handed down by juries on which many of them served. When the first district court session met in Shackelford County during June 1875, Judge Osterhout heard six horse theft cases. Three of the accused—including Charles McBride—were found not guilty.

Another case was discharged, and the judge issued fugitive warrants for two others who had fled before lawmen could apprehend them. Despite what citizens believed was the obvious guilt of the accused, their release was not attributable to a corrupt jury. The panel included men who controlled the local political structure, such as first-comer Joe Matthews and rising cattleman James A. Brock, who sat with other prominent citizens such as T. E. Jackson, John C. Jacobs, and George Wilhelm. Any number of explanations could account for the court's leniency. Although doubtful, Griffinites on the jury might conceivably have nursed a grudge over losing the county seat election to ranchers by letting the guilty men go unpunished. That sufficient evidence for convictions was lacking seemed unlikely, however, since most victims were caught with stolen stock. Perhaps sympathetic and even fabricated testimony helped set the accused free. Or, quite simply, nonstockmen on the panel might have felt that the penalty for taking a horse—normally one to ten years at hard labor—was too harsh for the crime. Under the philosophy of "jury nullification," they might have rendered "not guilty" verdicts rather than subject the accused to such extreme punishment.[8]

Measures were indeed taken to lighten the penalty for stock theft. The state legislature considered passing a law to assess a public whipping for a first conviction, whipping and branding for a second offense, and hanging for three-time offenders. Captain Robson jeered at the suggestion and chortled his own advice: "Hang 'em first, then if they persist in their innocent amusement, cremate them."[9]

In May 1876, Judge J. R. Fleming, fully aware of the explosive conditions, took the district court bench at Albany. He opened the session by delivering a stern lecture to the grand jury in which he reminded citizens of their responsibilities. "Nothing," he began, "can be as disastrous to the peace and well being of society, than the want of respect for, and confidence in the administration of justice." Alluding to the outbreak of vigilantism, he acknowledged that "whole communities have become impatient with the tardy justice meted out by the courts." He nevertheless affirmed the sovereignty of the law and appealed for restraint.[10]

Despite his admonition, the session ended on May 19 without a single conviction for stock theft. In almost a dozen cases the jury released every suspect who had not already fled the country. Upset citizens responded violently. Outraged by the failure of the court and emboldened by general approbation for "vigilante justice," new members—including a few townsmen—flocked to the secret society. About the first of June the opportunity to "initiate" them emerged. Sheriff Larn, back from Dodge City with two men who had escaped the posse at the Double Mountains, deposited his prisoners at the county jail in Albany. According to the *Echo*, about fifty men on foot and another twenty mounted ordered the guards to surrender their prisoners. The next morning suspects Bill Henderson and "Floyd" were found "dangling in the air" about a quarter of a mile from the town square. Captain Robson hollowly lamented that "it is at best a deplorable state of affairs when Judge Lynch is called to preside"; but in the next breath he quipped that so far the vigilantes "have made no mistakes."[11]

Many citizens later recalled brushes with the vigilantes or at least witnessing their handiwork. "Aunt Hank" Smith, who operated the Occidental Hotel, claimed that more than one morning a boarder snickered that "we have another man for breakfast hanging down yonder in a tree." Trooper Jacob Howarth told of having gone to the river for a bath only to see "a man hanging by the neck and riddled with bullets." Like Houston Faught, this one also sported a scorecard: "Horse Thief No. 8." Henry Herron, who eventually worked against the vigilantes, said that once he had asked a county laborer to identify two prisoners locked inside the courthouse. "A couple of horse thieves," was the reply. The next morning Herron saw them "hanging to an elm tree." Cowboy turned hunter Frank Collinson told of a more harrowing experience on the buffalo range. While he and partner Jim White were eating supper, vigilantes and Tonkawa Indians rode into their camp with a group of suspected stock thieves. One of them was prominent hunter and freighter George Causey, who had pleaded with the stock raisers to let White vouch for him. The affirmation apparently saved Causey's life. Collinson asserted that the mob led the other prisoners to a river bank and slashed their throats. He claimed that he saw one them later. "The skin on the neck was dry like old leather, but it showed plainly where the throat had been cut."[12]

Late in October 1876, Judge Fleming again lectured jurors upon concluding his second session of the district court—and with the same results. "It has been common for citizens to serve on the jury, try criminals, acquit them, [and] turn them loose upon society," he complained. Afterward these same jurors could be heard denouncing the courts "for the lawlessness and crime existing in the county." Decrying both the vigilantes and their supporters, he challenged citizens to act responsibly. Scarcely a month later, members of the secret society apprehended and hanged eleven suspected horse thieves just west of the military post. The *Fort Worth Daily Democrat* wrote that the mob had little trouble tracking the gang, as they were "burdened with twenty-seven stolen horses." The dispatch added that four more thieves from the same outfit were caught near Fort Sill, Indian Territory, and were being transported back to Fort Griffin, where "their show for life will be meager indeed."[13]

If the incident was a rebuttal to Fleming's admonitions, it was an emphatic but final statement. Although the clandestine workings of the vigilance committee left little room for more than speculation, a progression of events that followed the wholesale lynchings in December suggested that the campaign against common stock thieves had run its course. In February 1877, regional cattlemen formed an association that provided an orderly means to protect their property. Juries also began to return convictions later that year. Primarily though, the complexion of the secret society changed when members eventually realized that among their ranks was the most baneful offender of all. Unbeknownst to his fellow cattlemen, John Larn—along with John Selman—had established a network of stock thieves similar to the ones that the intrepid sheriff had so zealously worked against. The vigilantes, in one respect, had been nothing more than unwitting marionettes in helping Larn eliminate his competitors. When the awful truth became apparent, Clear Fork citizens felt compelled to use vigilantism for other ends as the defiant Larn and his confederates continued to use the extralegal force for their own purposes. His former associates, after failing to rein him in, resurrected the secret society to silence Larn as Texas Rangers were preparing to drop a net over the entire cabal.

On February 15, 1877, cattlemen from throughout the state's western frontier met at Graham to discuss matters of mutual protection and benefit. The next day they organized the Northwest Texas Cattle Raisers' Association. Foremost on their agenda was ending the epidemic of thievery. Committees divided the region between the Red and Colorado rivers into districts and persuaded stockmen not to drive cattle from their assigned ranges until they could gather for area-wide roundups. Members also agreed to hold any strayed animals they found until the owners could come and claim them. And before preparing to drive herds to market, members agreed to notify the three nearest stockmen in their district and authorize them to inspect brands. Before long, the association began hiring attorneys to prosecute suspected thieves and stationed men in Kansas to inspect herds as they reached market. Such safeguards eventually provided an effective alternative to vigilantism.[14]

Among ranchers sharing the 7th District, spanning the range north of Fort Griffin, were the Matthews and Reynolds clans—and John Larn. The stockraisers' association, as well as the efficiency of the vigilante movement, compelled the young brigand to adapt his clandestine operation to entirely new conditions. The methods that Emmett Roberts had observed him using several years earlier—that is, rounding up the cattle of ranchers on neighboring ranges—would no longer work, since almost everyone had endorsed the association's new practices. By the end of 1876, moreover, most outlaw gangs had learned to avoid the Clear Fork country. During the last week of the year the *Austin Weekly Statesman* wrote that "highwaymen are seeking security east of the Colorado."[15]

As a rancher, sheriff, and vigilante, Larn would either have to adopt legitimate ranging methods or appear ineffective as a lawman. In March 1877 he resigned his office, giving the excuse that he could not control Deputy Cruger, who had so poorly handled the killing of Larn's friend Billy Bland. The next month Larn accepted a job as Deputy Inspector of Hides and Animals, a position he shared with John Selman. Together they worked much of the Clear Fork country and were able to circumvent the new procedures established by the Northwest Texas Cattle Raisers' Association. As inspectors, Larn and Selman could shuttle animals from other districts onto their own range with ease and let the new sheriff worry about the continuing disappearance of cattle.[16]

That other stock raisers had long been ignorant of Larn's clandestine operation was almost certain, despite a growing cloud of suspicion. His marriage into the Matthews family and his efficient work as sheriff brought him prestige and respect. The coterie of vigilantes no doubt admired him as a leading force in the movement. Along with community leaders such as Judge Ledbetter, C. K. Stribling, and John C. Jacobs, Larn represented local Democrats at the party's state convention at Dallas in August 1876. To herald his aspirations he converted one of the ruins at old Camp Cooper into his "honeymoon cottage." And even though Larn had turned in his badge, the position of cattle inspector carried great responsibilities.[17]

Only slowly did stock raisers begin to realize the malignant character of their rising champion. The episode at Bushnob in 1872, reports from disgruntled men such as Emmett Roberts, and the harsh way Larn had dealt with thieves at the Double Mountains were not casually dismissed; on the other hand, such expediencies seemed well suited to this particular young fire-eater. About 1877, however, Larn's neighbors began to suspect that he was stealing their cattle to fulfill a beef contract to supply troops at the fort. And, whether true or not, more sinister tales began to circulate. One had Larn and Selman killing two men whom they had hired to build a rock fence; another added carpenter "Chips" Bendenger to the list of murdered laborers. The bodies of all three men were supposedly found floating in the Clear Fork. Among other stories, two were probably the same incident from different grapevines. The first asserted that a young Indian Territory man had tried to sell Larn and Selman a rustled herd; instead of paying up, they simply killed him and appropriated his stock. The other said that

a young man named Bryant, who had been running his animals
with the two miscreants, died "under mysterious circumstances,"
and they simply claimed his cattle.[18]

About 1877, Larn came into public view less often, but each
time it revealed the darker side of his character. Secrecy, of course,
hid the extent of his continued involvement with the vigilantes, but
the treatment of accused murderer and cattle thief James A. Brock
at the hands of the mob certainly bore the marks of Larn's influence.
The tragic and convoluted affair signaled a new direction in the
movement, away from simply lynching common stock thieves to
actually thinning the range of unwanted interlopers. The change
apparently provoked turmoil within the secret society. Clearly,
Brock for a while was targeted for a lynching, but others prevailed
in eliminating him by lawful means.

James A. Brock did not fit the mold of the typical Clear Fork
stockman. An Ohioan, he remained aloof from his Southern-leaning
neighbors and rarely mixed with them socially. His dress—a
stovepipe hat and clothes that an old pioneer remarked were "out
of place on the frontier"—also set him apart. A one-time Quaker
as well, he certainly disapproved of the secret activities that involved
many of his peers. And although Henry Herron remembered Brock
as somewhat mysterious and a "high hatter," he also commented
that he was a "serious, sober kind of fellow, and I think, a real
gentleman." Brock had arrived at the vanguard of the settlers' boom
during the mid-1870s and became a sutler's clerk at the fort. When
he seized upon the idea of becoming a stockman, he entered the
business by purchasing—for a pittance—the sore-footed stragglers
from northbound herds rather than gathering animals on the open
range. He then enlisted his cousins, Frank and Ed Woosley, to help
finance and establish a ranch southwest of Fort Griffin on Foyle
Creek. He next began buying parcels of land between Albany and
the Clear Fork and sent east for "a carload of fine blooded cattle."
Brock later claimed that by 1877 he and his cousins had amassed
two thousand head, "mostly half-blood Durhams." His work as
a "thorough going business man" won the praise of Captain Robson,
and in March 1877 he was appointed a delegate to a future meeting

of the new stock-raisers' association. Brock's successful practices no doubt peeved other ranchers, some to the point of alarm.[19]

Brock's ambitions for wealth and prominence, however, soon fell apart. He and the Woosleys began arguing over investments in the ranch and how much of the stock and improvements each man actually owned. Enmity between them boiled to the point where acquaintances openly predicted trouble. Then Frank Woosley abruptly vanished on May 22, 1877. That morning he had departed, with two saddle horses in tow, for a roundup at the SOD Ranch on the Clear Fork of the Brazos. At the Reynoldses' ranch on California Creek he stopped to ask where he could find the "cow outfit." Sallie Matthews directed him, and in her reminiscences noted that he "adjusted his saddle . . . and rode away. That was the last ever seen of him in West Texas."[20]

When some cowboys reported finding Woosley's extra horses heading back toward the Foyle Creek ranch, townspeople promptly accused Brock of foul play. Frank Collinson remembered that Ed Woosley readily spread the report that his cousin was responsible for the disappearance. He wasted no time issuing a reward of five hundred dollars for "any person . . . who will find the body of my brother, FRANK WOOSLEY, who is . . . supposed to have been murdered." Another chronicler commented that "the most absurd suspicions were converted into positive facts, and Brock was openly and almost unanimously charged with his kinsman's death." Griffinites conducted a thorough search of creek bottoms and prairies but found no trace of the missing man. A one-thousand-dollar reward that Brock posted for the discovery of his cousin only confirmed the general belief that no one would ever "turn up" the corpse.[21]

Because little evidence actually pointed to Brock, new Shackelford County Sheriff Bill Cruger and his deputy, Henry Herron, conducted a measured investigation. Volatile vigilantes acted more resolutely. While the officers were studying the situation, a faction of the secret society attempted to force a confession from "Uncle Nick" Williams, an African American ranch hand employed by Brock. Fitting him with a noose, they hoisted the man from the ground three times, almost killing him. Williams persisted, however, in proclaiming that the vigilance committee "would never force him to tell a lie."[22]

Old-timers recalled that attempts on Brock's life continued, but as events developed, the vigilantes did not have to resort to such measures. Fellow stockmen soon hit Brock with three counts of "sequestration," or cattle theft. The cases, which came to court in October 1877, suggested that his adversaries, if unable to agree on meting out "vigilante justice," could at least exercise "proper" measures to purge the range of this man whom they believed guilty of an unverifiable murder. In one case Brock faced two to five years at the state penitentiary for "leading away" a solitary cow belonging to a suspected member of the secret society, Judge J. C. Lynch. Among subpoenaed witnesses were Larn, Selman, M. V. (Mart) Hoover, and J. A. (Bud) Matthews. John Meadows, who lived north of Fort Griffin observed some of the activities of the vigilantes. Although quick to qualify his statement, he nevertheless claimed that "Bud Matthews was in it to a dead moral certainty, . . . and so was Mart Hoover, another brother-in-law of Larn's." Matthews, in fact, was at one time "captain of the old Fort Griffin vigilantes," according to John Jacobs. Court documents in another case suggested that Brock had been interrupted while conducting a roundup; he was charged with gathering about six hundred "variously branded" cattle that nevertheless included a "considerable portion" bearing his own brand. Brock, although certainly violating the spirit of the practices set by the Northwest Texas Cattle Raisers' Association, appeared to be caught on technicalities. Certainly, anyone inspecting cattle during a roundup on the open range could easily identify foreign stock.[23]

If jealous or self-righteous neighbors wanted to put Brock out of business, they succeeded. His cases dragged on for almost three years, and even though juries found Brock not guilty on every count, his business fell apart as he fought for his life and honor. In the October court session of 1877 he won a judgment against Ed Woosley, who had brought suit against him. But in and out of custody and fighting litigation at every turn, Brock was forced to

J. A. "Bud" Matthews and wife, Sallie. (Robert Nail Foundation Archives, supported by the Old Jail Art Center, Albany, Texas. Courtesy Watt Matthews)

sell his interest in the Foyle Creek ranch for one thousand dollars—a tenth of what he had rejected two years earlier. When the harried stockman finally disentangled himself from the legal system, he

embarked on an obsessive search for his missing cousin. Many
Clear Fork residents dismissed his gambit as histrionics designed
to regain some of the high regard that he thought he had once
enjoyed.[24]

Others tried for stock theft after the spate of vigilante killings
during 1876 found a more resolute jury. The same panel that found
Brock not guilty sentenced Charles Mussleman to five years at hard
labor for stealing cattle. The court also issued fugitive warrants
for several other men accused of taking cattle and horses. In 1878,
thirteen suspected stock thieves fled the county under indictments,
but four unlucky ones appeared in court and received penalties
ranging from five to ten years' hard labor at the state penitentiary.[25]

About the time that Brock's troubles began to multiply,
vigilantism changed directions once again as Texas Rangers finally
turned their energies to the Clear Fork country. The lawmen had
hoped that the movement would dissipate, but when Larn and
Selman began to drive small landholders from the range around
Fort Griffin, the Rangers could ignore the troubled area no longer.
Although they had observed the secret society since its beginning,
more pressing matters had diverted their attention. Indians and stock
thieves all along the frontier, bandits in South Texas, feuding citizens
in the Hill Country, and criminals such as Sam Bass, John Wesley
Hardin, and Bill Longley overwhelmed the undermanned and
underbudgeted force. Sometime during early summer 1877, Major
John B. Jones nevertheless added the troubled Clear Fork country
to the agenda of his Texas Ranger Frontier Battalion.[26]

Near present-day Throckmorton, Lieutenant G. W. Campbell,
at the head of twenty-five to thirty men, established a camp on
Elm Creek and started his investigation. By this time members of
the vigilance committee had evidently reassessed their situation.
The illicit activities of their renegade former sheriff were now
clearly evident, and the Rangers' probing no doubt gave them pause
as well. When Campbell declared that he would pursue a complaint
against Larn and Selman for butchering and dumping the hides
of stolen cattle, some "concerned citizens" stepped forward to help
the lawmen search the area surrounding Larn's ranch house. John

Stock certificate showing Woosley's brand; the Monroe Cattle Company was only one such outfit that gained from the cousins' misfortune. (Robert Nail Foundation Archives, supported by the Old Jail Art Center, Albany, Texas)

Chadbourne Irwin, who was with the local men, recalled that "Larn started cursing our entire bunch . . . and dared them to come through the yard." With Larn's henchmen "Tom Cat" Selman, Tom Merrill, and others inside the house, the party thought better and made its way to the river bank, where it found six hides. Although Larn and Selman accompanied the Rangers to Fort Griffin, the compliant justice of the peace court allowed the pair to go free. For their effort, the Rangers earned the enmity of the accused outlaws and the contempt of local citizens.[27]

Campbell afterward grew more wary, and as he relentlessly pressed his inquiry, the investigation began to implicate some of the area's most prominent citizens. The sensitivity of the matter soon had everyone looking to Twelfth District Court Judge J. R. Fleming for help. Chastened members of the secret society begged him to help extricate them. Campbell also placed his trust in Fleming and worked zealously to bring every guilty citizen to justice. To Major John B. Jones in Austin, the lieutenant wrote, "There are men in Shackelford and adjoining counties that will come up and give in their evidence when these parties are arrested." But until then, he noted, "they are afraid to say anything." These frightened opponents of the mob no doubt read or even heard Fleming condemn the vigilantes in his lectures to jurors and assumed that he, like Campbell, would assure justice. The old frontier judge, however, fell on the side of the ruling clique. On May 1 he appealed to Governor Richard Bennett Hubbard to apply executive pressure to have the lieutenant and his outfit transferred to another county.[28]

Before the intrigue was executed, the situation worsened. On June 15, 1878, Ranger Sergeant J. E. Van Riper wrote an alarming letter to Major John B. Jones apprising him of recent developments. In a dire tone Van Riper declared that Larn and Selman had promised to "exterminate and drive the farmers from the country." Men were indeed "mysteriously disappearing." Gunmen in the gang, moreover, had made a practice of "riding at midnight into the door yards of peaceable citizens and discharging their firearms," often killing the milch cows and calves that settlers had penned beside their homes. "Continually," grangers were "finding their horses and cattle shot down on the prairies." Underscoring his appeal, Van Riper added that the legal community had ignored the settlers' grievances. Fleming, of course, was doing nothing, and according to Lieutenant Campbell the majority of county officers were either active or former members of the secret society. Even the coroner—a "known vigilante"—examined a body found floating in the Clear Fork and pronounced the death a drowning accident, despite the testimony of Texas Rangers who claimed that the corpse "bore marks of violence." Concluding the letter, Van Riper warned that both outlaws and farmers now "travail the country in squads, well armed—trouble is hourly expected."[29]

At this critical juncture, Lieutenant Campbell received the new marching orders that Fleming had arranged through the governor. Before leaving the Clear Fork country the frustrated Ranger wrote Major Jones affirming Van Riper's report and added a few parting comments. He obviously did not realize the powerful and unseen hands moving events behind the scenes. Campbell, in fact, had been reporting to Fleming on the direct order of Adjutant General William Steele, who commanded the entire Ranger organization. The lieutenant in his letter laid out the plan that he had confided to the judge, no doubt providing Fleming with a measure of self-vindication. Campbell repined that "we would have had plenty of evidence" to bring in "some forty in number." Somehow, he continued, the "vigilance party have found out all about what has been going on." The ever-faithful Ranger lieutenant had assured the grangers that Major Jones would personally come to their rescue. He also commented that Clear Fork men were passing rumors that his Rangers had been dishonorably discharged and were openly boasting that they had forced his company to disband. The lieutenant ended by saying that he would rather have remained on duty without pay than suffer such humiliation.[30]

Despite the departure of Campbell and all but six men, Sergeant Van Riper continued to campaign with the skeleton force. Ranger Newt Jones asserted that the crew had prepared to meet in Albany early in July 1878 to strike a deal with Larn and Selman. The two outlaws, possibly because they felt that their one-time allies had betrayed them, supposedly agreed to turn state's evidence. Jones claimed that they had volunteered to "show us the bones of the men who had never been buried."[31]

The affair reached a climax, however, before the meeting could take place. A local posse led by Sheriff Cruger obtained warrants for Larn and Selman without the Rangers' knowledge. Before dawn a party of men stealthily surrounded Larn's ranch house, and when he eventually walked to his cowpen, they followed, and Cruger informed him that he was under arrest. Possibly thinking that the writ was part of his agreement with Sergeant Van Riper, Larn handed over his gun and belt. Phin Reynolds heard that when Larn realized Albany, and not Austin, had summoned him, Larn began to tremble and inveighed bitterly that he would not have surrendered had he known sooner. Selman, apprised of the situation, made his escape before the party could deliver the second warrant. That day the blacksmith fitted Larn with shackles, and jailers placed their prisoner in the picket cell at the county seat. Then, sometime during the night, the vigilance committee claimed its last victim. About a dozen men wearing slickers, their faces covered by bandanas, entered the crude jail and emptied their guns into John Larn. On July 5, Robson's *Frontier Echo* conceded only a curt dispatch to the shocking incident: "At night a party of armed men went to the jail and shot Larn to death. Of the charge against the man we are unable to learn anything definite."[32]

For several days Van Riper and his men attempted to gather evidence in the case, but the machinations of the vigilance committee and their powerful supporters blocked the Rangers' efforts. Arriving at Griffin, the lawmen got a cold reception from Constable John Poe, a supposed vigilante himself. Ranger Newt Jones then pulled aside Glenn Reynolds, who was standing with a posse that had just come into town after failing to bring in John Selman. Reynolds, the Ranger asserted, confided that members in the secret society "would kill us just the same as they would Larn." When a man approached Rangers Jones and Jack Smith, offering them a bribe to drop the investigation, Smith "started

cursing him and told him we did not want that kind of money."
After meeting silence at every turn, the frustrated Texas Rangers
left for Austin several days later to file their report and await a new
assignment.[33]

Toward the end of July, Ranger Captain G. W. Arrington arrived
at Griffin with orders to cooperate with local authorities. He found
Clear Fork citizens docile and helpful, no doubt because the Rangers
had allowed the affair to pass. To Major Jones he reported, "I am
satisfied that at one time nearly everybody belonged to the mob—but
the good men are now satisfied that law and order can be maintained
without the lynch law."[34]

The secret society had won, but the moral and ethical costs
were high. From the crude picket cabin of the justice of the peace
all the way to the governor's mansion, the ruling clique compro-
mised the integrity of the law to cover past mistakes and to preserve
their standing in the community. In the course of their activities
members of the secret society violated the civil rights of guilty and
innocent alike, and quite literally they apparently "got away with
murder." With the likely exception of Larn, even the obviously guilty
vigilante victims may not have committed crimes punishable by
death. The *Echo*, in fact, noted on March 15, 1878, that the state
had executed only two convicts in the year before Larn's slaying.
Otherwise honest men stood idly by as Larn and Selman orch-
estrated the persecution of grangers. And because his own
commanders had connived with Clear Fork citizens, Lieutenant
Campbell helplessly endured public humiliation. Finally, members
of the mob executed John Larn to cover their own crimes and
afterward intimidated anyone who threatened to expose them.

Less than a year after the affair ended, people began to whisper
that vigilantes would soon strike again. Judge Fleming seized the
occasion to deliver yet another lecture to the grand jury when his
district court convened on May 12, 1879. He began by congratulating
fellow citizens for dealing admirably with the chaotic social
conditions following Reconstruction and rapid settlement. But
changing his tone, he decried vigilantism as "a disease in the body
politic, that is pregnant with ruin and disaster." Referring to the

recent experience, he stated that the court could not execute its duties in an environment where "officers and citizens of the country are awed into quiet and peaceable submission to such outrages." Offering a glimpse of the future, he predicted that "jurors will be intimidated, witnesses assassinated, peaceable law abiding citizens shot down, and life and property destroyed" if the "fires of passion" were kept burning. He closed by reminding jurors that arresting and bringing criminals to trial was futile without holding guilty parties liable for their crimes. This time they listened.[35]

James A. Brock, by the way, was innocent. Secure in that knowledge, he never abandoned hope that someday, by undying persistence, he would find the man he was accused of murdering. This postscript to the affair, however, took him fourteen exhaustive years. Along with the one-thousand-dollar reward that he had posted for finding Woosley, Brock distributed cards with his cousin's description to lawmen across the United States as well as Mexico and Canada. To facilitate his search, he subcontracted a six-hundred-mile U.S. mail route that placed him in touch with countless travelers and transients. Finally, he left Northwest Texas to investigate the most promising leads. When resources ran low, he was able to continue the search by working at "everything from driving a freight wagon to slinging a pick."[36]

Early in the summer of 1891, Brock received the news for which he had long awaited. A Georgia detective, G. B. Wells, by chance encountered Woosley while in Arkansas searching for another man. Immediately, he wired Brock: "Have one of your cards and am sure I have the man wanted." Brock's almost desperate reply importuned: "When you are sure you have him located I will go for him. Don't arrest but keep spotted. . . . He is an infidel."[37]

Brock hastened to Arkansas, joining Wells and a sheriff. The three men caught a train unaware that Woosley, returning to his Benton home from a business trip, was also on board. At a stopover in Augusta, Brock was depositing his six-shooter with the station agent when, glancing about, he recognized his cousin. Viscerally jolted, he nevertheless managed to take up the gun and accost Woosley; Wells and the sheriff approached the astonished fugitive from either side. The search was over.[38]

The captors apprised their bewildered prisoner of Brock's plight; in turn, Woosley cooperated, responding without hesitation to a spate of questions and comments. He even agreed to accompany Brock and Wells to Ohio in order to help restore his cousin's reputation. Regarding his unexplained departure, however, Woosley would only concede that he had been "depressed." He claimed that most of the hiatus immediately following his flight was a blank and that his first recollection was "laying sick for some time" at Jewett, a small town east of Waco, Texas. Upon recovering, Woosley had drifted to Benton, Arkansas, where a pottery manufacturer gave him employment. The two, in fact, became intimate friends, and Woosley even nursed the man through years of poor health. Upon the potter's death, Woosley helped the widow manage the business, eventually married her, and became a prominent and well-respected businessman in the community.[39]

At the cousins' hometown of London, Ohio, the matter had been a topic of debate for almost a decade and a half. Interest redoubled as the late-breaking developments became known. Then news reached London that Brock and Woosley were on their way. With the hour of their arrival drawing near, a large crowd gathered at the depot to meet the eleven o'clock Little Miami train. As it steamed into the station, men and women rushed to the platform to see for themselves whether the report was true. Friends and acquaintances of the cousins recognized them immediately; well-wishers in particular mobbed Brock, showering him with congratulations. Reporters dramatically recounted his reaction "at the hour of his final triumph," noting that "he was overcome with emotion and cried like a child." With Brock's vindication the last tragic ghost of the vigilance committee had been laid to rest.[40]

Frank Woosley, allegedly murdered by cousin James A. Brock. (Courtesy Marjorie Kirkwood)

A serene James A. Brock poses with his children at London, Ohio, 1891. (Courtesy Marjorie Kirkwood)

CHAPTER TEN
JUST PLAIN OL' FOLKS, 1875-1880

ALONGSIDE THE WILD, colorful, and sometimes violent "underworld" that flourished in Northwest Texas, a more prosaic society gradually arose that better represented life in the nascent villages and developing countryside. Beginning in 1875 "*Echo* Man" Captain George W. Robson visited the edge of the plains on several occasions, each time returning to Jacksboro with a more favorable impression of the people who inhabited the frontier. In 1879, Robson moved his newspaper to Fort Griffin and for three years chronicled the side of life that lawlessness had so long overshadowed. Others also left records or later recorded their thoughts and experiences. Collectively, their story presented a broad picture of social life in the Clear Fork country during and after its heyday.

The ranchers and farmers who settled on the Rolling Plains during the late 1870s and early 1880s found a different environment than that of their precursors, who just a few years earlier had crossed the treeline with the parade of surveyors, soldiers, prospectors, hunters, and assorted adventurers. The bison, of course, had suffered near extinction, but the great slaughter was only the most visible natural debacle because of its socioeconomic impact. Other animals all but disappeared as well, barely surviving the years of indiscriminate hunting.

Plainsmen often recounted their observations regarding the variety of wildlife and the destruction of many species. According to one chronicler, deer were "as numerous as cattle are now," and antelope ranged in herds as large as "two or three thousand." John Cook, a participant in this tragic waste, remembered that bears and panthers ranged the canyons and brakes in prolific numbers and that raccoons, polecats, coyotes, and wolves were "ever present." Like the first wave of men who ventured beyond the treeline in the postwar period, latecomers also shot such trophies and pests indiscriminately.[2]

Eagles, though rare, were also a favorite target of hunters; they prized the bird for its "oil," supposedly an ideal gun lubricant. The feathers also provided a valuable commodity for bartering with Indians. Cook told how he once stalked an eagle preoccupied with a jackrabbit clutched in its talons. "I drew a fine bead, and fired," he remarked, and then watched as it "plunged over the crag and rolled to the bottom—dead."[2]

Cook also recounted several cases of the shooting of panthers. He and some companions on one occasion wounded a particularly large animal. Dragging its entrails, the big cat dashed for a cave, where all night long it "whined and sighed," every once in a while making a noise "like a long-drawn-out yawn." An ear-piercing scream "like a woman in distress" accompanied its contortions just before death silenced it. After skinning the panther and stuffing the hide with buffalo hair, the hunters placed marbles in its eye sockets. This was the very specimen that startled "Charley" and other hung-over revelers at Griffin who had passed out on the banks of the Clear Fork.[3]

Several old-timers recalled the less lamented but still wholesale annihilation of wild turkeys. Jet Kenan, who had gone to the foot of the High Plains "in search of adventure," possessed beautiful memories of "great flocks . . . emerging from the brakes on cold mornings, the ground covered with snow." He and others remarked how they seemed "little afraid of man." Cook told how the gentle birds wandered into camps and ate feed alongside the horses. Thousands of turkeys, he claimed, gathered below his camp at night—"they came in droves from all points of the compass." When the wave of casual and nonprofessional hunters descended on the range, they exhibited even less concern for wildlife than did the experienced hunters. For these self-proclaimed sportsmen, turkeys provided easy targets. One plainsman decried the prodigal methods of the slaughter. On more than one evening he saw gun-wielding groups sweep the outline of trees where thousands of the birds were roosting. The sickening sound of thuds and fluttering lasted throughout the night. Morning's light revealed the disgusting sight of the ground covered with dead turkeys and the woods full of wounded ones. After settlers introduced large numbers of hogs to the country abount 1876, the wild turkey population dwindled even more rapidly. The swine possessed an insatiable appetite for eggs, and their proficiency in locating turkey nests all but eliminated the birds.[4]

In 1878, Henry Herron, who had caught a wagon headed back to Fort Griffin from the buffalo range, had camped with the teamster and another traveler near present-day Colorado City. Hearing the novel sound of a rooster at a nearby river bank, they investigated and found a coop tied to the back of a prairie schooner belonging to a couple with a little girl. Herron commented that in six months on the range these were the only females he had seen. Others were already there, however, and many followed. The previous year, hunter John St. Clair had become enraptured of a young woman named Church who accompanied her parents to the plains. Her father did not object to the lovers' engagement, but he did resist the breakup of his family. Leading Mr. Church to believe they were taking a "short ride," the couple traveled two hundred miles to Albany, where they were married.[5]

On one occasion John Cook stayed at the camp of an Arkansas family. Even though the husband directed the operation, his wife was boss in her own domain. She provided the arrangements for their guest, managed the children, tended chickens, and prepared meals—even dictating how much food each person received. The unusual conditions certainly challenged contemporary notions of domesticity, but they did not entirely upset the traditional division of family duties. Although plainswoman Ella Dumont enjoyed shooting turkeys with her Winchester, she nevertheless kept her primitive dwelling "clean and comfortable" and made sure that her children would not become as wild as their surroundings. Increasingly, women such as Dumont and the others helped replace the raw camps on the bison range with homes.[6]

Even the crudest dwelling could be transformed into a tidy home under a woman's supervision. Ella Dumont, whose first residence on the Rolling Plains was nothing more than a tipi constructed of poles and buffalo hides held together by rawhide thongs, declared that "a more clean and comfortable little home you could not find in any of the eastern cities." The packed and hardened clay floors of dugouts, when covered by straw and topped with tow sacks, looked quite presentable. Sometimes paint added color and durability to a bare floor. Buffalo hides and canvas, as well as newspapers and magazines, provided covering for walls and ceilings. From the soft, green wood that lined creeks and riverbanks women and their menfolk fashioned chairs, tables, mantles, shelves, and boxes.[7]

Despite such a spartan life-style, men and women in the economically depressed 1870s—especially rural Southerners—saw nothing but opportunity in the opening of West Texas. Families who pioneered the budding ranches, farms, and communities became the architects of a new society. In July 1877 a *Dallas Herald* correspondent toured the land up to the plains and issued a glowing report on "our own beautiful and flourishing frontier." Already families with "the means necessary to purchase and fit up a small farm" had dropped roots along its length. "All that is needed to make the country bloom," he asserted, "is the application of muscle directed by intelligence." The newsman seemed surprised that the pastoral life on the frontier contrasted so sharply with reports of a wild and lawless country. "The actual settlers," he wrote, possessed a repugnance to lawlessness equal to that of "the oldest settlement in New England."[8]

The next month a correspondent with the *Fort Worth Democrat* visited Griffin and issued a similar report. While admitting an occasional violent encounter, he maintained that "a more law-abiding people cannot be found." He crowed, moreover, that "it is impossible to do justice to the natural advantages of this embryo city." His list of the goods, services, and community facilities at this outpost evinced rapid progress, as did the comment that "substantial rock and frame buildings" were replacing the town's "earth-covered picket houses." Like the countryside, the town also received a stable current of men and women who steadily eroded the dross of society.[9]

Until 1875 few communal activities existed in the Clear Fork country; children attended school, and occasionally a dance or wedding at the home of a rancher or some activity at the post would draw a gathering. By the end of the decade, however, the country was all but joined with the interior, and the variety of life reflected the strides of progress. Churches, fraternal lodges, schools, and any number of businesses arose in the new communities. As early as 1877, citizens at Fort Griffin accepted the donation of a site "for the purpose of erecting a church for all denominations"; during the week, children attended school in the two-story rock structure, and on the Saturday night "on or before the full moon" the Masons met upstairs. Albany also erected a Masonic lodge and pursued other diversions. At the home of Professor McConnell, citizens sometimes gathered on Friday nights to compete in spelling bees. Townspeople even formed a "dramatic club" that normally performed when the population swelled during the term of the district court. And like citizens on the Clear Fork, men and women at the county seat enjoyed reading about community events in their own newspaper, the *Albany Tomahawk*, which rolled off the press barely a month after Robson's first issue from Fort Griffin.[10]

Like families everywhere, those on the frontier looked forward to holidays. The Fourth of July was an especially festive occasion. In 1879 soldiers at Fort Griffin fired a thirteen-gun salute at dawn and again at dusk, while the rest of the day young boys and girls filled the valley with the resounding pops of firecrackers. That night "Master Albert Hervey" entertained the children with a "show and dance." People at Albany enjoyed a picnic hosted by the temperance society and later flocked to the home of George Wilhelm for a dance. Captain Robson exclaimed that folks in older states believed "that a gathering of the people on a public day is a failure in Texas unless a number of men are killed." Regarding this occasion, however, he gloated that "not one pistol shot was fired in Fort Griffin or in Albany yesterday." Breckenridge was even quieter;

fireworks ordered for the Fourth did not come until October, but when they did arrive, townspeople held a second celebration "to the no small delight of the urchins."[11]

Later in the year, people filled the streets of Fort Griffin in "bracing but good weather" on the day before Christmas. At the well-stocked dry goods stores they bought rocking horses, little wagons and wheelbarrows, drums, harmonicas, and a variety of toys for their children along with useful gifts for grown-ups. Many families left their ranches and farms to attend a celebration that evening at the community building. So many people had come to town, in fact, that accommodating them all proved difficult. Local women had spent weeks preparing for the event; they had draped the doors and windows of the hall with evergreen boughs and placed "mottoes and emblems" about the large, open room. In the center stood a tree decorated with lights and gifts. The hostesses had raised almost a hundred dollars for presents and promised that no child would leave disappointed. Their preparations also included a supper to help pay for church pews. When Santa Claus appeared, "clad in his furs, his long gray beard glistening with frost, a shout went up from a hundred little throats." The children were afterward sent to bed happy while grown-ups cleared away the tables and chairs. "Soon the floor was covered with merry dancers, moving to the dreamy music of the waltz." Again in 1880, Griffinites held a similar celebration, and this time the "colored people were not behind their white neighbors in preparing amusement for their children." At the home of Elijah Earl, they, too, had a "fine tree, beautifully decorated, and literally covered with presents."[12]

For African Americans, Emancipation Day provided an occasion that was all their own. In 1879 about a hundred of them from Shackelford and adjoining counties gathered to celebrate the holiday at a grove on the Clear Fork, two miles from Fort Griffin. While everyone enjoyed a picnic lunch, Elijah Earl and William Jones delivered what the *Echo* called "appropriate addresses." School children also "spoke their pieces in a creditable manner." The observance, however, was interrupted when three drunk black men—one brandishing a six-shooter—rode their horses into a group

Elijah Earl, former buffalo soldier, prominent in the Clear Fork's
African American community. (Robert Nail Foundation Archives,
supported by the Old Jail Art Center, Albany, Texas)

of women. The younger people had hoped to cap the celebration
with a dance in town, but the continuing menace of the party
crashers precluded it.[13]

People enjoyed other activities besides holidays. Men and
women, almost always accompanied by their children, attended
picnics, dances, and camp revivals. Adolescents found frequent

opportunities for horseback riding and dances. T. E. Jackson seemed always willing to clear his mercantile building for the young people. Lulu Graham cherished one particular evening at the old pioneer's store; like many young women who attended such impromptu gatherings, she met her future husband there. Phin Reynolds remembered less fondly a dance at the stone school and lodge building. "Dancing the square" with Carrie Doulette—"a heavy swinger"—he spun the girl too hard, throwing her to the floor. "She refused me any more dances," he commented wryly.[14]

Fishing was a favorite pastime of young and old alike; the *Echo* recorded many examples of good catches in the Clear Fork and its tributaries. Notably eventful was the aborted fishing excursion of six Griffinites overtaken by a sudden storm. One of them told Robson that the wind shifted violently from south to north and in "fifteen or twenty minutes" hail, falling with enough force "to knock a man down," turned the prairie from green to white. While the bruised occupants of the wagon tried to rein in their uncontrollable horses, one of them, George Matthews, reportedly prayed aloud. Whether by luck or providence, the storm abated immediately.[15]

Despite civic progress, the saloons remained Fort Griffin's most popular attraction. Most children, of course, were forbidden to ford Collins Creek, which led into the business district; few of them, therefore, possessed any firsthand knowledge of the town's deviant side of life. Their days were filled with more puerile activities. Kids of all ages played together, and adults often organized dances and games for them. On one happy occasion a man arrived in town with two trained bears, which he wrestled and drilled through many tricks. One of them, a particularly gentle animal, he allowed the children to ride. A youngster, Ida Grace, later recounted that the bear climbed a big pecan tree across from Thorp's blacksmith shop, and "it took a lot of coaxing to get him down."[16]

Other mundane activities included playing croquet or any variety of games and amusements. W. B. Champlin fondly recalled hunting rabbits alongside Collins Creek with "the Thorp boys" and venturing to Mill Creek after catfish, perch, and bass. He also remembered walking to school with a gang of boys who begged for a sip of "blackberry cordial" that two brothers had somehow acquired. Annie Zug told of more onerous walks to school on days when trail herds passed by the edge of town, kicking up so much dust that the children could barely see. Ida Grace sometimes sat on a fence with her brothers for hours watching the cattle drift by. Infinitely more exciting was witnessing the Tonkawas' war rituals. Sometimes at night children climbed the hill at the military post, where they could take in the drums and shouts of the Indian dancers illuminated by flickering bonfires.[17]

But life for children was not all carefree. They helped prepare meals, tended animals, and labored in the fields. Tragedies, while rare, nevertheless resulted sometimes from burdening them with chores beyond their abilities. Mrs. George Wilhelm related the gruesome death of a boy thrown by a wild horse. Near the brow of the post hill he had been trying to break the animal, and somehow one of his feet had become entangled in a stirrup as he fell. The horse, she recalled, dragged him down the hillside and dashed his head open against the rocks. Equally horrifying was the death of eleven-year-old Annie Martin, who lived with the Hammond family near Fort Griffin. The young girl, left in charge of the house, had grown impatient waiting for a cook fire to burn. When she poured about half of a five-gallon can of coal oil onto it, the contents of the can exploded. The child, in flames, ran into the yard, "her entire body . . . burned into one immense blister," according to the *Echo*. Although the family rushed her to post surgeon Dr. Powell, he could do little to save her.[18]

Many families suffered the loss of children, and with so many hazards in the open countryside, the safety of young people was a constant source of worry. In the same editions that carried advertisements for merchant J. M. Cupp and land agent C. K. Stribling, the *Echo* mourned infants their families had just buried. Only luck saved the life of George Newcomb's young daughter. A rattlesnake that had crawled into the outhouse bit her between the eye and the bridge of the nose. Local physician Dr. Shell, who by chance had stopped to water his horse at the family's well, was

Children Annie Zug and Ida Grace. (Robert Nail Foundation Archives, supported by the Old Jail Art Center, Albany, Texas. Courtesy Helon Maxson Farmer)

able to treat her at once. Mischief was also responsible for many accidents. A live round in a toy gun, for example, left a boy wounded when a group went "buffalo hunting" in the Champlins' living room. The exploding cartridge also set a tablecloth on fire, almost resulting in an even larger tragedy. Captain Robson colored with humor the concern of a mother who had warned her son not to go swimming in the Clear Fork. When he came home with wet hair, the boy told her that he had gotten sweaty playing on the wool sacks at Conrad's; she did not accept the explanation that his shirt had "got on inside out" when he "crawled under the fence." Muttering something about "not crawling out of a whipping," she proceeded to spank him with a shingle.[19]

Raising children commanded much of women's time, and with few exceptions other domestic duties filled the rest of their days. Preparing meals and keeping up with cleaning and laundry comprised a full-time job. A few fortunate families hired servants or opened their homes to young single women, who helped around the house. Lucky was the woman who could delegate duties to older children. Neighbors often lived nearby, providing company and sharing the burdens of maintaining a household. Lulu Wilhelm and her family for a time lived in a Fort Griffin enclave of "four small, neat cottages." She and a Mrs. Steele raised vegetables that added a welcome variety to their families' diets. They threw their waste water on the plot "so that it grew and was a very nice garden." Mrs. Wilhelm also enjoyed the rare luxury of owning a sewing machine and an organ sent to Fort Griffin by her grandfather, who lived in Kentucky.[20]

The women's sphere, although confined largely to the home, extended occasionally into the business sector. Such endeavors normally projected from their traditional roles. Both a dressmaker and a seamstress owned shops at Fort Griffin. Some women helped operate family-owned concerns. Several others shared the responsibility of running hotels. On a trip to Fort Griffin in 1878, editor Robson praised Jack Swartz, who owned the Planters Hotel, mentioning that his "estimable wife" helped him. "Aunt Hank" Smith ran the Occidental Hotel virtually by herself, while her husband, Henry, pursued other interests. Many duties of operating a boardinghouse were best performed by women, and many aspects of the business were theirs almost exclusively. Jet Kenan remarked that a Mrs. Owsley ran a boardinghouse and restaurant, adding that her husband and partner held no "regular job." Charlotte Thompkins, of course, owned at least part interest in a boarding house and saloon, and Kate Gamel owned a brothel. As entrepreneurs, these two were exceptions, but even their endeavors encompassed the woman's sphere, however ignoble. Many unskilled women, largely African Americans, worked as servants and laundresses; both were legitimate pursuits, yet neither was especially esteemed. Many prostitutes also claimed the title of laundress to mask their profession, but others unabashedly listed their occupation as "courtesan."[21]

A sizable population of single men at Fort Griffin experienced a different kind of home life. Jet Kenan doubted that "Uncle Billy" Wilson, although "loved and respected," ever saw the inside of a typical home while living there. Kenan, who became a pharmacist, lived and worked out of his long, rambling quarters on Griffin Avenue. Like many businessmen, he regularly extended hospitality to friends and travelers, "both men and women." Cowboys routinely threw a saddle blanket wherever vacant space allowed. Kenan himself enjoyed sleeping on his lean-to back porch in all but the coldest weather, often sharing a narrow bunk with a friend. "How we slept I do not know," he commented, with the "coming and going all night and part of the day time." The traffic included Taylor Bradley, who ran a business a couple of doors down the street. A very lethargic man, he reportedly spent most of the day in a hammock, but every morning, "as early as he could," Bradley walked over to Kenan's to learn what had transpired in the Flat the previous evening.[22]

For first-comers who had endured privation and Indian raids, the mid-1870s saw them finally reaping the benefits of persistence. Influence as well as relative affluence marked their success. Officers at Fort Griffin continued to entertain herder folk at the post and visited them in their homes. Generally, stockmen remained a mobile group, but those who dropped roots began to build comfortable dwellings of rock and milled lumber. Some homes included appointments and innovations such as beveled glass, sinks, and gas lamps hung from ceilings; one even boasted a well accessible from indoors. Several ranchers held county offices, and many contributed generously to civic causes. While the women saw to their children's education and arranged church functions, the men formed organizations such as the Northwest Texas Cattle Raisers' Association and local Masonic chapters. Where once a trip into Weatherford or Fort Worth for milling and supplies placed the entire family in peril from Indians, prosperous ranchers could now afford the extravagance of a leisurely journey.[23]

Just before 1880, George and William Reynolds and their wives traveled to Chicago. The *Echo* reported that while the women embarked on "a little shopping expedition," the stockmen received twenty-five carloads of "fat cattle" they had shipped earlier. Successful herder folk steadily extended their operations throughout the Southwest and the Great Plains, venturing to places as diverse as Arizona, Ohio, Alabama, and Connecticut for business and pleasure. In 1893 the Reynoldses returned to Chicago, this time taking their entire families, with servants in tow, to attend the World's Columbian Exposition.[24]

Life for the most successful herder families softened considerably as the frontier joined the interior. While managing large operations certainly consumed the energy of ranchers, their able foremen increasingly relieved them of many pressures. The wives and dependents of wealthy ranchers certainly enjoyed more leisure than they had known in earlier times. Servants performed tedious household chores, freeing the women for more pleasant pursuits. Even some of the duties of motherhood were delegated to others. An "old negro mammy, Aunt 'Melia," nursed the Matthews children; the family also employed governess Prudie Hall to instruct the young girls in voice and dance and to teach them to play the organ. Sallie Matthews recalled that the sons and daughters of the patriarchs often visited friends for several days at a time. "There was never any great hurry to be going," she commented. Her life changed upon marrying and moving to sparsely populated Haskell County. When she realized just how lonely her new life would be, she "could not keep the tears from flowing."[25]

Nothing demonstrated social change more clearly than the contrast of weddings celebrated between two sets of Reynoldses and Matthewses in 1867 and 1879. The first one briefly broke the pioneers' mood of living under siege. At the nadir of their experience on this frontier, people trickled cautiously into Picketville over three days from places throughout the Clear Fork region to see George Reynolds marry his Betty. A more elevated mood surrounded the second wedding, between William Reynolds and Susan Matthews. This one drew a crowd of about 150 guests—all invited. While they, like the earlier revelers, "chased the glowing hours with flying feet," this time the coffee was not served in washtubs, and silk and lace had replaced homespun. And instead of relying on the guests to pool their food, the families of the bride and groom hired a manager to supervise the cooking of copious quantities of meat and "pies by the dozen." They also sent to Fort Worth for a French dressmaker. Only for lack of space did the *Echo* fail to describe the "costumes" worn by the female guests for "the benefit of our Eastern friends who believe there is no culture or refinement on the frontier." The land, however, showed it still possessed a raw side. When a special stage carrying a group of women back to Fort Griffin became stuck in the river, the passengers ingloriously disembarked at midstream. Such a hardship might have evoked pathos for the already tormented pioneers, but for their more well-heeled progeny the scene took on comic proportions. According to the *Echo*, several of the women fell into the "freezing water of the Clear Fork" and had to "scramble up the steep bank, tearing their clothing on the briars." With no other transportation, they " 'hoofed' it nearly two miles" into town.[26]

Not many weddings, of course, were as stately. The *Echo* casually announced unions such as the one between James Draper and Mary Cooper, who "tied the knot" at the Planters Hotel on Griffin Avenue. Ida Grace, whose father was justice of the peace, recalled playing in the yard with some other children when a couple pulled up to the house in a buggy. Calling out the J.P., they remained in their vehicle while he performed the ceremony. When bartender Paul Hoeffle married a Jacksboro widow, a group of "friends" followed them to Albany, where the pair planned to honeymoon. That evening, about 10:30, the pranksters "turned loose" making "devilish noises." The bride became alarmed and fled to a neighbor's house, but Hoeffle accepted the shivaree with good humor.[27]

Even though the influx of settlers helped pacify the backcountry, civilization did not come all at once. When the Graham family acquired old Fort Davis about 1875, they did not feel comfortable traveling to Griffin without taking along their Springfield rifle. On their first Sunday trip the family piled into the "job wagon" to attend church. About halfway to Griffin they came upon two trees near the road, each with the corpse of a suspected horse thief suspended from its branches. Stoically, they passed them by and proceeded to church.[28]

Before Griffinites erected the Masonic lodge, church services were held out-of-doors or in a picket building. The Grahams attended the latter. Their daughter Lulu recalled that seats were fashioned from logs split down the middle and raised by stobs. Circuit riders of various denominations included Griffin on their routes, sometimes preaching once a month and other times more frequently. In 1877 a Methodist circuit rider from Weatherford published his "appointments," including Fort Griffin at the farthest stop. From his base in Albany, the Reverend Ezell, a Presbyterian minister, rode a loop that embraced Griffin, Buffalo Gap, and Camp Cooper. Camp meetings along the Clear Fork were among the most popular events of the summer months. Missionary Baptist leader A. A. Hilliard had such success at his "river revival" that he established a permanent church at Fort Griffin. Rural dwellers often pitched tents or spread bedding in the open air. Some even hauled iron ovens, which they heated on beds of coals, at the site. The Graham girl recalled that sometimes the rains would swell Paint Creek upriver from the camp, and the runoff turned the Clear Fork "red as blood."[29]

The fervor that marked such gatherings found another outlet in local temperance organizations. As early as 1875 Robson—quite a tippler himself—chided Fort Griffin correspondent Sam Stinson for joining the movement. Calling his friend "the False Prophet" for his newfound zeal and the biblically styled prose of his reports, the editor predicted that Stinson's abstinence would provoke "weeping and wailing and sack cloth & such" in the saloons on Griffin Avenue. The movement, however, was quite serious and inspired the state legislature to enact so-called Sunday laws, a local-option bill encompassing a number of vices. In 1877, Robson moralized at length over the absurdity of trying to enforce an elevation of moral standards. As the debate grew, men and women rallied around both sides of this emotional issue. An outgrowth of the "righteous" cause, the United Friends of Temperance, took on all the trappings of a social or religious organization. Branches at Fort Griffin and Albany held picnics and regular meetings. Robson reported in 1879 that the fifty-two members of the "Albany Council" gathered every Thursday night, while the "anti-Temperance boys"—with bottle in hand, no doubt—held their own impromptu meeting "outside in the dark."[30]

The participation of frontier folk in contemporary social movements demonstrated that conditions were improving. Among the new immigrants were many farm families who joined Granger organizations; they were reluctant, however, to disclose membership roles or the time and place of their meetings. On the other hand, most citizens followed politics eagerly. Both the *Echo*—a weekly— and the *Fort Worth Daily Democrat* vigorously supported the Democratic party and kept readers abreast of the latest developments. While the *Echo*, published in Jacksboro until 1879, enjoyed a wide readership in the backcountry, more Griffinites subscribed to the daily paper than did the citizens of any other community west of Fort Worth. In 1876 local voters sent six delegates to the Democratic convention in Dallas to represent Shackelford and its attached counties. Two years later, when "Greenbackers" threatened to upset the state's one-party voting pattern, the spirited contest did not fail to quicken the pulse of citizens at the plain's edge. When the two camps announced their platforms, Robson printed an extra hundred copies to satisfy the demands of eager readers. Even though none of the frontier counties sent representatives to the challengers' state convention in August, the support of local luminaries lent credibility to the upstarts. Judge J. R. Fleming, for example, ran for the state senate on the Greenback ticket. Introducing himself as "a good soldier in the Confederate army" and a lifelong Democrat who "has seen the error of his way and repented," he accused his opponents of being "controlled by bankers in the interest of capital." A decade of Reconstruction and Republican rule, along with stockraisers' opposition and pockets bulging with hide and trail money, however, only steeled the well-entrenched party to the challenge.[31]

Of more immediate concern to cattlemen were industry-wide matters arising from open-range conditions. Accounting for strays, assuring proper inspections, and guarding against theft were problems shared by all ranchers. Forming the Northwest Texas Cattle Raisers' Association solved many of their problems. Unlike the farmers' Grange, the ranching group held few social functions and did not often flirt with politics. On the other hand, businessmen and politicians did not dare turn a deaf ear to the occasional utterances of the association, whose voices included those of the region's ruling clique. When Secretary J. C. Loving called a meeting to protest steep railroad rates, he suggested that Texas cattlemen might consider driving their steers to another road. The thinly veiled threat received prompt attention.[32]

In August 1878, Fort Griffin hosted a two-day meeting of the cattlemen's association, attended largely by delegates. Townspeople had expected up to three hundred visitors, and even though the crowd was smaller than anticipated, it nevertheless stretched accommodations. The Planters Hotel and other lodging facilities—including the two wagon yards—filled up quickly; the overflow gratefully slept on floors and countertops in Griffin business houses, covered with blankets that merchants had pulled from their shelves. The proud townspeople showcased their new stone lodge and schoolhouse, where the meeting was held, by decorating the hall with evergreens, flags, and pictures. The thoughtful hosts also assured adequate seating and even provided stationery for association officers and newspaper correspondents. Even though the "*Echo* Man" described Fort Griffin as "rather dull," the event was enlivened by the tumultuous row involving Zeno Hemphill and the local authorities.[33]

The gathering at Fort Griffin notwithstanding, Albany was actually the nerve center for the regional cattle trade into the 1880s. In 1875 the Texas legislature created fifty-six counties in West Texas, attaching over a dozen to Shackelford while they remained unorganized. From Albany, officers of the courts appraised land, set taxes, and administered the settlement of thousands of square miles. Stock raisers, who radiated westward, traveled to the Shackelford County courthouse to register brands and "ear wattles," log transactions, settle disputes, and conduct other official business. Gradually, as the country "settled up," Albany's influence waned. Callahan, Taylor, and Throckmorton organized by 1880; two years later, Mitchell, Nolan, Jones, Howard, and Andrews counties had broken off. Six others—including Stonewall, Fisher, Scurry, Borden, Dawson, and Gaines—remained attached for a while longer, but by then other centers had arisen that overshadowed the influence of Shackelford's county seat.[34]

Although businessmen, farmers, sheepherders, and hog raisers spread throughout the Rolling Plains and into the Southern High Plains, the cattle industry had more influence on bringing the region to fruition more than did any other enterprise. Whereas much of the land up to and beyond the treeline had been unknown in 1870, livestock grazed over nearly the entire region by the end of the decade. The plains, rich in natural pasture during these wet years, proved especially well suited to stock raising. The origins of cattlemen varied little from the earlier-established patterns. In 1880 well over 80 percent of stock raisers in Shackelford and Throckmorton counties hailed from Southern states. For the larger region of the Rolling Plains and beyond, North and East Texas continued to provide a staging area for the great majority of ranchers. Still, several herders reached the plains from other locations; in fact, the area's largest outfit, "the Millet Brothers & Irwin," drove herds up the Western Trail from South Texas to a vast range covering parts of Baylor and Knox counties.[35]

The Clear Fork country provided a natural gateway to this inviting land. The *Echo* routinely reported the movements of cattlemen as they steadily peopled the region. Typical of Robson's entries was a comment in August 1879 that several Palo Pinto and Young county cattlemen had passed through Fort Griffin on their way "to select less crowded ranges" on the plains. The next month he noted that "three to six herds of cattle have passed through Albany every week, going west." Many of them, he announced, were destined for ranges as far away as the Cap Rock, more than 120 miles northwest of Fort Griffin. Ranchers occasionally returned for supplies and submitted glowing reports of the favorable conditions beyond the treeline, beckoning others to the vast grasslands.[36]

As the ranges became crowded, ranchers were somewhat slow to adjust. Cattlemen, satisfied with long-established open-range traditions, did not amass monolithic, proprietary spreads during the settlers' boom of the 1870s. Owners of the largest herds, however, did continue to run their animals freely over vast, nebulous ranges, provoking complaints from some of the minor herders. The marginal stockmen asserted that during roundups the larger concerns drove away or branded over their cattle; others, however, defended the system, asserting that all cattle owners could attend the communal event and guard against such practices. According to chronicler Don Biggers, four big outfits, which included those of William Hittson and Judge J. C. Lynch, covered a range of about one hundred square miles in the Clear Fork country during the late 1870s. Scattered throughout the land, he contended, were families who farmed and ran small herds with little interference from their influential neighbors. But among the biggest ranchers, Sallie Matthews asserted that when some of the newly arrived outfits tried to "crowd out" and intimidate first-comers, the interlopers soon found that "they had made a grave mistake." Millet and Irwin, however, did usurp the range of Mart Hoover, forcing the pioneer rancher to move his operation and build new branding pens. Matthews claimed that eventually, the powerful cattlemen learned to share the range peaceably.[37]

Although isolation, hard work, and peril continued to characterize the lives of cowboys, they nevertheless enjoyed the benefits of the country's rapid settlement. Their lonely routine consisted largely of patrolling the limits of the home range. Line riders, generally two to a camp, lived in spartan dugouts or cabins placed at the limits of the home range. Each day they rode in opposite directions, meeting their counterparts from the adjoining camps. While staying on constant alert for rustlers, they also prevented cattle from straying. Managing these tasks was not simple. Newton Jones, left in charge of three thousand painstakingly gathered head, watched in distress as the herd stampeded. The foreman, however, told him not to worry; they could "get them in the spring." Visits by travelers and other cowboys as well as dances and roundups occasionally broke the monotony of their isolation. The *Echo* issued a report of a roundup at the J. C. Lynch range attended by 150 cowboys from seven surrounding counties. They gathered at Albany—a rare treat for the lonely ranch hands—before addressing the task at hand. Sallie Matthews told how the women sometimes planned a "surprise for the boys" who worked on their range. After cooking a special dinner, they ventured into the field, where they all ate together, "making a gala day of it." The men surely enjoyed the culinary change of pace. Ranchers provided the men with a diet high in fat and starch; almost every meal consisted of flour, bacon, beef, and molasses washed down with coffee.[38]

Increasingly, cowboys found themselves sharing the range with grangers, who appropriated the fertile brakes and streams for their small farms and sprinkling of cattle and hogs. At the same time that stockmen grazed their animals over the entire countryside, absentee owners of large tracts frequently persuaded officers of the court to remove the marginal settlers who had squatted on their land. And even though the state legislature, in 1873, had passed a trespass law that held stockmen liable for damages to unfenced crops, West Texans ignored the statute. In 1878, in fact, officials in Shackelford County held a vote that tested the act. When Captain Robson noticed that some of the "nestors" had erected brush fences on rangeland, he suggested that they "would be better off had they remained in the settlements where they could rent improved places." Robson alternately praised and disparaged farmers. Every edition of his paper carried a glowing assessment of the fertile land and its potential for farming. Occasionally, however, he included an entry such as: "The gentle Granger is now putting in his *crap*." The newspaperman clearly recognized the preeminence of the big stock raisers, and where their interests conflicted with those of farmers, he consistently sided with the ruling class.[39]

Alongside the burgeoning Anglo population, almost a hundred Tonkawa Indians, augmented by a score of Lipan Apaches, continued to eke out a meager existence. The dwindling tribe that had numbered almost 150 when it straggled into Fort Griffin in 1868 seemed miscast amid the vibrant activity of the white newcomers. Once the Indian war had ended, the secretary of war refused to continue allocating rations to the Tonkawas because they were not on active duty; the secretary of the interior likewise refused to take responsibility for them because they did not live on a reservation. General Edward Ord pointed out the irony of former hostiles "loaded down with presents" at the same time that the loyal Tonkawas were starving. A succession of Fort Griffin commanders became overseers of the tribe's welfare, but the Indians' poverty and cultural decline steadily worsened.[40]

Casual observers disparaged the Tonkawas' fondness for liquor and found their personal habits loathsome. Late in 1879 the *Echo* reported that "Monday a number of Tonks managed to get hold of some whiskey and soon the town was full of half-drunk Indians." When their revelry grew boisterous, the Griffin constable placed seven of them in jail to "cry, sweat and sober off." The next morning after "a kick and cuff he set them at liberty." Tribesmen had grown accustomed to suffering punishment for such behavior. A perplexed Tonkawa named Jack, upon being forced to pick up garbage for shooting arrows across a public street, reportedly asked: "What for me do that, me no drunk." Regarding their personal hygiene, a resident commented that "squaws did their wash" by simply wading into the river and then hanging the clothes on the limbs of trees to dry; when they wanted to "clean up their camps they just moved to a new one." In 1877, when the *Daily Democrat* learned that a group was visiting Fort Worth, the paper declared that "they are noted thieves as well as beggars," and warned: "Watch out for them."[41]

Despite their decline, the Tonkawas had grown comfortable in their relationship with the whites and attempted to carve a niche in the frontier society. Long-time residents, grateful for their service, embraced them as worthy dependents. Griffinites enjoyed watching them race their horses past houses on the fringe of the settlement, and a few townsmen earned the privilege of joining their ceremonies. Leaders of the tribe, anxious to perpetuate a source for luxuries such as raisins and calico, even promised some lucky Anglos that they could inhabit the "unbroken wilderness" of their afterlife as storekeepers. In 1880, even though the menace of raiders had long subsided, several proud men still listed their occupation as scout. Perhaps they awaited another occasion like the one scarcely three years earlier, when they helped crush the Comanches who had ended that season's bison harvest. Other warriors changed their occupation to "hunter." The Tonkawas occasionally accompanied ranchers on expeditions to the plains; in 1879 the *Echo* mentioned that a group had joined Joe Matthews and W. P. Vandervert on a bear hunt. Many wandered the plains without escort, at times frightening men unfamiliar with the tribe. A brother of Theodore Roosevelt, who had arranged a buffalo hunt, at first recoiled in fear when an Indian walked brazenly into his camp; announcing that he was a "Tonk," the tribesman proceeded to help himself to the crew's stew.[42]

For their service and loyalty to the whites, the Tonkawas aroused many champions for their plight. As early as 1876, when the federal government cut their aid, the *Dallas Daily Herald* outlined their record of service and urged the state to come to the aid of the tribe, which, it declared, "has nearly been exterminated on her behalf." People periodically voiced similar expressions of sympathy. In 1881, when the reduction of the post became imminent, Clear Fork area residents circulated a lengthy petition requesting the state to appoint a permanent agent, appropriate three thousand acres, and allocate ten thousand dollars for fencing, quarters, farm implements, food, and clothing. Later that year, Captain Robson pleaded their case, asking: "What will become of the Tonks?" Yet another panegyric commending the Tonkawas ended with a plea to the secretary of the interior to assure them a place in Texas. Every appeal, however, was ignored.[43]

As a group, African Americans in the Clear Fork country did not enjoy the admiration and gratitude that local whites accorded the Tonkawas. Anglo citizens were readily willing to admit that the blacks, like the Indians, were an inferior race, but stopped far short of treating them as dependents. All but a handful of the hundred-odd black civilians living in Shackelford County in 1880 resided in the vicinity of Fort Griffin. Four black people and one Hispanic family, in fact, were Albany's only nonwhites. Many former buffalo soldiers remained near the post after being discharged. The families of these men often joined them, and most erected small homes on the "town side" of Collins Creek in a subdivision that had existed since the town was first platted. Other black people were scattered about town. Lulu Wilhelm remembered that a group lived in "three little houses right in a row" amidst an enclave of white residents. Griffin's mulatto barber, Elijah Earl, lived next to a bartender and his wife near the Clear Fork crossing, and an elderly black woman lived alone on a hill near the post.[44]

As in most communities, the average black or mulatto citizen at Fort Griffin held a menial job, but several achieved distinction in more substantial endeavors. Single women worked largely as servants and cooks, some for the area's large ranches. Men, too, were employed as cooks, but many more, such as "Old Nick," who worked for James A. Brock, were ranch hands; others were laborers. Several owned farms and ran a few cattle and hogs. Others identified themselves as teacher, minister, freighter, porter, blacksmith, and barber. Such jobs likely did not sustain their large families—often seven or eight to the household. Many, such as "Nigger Charlie" Fowler, who hauled wood to the fort, found odd jobs and daywork to help ends meet.[45]

African Americans infrequently interacted with whites socially, a practice that both races accepted for different reasons. Local affairs, like the two Christmas Eve parties in 1880 as well as dances and picnics, were celebrated separately. Black people also sent their children to a segregated school. In other parts of Texas with larger African American populations, the minority enjoyed associations such as the Colored State Grange, the Colored Farmers' Alliance, and even limited membership in the Knights of Labor. At Fort Griffin, however, about the only formal communal focus for black citizens was the American Methodist Episcopal Church; in 1878 the baptism of four women by Reverend Shepherd Middleton merited a line in the *Echo*.[46]

Whites, out of prejudice and fear, kept African Americans at arm's length. Even though Captain Robson eagerly sought printing work, he published the notice: "No JIM CROW work at this shop." Anglos, convinced of the blacks' "natural inclination toward violence," heartily recommended discouraging disruptive behavior by extreme measures. The *Echo* reprinted an article from the *Fort Worth Daily Democrat* that suggested "castration and fire" would be fitting punishment for any "Negro" who raped a white woman. The entry was obviously a warning. As elsewhere in Texas, whites at Fort Griffin were still apprehensive about the recent taste of freedom that African Americans had won. Mahalia Dedmon, a former slave who moved to the Clear Fork after the Civil War, remarked that the behavior of local blacks caused her to fear that they would indeed be "returned to slavery."[47]

Such concerns were seldom well grounded; Anglos were quick to remind any forgetful African Americans of the prevailing caste. Jet Kenan told of a white transient who once walked into a near-empty Griffin saloon and invited a black man, Alan Dudley, to join him for a drink. Bartender John Hammond, somewhat bemused but fully annoyed, served them. The drinkers, related Kenan, "tipped glasses and down their throats went the liquor." After the white man departed, Hammond railed at Dudley for the egregious breach of etiquette. The black man's tactful explanation spoke volumes about race relations at Fort Griffin. "Mr. John," he supposedly stated, "I knowed he was nothing but white trash and I drank with him just to show you how low down he was."[48]

A few blacks, to their grief, were reminded more harshly that power and justice belonged to Anglos alone. The incident involving Captain Lincoln and infantryman Charles McCafferty in 1879 illustrated only the most extreme miscarriage of justice. In contrast to a fine assessed Griffinite "Major" Hinkle for "knocking down an insolent darkey" was an incident at Albany in which attorney R. A. Jeffries beat a black woman over the head with a log, sending her crawling to a nearby residence for help. The court, after examining the evidence, determined that "he probably did assault her," but also asserted that clearly "he was fully justified."[49]

Some former Clear Fork people nevertheless remembered more pleasant incidents and associations between the races. Upon stopping at Griffin on his way to Fort Concho, Lieutenant Henry Flipper—the only black officer in the U.S. Army—led a "sextet" that serenaded the townfolk one summer evening. A "colored boy" who broke horses for stable owner Pete Haverty earned the reputation as "the pluckiest and grittiest fellow we know of," according to the *Echo*. And Jet Kenan seemed to regard Elijah Earl as an esteemed acquaintance; he described the barber and former soldier as a "very intelligent, courteous, likable fellow." Both Kenan and Joe Matthews openly claimed the friendship of a man named Sutton. The rancher remarked that he kept a very clean place "for a Negro man" and was never reluctant to stop there for a meal.[50]

In the new communities across the Rolling Plains, African Americans were fewer than at Fort Griffin. The town on the Clear Fork, in fact, differed from its neighbors in many respects. Griffin represented the transition between raw frontier and "refined" community. While businessmen attempted to diversify the local economy, they were unwilling to abandon entirely the pursuits that had brought the town both wealth and a dubious reputation. Tolerance for saloons and brothels turned away many prospective inhabitants, who found other places more inviting. Increasingly, institutions such as the military post and the long drive as well as the presence of the Tonkawa Indians and grizzled frontiersmen seemed more and more out of place as moderninity changed the face of society. While many of the budding communities suffered growing pains marked by occasional lawlessness, disruptions were comparatively minor; residential and business districts, moreover, did not start out as collections of haphazardly strewn picket buildings. Unlike San Angelo, Griffin's sister post town in the shadow of Fort Concho, the Clear Fork center boasted neither county seat nor railroad. The rollicking life in the once lively frontier metropolis gave way to lethargy as competing towns enjoyed the fruits of expanding settlement and community development.

CHAPTER ELEVEN
SETTLING UP, 1879–1887

AS THE 1870s CAME TO AN END, the edge of the plains was "fast settling up," in the words of boosters, and the potential for expanding into the Rolling Plains, the Southern High Plains, and even the trans-Pecos seemed limitless. Over the next decade railroads would cut through the grasslands, cattle would fill up the open spaces, farmers would plow the bottomlands, and towns would mushroom where just a few years earlier such scenes would have been inconceivable. The welter of activity nevertheless deceived hopeful newcomers. Even the best land along the Clear Fork had disappointed most earlier pioneers. Stock raisers, farmers, townspeople, and absentee capitalists who counted on a good life and unabated prosperity would learn the same lessons as those who had come before them. Some would do well and stay, but many more would fail and move on. In any event, the formative development of the Clear Fork country, at least, would be complete by the end of the 1880s, and the experience of its pioneers would leave an indelible mark on the regional character of West Texas. The history and ways of life in the larger region were—and would continue to be—checkered by cycles of great expectations and successes as well as great disappointments and failures.

When the new decade began, Fort Griffin remained the most prominent town in western Texas, but clearly it had lost the vibrancy that had once made it the unrivaled center of the frontier. Just before 1880 Captain Robson estimated that business over the previous winter had not exceeded "the trade of a single day during the hurrah times." In fact, he admitted that it had been the "darkest hour in the history of Fort Griffin." The list of failed businesses included two big merchant stores, four saloons, a boardinghouse, and the tannery. The "floating population" had all but disappeared as well. Yet despite the dreary reality, Robson foresaw a land "dotted with farm houses, grain fields, herds of cattle, horses and sheep." At the center of this activity, he promised, would be Fort Griffin. "Our town will jingle with the music of the mill, the furnace and the factory." Immigrants indeed continued to settle in the surrounding countryside, and even people as far away as the Cap Rock traded at the river bottom village. One of the merchants who had departed returned late in 1879, explaining, "I found no place as good as Ft. Griffin for business."[1]

Griffinites futilely clung to the belief that they could survive the rapid social and economic changes that were transforming the region, but they pinned their hopes on fortuity and continued business as usual. In March 1879, Robson cheerfully reported that "in spite of hard times the music still goes on at Casino Hall." A month later the owner closed the saloon and headed for Leadville, Colorado, even as Gus Huber of the Hunters' Retreat traveled to Fort Worth for supplies and new bar furniture. Griffin was no doubt a lonelier place when some prostitutes left for Mobeetie, the parasitic settlement attached to Fort Elliott in the Texas Panhandle. Jules Hervey and his sister, who had made a living by staging variety performances, also boarded a stagecoach after selling her furniture at public auction. But later in the year, as the trail traffic picked up, Charley Meyer reopened the Cattle Exchange Saloon. "The crack of billiard balls and clink of glasses," Robson crowed, was "making a fine accompaniment to the hum of many voices." The following year, in July 1880, the editor took exception to the boast of a saloon in Gonzales, Texas, that claimed its receipts were the highest in the state. "Pull down your sign—it won't win," Robson bellowed. "There's a little town on the frontier called Griffin, with only two saloons in it, both of which will add $10 to those figures and then beat that."[2]

As long as cowboys kept driving their herds up the Western Trail, business indeed thrived in the last pair of taverns. But the "laughter, songs, and miserable music" that not so long ago had reverberated through the valley now echoed hollowly. The streets had grown quiet enough that the "loud and vulgar" revelry of drunken men and women irked the editor to demand: "Dry it up." And no longer could the remaining kingpins of Griffin's underworld escape the same rigid standards that governed the rest of the community. Robson came to the defense of three local men fined for "gaming," complaining that they should have been warned that the law would be enforced. When "Hurricane Minnie" found a suitor to replace the long-gone "Hurricane Bill," the new couple ended up in court facing charges of adultery.[3]

A more nettlesome problem sprang from herders and others who no doubt wanted to be able to tell their grandchildren about the wild times they had once spent at Old Fort Griffin. The *Echo* continually decried their antics and random gunfire. Sometimes revelers just wanted to annoy the constable; other times they shot at birds, rabbits, or objects on the street, such as the glass insulators atop the telegraph poles. Once Robson scolded some men whose "uncomfortably close shots" forced two women to seek the shelter of a nearby house. The many incidents of cowboys trying to "take the town" prompted a stern lecture from the "*Echo* Man": "You damn the Mexican and ape him by running your horses and firing your guns and pistols, just to hear them roar; you despise the half-naked, lousy Indian and then try to mimic his unearthly yell." Such admonitions went unheeded. A few months later some cowboys stormed through the fort, guns blazing, and accidentally wounded a sentry in the knee.[4]

Despite townspeople's every effort, Griffin could not overcome its notoriety. Lawlessness, though infrequent, continued to reinforce outsiders' negative perceptions, contributing further to the town's demise. During 1879 the killings of "Cheap John" Marks and Charles McCafferty captured wide attention. The next year the moribund little village suffered two more incidents that rivaled any of the "spectacular" killings that occurred against the colorful backdrop of Griffin's heyday.

The first evolved out of a drunken spree, when African American cowboy Dick Bell inexplicably mounted his horse and

shot a boy's pet, then harassed a black teamster and some buffalo
soldiers before a posse cornered him in a mesquite thicket. A
running gunfight through the town followed, whereupon Bell took
several wounds; as he wheeled around to face his pursuers, he
accidentally shot his own horse and then went down himself. Some
men loaded Bell onto a discarded door and left him to die at the
home of an elderly black woman. Miraculously, he recovered. The
Echo reported that Dr. Powell removed a bullet from his face and
that he was "carrying six more balls in his body but is doing well."
So well, in fact, that Bell escaped, followed by wild stories that
he had killed "an even dozen men."[5]

About a month later, at Gus Huber's saloon, Fort Griffin lost
its only lawman in the line of duty. Gambler Ed Forrest, after
beating another patron with a cue stick, exchanged shots with
Constable John Birdwell and Deputy Cy Abel. A witness testified
that when the deputy tried to intervene, Forrest told him, "Step
up, Cy Abel, you son of a bitch, I can give you what you want."
Abel backed out of the door, but when the fight was over, Birdwell
found him across the street at the meat market sprawled over a
chopping block, dead.[6]

Other developments were even more responsible for leading
to Griffin's steady decline. Among them was a devastating flood
in 1879. Old pioneers like Joe Matthews, who had seen other "trash
movers," had long warned of such a calamity. Townspeople
nevertheless felt thankful when the heavy rains began to fall on
June 20; all spring they had suffered from a drought. By evening,
however, both the Clear Fork and Collins Creek had risen out of
their banks. Soon a three-foot torrent was sweeping through the
town, carrying away wagons, fences, farm machinery, and anything
else not securely fastened. Just before 10 P.M. some men fired their
pistols to alert everyone who had not yet realized the danger. Captain
J. B. Irvine then sent a squad of soldiers to help townspeople
evacuate the river bottom. Against the swift current men groped
in the darkness toward the voices of stranded women and children,
as others scrambled for trees or made their way to the two-story
stone lodge and school. The flood claimed two lives and cost

townspeople upwards of four thousand dollars. Many businessmen and residents rebuilt, but the disaster convinced others that their destinies lay elsewhere.[7]

Griffin's greatest setback, at least psychologically, was the reduction of the military post less than a year later. The event was inevitable. The state legislature had recently declared Shackelford County no longer part of the frontier. The number of soldiers occupying the post, moreover, had already been trimmed considerably; at times as few as fifteen infantrymen comprised the garrison. To recognize the occasion, Captain Robson composed a solemn eulogy, writing in part: "At sundown, May 31, 1881, the flag at the United States military post known as Fort Griffin, was taken down, never again to be unfurled over military forces at that place." The next day Captain Irvine marched his 22d Infantry toward Fort Concho before leading them on to Fort Clark in South Texas. The soldiers, unable to find a freighter for the long trip, left behind a large quantity of both government and personal property, which they either sold or gave away. Despite the shaky beginning, Fort Griffin and its namesake had eventually established cordial relations. And even though the post had long ceased to be much of an economic asset to the civilian community, townspeople were genuinely sad to see the troops go. Women expressed particular sorrow at saying goodbye to Mrs. Irvine. The captain's wife had taught Sunday School for two years, and when she departed, the class was discontinued.[8]

After the flood, but before the troops left, B. B. Paddock of the *Fort Worth Daily Democrat* visited the Clear Fork country. He wrote that "Griffin is not the bustling place that we first knew it . . . in the palmy days of the buffalo hunt." Even then he noted that the fort looked "quiet and almost deserted." By contrast he traveled to the lively county seat of Albany, where he was impressed by the many "substantial and neat" dwellings. A Professor Cary was completing two stone buildings, one on the square for his new business and the other for his residence. Former Griffinite Sam Stinson, who had just bought a saloon, was busy repainting the sign—a steer head that looked "as though it had 'shed off.' " And although Paddock remarked that "Shackelford County will long remain the home of the cowboy," he also asserted that it possessed fertile valleys and was "one of the best watered counties in the state." Captain Robson, noting that some local grangers had come into Albany to sell their goods, added that such newcomers were "fast exploding the theory that Shackelford is not a farming district." Still others took up any number of pursuits. Breeder Henry White and his family brought a thousand head of horses from Belton and built a neat two-story residence on the west side of town. Other men and women arrived continually, filling professional needs and providing goods and services.[9]

While Albany and Fort Griffin competed for preeminence, other communities at the edge of the plains nurtured similar rivalries. In Throckmorton County during 1879 its budding namesake vied for the administrative seat with Williamsburg, a farming community founded the previous year by four hundred Pennsylvanians. Even though the town of Throckmorton won the contest, its victory proved less destructive to the colony of northerners than a dispute between speculators over rights to broker lots. As they fought over title to the land, the town languished. Toward the end of the year a traveler exclaimed that a solitary well betrayed the only evidence that Williamsburg had ever existed. The new county seat meanwhile buzzed with activity. Several Griffinites relocated there and took Frank Conrad's mercantile building with them. The two-story frame structure served as the first courthouse, and by September, Throckmorton had added a post office, general store, boot and shoe shop, restaurant, and several dwellings. This is "a model county," the *Echo* reported; in its first session "the grand jury failed to find even one indictment."[10]

The same experience attended the activities of town builders in Callahan County, bordering Shackelford to the south. Just before the county organized in 1877, citizens had founded two communities. Although Belle Plain won the county seat, its rival, Callahan City, prospered briefly. The latter had even established a newspaper and a post office but could not survive in the shadow of its successful neighbor and all but withered three years later. In 1879, Belle Plain

impressed a party from East Texas as the future "city of the frontier."
Everywhere homes and businesses were going up, several constructed of sturdy native limestone. One of the visitors declared
that in two hours citizens had raised sixteen hundred dollars for
building a combination church, schoolhouse, and fraternal lodge
and that townspeople were also preparing to erect a mill. Both
projects eventually succeeded; in fact, the community building was
for a time the largest structure west of Fort Worth. Later in the
year a correspondent reported that the boom had continued and
that the town was "full of strangers" bidding for contracts to erect
public buildings. Among them was the Belle Plain Academy, touted
in 1880 as "one of the best schools of western Texas."[11]

Similar reports emanated from Seymour, Buffalo Gap, and
Coleman, where building booms and successful county seat
elections whetted the same ambitions. But railroad barons in distant
boardrooms, not the men and women who occupied the land,
actually controlled the destinies of West Texas towns. Even as late
as 1880, however, few would have believed it. When Thomas Scott
announced the previous August that his Texas and Pacific Railroad
had issued twenty-four million dollars in bonds to complete the
road "from Fort Worth to the Pacific Coast," Captain Robson
greeted the news skeptically. "This looks very much like a case
of whistling to keep the courage up," he hooted. Scott was not the
first to air such a lofty goal. Many times railroad men had made
boastful claims, and surveying crews had been traipsing over the
land since before the Civil War without resulting in a single foot
of track. The "*Echo* Man" also knew that Congress had recently
turned down the T&P's appeal for federal aid. The line, moreover,
had only reached Fort Worth in 1876 after standing frozen on the
outskirts of Dallas since 1873; now, as the decade ended, it was
still no closer to West Texas than it had been four years earlier.[12]

New developments, however, assured the road's success. Early
in 1880 financier Jay Gould and a partner bought the T&P from
Scott for $3.5 million. With the experienced Gould directing
operations, construction crews exploded across the Cross Timbers,
Rolling Plains, and trans-Pecos. At the same time, Collis P.

Huntington's Southern Pacific was building eastward from California. Feverishly, the two lines raced to lay track in order to claim as many miles of empty grassland and desert as their "first rights" to the land would allow. In June, thirty miles beyond Fort Worth, the long-awaited engine puffed up to the new depot at Weatherford amid wild celebration. By Christmas it had reached the hastily conceived town of Baird, 109 miles farther west. By the summer of 1881 it had leapfrogged another 127 miles, leaving behind it such tent cities as Abilene, Sweetwater, Colorado, and Big Spring. The line quickly pushed another 250 miles through all but uninhabited country, finally linking with the Southern Pacific at Sierra Blanca on December 16, 1881.[13]

Even as the tracks approached the edge of the plains, nobody seemed to know the exact route the T&P would take. Town fathers in Griffin and Albany, and in each of the area's newer communities, hoped for a terminal on the transcontinental railroad, but they could not afford the inducement of issuing bonds. Neither did they take into consideration the nature of the business. Road builders, though handsomely rewarded with land, nevertheless faced tremendous expenses. The T&P received over five million acres of Texas acreage, yet the terms required the company to dispose of it quickly—otherwise the unsold portion would revert to the state. And even though Gould's railroad circumvented its agreement by selling huge tracts to land companies organized by preferred stockholders, the T&P was still left holding countless acres of marginal real estate. When other lines began to crisscross it, competing land sales drove prices down even further. Surveying and perfecting patents cost the railroad about $1.00 an acre, and with the arid and sparsely settled land commanding between $1.50 and $2.00 per acre, the huge grant fell short of the windfall that critics of such "giveaways" decried. Road builders naturally avoided laying track through places where others already owned the land; preexisting towns, of course, meant money out of their pockets.[14]

The sudden explosion of town building along the length of the new road inspired the same excited observations that only a year or so earlier had attended the founding of places up and down the edge of the plains. The character of the new towns, however, reflected a more formidable but somewhat rougher influence. In November 1880 a correspondent in Eastland, between Weatherford and Baird, wrote: "The little town that was hid in the brush is transformed into a busy railroad town." A few months later a traveler noted that in Baird "several large and imposing buildings are going up." And while another complained that the many saloons there impeded "thrift and industry," he marveled that "when anyone goes away for a few days, they always express astonishment on their return." Abilene, commented a reporter, was also "a live town" with a "Red Light" about a mile from its burgeoning collection of hastily erected dwellings and businesses.[15]

In February 1881, Captain Robson journeyed to the tracks of the Texas and Pacific to report firsthand its progress. On the way to Sweetwater, his first stop, he passed through the Jones County village of Brazos City. A year earlier its founders, believing they were situated on the railroad route, had petitioned for the county seat. They now found themselves twenty-five miles north of the line, holding down a ramshackle house and one "poor" store.[16]

The town of Colorado presented a far different scene. Already the temporary seat of Mitchell County, it had four hotels and a restaurant, a feed and wagon yard, a grocery, a general merchandiser, two law offices, a doctor, a printing office, and five saloons. Most of the structures were portable, built in sections, although frame buildings were replacing them. Everywhere the sound of hammers and saws filled the air. Robson ran into several former Griffinites in Colorado such as bartender turned "capitalist and speculator" Paul Hoeffle, attorney R. A. Jeffries, and former constable John Birdwell, who had turned in his badge for a saloon apron. Gus Huber had also abandoned his recently refurbished Hunters' Retreat for this lively spot. Yet another old acquaintance had become a local judge and owned one of the hotels.[17]

Proceeding to Big Spring, Robson noted the same type of activity beginning to gain momentum there. On the return trip he visited Abilene, "the future great," which then consisted of about forty houses and tents. Robson exclaimed that the T&P proposed to build "extensive shipping pens and make this the cattle market for all the country east of the Colorado river."[18]

In the wake of the railroad boom many once promising communities either withered or disappeared entirely. Belle Plain, where about three hundred inhabitants opened the decade with bright hopes for the future, was almost a ghost town just a few years later. In April 1880, when tracks were still being laid between Fort Worth and Weatherford, its *Clarendon* noted that a railroad crew was building a section house three miles north of Callahan City. "We didn't get the road in the heart of our city, still it is right in our suburbs, and that is where it should be," commented the editor. Perhaps expressing hope rather than conviction, he continued, "As the surrounding country becomes developed, our thriving town will naturally keep pace with it." Almost a year to the day, the *Clarendon* put out its first edition from Baird; the county seat soon followed.[19]

Far-sighted civic leaders in Albany took steps to see that their town would not experience the same fate as that of Belle Plain. When the T&P bypassed them, citizens began at once to induce the Houston and Texas Central Railroad to extend its line into the Clear Fork country. The road, which headed northwest from near Waco, had projected possible routes into the Panhandle, hoping to connect with one of the east-west lines into New Mexico and Colorado. The company, however, ran into financial trouble and was fortunate to locate its northern terminus at the T&P town of Cisco, thirty miles short of Albany. At the Shackelford County courthouse, area citizens held a railroad meeting in April 1881 and agreed to pledge a right-of-way through Albany as well as land for a depot, sidings, and turnouts. The committee convinced H&TC executives that the extension would be profitable. They argued that as a cattle-shipping point the Clear Fork country was "second to none." They also asserted that immigrants would be enticed by their fertile soil, clear water, abundant coal, and limitless limestone for building material.[20]

Albany's success kept its building boom going while other towns bypassed by the T&P saw activity all but cease. As townspeople looked forward to the completion of the track on December 16, 1881, the *Echo* reported that hotels, residences, and business "are going up on all sides." Shortly after the first train arrived from Cisco, carrying dignitaries and other excited passengers, the H&TC's Major Cave delivered a short speech. Pointing to the natural resources, healthful climate, and splendid scenery of the Clear Fork country, he proclaimed that the region in twenty years would be "the most densely populated portion of the State." Four days after the ribbon cutting, merchants from as far away as Waco, Houston, and Galveston braved a heavy rain and "fierce norther" to bid on the sixty-odd lots auctioned off that day by the railroad. A month later the *Echo* reported that Albany's growth remained "steady and rapid."[21]

For Fort Griffin the railroad had been its last hope. When the Texas and Pacific bypassed it, and the Houston and Texas Central failed to reach it, the former "metropolis of the plains" rapidly degenerated. Most businessmen saw no point in remaining on the Clear Fork when so many opportunities beckoned in other places. Frank Conrad timed his move to the county seat with the dedication of the new H&TC terminus. On December 10, 1881, he announced: "We will move into our new store at Albany next week, when we will open the LARGEST, MOST COMPLETE and CHEAPEST stock of goods ever shown in Shackelford county." Others had already departed or soon followed. In little more than a month Captain Robson called it quits as well. "It is suicidal financially to longer continue the publication of the *ECHO* at this place," he informed readers. And while he asserted that business "in the near future will be better than ever," he concluded: "We do not wish to starve to death awaiting it." Afterward Fort Griffin was little more than a seedy hamlet where drovers and local ranchers and farmers could obtain supplies and cowboys with passing trail outfits could "get serviced." But even much of that trade soon dried up. The railroads, of course, cut into the cattle trailing traffic, and when the new Potter-Bacon Trail into the Panhandle splintered northwestwardly at Albany, it bypassed Griffin altogether. Finally, in December 1883 some young local men ordered the last prostitutes to leave town or "face a tar and sanding."[22]

Early street scene at Albany. (Robert Nail Foundation Archives, supported by the Old Jail Art Center, Albany, Texas)

Other evidences of the frontier also began to disappear. A few months before the troops abandoned the military post the *Echo* reported: "The Tonks are camped about six miles from town on Uncle Joe Matthews' ranch." For three more years the tribe struggled to survive in the Clear Fork country. Cut off from most federal aid, they were nearly starving; their aged medicine man provided the Tonkawas' only care. During that time they celebrated only three births but mourned four deaths. And although former warriors occasionally accompanied a sheriff's posse, they could find no other work. Even when poverty forced them to abandon their nomadic life-style, a drought all but wiped out their crops. In 1884 the government established a reservation in Indian Territory for the seventy-eight surviving members of the tribe and their nineteen Lipan dependents. That October troops from Fort Clark drove the Tonkawas from their tipi village and herded them onto a train at Albany. Waiting for the transfer at Cisco, they looked consummately out of place to a woman who remembered watching the "squaws . . . picking the lice out of their children's hair."[23]

Once again, during 1881 and 1882, the bison provided a final resource rush. This time, however, it was not for the hides, tongues, and meat, but for the bones that had lain bleaching in the sun for half a decade. Fertilizer plants ground them into bone meal; refineries extracted the calcium phosphate to decolor sugar; manufacturers used the ash to produce bone china; and factories used the firmest remains to fashion buttons. Even before hunters had completed the slaughter, men had freighted bones to San Antonio and Dodge City. Seldom afterward did ranch hands go to market for supplies without hauling a load. But when the T&P crossed the Rolling Plains, a "bone bonanza" exploded. A hundred skeletons weighed about a ton, and with such a unit bringing six dollars, men rushed to harvest the commodity. Soon the plains were dotted by the camps of gatherers, and roads were lined with their bone-laden wagons. Briefly, Griffin flourished as a "bone hub," or collecting point. The great white mounds, piled where hides had once awaited freighters, provided a ghostly and almost perverse spectacle. In January 1882, Robson noted that every day "there are ten to fifteen wagons in town loaded with bones, all bound for the railroad." Former Griffin merchants Charley Meyer and Frank Conrad, who profited from the slaughter, now directed much of the bone traffic from their new stores in Albany. The H&TC terminus became the area "bonehead," competing with shipping points at Abilene, Baird, and other T&P towns on the plains. Like the previous resource rush, this one also ran its course rapidly, although people occasionally gathered enough bones to ship a carload until just after the turn of the century.[24]

By the time the railroad opened the Rolling Plains, the Clear Fork country had joined the mainstream of contemporary life. Telegraph service came to Albany during the first month of 1882, and the next year a local merchant became the area's first telephone customer. Boys and girls and even grown men played baseball and ate ice cream. And the railroad provided easy access to distant centers. Almost any luxury that could be loaded aboard a flatcar could be found in homes and businesses in the county. The ordinary affairs of townspeople, ranchers, and farmers in the Clear Fork country differed little from that of their neighbors throughout West Texas, although some of the more recently settled places suffered brief spasms of violence and lawlessness.[25]

For awhile Albany tried to keep pace with Abilene, but it quickly became apparent that the regional center was gravitating toward the newer town. And although the fortunes of towns and counties varied, homogeneity was nevertheless shaping the human experience in this part of the state during the 1880s. Part of that experience, which came during mid-decade, was the same harsh lesson that their predecessors had learned—the land possessed two faces.

The most radiant visage of West Texas smiled broadly for wealthy outsiders who boarded T&P trains to see for themselves the El Dorado they had heard so much about. The timing could not have been better—or more deceptive. Good weather during 1881 produced luxuriant grass and fat cattle in 1882. The pressing demand for beef in Europe that had already attracted a spate of absentee ranchers on the Middle and Northern Plains enticed speculative fever on the Southern Plains as well. The flood of foreign and

A panoramic view of Albany, 1885. (Robert Nail Foundation Archives, supported by the Old Jail Art Center, Albany, Texas)

eastern capital prompted experienced Texas cattlemen to join the reckless development of the land, and soon the overstocked range was brimming with cattle.[26]

Barbed wire, windmills, and scientific management facilitated the boom of the early 1880s. Although grangers and small stock raisers occupied some land along the watercourses, the vast empty spaces between the streams had little utility for small operators. Large ranchers, however, acquired or leased the expansive tracts and drilled wells at costs that others found prohibitive. Fences and tanks enabled them to begin improving their stock. In 1885 a Washington official wrote a rancher, inquiring whether progress was being made toward introducing "high-bred bulls." The stockman responded: "There are but few, very few, of the old long-horn Texans in the State." Cattlemen had indeed begun specializing in all sorts of breeds. A ranch might have nothing but Durhams, like the one on Foyle Creek that "Colonel" Godwin bought from James A. Brock. Others raised Holsteins, Devons, Brahmas, and other breeds. Albany, in fact, became known as "Home of the Hereford."[27]

The furiously paced economic expansion continued until 1885, when conditions abruptly reversed. Texas cattle that sold in 1880 for seven dollars a head, sold for eleven dollars in 1881, sixteen dollars in 1882, and twenty-five dollars in 1883. In 1884 the market reached a plateau. Prices then plummeted, bottoming out at three dollars a head in 1886, as the first of many "die-ups" prompted stock raisers to dump their starving animals on an already glutted market. "For nine miserable years," remarked old-time chronicler Don Biggers, "it seemed that every power on Heaven and earth had turned against the cowman." The first misfortune was a series of blizzards that swept the overstocked and underwatered land. In many places cattle drifted southward until reaching the fence lines, where they piled up in a frozen mass, forming a bridge for others to walk over. When the weakened and thirsty survivors reached the rivers, they plunged into the water but could not reach the bank. Biggers commented that the Pecos in the spring of 1885 was "a revolting mess of carrion and ruin," and everywhere the country was "full of bleating, starving, motherless calves." As bad as the die-up of 1884 had been, it paled in comparison to the one that occurred during the drought of 1885–86. From the Canadian border to the Rio Grande, carcasses covered the Great Plains.[28]

For twenty-three months—from June 1885 to April 1887—the sky grew stingier than anyone could remember. Ranchers, even though suffering terribly, at least found solace in seeing the range thinned of unwelcomed competitors and grangers. The drought's effect on reversing migration was second only to the Indian raids during the two years after the Civil War. In some places the exodus reached dramatic proportions. Shackelford County, particularly hard-hit, began the decade with 2,037 people and ended it with 2,012; just before the prolonged dry spell, however, an enthusiastic booster published a pamphlet claiming that 5,000 resided there, about half of them farmers. A New Yorker who visited Northwest Texas in the autumn of 1886 claimed to have counted forty-five eastbound wagons passing through Jacksboro in a single day.[29]

The human suffering was pitiable. Many businesses failed, throwing people out of work. With their savings gone and their gardens withering, families began offering land and possessions to gain subsistence, but few found buyers. The money that Clear Fork country citizens normally raised for buying Christmas presents for area children provided them food and clothing instead. Farmers found the drought particularly severe. For over a hundred days during the growing season of 1886, Shackelford County saw nothing more than an occasional sprinkle. After a late autumn rain answered their prayers, thankful citizens offered assistance to farmers in Haskell County. At first their prideful neighbors refused relief, but two weeks later the beleaguered grangers met and declared that any act of kindness would be humbly accepted. At Hulltown, near old Mugginsville, a man wryly commented that unless it rained soon the twenty-odd members of the local Farmers Alliance might be expelled, "as none can claim to be farmers." Two days after Christmas twenty-one county representatives met at Albany to organize aid for the drought-stricken region; a committee concluded that up to "30,000 people were utterly destitute and that $500,000 would be needed for relief."[30]

An outgrowth of that assembly was a controversial mission undertaken by Presbyterian minister John Brown of Albany to solicit aid. Traveling to Chicago; New York; Washington, D.C.; and other cities, he met with ministers and citizens' groups, spreading a woeful tale of suffering and distress. His trip raised thousands of dollars and carloads of supplies; he even convinced Red Cross President Clara Barton to make an inspection tour of the region. Farmers and most townspeople fervently praised the minister for his work, but others responded angrily. Boosters excoriated him, fearful that he would reaffirm the perception of the plains as the "Great American Desert." Stock raisers, worried that Brown's jeremiad would cause a further drop in beef prices, sabotaged his efforts in the North. And while he was in New York, the Gould syndicate, trying to protect its land investments and the T&P, pleaded vainly with Brown to drop his campaign.[31]

Consistent rains during April and May of 1887 finally broke the drought. The Texas legislature further alleviated the suffering by appropriating one hundred thousand dollars for the relief of thirty-seven counties, mostly in West Texas. Afterward other dry spells would plague the region, but those who remained were better prepared.

Old-timers could no doubt have warned those new to the area that settling the Clear Fork country and the land beyond it carried great risks. Probably few would have listened anyway. Like first-comers, others would bring with them the same optimism and tenacity by which pioneers conquered the native peoples and withstood the elements. People in the Clear Fork country, like other West Texans, would eventually learn to cheat nature by irrigating and developing dry farming methods as well as exploiting rich reserves of oil. Even the ruling clique of ranchers would have to learn to adjust to the new age by purchasing their land and continuing to adopt new technologies and techniques, and then readjust as many of their large holdings broke up. Their sons and daughters would also have to make way for, or join, a new upper class of industrialists, mercantilists, bankers, and professional people who would make decisions affecting the region's future. And all of them, of course, would continue to be at the mercy of market forces determined by distant seats of political and financial power.

Still, nothing would dictate success and failure more than the land itself. The mercurial events that unfolded between 1880 and 1887 in many respects bridged the experience in the Clear Fork country with the continued development of the larger region. Like others before them, hopeful West Texans would pour into this inviting land only to realize too late its fickle nature. The successors of Jesse Stem, Newton C. Givens, James A. Brock, and a parade of long-forgotten pioneering men and women would reap the bittersweet legacy of conquest from the alternately generous and miserly land. Through cycles of bountiful cotton harvests and plagues of boll weevils, through "gushers" and "dusters" during oil booms and busts, and through wet years and dry ones, others would come and write similar chapters of great successes and abysmal failures. Many others would come with smaller hopes and aspirations and quietly accept what the land would yield.

CONCLUSIONS
CASTING LIGHT ON THE
"VANISHING SHADOWS OF
THE TEXAS FRONTIER"

IN 1909 former Albany journalist Edgar Rye penned a partly biographical, partly fictional retrospective, *The Quirt and the Spur.* A prized jewel today on many a collector's shelf, the volume dramatized Clear Fork country life in the late 1870s, when supposedly "liquor flowed freely" and "insults, real or imagined, were repaid in lead." Complaining about a lack of sources, Rye admitted that "all that has passed on before appear to me as vanishing shadows, . . . too far away to grasp the details, yet . . . clear enough to . . . allow imagination to supply the perspective."[1]

Time, ironically, rather than dimming memories further, has become an ally in illuminating the dark corners of the Clear Fork's heritage. After Rye came men and women with a sense of urgency who labored to record the thoughts of old-timers. Through the years, descendants of former pioneers have shared letters tucked away in old family Bibles and found other treasures in dust-covered trunks and long-forgotten shoe boxes and bureau drawers. Historians, too, have continually ferreted out fresh information. Future finds will be forthcoming as well. Files at Albany's Old Jail Art Center grow thicker by the year, and serendipity has not likely run its course. Certainly researchers will continue to mine the archives.

New perspectives, too, have stirred historians to reassess the frontier of Edgar Rye and later writers who eagerly pandered to popular appetites whetted by dime novels, Wild West shows, and Hollywood horse operas. A growing body of fresh interpretations, in fact, has lately challenged the traditional focus on great *men* and sensational events. Eschewing the frontier fixation and a romantic style, the "new western" history has demanded that scholars increase the vitality of the search for meaning in the region's past. It insists on a more balanced view that includes women as well as men and minorities as well as Anglos. It broadens the story to include the economy, the environment, big government, and big business in an unbroken story that continues to the present.[2]

In this intellectual environment, *A Texas Frontier* explores more than three decades of formative development in a region where Texans—mostly white male Texans—struggled to wrest the land from the native peoples and imprint an Anglo culture. Even though this particular study is more akin to the West of traditionalists such as Frederick Jackson Turner, Walter Prescott Webb, and Ray Allen Billington, it nevertheless reflects expressions of an historiographical trend that has forced scholars to reexamine this field.

University of Toledo Professor Gerald Thompson, a proponent of the "new" history, drew the analogy that historians, like psychologists, "recognize that formative experiences have a great impact upon the nature and character of the adult." This is certainly true of the American West. And while *A Texas Frontier* falls short of extending the story to the present day, the introduction, "Marlboro Country," nevertheless demonstrates how the formative development of the Clear Fork country survives in the everyday life of its present-day inhabitants. Such a view underscores the significance of the frontier experience and its lingering influence.[3]

The text itself, the record of that formative development, is in part at least a response to the need identified by Susan Armitage of Washington State University for regional syntheses grounded in social history. Such studies, she argued, should help explain how ordinary people approached the land and its original occupants, how they adapted to their particular western locale, and how they dealt with the conflicts that arose from their occupation.[4]

The prevailing ideas and attitudes of the era in which historians write, of course, influence their interpretations. In this respect, *A Texas Frontier* is typical—a product of the times. The earliest works depicting life in the Clear Fork country were characterized by a bias demonstrated in the works of Edgar Rye and fellow turn-of-the-century journalist Don Biggers. Their readiness to include sensational but unsubstantiated episodes produced a mythical Clear Fork country that has survived to the present day.

In his introduction to the 1967 reprint of *The Quirt and the Spur*, Texan scholar James M. Day wrote that several prominent historians had "found Rye's book to bear the stamp of authenticity." In most cases, however, their reliance on the uncorroborated tales should have drawn criticism for dubious research rather than kudos for the early-day author. As an interpretive tool, *The Quirt and the Spur* helped ingrain the image of the Wild West. Day, even though quick to point out the fallibility of the text, nevertheless called it a "true pageant of the West Texas frontier of the 1870s."[5]

Don Biggers's efforts to enlarge his boyhood memories of the West Texas frontier resulted in several works. He was not yet a teenager when Griffin was at its peak, but he had caught glimpses of the town and the range while accompanying his father on trips. Texas historian Seymour V. Connor wrote in a biographical sketch that Biggers's "attempts to preserve . . . the campfire tales he had heard" resulted in *History That Will Never Be Repeated* (1901) and *From Cattle Range to Cotton Patch* (1905). Perhaps Biggers's most notable work was *Shackelford County Sketches,* which appeared in 1908. Like Rye, who had once employed him at the *Albany News,* Biggers recounted without question some old-timers' tales that fostered the impression of Fort Griffin as a place of casual and gratuitous violence. Unlike Rye, however, he left a creditable record of early settlers who established the area's first ranches and inhabited places such as Fort Davis and Picketville; he was also the first to acknowledge that African Americans as well as Tonkawa Indians shared the land with Anglos. Still, all these images, side-by-side, seemed to legitimize the salient aspects of violence.[6]

Despite more than eight decades of scholarship built upon these cornerstones, the impact of the early-day writers still weighs heavily. As late as 1992, Charles Robinson III was still perpetuating the legendary hellhole of Rye and Biggers in his *Frontier World of Fort Griffin*. Ignoring the county and district courts as well as Texas Rangers and the fort's troopers, he asserted that Justice of the Peace Edgar Rye "represented the legal system in Shackelford County." His view of the vigilantes, "solid, respectable citizens," was that they were just doing what they had to do. To Robinson's credit, he included chapters that dealt with "downtown merchants" and "life among the law abiding," yet such images as the hanging tree cast long shadows that leave his ordinary Griffinites in the penumbra of a much larger, romantic myth.[7]

Local lore has inspired unending speculation about several larger-than-life figures who passed across the Clear Fork scene. None have proved more titillating than notorious woman gambler Charlotte Tompkins, who in 1994 once more broke hearts and pocket books in Cynthia Rose's *Lottie Deno*. Rose's undocumented work glorified the gambling queen's hackneyed image and repeated such easily refuted anecdotes as her apocryphal dalliance with Doc Holliday along with some spurious troubles he supposedly suffered at Fort Griffin. Rose also had Lottie leaving town in 1877 with a trunk full of gambling proceeds, even though records show that a year later she was still in Shackelford County trying to convince the district court judge that her "Gus" was just a boardinghouse. The author, moreover, drew nothing from the rich body of gender studies now emerging in western history.[8]

Such portrayals are forgivable; they merely uphold a tradition of western writing that reinforces an American creation myth in which men in white hats triumph over the elements and easily identifiable bad guys. On the other hand, few regions have produced such a thorough and wide-sweeping local history as that which exists for the Clear Fork country. Since 1925, contributors to the *West Texas Historical Association Yearbook* have gleaned statistics, interviewed surviving pioneers, conducted archaeological studies, and combed through mountains of business and personal records, archival sources, and newspapers in an effort to preserve the region's heritage.

Several writers have produced admirable overviews. The most thorough is Carl Coke Rister's *Fort Griffin on the Texas Frontier* (1956). While it emphasized military history and the Wild West at the expense of social movements and the mundane side of life, it nevertheless outlined the sweep of local history. In *Alkali Trails* (1930) William Curry Holden commendably profiled some of the social and economic history of West Texas and the Clear Fork country, addressing topics as diverse as frontier amusements, immigration, droughts, and journalism. His text, however, is full of happy and courageous but longsuffering "Nordics."

The most critically celebrated book on this land is *Interwoven* (1936), in which Sallie Reynolds Matthews chronicled the years of her life. To women, recent historians assert, the West was a place, not a process; in this respect Matthews addressed many aspects of frontier life that male authors of her era routinely overlooked. Although she avoided broaching many unpleasant topics, such as her family's involvement with the vigilantes, the resulting inter-pretation is nevertheless in many ways an accurate picture of the late-nineteenth-century Clear Fork country that "new western" historians have applauded. On the other hand, it depicts the story from the perspective of the successful few, seldom revealing what life was like for the vast majority.

Lately, Francis Mayhugh Holden has appended this work. Her *Lambshead before Interwoven* (1982) attempted to provide a context for the herders' ascendancy, complementing and illuminating the earlier work. Like Sallie Matthews, however, her sensitive and thoughtful work was a paean to the land's first-comers and was not intended to portray the lives of plain, ordinary folk.

Eminent West Texas historian Rupert N. Richardson gained his deserved reputation for a more widely encompassing view and a sympathetic portrayal of native peoples. *The Comanche Barrier to South Plains Settlement* (1933) is in many ways as fresh today as when it was penned. His *Frontier of Northwest Texas* (1963), which treats the Clear Fork country as part of the larger region, provided a broad overview most esteemed for its survey of the antebellum period. And Richardson, virtually alone among West Texas historians, resisted advancing the image of casual violence. He did so, however, by largely ignoring the topic.

Where Clear Fork African Americans are concerned, few regional writers have depicted them sympathetically. In 1926, when trooper Jacob Howarth mentioned the 10th Cavalry in his reminiscences, either he or an editor used the parenthetical reference "nigger" to distinguish them from the Anglo soldiers. In a 1939 article on frontier social conditions, the author attributed the blacks' inability to enter the mainstream of life to laziness and a failure to manage the condition of freedom. Even though attitudes are changing, local authors have recently referred to African Americans as "coloreds" and "Negroes."

The early interpretations and more recent faux pas only reinforce what cultural geographer D. W. Meinig concluded about the monolithic Anglocentrism of the region's inhabitants. He called this area "the purest example of the 'native white Anglo-Saxon Protestant' culture in Texas." The early day non-Anglo population, consisting of former slaves brought into the region by the first immigrants as well as the buffalo soldiers, Tonkawas, a sprinkling of Hispanics—and a solitary Chinese launderer who lived at Fort Griffin—was small in comparison to that of the whites and so dominated by the ascending culture that the non-Anglo presence was subordinated in the process of regional development.[9]

As in the case of many areas in the West, no aspect of Clear Fork country history has been more misinterpreted or misrepresented than violence. Make no mistake about it: by frontier standards this was a violent place. But the incidents that writers have portrayed, often spread over three decades, leave the impression that such anecdotes were just representative—that they happened all the time. And no wonder, when considering testimony such as that left in 1930 by frontiersman R. A. Slack: "A killing was one of the ordinary, expected events of the night [at Fort Griffin], on which the comments were over, and the incident closed by the time the blood had been mopped up from the floor."[10]

On the contrary, violence was outside the normal experience of pioneers, and hardly any story went unrecorded in some form. Seldom, however, do the tales encompass the larger everyday environment in which the acts took place, or the reactions of townspeople and the legal community to bloodshed. A "strain of violence" certainly coursed through the history of the Clear Fork country, but not in the numbers and not in the manner that writers have suggested.

Many writers have mistakenly assumed that in an environment where drinking, gambling, and prostitution were so weakly regulated, violence was accepted casually as well. When Charles Robinson III, for example, asserted that fights and "an occasional killing" were merely "part of the risk of doing business" in Griffin's heady economic environment, he was only echoing what others had long believed. J. Marvin Hunter, best known for *The Trail Drivers of Texas*, said this "wicked little metropolis" was devoid of the "restraints of . . . law enforcement." Even Carl Coke Rister wrote that "here the revolver settled more differences among men than the judge."[11]

This exaggerated reputation, set in motion by Rye and Biggers, gained momentum in the reminiscences of old-timers and afterward was eagerly perpetuated by writers and historians. Frontiersman Frank Collinson called Griffin "the wildest and most colorful of all the border towns . . . from Dodge City, Kansas, to Ogallala, Nebraska." The testimony seems impressive until considering that Collinson's lone trip to the Central Plains was in 1874, after the bison slaughter had waned and before the railroad made Dodge a "cow town." And Emmett Roberts, while an authority on range conditions, knew little about Fort Griffin. When he declared that "robbers" would "throw a blanket over your head and take your money in a flash," he was no doubt repeating what he had heard. From another reminiscence a writer reached the absurd conclusion that gun- and knife-wielding Tonkawas "in a state of beastly intoxication" made it unsafe to go into Fort Griffin unarmed.[12]

The image of the Northwest Texas frontier as a place where sensational violence occurred regularly was contemporary, especially in the 1870s, further validating misperceptions. The columns sent to the *Dallas Daily Herald* by "Comanche Jim" Grahame represent extreme examples. His colorful descriptions of killers as "full of old rye and the devil" and hanging victims as "hard looking sights" made fatal incidents seem almost comical. Upon Johnnie Golden's killing, he mentioned nonchalantly that "it was amusing to hear men, while standing around the body of Golden, call it nothing and then begin to relate their border experience in Kansas." Writers—including this one—have naturally found Grahame a good source for a quote.[13]

Typical of misrepresented incidents, a myth grew around the killing of "Cheap John" Marks. As the peddler lay dying, according to the deposition of accused murderer Frank Schmidt, he begged his supposed killer to give him his slippers. Schmidt obliged, but claimed that since the dying request rendered him barefoot, he took Marks's boots; he had left his own in the wagon that a companion had taken to Fort Griffin. The incident gave rise to the story that Schmidt had followed Cheap John onto the plains and callously killed him for nothing more than that pair of boots.[14]

The raw social environment certainly magnified stories of violence, and through repeated tellings many exaggerated and even outright spurious tales acquired an air of credibility. A Young County sheriff supposedly pursued one "Buffalo Bill" to Fort Griffin, where the pair "squared off" with Winchesters; the lawman fell from a bullet to the heart, Bill from a shot to the center of his forehead. The strange silence of newspapers, legal records, and all but one old-timer, who repeated the story from hearsay, argue convincingly that even if the killing occurred, it did not unfold quite so dramatically.[15]

In another instance a local court reportedly delivered an adverse decision against defendant John B. Carn, who "knocked out the judge, the clerk, and the opposing attorney" and simply walked out of the courtroom and never suffered reprisal. The incident could not be found in the November 2, 1876, *Frontier Echo* (Jacksboro) that the author cited; the paper did, however, relate what happened when Mike O'Brien tested the court. Defending himself against a minor charge, he started, "Well, fellers, I'm not much of an orator, but d____d if I don't give you a blast anyhow." The judge sternly warned that he would fine O'Brien for "swearing" before the jury could even rule, demonstrating the narrow latitude that actually existed.[16]

The most celebrated yarn that storytellers manufactured involved Doc Holliday and his supposed evisceration of a fellow poker player and escape from a lynch mob. District Court records show that in 1875 Doc indeed fled Fort Griffin, but merely to avoid a "gambling and liquor" charge. Had he returned afterward, he would have had to face the local court. The more deviant act, which supposedly included the torching of a downtown building to cover his flight, would have brought another "alias capias" in the court records as well as word-of-mouth notoriety in local people's recollections.[17]

Even after deducting all the false accounts and discounting the blithe clichés and colorful phraseology of writers, few places in the West could best the Clear Fork country for its scale of violence. Early confrontations with Indians as well as the rash of antebellum slayings attributed to the Old Law Mob were surpassed by more intense episodes after the war. For a brief period, when in 1872 the military refused to become involved in civil affairs, the Flat was virtually without law. Later, after the town of Fort Griffin grew to several hundred people, the area continued to suffer murders. Don Biggers set the Clear Fork country's unlikely total of killings at fifty-five for a twelve-year period. His digest, however, included several incidents that seemed to be different versions of the same story as well as others that are unverifiable or clearly apocryphal. Nevertheless, these include such episodes as the Bushnob "massacre" and its sequel, the killing of Johnnie Golden, the "Shooting Bee," and the slayings of quartermaster clerk June Leach, Thorndale man Andrew Brownlee, and trooper Charles McCafferty. Sociopaths such as John Larn and John Selman were certainly responsible for some mysterious disappearances. In few places, moreover, would the legal community have refused to investigate a string of grisly slayings because it might implicate dozens of the community's "best citizens" working behind the aegis of vigilantism.

In a recent essay appropriately titled "Violence," noted scholar Richard Maxwell Brown argued that vigilantes normally felt "conditions of frontier and western disorder" justified their actions. He contended that "at the core of the ideology" was a right to "preserve the community against outlaw activity." Members of such extralegal movements, working in an environment where the law was ineffective, even went so far as to believe that a "doctrine of popular sovereignty" excused their excesses.[18]

None of these rationalizations, however, absolve the Clear Fork's vigilantes. A ranching elite clearly dominated local politics and society, and it controlled an earnest legal system that worked on its behalf. Even if conditions at times seemed chaotic, outlawry never seriously threatened life and property beyond the means of the legal community. Far from a noble cause, the vigilante movement apparently arose out of nothing more than impatience and the willingness of Clear Fork men to become seduced by the charismatic, but deranged, John Larn. Cleaning up after the deposed instigator only added shame to an already reprehensible episode. In stark contrast stand the efforts of their more level-headed neighbors in the Cross Timbers who corrected the same problems by spearheading a move to create the Northwest Texas Cattle Raisers' Association.

In sum, the bloodletting that shaped a significant part of the Clear Fork's history provides a fertile field for reexamining western violence. The reputation of this Texas frontier, of course, has been fueled in large part by a romantic vision that never existed. Still, it possessed nearly all the lurid ingredients for which Wild West enthusiasts could hope, demonstrating why such long-held assumptions regarding violence are so difficult to overcome. In such a socially volatile environment where gun-toting was ubiquitous, however, the number of fatal confrontations might arguably seem negligible. And far from a place where "shootings were so common . . . that no attempt was made to explain fully why"— as one prominent historian wrote—a credible legal framework did exist. Crimes such as rape, domestic violence, and assaults against the weak, elderly, and defenseless either seldom occurred or went largely unreported, further mitigating the rough image.[19]

In joining the debate, writers and historians need to focus more on the reactions of citizens, measures taken by the legal community, and the consequences to society. All too often, when examining local legends like the one involving Lottie Deno and Johnny Golden, "inquiring minds" have dwelt upon such imponderables as their romantic link rather than exploring the social conditions that led to a momentary breakdown of law and order. Only by probing the more substantial issues can the significance of violence in the western experience be properly assessed.

Another exaggerated aspect of this regional history has been the importance of the post Fort Griffin (see Appendix B). Militarily, economically, and socially it was not as influential as writers have asserted. Although the presence of federal troops discouraged large-scale invasions, official reports show that between 1867 and 1875 patrolling soldiers encountered Indians on only eight occasions. Well into the 1870s, in fact, small raiding parties depredated seemingly at will because the fort's command was slow to respond and the troops were cumbersome in the field. The army's task was certainly not impossible, as demonstrated by Texas Rangers, who in 1874 intercepted fourteen of about forty raiding parties. Only with the collapse of President Grant's Peace Policy did the army complete its work—and not by patrolling the Clear Fork country, but by campaigning against the Plains Indians where they lived.

Compared with Forts Richardson and Concho, Griffin's impact on the local economy was negligible. The most lucrative government awards were normally filled by distant contractors. Not only did commercial activity remain insignificant during the post's most active years, but also Griffin's commanders worked diligently to suppress the emergence of a business district adjoining the government reservation. Granted, the troops' presence did nurture a civilian settlement, but the emergence of Albany at the same time that D. M. Dowell launched his real estate scheme demonstrated that conditions had grown ripe for a town regardless of the security that federal troops provided.

The social impact of the garrison was marginal as well. Although officers and herder folk profited by mingling socially and establishing schools, the military-civilian association went only so far. Contact between enlisted men and civilians was discouraged, and the government trimmed the troop strength just before the settlers' boom. After their enlistments expired, white soldiers normally returned home or went elsewhere. African Americans who remained, however, modified the racial mix, and this was likely Fort Griffin's most enduring social significance.

Far more important in shaping the region's history were stock raisers, who set the tone for cultural imperialism (see Appendix F). Very early in the regional history, cow hunters established a social and economic preeminence, yet their nomadic nature and sparse numbers obscured their hegemony over the vast area. Herder folk alone learned to adapt to the unfamiliar environment while persisting through the social dislocations of Indian raids and the Civil War. Afterward they successfully adjusted to the challenges of Reconstruction. Once the region began maturing, they asserted their political sovereignty by locating the county seat at Albany, rebuffing the powerful merchant class that arose at the town of Fort Griffin. The formative period ended on the same course as it began—with a ranching-based economy and a local society controlled by stock raisers.

From the late 1870s until the drought of the mid-1880s, however, waves of farmers and small landholders challenged the existing order—and the ruling clique successfully resisted. Perhaps the vigilante affair turned so ugly in part because large-scale ranchers were reluctant to intervene on behalf of intimidated settlers who were threatening to break up the open range. Ranchers were certainly quicker to save face than register alarm or indignation as their less well-heeled neighbors suffered incidents such as stalkings and the work of gun-firing "nightriders" trampling into their dooryards. Later, of course, ranchers sabotaged the efforts of Presbyterian minister John Brown when he sought relief for drought-plagued farmers. This time nature, normally an implacable foe, actually helped the ruling clique reassert its sovereignty.

The stock raisers and others who migrated to the Clear Fork country were mostly Southerners, but the society that emerged was western—and it became that way only after a long and tortuous environmental, social, and economic process. The first inhabitants to arrive established familiar patterns of rural Southern life. Adapting them to the unfamiliar land was obviously a distinguishing factor between the sections. The most successful herder folk set up ranching operations that arguably became the western equivalent of the Southern plantation, yet with important differences. Both were self-contained, but herder folk did not erect dwellings on the scale of plantation houses—at least at first because they rarely remained in one spot. Neither did they significantly extend slavery to constitute a work force. The small population of African Americans certainly differentiated West and South demographically.[20]

The largely Anglo society that was emerging found some other conditions democratizing. In both the West and the South the elite were concerned with providing for their children's education, and both commonly hired tutors; yet where many Southerners sent their offspring to distant centers of learning, Westerners cooperated locally to provide education. Less affluent people enjoyed the benefit, increasing the literacy of the general population. Horseback riding provided another social leveler. Footbound common folk, forced to look up to their equestrian "betters" in the aristocratic South, found themselves eye-to-eye astride snorting mounts when they came West. Communal activities, too, melted away some of the Old South's pretensions. The immense and sparsely settled land for a long time made welcome guests out of the plainest of ordinary folk. Matters of defense fostered this democratizing effect as well. Dealing with Plains Indians, of course, was as distinctly "western" as the arid and treeless land itself.

Nothing did more to transform Clear Fork country citizens into Westerners than the experience of the Civil War and Reconstruction. On the eve of disunion, however, they were solid Southerners. Many historians, notably Rupert Richardson and Floyd Ewing, Jr., argued that just before the war, frontier people harbored Unionist sentiments because of the presence of Peters colonists along the northern line, German colonists on the southern fringe, and the fear of Indians along the entire length. Yet in North and Northwest Texas, demographic diversity waned the farther west that people settled. Despite the mortal threat of raiding parties, backcountry folk demonstrated an unwavering support for the South. Palo Pinto's unanimous vote to withdraw from the Union cannot be entirely attributable to secessionist pressure, as Richardson and Ewing asserted, unless secessionists were firmly in the majority. That Camp Cooper was the only frontier post to experience a popular uprising against U.S. troops was no historical accident either. Southern sympathy may have been diluted elsewhere, but ardent rebels in the Clear Fork country demonstrated their loyalty by renaming Buchanan County in honor of Confederate Vice-President Alexander Stephens, and later by naming their little citizen post after President Jefferson Davis.[21]

The subsequent experience, however, cleaved the western hinterland from the interior. While friends and relatives throughout the South were fighting Yankees, people on the edge of the plains were contending with Indians. Afterward, when the rest of Texas and the South were resisting military occupation, people in Northwest Texas were begging to be occupied. And when the Northern troops finally came, Clear Fork citizens rode with them on patrols, dined and danced with officers and their wives at the post, and entertained them in their homes.

The experience in the Old South of a humiliating federal occupation and the self-searching obsession with the "lost cause" hardly affected the Clear Fork country and West Texas. The sectional row that occurred in 1875 between troopers and townspeople at the Flat was but a footnote in the reminiscences of old-timers. In contrast, John Cook described how a variegated group of buffalo hunters celebrated the Fourth of July in 1877. They constructed an American flag from shirts and flour sacks and fashioned stars out of the tinfoil from their plug tobacco. "I fit agin it wunst, but it's sacred now," one of them commented. Another catalyst for the sectional split was the Panic of 1873. Subsequent events caused the South to slip even farther into institutional and economic lethargy, while at the same time West Texas was transformed by the bison slaughter, trail driving, and ranching and settlers' booms.[22]

The Clear Fork country nevertheless retained many Southern ways of life despite its westering experience. Some might have "done forgot that Civil War," as Griffin ranch hand John Meadows commented, but he for one was "from down there in Alabama, where a kid didn't suck nothing but Democratic breasts." From physicians to stonemasons, Northerners were well-represented in professional and skilled positions, yet the bulk of the population remained largely Southern and rural. Most inhabitants embraced a Southern type of evangelism, but other denominations were not without representation. The South produced almost all of the local attorneys and politicians, assuring that familiar laws and institutions would perpetuate the dominance of the ruling clique. Stribling and Kirkland, for example, were Southerners, and Judge Fleming had been in Texas since 1846. When he bolted the Democratic party for the Greenbacks, Fleming pointed to his service as a Confederate soldier to bolster his campaign. His Southern ties no doubt influenced him later to protect members of the vigilance committee even though he openly decried their high-handed actions. The slaying by, and subsequent acquittal of Captain Lincoln, who killed black trooper Charles McCafferty, also demonstrated solidarity of section by race.[23]

No X, of course, can be placed on a map to say "here is the spot where South turned West." No other place, however, better demonstrated the process of adapting the older culture to the land than did the Clear Fork country. Certainly all of the territory between the Western Cross Timbers and the Concho country shared much of this legacy. All suffered Indian raids, provided bases for cavalry companies, and experienced the long drive; all, too, possessed larger numbers of Southerners than any other group and retained many folk ways of the Old South. The Cross Timbers, however, closer to the interior, was much better suited to farming, and its racial mix of Northerners, Peters colonists, and African Americans made it more diverse. The impact of the bison boom, moreover, was negligible compared with that in areas farther west. At the other end, the Concho country was not solely part of the steady concatenated South-to-West expansion that diffused through the Cross Timbers and into the Clear Fork country. The main roads into the Concho territory extended through the large Hispanic and German settlements of South and Central Texas and the Hill Country, thus diluting its "Southernness."

Certainly by the end of the formative period the Clear Fork country had begun to develop western characteristics that distinguished it from the parent culture of the Old South. Yet just as certainly, the emergence of a society that looked at itself as distinctly West Texan was still to emerge. Beyond the edge of the plains everyone was a newcomer, and the process of settlement was just beginning. Dry farming and irrigation as well as a record of town building and rural development, mercantilism, and mineral production would eventually sever emotional ties with distant places and build new ones.

At the core of their attitudes and outlooks, West Texans would embrace a fundamental distinction bridged in large part by the history of the Clear Fork country. Theirs was a land of forward-looking conquerors; the older culture was a land of the vanquished. The difference has been profound. Where Southern children play "Johnny Reb and Billy Yank," western children play "cowboys and Indians"—and the cowboys win every time.

	Average Garrison Strength	Officers Killed in Action	Officers Dead of Disease	Enlisted Men Killed in Action	Enlisted Men Dead of Disease	Deserters
1867	273	0	0	0	4	19
1868	256	0	0	0	4	31
1869	201	0	0	0	2	5
1870	308	0	1	1	7	24
1871	445	0	0	0	9	86
1872	340	0	0	5	5	35
1873	312	0	0	2	8	56
1874	469	0	0	1	8	24
1875	277	0	0	0	2	12
Totals	320	0	1	9	49	292

NOTE: Together with the list of Engagements (Appendix B), these statistics demonstrate Fort Griffin's minimal role as an offensive force in eliminating Plains Indians from the Clear Fork country. Both engagements and combat deaths were few. "Killed in action" meant while on duty, regardless of whether a soldier was killed in battle or while walking picket at the fort itself. Of the five men "killed in action" during 1872, one died in battle and another later died of wounds. Two others died of wounds *not* received in battle, and yet another died of an accidentally self-inflicted wound while on an expedition. The two "killed in action" in 1873 were not battle casualties either, and the single "killed in action" in 1874 was actually a drowning. Of all soldiers'

298 APPENDIX A

deaths, fifty occurred as a result of disease (about six per year), and only three dead—all enlisted men—were actually combat fatalities. The three killed in combat included one unnamed private of the 24th Infantry in January 1870; Private John Kelly (4th Cavalry), killed "by Indians" on the North Fork of the Red River on September 29, 1872; and Private John Dooras (4th Cavalry), who died of wounds received on September 29, 1872, on the North Fork of the Red River. During the brief uprising in 1877, Comanches killed Charles Butler (10th Cavalry) on May 4 at Lake Quemado, Texas.

The campaigns to end Plains Indians depredations in Texas concluded in 1875. The military presence maintained afterward largely guarded against renewed hostilities, and patrols decreased steadily. In 1876 more than two hundred troops were stationed at Fort Griffin, but by the end of 1877 just over eighty soldiers manned the post. From 1878 to 1881 the garrison strength ranged from twenty-one to sixty-one men. Desertions fell off, too. In 1876 only five took flight, and afterward commanders reported only one desertion each in 1877, 1879, 1880, and 1881.

SOURCE: Compiled from Post Returns, Fort Griffin, Texas, Microfilm 617, roll 429, National Archives, Washington, D.C.

APPENDIX B
ENGAGEMENTS BETWEEN
FORT GRIFFIN PATROLS
AND INDIANS, 1867–1875

Deep Creek, October 17, 1867, 6th Cavalry (Companies F, I, K, L); commanding officer W. A. F. Ahrberg; three Indians killed, one captured

Paint Creek, March 6, 1868, 6th Cavalry (Companies F, I, K); commanding officer Captain A. R. Chaffee; seven Indians killed, two enlisted men wounded

Paint Creek, near the Double Mountain Fork of the Brazos, May 7, 1869, 35th Infantry and Indian scouts; commanding officer Captain G. W. Smith; fourteen Indians killed

January 1870, place not listed; unnamed enlisted man of 24th Infantry killed

North Hubbard Creek, April 3, 1870, 4th Cavalry (Company F); commanding officer Wirt Davis; two Indians killed, four wounded

Mount Paso, July 14, 1870, 4th Cavalry (Companies D, F); commanding officer Wirt Davis; one Indian killed

North Fork, Red River, September 29, 1872, 4th Cavalry (Companies A, D, F, I, L); campaign with troops from Fort Richardson; 23 Indians killed, 120 Indians captured, one enlisted man killed

Elm Creek, December 5, 1873, 10th Cavalry (Company D); four Indians killed, sixteen captured

Double Mountain Fork, Brazos, February 5, 1874, 10th Cavalry (Companies D, G), 11th Infantry (A, F); ten Indians killed

Salt Fork, Red River, October 9, 1874, 11th Infantry (Companies A, F), no casualties

SOURCE: Compiled by the U.S. Army Adjutant General's Office from official reports, *Chronological List of Actions, &c., with Indians from January 15, 1837, to January, 1891;* also, Post Returns, Fort Griffin, Texas, Microfilm 617, roll 429, National Archives, Washington, D.C.

APPENDIX C
RANKING OFFICERS,
FORT GRIFFIN, 1867–1881

Bvt. Colonel S. D. Sturgis, 6th Cavalry, July 1867–March 1868

Captain Adna R. Chaffee, 6th Cavalry, April 1868

Captain Malcolm McArthur, 17th Infantry, May 1868

Bvt. Colonel S. B. Hayman, 17th Infantry, June 1868–April 1869

Captain John Lee, 4th Cavalry, May–July and September 1869, and December 1869–March 1870

Captain J. W. Clous, 38th Infantry, August and October–November 1869 and April–May 1870

Bvt. Major Theo Schwann, 11th Infantry, June 1870 and January 1874, August–November 1874, and March–July 1876

Bvt. Lieutenant Colonel Charles A. Whiting, 6th Cavalry, August–December 1870

Captain James Biddle, 11th Infantry, January 1871

Colonel W. H. Wood, 11th Infantry, February 1871–November 1872

Lieutenant Colonel G. P. Buell, 11th Infantry, December 1872–July 1873; September 1873; November–December 1873; February–May, July, and December 1874; January–February 1875; and October 1875–February 1876

Captain George L. Choisy, 11th Infantry, August 1873 and June 1874

Major D. B. McKibbins, 10th Cavalry, October 1873 and August–September 1875

Captain J. B. Van de Weile, 10th Cavalry, March and May 1875

Lieutenant Colonel J. W. Davidson, 10th Cavalry, April and June–July 1875

Captain Philip L. Lee, 10th Cavalry, August 1876–March 1877 and May–June, August, and November–December 1877

Lieutenant S. R. Colladay, 10th Cavalry, April, July, and September 1877

Lieutenant J. F. Stretch, 10th Infantry, January–April 1878

Captain S. H. Lincoln, 10th Infantry, May 1878–March 1879
Captain J. B. Irvine, 22d Infantry, April 1879–May 1881

SOURCE: Compiled from Post Returns, Fort Griffin, Texas, Microfilm 617, roll 429, National Archives, Washington, D.C.

APPENDIX D
GARRISON TENURES,
FORT GRIFFIN, 1867–1881

4th Cavalry, Company D, May 1869–May 1872, January 1875
4th Cavalry, Company F, May 1869–March 1871, September 1872–May
  1873
4th Cavalry, Company H, September 1870–May 1873
6th Cavalry, Company B, July 1870–May 1871
6th Cavalry, Company F, July 1867–March 1868, July 1870–May 1871
6th Cavalry, Company I, July 1867–September 1868, November
  1868–March 1869, May–September 1870
6th Cavalry, Company K, July 1867–March 1869
6th Cavalry, Company L, July 1867–March 1869
9th Cavalry, Company A, August–September 1874
9th Cavalry, Company B, August 1871–February 1872
9th Cavalry, Company E, August–September 1874
9th Cavalry, Company F, August–September 1874
9th Cavalry, Company G, August 1871–February 1872
10th Cavalry, Company A, August 1874
10th Cavalry, Company B, March 1875–September 1876
10th Cavalry, Company C, May–December 1873
10th Cavalry, Company D, May 1873–September 1874, October 1874,
  March 1875
10th Cavalry, Company E, March 1875–September 1876
10th Cavalry, Company F, March–September 1874, March 1875
10th Cavalry, Company G, December 1873–January 1875, August
  1876–January 1878
10th Infantry, Company E, January 1878–April 1879
11th Infantry, Company A, October 1870–March 1877
11th Infantry, Company F, October 1870–March 1877
11th Infantry, Company G, June 1870–March 1877

17th Infantry, Company C, May 1868–March 1869
17th Infantry, Company F, June 1868–March 1869
17th Infantry, Company S, June 1868–March 1869
22d Infantry, Company A, April 1879–May 1881
24th Infantry, Company E, July 1869–July 1870
35th Infantry, Company E, March 1869–June 1869
35th Infantry, Company F, May 1869–June 1869
38th Infantry, Company B, July–November 1869
38th Infantry, Company E, July–November 1869

SOURCE: Compiled from Post Returns, Fort Griffin, Texas, Microfilm 617, roll 429, National Archives, Washington, D.C.

APPENDIX E
SUMMARY OF CHARGES
AND SPECIFICATIONS

	1870	1871	1872	1873	1874	1875	1876	1877
Murder	1	0	0	0	0	0	1	0
Assault	1	3	n/a	5	3	6	3	0
Desertions	24	86	35	56	24	12	5	1
Theft	8	7	7	14	n/a	4	2	1
Sleeping on watch	2	3	n/a	4	6	3	5	6
Drunk on duty	11	18	21	27	8	4	2	0
Leaving duty post	1	2	8	3	2	6	0	0

NOTE: These statistics involve the actions of soldiers only; violence among soldiers and civilians is not included. Returns for the years 1867 through 1869 were incomplete, yet desertions *were* logged and totaled nineteen, thirty-one, and five, respectively. Murders, clearly, occurred infrequently. Illustrative of assaults, 1873 included five typical incidents: a soldier charged with beating another over the head with a carbine, a choking incident, a captain striking an enlisted man with a ruler, and two fistfights. More severe cases were extremely aberrant. Charges of theft were largely for items taken by soldiers who deserted with federal property, including their clothing, arms, and the horses on which they fled. Many incidents of drunkenness involved repeat cases, including several habitual offenders. The peak of activity at the fort and the heyday of the Flat overlapped during 1875, 1876, and part of 1877, yet statistics do not reflect a particularly corrupting influence on the garrison.

SOURCE: Compiled from Record Group 393, Charges and Specifications, FG; Medical History of the Post, FG; and, Post Returns, FG, Microfilm 617, roll 429, National Archives, Washington, D.C. Returns for 1867–1869 incomplete.

APPENDIX F
SELECTED STATISTICS FROM
UNITED STATES CENSUS DATA

<u>Eighth Census, 1860</u>

<u>Buchanan (Stephens), Shackelford, and Throckmorton Counties</u>

Total population of persons over eighteen years old:	163
Nonwhite population:	2.5%

Of all reported occupations (excluding homemakers):

Cow hunters/stock herders	67.7%
Farmers	27.9%

	Birthplace of men and women over eighteen years old	Cow hunters/ stock herders
The South	107 (66%)	32 (70%)
Border States	28 (17%)	6 (13%)
The North	12 (7%)	3 (7%)
Foreign	16 (10%)	5 (10%)

<u>Ninth Census (1870)</u>

<u>Stephens and Shackelford Counties</u>

Total population of persons over eighteen years old:	239
Nonwhite population	10.1%

Of all reported occupations (excluding homemakers):

Cow hunters/stock herders	84.6%
Farmers	8.9%

	Birthplace of men and women over eighteen years old	Cow hunters/ stock herders
The South	158 (66%)	79 (67%)
Border States	43 (18%)	15 (14%)
The North	23 (10%)	5 (5%)
Foreign	15 (6%)	5 (5%)

Tenth Census, 1880

Shackelford and Throckmorton Counties

Total population of persons over eighteen years old: 1,420
   Nonwhite population: 10.2%

Of all reported occupations (excluding homemakers):
   Cow hunters/stock herders 40.1%
   Farmers 34.0%
   Noncow stock raisers (sheep, hogs, horses) 9.9%
   Nonagribusiness occupations 16.0%

	Birthplace of men and women over eighteen years old	Cow hunters/ stock herders
The South	888 (63%)	247 (69%)
Border States	233 (16%)	74 (20%)
The North	206 (14%)	29 (8%)
Foreign	93 (7%)	9 (3%)

NOTE: Clearly, Southern roots and a herding tradition ran deep during the formative development of the Clear Fork country. Southern states in this analysis included Alabama, Arkansas, Georgia, Florida, Louisiana, Mississippi, North Carolina, South Carolina, Tennessee, and Virginia. Texans were counted as Southerners for the 1860 and 1870 profiles only. By 1880 native Texans were so numerous as to skew the statistics; hence, Texans for this profile were counted according to their paternal origin. The Border states included Kentucky, Maryland, and Missouri. Northern states included Connecticut, Illinois, Iowa, Kansas, Maine, Massachusetts, New Jersey, New York, Ohio, Pennsylvania, and Vermont. Foreign countries included Austria, Bavaria, Canada, England, France, Germany, Holland, Ireland, Italy, Mexico, Poland, Prussia,

Saxony, Scotland, Sweden, and Switzerland. Excluded from all the profiles were active soldiers and other military personnel; excluded from the 1880 profile were eleven citizens from western states, the District of Columbia, and Indian Territory.

The counties in these statistical analyses vary. For Buchanan/Stephens County, included in the 1860 and 1870 profile, only the middle and western precincts (that is, excluding the eastern precinct) were included, because the nascent development of the Clear Fork country formed strong demographic and administrative ties as men and women migrated primarily from east to west along the watercourses and valleys. By 1880 Shackelford and Throckmorton counties by themselves better represented the Clear Fork country. By then these two counties had provided hunters, ranchers, and settlers an entrepôt for expanding beyond the treeline; moreover, they became a primary destination for those who diffused into the region north and south as well as westward. By that time, too, Stephens County had established characteristics either distinct or more closely related to the Cross Timbers counties of Young and Palo Pinto. Throckmorton County did not post returns for the 1870 census and could not be included in that profile.

The flowering of a distinctive culture can be seen in the enumeration of occupations included in the 1880 census that were not listed in those of 1860 and 1870. In 1860, skilled and professional persons included only a blacksmith and two teachers. In 1870 a physician, carpenter, brewer, and salt maker joined them. New occupations in 1880 included accountant, artist, attorney, barber, dentist, dressmaker, grocer, gunsmith, druggist, hostler, merchant, painter, preacher, printer, publisher, railroad contractor, saddler, saloonkeeper, seamstress, shoemaker, stonemason, surgeon, tanner, telegrapher, watchmaker, and any variety of specialty laborers, clerks, and county, state, and federal officials. Still, in 1880, despite the settlers' boom and a proliferation of new jobs, stock raising continued to employ more citizens than any other occupation.

NOTES

ABBREVIATIONS USED IN NOTES

AG	Adjutant General
AAG	Assistant Adjutant General
AAAG	Acting Assistant Adjutant General
CAH	Center for American History, University of Texas at Austin
FG	Fort Griffin
IO	Indian Office
LC	Library of Congress
LS	Letters Sent
LR	Letters Received
NA	National Archives, Washington, D.C.
NC	Robert Nail Foundation Collection, Albany, Texas
NHML	Nita Stewart Haley Memorial Library, Midland, Texas
PPM	Panhandle-Plains Historical Museum, Canyon, Texas
PPHR	*Panhandle-Plains Historical Review*
PMH	Post Medical History of Fort Griffin, Texas
RG	Record Group
SL	Soule Letters, NC
SP	Cornelius Stribling Papers, Center for American History, University of Texas at Austin
SWHQ	*Southwestern Historical Quarterly*
TSA	Lorenzo de Zavalla State Archives, Austin, Texas
WP	Webb Papers, Hardin-Simmons University, Abilene, Texas
WTHAY	*West Texas Historical Association Yearbook*

INTRODUCTION

1. Notes, by author, from Fandangle Parades, 1989, 1992, 1993.

2. T. R. Fehrenbach, *Lone Star: A History of Texas and the Texans*, 536–37; John Myers Myers, *Doc Holliday*, 68–71; Ian Frazier, *Great Plains*, 86–87.

3. *Fort Worth Daily Democrat*, Aug. 6, 1879.

4. George W. Bomar, *Texas Weather*, 207.

5. Author's conversation with GTE marketing executive Stacey Dees; H. H. McConnell, *Five Years a Cavalryman; or, Sketches of Regular Army Life on the Texas Frontier, Twenty Odd Years Ago*, 46–47.

6. For a good critique of the Fort Griffin Fandangle, see Fane Downs, "Fandangle: Myth As Reality," *WTHAY* 54 (1978): 2–9.

7. *Frontier Echo* (Jacksboro), Feb. 11, 1876.

CHAPTER ONE

1. William B. Parker, *Notes Taken during the expedition commanded by Capt. R. B. Marcy, U.S.A., through unexplored Texas, in the summer and fall of 1854*, 126.

2. Ibid., 121, 128, 132, 137, 143–44.

3. Ibid., 88.

4. Elizabeth John, *Storms Brewed in Other Men's Worlds: The Confrontation of Indians, Spanish, and French in the Southwest, 1540–1795*, 305–307; Ernest Wallace and E. Adamson Hoebel, *The Comanches: Lords of the South Plains*, 276–77.

5. Walter Prescott Webb, *The Great Plains*, 52–67; Fred A. Shannon, *Critiques of Research in the Social Sciences*, vol. 3, *An Appraisal of Walter Prescott Webb's "The Great Plains": A Study in Institutions and Environment*, 53–54; Wallace and Hoebel, *Comanches*, 307; W. W. Newcomb, *The Indians of Texas: From Prehistoric to Modern Times*, 174–76; Donald E. Worcester, "The Spread of Spanish Horses in the Southwest, 1700–1800," *New Mexico Historical Review* 20 (Jan. 1945): 8–9.

6. Sallie Reynolds Matthews, *Interwoven: A Pioneer Chronicle*, 4th ed., 4; Edward Everett Dale, *The Range Cattle Industry*, 34; Webb, *Great Plains*, 3–9ff.

7. R. C. Crane, contrib., "Report of Captain R. B. Marcy, of the Fifth Infantry, United States Army, on His Exploration of Indian Territory and Northwest Texas," *WTHAY* 14 (1938): 117. The focus of this study—the Clear Fork country—overlaps the two regions that Marcy noted. Its boundaries are indeterminate because history, rather than any unique geographic characteristic, sets it apart. The area rests partly within the "Osage Plains" or "Lower Plains" (bounded on the west and northwest by the Cap Rock Escarpment) and partly within the Western Cross Timbers to the east. It is within the Clear Fork country that settlers reached the end of the treeline, or the farthest point where significant belts of deciduous forests grow naturally. See Terry G. Jordan et al., *Texas: A Geography*, 9, and Webb, *Great Plains*, 27–33ff.

8. Randolph B. Marcy, *Thirty Years of Army Life on the Border*, 206, 208; Lieutenant Colonel Robert E. Lee, Camp Cooper, to wife, Aug. 2, 4, 1856, June 29, 1857, in M. L. Crimmins, "Robert E. Lee in Texas: Letters and Diary," *WTHAY* 8 (1932): 7, 17; Crane, contrib., "Marcy's Report of Northwest Texas," 121.

9. Marcy, *On the Border*, 208–209.

10. W. S. Nye, *Carbine and Lance: The Story of Old Fort Sill*, 19.

11. Ferdinand Roemer, *Texas: With Particular Reference to German Immigration and the Physical Appearance of the Country*, 324.

12. Rupert N. Richardson, *The Comanche Barrier to South Plains Settlement: A Century and a Half of Savage Resistance to the Advancing White Frontier*, 122–27ff.; Minutes of the Council at the Falls of the Brazos, Oct. 7, 1844, in Dorman H. Winfrey and James M. Day, eds., *The Indian Papers of Texas and the Southwest, 1825–1916* II, no. 75, 103–14ff; H. P. N. Gammel, ed., *Laws of Texas*, II, 1192–96.

13. Marcy, *On the Border*, 43–44; Newcomb, *Indians of Texas*, 350–52; Richardson, *Comanche Barrier*, 23, 128–30, 144.

14. Richardson, *Comanche Barrier*, 133; Report of Benjamin Sloat, Indian Agent, July 12, 1845, no. 251, pp. 283–86; Sloat to Thomas G. Western, Indian Affairs, Aug. 18, 1845, no. 290, pp. 325–26; Report of a Council with the Comanche Indians, Trading House, Post No. 2, Nov. 23, 1845, no. 376, pp. 411, all in Winfrey and Day, eds., *Texas Indian Papers* II; John Salmon Ford, *Rip Ford's Texas*, 449.

15. Walter Prescott Webb, *The Texas Rangers: A Century of Frontier Defense*, 20; Seymour V. Connor, *The Peters Colony of Texas*, 16–17.

16. Connor, *Peters Colony*, 20, 54, 95; Rupert N. Richardson, *The Frontier of Northwest Texas*, 46–49.

17. Connor, *Peters Colony*, 114–15, 119, 307; *Eighth U.S. Census, 1860*, Schedule I, Population, Texas, VIII (microfilm), Buchanan County, 347–50; Shackelford County, 350, reel no. 1302; Throckmorton County, 402–404, reel no. 1308 (hereafter cited as *U.S. Census, 1860*, followed by county); Thomas Lambshead to G. W. Manypenny, May 1, 1856, IO (microfilm), LR, CAH; Marcy, *On the Border*, 207–208; Parker, *Through Unexplored Texas*, 192.

18. Sloat to Western, July 24, 1844, no. 262, pp. 298–99; Sloat to Western, Aug. 18, 1845, no. 290, pp. 325–26; L. H. Williams to Western, Aug. 20, 1845, no. 291, pp. 326–27, all in Winfrey and Day, eds., *Texas Indian Papers* II; Richardson, *Comanche Barrier*, 136–37, 144–46.

19. Torrey and Brothers to Western, Sept. 15, 1845, no. 318, p. 360, in Winfrey and Day, eds., *Texas Indian Papers* II; Robert S. Neighbors to W. Medill, Commissioner of Indian Affairs, June 22, 1847, S. Exec. Doc. 1, 30th Cong., 1st sess., serial set 503, p. 892.

20. Neighbors to Medill, June 22, 1847, S. Exec. Doc. 1, 30th Cong., 1st sess., serial set 503, pp. 893–96; "Texas Indians"—Report of P. M. Butler and M. G. Lewis, Aug. 8, 1846, H. Doc. 76, 29th Cong., 2d sess., serial set 500, p. 3.

21. Nye, *Carbine and Lance*, 19; Ford, *Rip Ford's Texas*, 116; James Shaw to Sam Houston, Oct. 2, 1844, in Winfrey and Day, eds., *Texas Indian Papers* II, no. 74, p. 102; Marcy, *On the Border*, 43–45.

22. Marcy, *On the Border*, 44; J. R. Webb interview with John Chadbourne Irwin, Fall and Winter 1934, WP (hereafter cited as Irwin interview unless otherwise indicated by different date or author); Ford, *Rip Ford's Texas*, 115–16.

23. M. L. Crimmins, ed., "W. G. Freeman's Report on the Eighth Military Department," *SWHQ* 53 (Apr. 1950): 470-73; Oliver Knight, *Fort Worth: Outpost on the Trinity*, 5-10.

24. Richardson, *Frontier of Northwest Texas*, 68, 95; Report of General William G. Belknap, to General Persifor F. Smith, July 7, 1851; Lieutenant Clinton Lear to Mary Lear, Nov. 14, 19, 1851, all in John H. Shirk, "Mail Call at Fort Washita" *Chronicles of Oklahoma* 33 (1955): 22, 27-28.

25. Crimmins, ed., "Freeman's Report," *SWHQ* 53 (Apr. 1950), 448-53; Carl Coke Rister, "The Border Post of Phantom Hill," *WTHAY* 14 (1938): 3-13ff.

26. Jesse Stem to Rutherford B. Hayes, Oct. 5, 1850, May 2, 1852, in Watt P. Marchman and Robert C. Cotner, "Indian Agent Jesse Stem: A Manuscript Revelation," *WTHAY* 39 (1963): 117-18, 145, 148.

27. Stem to Hayes, May 2, 1852, in Marchman and Cotner, "Jesse Stem," 148; Glyndon G. Van Deusen, *Horace Greeley: Nineteenth Century Crusader*, 173; David M. Emmons, *Garden in the Grasslands: Boomer Literature of the Central Great Plains*, 128.

28. Richardson, *Frontier of Northwest Texas*, 78-79; Stem to Hayes, May 2, 1852, in Marchman and Cotner, "Jesse Stem," 145-46.

29. Stem to wife, Nov. 25, 1851; Stem to Hayes, May 2, 1852, in Marchman and Cotner, "Jesse Stem," 142, 148.

30. Marcy, *On the Border*, 203-205.

31. Marchman and Cotner, "Jesse Stem," 147-48; W. C. Holden, "Frontier Defense, 1846-1860," *WTHAY* 6 (1930): 47.

32. Holden, "Frontier Defense, 1846-1860," 52; Richardson, *Frontier of Northwest Texas*, 78-80; Marcy, *On the Border*, 208.

33. Stem to Hayes, May 2, 1852, in Marchman and Cotner, "Jesse Stem," 149.

34. *Northern Standard* (Clarksville, Texas), June 11, 1853; Jerry Thompson, *Henry Hopkins Sibley: Confederate General of the West*, 96-98.

35. Marchman and Cotner, "Jesse Stem," 152; Richardson, *Frontier of Northwest Texas*, 84.

36. Richardson, *Frontier of Northwest Texas*, 68, 95; C. C. Rister, "The Border Post of Phantom Hill," *WTHAY* 14 (1938): 9; Kenneth F. Neighbours, "Robert Simpson Neighbors in Texas, 1836-1859: A Quarter Century of Frontier Problems" (Ph.D. diss., University of Texas at Austin, 1955), 254.

37. Resolutions from P. H. Bell to U.S. Congress, Feb. 7, 1850, in Winfrey and Day, eds., *Texas Indian Papers* III, no. 91, pp. 114-19; Holden, "Frontier Defense, 1846-1860," 41, 49.

38. "Support of the Army—Message from the President of the United States," Franklin Pierce, Aug. 21, 1856, H. Exec. Doc. 1, 34th Cong., 2d sess., serial set 864, pp. 1-3; Charles P. Roland and Richard C. Robbins, eds., "The Diary of Eliza (Mrs. Albert Sidney) Johnston," *SWHQ* 60 (Apr. 1957): 465.

39. Carl Coke Rister, *Robert E. Lee in Texas*, 13-14, 19, 22-23; RQ 94, Camp Cooper, Post Returns, NA, (microfilm 617, roll 253).

40. Marcy to Pease, Jan. 10, 1855, in Winfrey and Day, eds., *Texas Indian Papers* III, no. 127, pp. 192-93; Shirk, "Mail Call," 28.

41. Richardson, *Comanche Barrier*, 215–17; Report of Marcy and Neighbors to Bell, Sept. 30, 1854, no. 125, pp. 186–90; Marcy to Pease, Jan. 10, 1855, no. 127, pp. 192–93, in Winfrey and Day, *Texas Indian Papers* III.

42. Rupert N. Richardson, "The Comanche Reservation in Texas," *WTHAY* 5 (1929): 51–54; Hill to Neighbors, Mar. 31, Apr. 3, 1855, IO, LR.

43. Neighbors to Pease, Dec. 7, 1854, in Winfrey and Day, eds., *Texas Indian Papers* III, no. 126, pp. 190–91.

44. Richardson, *Comanche Barrier*, 217; Patricia Limerick, *The Legacy of Conquest: The Unbroken Past of the American West*, 189.

45. S. P. Ross to Neighbors, Jan. 9, 1856, IO, LR; Neighbours, "Neighbors," 396, 425, 436.

46. Neighbors to G. W. Manypenny, Sept. 18, 1856, "Report of the Secretary of Indian Affairs," in S. Exec. Doc. 1, 34th Cong., 3d sess., serial set 875, pp. 724–27.

47. Baylor to Neighbors, Mar. 14, 21, 1857, IO, LR.

48. Statement, Thomas Lambshead and J. N. Gibbins, Clear Fork Camp, Mar. 30, 1858, IO, LR, cited in Kenneth F. Neighbours, *Robert Simpson Neighbors and the Texas Frontier*, 193; Douglas Southall Freeman, *Robert E. Lee: A Biography*, I, 364; Richardson, "Comanche Reservation," 54–55, 58–61; Marcy, *On the Border*, 204.

49. Neighbours, *Neighbors*, 153, 159, 163, 174–77, 181.

50. Jerry Don Thompson, *Colonel Robert John Baylor: Texas Indian Fighter and Confederate Soldier*, 4–6, 20–21, 24–34; Neighbours, *Neighbors*, 159.

51. Lee to family, Apr. 12, June 28, 1856, in Crimmins, "Robert E. Lee Letters," 5.

52. Ford, *Rip Ford's Texas*, 232–36; Report of John S. Ford to H. R. Runnels, May 22, 1858, in Winfrey and Day, eds., *Texas Indian Papers* V, no. 169, 233–38; J. W. Wilbarger, *Indian Depredations in Texas*, pp. 320–26, 329–32; Webb, *Texas Rangers*, 155–57.

53. A. Nelson to Captain, Apr. 13, 1858, in Winfrey and Day, eds., *Texas Indian Papers* V, no. 165, pp. 228–29; Neighbours, *Neighbors*, 223–24, 227, 242–45; J. J. Sturm to Ross, Dec. 28, 30, 1858, S. Exec. Doc. 2, 36th Cong., 1st sess., serial set 1023, pp. 588–90; Joseph Carroll McConnell, *The West Texas Frontier; or, a Descriptive History of Early Times in Western Texas* I, 325–27; Thomas T. Ewell, *History of Hood County*, 16–17; Mary Whatley Clarke, *Palo Pinto Story*, 7.

54. Richardson, "Comanche Reservation," 70.

55. Neighbours, *Neighbors*, 282–292ff.; Neighbours, "The Assassination of Robert S. Neighbors," *WTHAY* 34 (1958): 38–49.

CHAPTER TWO

1. McConnell, *West Texas Frontier* II, nos. 330, 333.

2. Ibid., no. 334; Matthews, *Interwoven*, 4–5; R. E. Sherill, "Early Days in Haskell County," *WTHAY* 3 (1927): 22–23.

3. *The White Man* (Jacksboro), Sept. 13, 1860; Matthews, *Interwoven*, 38.

4. Ida L. Huckabay, *Ninety-Four Years in Jack County, 1854–1948*, 60–66; McConnell, *West Texas Frontier* II, nos. 346, 348, 349, 350.

5. *White Man* (Jacksboro), Sept. 15, 1860; Richardson, *Comanche Barrier*, 265–66; McConnell, *West Texas Frontier* II, no. 351.

6. McConnell, *West Texas Frontier* II, nos. 307, 351; Wilbarger, *Indian Depredations in Texas*, 335–39; Lee to family, Apr. 12, June 28, 1856, in Crimmins, "Robert E. Lee Letters," 5.

7. Richardson, *Comanche Barrier*, 122–27; Minutes of Council, Oct. 7, 1844, in Winfrey and Day, eds., *Texas Indian Papers* II, no. 75, pp. 109–12.

8. Ben G. O'Neal, "The Beginnings of Fort Belknap," *SWHQ* 61 (Apr. 1958): 511; W. L. Ormsby, *The Butterfield Overland Mail*, 47; Richardson, *Frontier of Northwest Texas*, 112–13.

9. J. R. Webb interviews with Phin Reynolds, May 1936 and April 1938, WP (hereafter cited as Reynolds interview unless otherwise indicated by different date); Belknap to Smith, July 7, 1851, in Shirk, "Mail Call," 22.

10. Roscoe P. Conkling, *The Butterfield Overland Mail, 1857–1869* I, 32–41ff.; Rupert Richardson, "Some Details of the Southern Overland Mail," *SWHQ* 29 (July 1925): 14.

11. Conkling, *Butterfield Mail* I, 289–91.

12. Ibid., 320–22; *U.S. Census, 1860*, Stephens County; Connor, *Peters Colony*, 255.

13. Ormsby, *Butterfield*, 47–48.

14. Conkling, *Butterfield Mail*, I, 128; Richardson, "Details of the Mail," 14; Richardson, "Comanche Reservation," 60–61; Rupert N. Richardson, "Saga of Camp Cooper," *WTHAY* 56 (1980): 22; Rupert N. Richardson, "The Southern Overland Mail, Conveyor of News, 1857–1861," *WTHAY* 34 (1958): 32.

15. Conkling, *Butterfield Mail* I, 131–33; Odie Minatra interview with John Chadbourne Irwin, Sept. 1935, WP; Ormsby, *Butterfield*, 42.

16. Conkling, *Butterfield Mail* I, 322–27; Ormsby, *Butterfield*, 48; Irwin interview; *U.S. Census, 1860*, Throckmorton County.

17. Irwin interview; *U.S. Census, 1860*, Buchanan, Shackelford, and Throckmorton counties; Connor, *Peters Colony*, 307; Neighbours, "Indian Reservations," 15.

18. Lee to wife, Aug. 2, 4, 1856; June 29, 1857, in Crimmins, "Robert E. Lee Letters," 7, 17.

19. Lee to family, Aug. 4, 1856; June 9, 22, 1857, in ibid.

20. Wilbarger, *Indian Depredations in Texas*, 335–39; Irwin interview with Minatra; McConnell, *West Texas Frontier* II, no. 351.

21. Irwin interview with Minatra; McConnell, *West Texas Frontier* II, no. 201; *U.S. Census, 1860*, Throckmorton County.

22. McConnell, *West Texas Frontier* II, no. 201; Neighbours, *Neighbors*, 210; *U.S. Census, 1860*, Buchanan, Shackelford, and Throckmorton counties; Irwin interview with Minatra; Gammel, ed., *Laws of Texas* IV, 908–10.

23. Holden, "Frontier Defense, 1846–1860," 64–66; *Dallas Herald*, Sept. 1, 1858; *The White Man* (Jacksboro), Sept. 15, 1860.

24. Ben O. Grant, "Citizen Law Enforcement Bodies: A Little More about the Vigilantes," *WTHAY* 39 (1963): 158–59; *The White Man* (Jacksboro), Sept. 15, 1860; Irwin interview.

25. Marcy, *On the Border*, 206; Webb, *Great Plains*, 17–21ff., 27–32ff.; Don H. Biggers, *Shackelford County Sketches*, 3–4.

26. G. W. Cullum, comp., *Biographical Register of the Officers and Graduates of the U.S. Military Academy at West Point, New York*, 266–67; Ormsby, *Butterfield*, 49; Rister, "Phantom Hill," 9.

27. Parker, *Through Unexplored Texas*, 215–17; Barbara Neal Ledbetter, *Fort Belknap, Frontier Saga: Indians, Negroes and Anglo Americans On the Texas Frontier*, 41, 47.

28. Biggers, *Shackelford County Sketches*, 56–58; Matthews, *Interwoven*, 27–28.

29. Matthew Leeper to Neighbors, Mar. 27, 1858, IO, LR; Matthews, *Interwoven*, 27; Rister, *Fort Griffin*, 34–35; Biggers, *Shackelford County Sketches*, 56–57; Holden, *Lambshead before Interwoven*, 38–39, 200–201; Neighbours, "Simpson in Texas," 492–93. In recent times the issue has been clouded by the discovery of some apparent foundations on the "Bake Oven pasture" along Paint Creek.

30. Leeper to Neighbors, Mar. 27, 1858, IO, LR; Freeman, *Lee* I, 360, 364; Rister, *Lee in Texas*, 89–90.

31. Amelia W. Williams and Eugene C. Barker, eds., *The Writings of Sam Houston* VII, 164–65.

32. James K. Greer, *A Texas Ranger and Frontiersman: The Days of Buck Barry in Texas, 1845–1906*, 124.

33. Ford, *Rip Ford's Texas*, 216–17; Cullum, *Biographical Register*, 266–67; C. C. Rister, *Fort Griffin on the Texas Frontier*, 35–36.

34. Terry G. Jordan, *Trails to Texas: Southern Roots of Western Cattle Ranching*, 3.

35. *Dallas Herald*, June 15, 1859.

36. Richardson, *Frontier of Northwest Texas*, 209; Neighbours, *Neighbors*, 282, 288–89.

37. Newcomb, *Indians of Texas*, 189–91; Irwin interview.

38. Irwin interview; Matthews, *Interwoven*, 28.

39. Governor Sam Houston to Mr. Floyd, Apr. 14, 1860, in "Troubles on the Texas Frontier," H. Exec. Doc. 81, 36th Cong., 1st sess., serial set 1056, pp. 90–92.

40. Ernest W. Winkler, ed., *Journal of the Secession Convention of Texas, 1861*, 89–90; Greer, *Buck Barry*, 126; Newcomb Family Diary, July 4, 1865, typed copy, NC (hereafter cited as Newcomb Diary; all entries by Sam Newcomb unless otherwise indicated). For a different interpretation, see Floyd F. Ewing, Jr., "Unionist Sentiment on the Northwestern Frontier," *WTHAY* 33 (1957): 60–62, and Ewing, "Origins of Unionist Sentiment on the West Texas Frontier," *WTHAY* 32 (1956): 21; Gammel, ed., *Laws of Texas* IV, 908–10, 930–34, 959, 966.

41. Henry E. McCulloch to John C. Robertson, Mar. 7, 1861, pp. 374–79; McCulloch to E. W. Rogers, Mar. 7, 1861, p. 379; McCulloch to Robertson, Mar. 9, 1861, pp. 380–83, all in Winkler, ed., *Secession Journal*.

42. For a different interpretation, see Rister, *Fort Griffin*, 30–31.

43. D. S. Howell, "Along the Texas Frontier during the Civil War," *WTHAY* 13 (1937): 88.

CHAPTER THREE

1. W. C. Holden, "Frontier Defense in Texas during the Civil War," *WTHAY* 4 (1928): 31; Richardson, *Frontier of Northwest Texas*, 251-53.

2. *U.S. Census, 1860*, Buchanan, Shackelford, and Throckmorton counties; *Ninth U.S. Census, 1870*, Schedule I, Population, Texas, XI (microfilm), Shackelford County, 120-27, reel no. 1604; Stephens County, 467-71, reel no. 1605 (hereafter cited as *U.S. Census, 1870*, followed by county). During the decade, Buchanan County was renamed Stephens; Throckmorton County returned no census data for 1870.

3. Biggers, *Shackelford County Sketches*, 58-59; Matthews, *Interwoven*, 9.

4. Newcomb Diary, Mar. 14, 31, 1865; Matthews, *Interwoven*, 30; Biggers, *Shackelford County Sketches*, 58-60.

5. Irwin interview; Ben O. Grant and J. R. Webb, contribs., "On the Cattle Trail and Buffalo Range: Joe S. McCombs," *WTHAY* 11 (1935): 94; David J. Murrah, *C. C. Slaughter: Rancher, Banker, Baptist*, 12; Richardson, *Frontier of Northwest Texas*, 46-59, 110-11; 120; Biggers, *Shackelford County Sketches*, pp. 5-8.

6. Jordan, *Trails to Texas*, 41-45, 51, 54-55, 156; D. W. Meinig, "The Continuous Shaping of America: A Prospectus for Geographers and Historians," *American Historical Review* 83 (Dec. 1978): 1190-91; John D. W. Guice, "Cattle Raisers of the Old Southwest: A Reinterpretation," *Western Historical Quarterly* 8 (Apr. 1977), 167-75; Frank L. Owsley, *Plain Folk of the Old South*, 26; Sam B. Hilliard, *Hog Meat and Hoecake: Food Supply in the Old South*, 116-17.

7. Jordan, *Trails to Texas*, 43-45; Owsley, *Plain Folk*, p. 26; Forrest McDonald and Grady McWhiney, "The Antebellum Southern Herdsman: A Reinterpretation," *Journal of Southern History* 41 (Apr. 1975): 156.

8. Jordan, *Trails to Texas*, 83-85, 87, 91, 98, 107, 118-22ff.; McDonald and McWhiney, "Southern Herdsman," 156; Guice, "Cattle Raisers," 184. For an opposing interpretation, see Sandra L. Myres, "The Ranching Frontier: Spanish Institutional Backgrounds of the Plains Cattle Industry," *New Spain's Far Northern Frontier: Essays on Spain in the American West, 1540-1821*, ed. David J. Weber, 79-94.

9. *U.S. Census, 1860*, Buchanan, Shackelford, and Throckmorton counties; *U.S. Census, 1870*, Shackelford and Stephens counties; Jordan, *Trails to Texas*, 51, 54-55; Matthews, *Interwoven*, 2.

10. Matthews, *Interwoven*, 1-3; James Cox, *Historical and Biographical Record of the Cattle Industry and the Cattlemen of Texas and Adjacent Territory* II, 339-40.

11. *U.S. Census, 1860*, Buchanan, Shackelford, and Throckmorton counties.

12. Richardson, *Frontier of Northwest Texas*, 129, 144, 146; Cox, *Cattle Industry of Texas* II, 399; Jordan, *Trails to Texas*, 3.

13. Minutes of County Court, Jan. 21, 1878, vol. A, Shackelford County, Texas (hereafter cited as County Court); McDonald and McWhiney, "Southern Herdsman," 157-58. In 1873, the Texas legislature did pass a statute holding stockmen liable for damage to unfenced crops, but it did not raise the issue of fencing. Gammel, ed., *Laws of Texas* VII, 11.

14. Matthews, *Interwoven*, 33; Newcomb Diary, January 1, 1866; Jordan, *Trails to Texas*, 25–26; Irwin interview.

15. Biggers, *Shackelford County Sketches*, 51–52; Jordan, *Trails to Texas*, 12, 34.

16. J. Evetts Haley, *Charles Goodnight: Cowman and Plainsman*, 19–20; Richardson, *The Frontier of Northwest Texas*, 150.

17. Grady McWhiney, *Cracker Culture: Celtic Ways in the Old South*, 139–40; Jordan, *Trails to Texas*, 31–32; Reynolds interview.

18. McConnell, *West Texas Frontier* II, no. 447.

19. Ibid., no. 405.

20. Ibid., no. 426.

21. See Holden, "Frontier Defense in Texas," 16–31. The most recent and complete work is David Paul Smith's *Frontier Defense in the Civil War: Texas' Rangers and Rebels*.

22. Kenneth F. Neighbours, "Elm Creek Raid in Young County, 1864," *WTHAY* 40 (1964): 83–89; Ledbetter, *Belknap Saga*, 111–21; Wilbarger, *Indian Depredations in Texas*, 449–52; Greer, *Buck Barry*, 175–79; *War of the Rebellion: A Compilation of the Official Records of the Union and Confederate Armies*, Ser. I, XLI, pt. I, Reports, 885–86 (hereafter cited as *OR*); William R. Peveler, "Diary of William R. Peveler," typescript copy, CAH.

23. Carrie J. Crouch, *A History of Young County, Texas*, 40; Ledbetter, *Belknap Saga*, 117–18; Wilbarger, *Indian Depredations in Texas*, 449–52.

24. Crouch, *Young County*, 38–40; Wilbarger, *Indian Depredations in Texas*, 449–52; *OR*, Ser. I, XLI, pt. I, 886.

25. Greer, *Buck Barry*, 175; Crouch, *Young County*, 38; Ledbetter, *Belknap Saga*, 118–19.

26. Newcomb Diary, Mar. 1, 2, 1867.

27. Ibid., Jan. 1, 1865; Clifton Caldwell, *Fort Davis: A Family Frontier Fort*, 10–11; Biggers, *Shackelford County Sketches*, 17–18; Wilbarger, *Indian Depredations in Texas*, 449; Reynolds interview.

28. Newcomb Diary, Feb. 17, 1865; Biggers, *Shackelford County Sketches*, 18, 32–33; Bill Sumners, comp., *Inventory of County Records, Stephens County Courthouse*, 1.

29. Newcomb Diary, Jan. 1, 1865; *U.S. Census, 1860*, Buchanan County; Irwin interview; Reynolds interview.

30. Irwin interview; Reynolds interview.

31. Irwin interview; Newcomb Diary, Nov.–Dec. 1865.

32. Newcomb Diary, Jan. 1, Mar. 1, 13, Apr. 19, 27, 1865.

33. Ibid., Jan. 29, Aug. 26, Oct. 1, Dec. 24–27, 1865; *U.S. Census, 1860*, Buchanan County.

34. Newcomb Diary, Feb. 8, 17, Mar. 2, 1865.

35. Ibid., Oct. 3, 1865; *U.S. Census, 1860*, Buchanan and Shackelford counties.

36. Newcomb Diary, Mar. 2, Nov. 25, 28, 1865; Irwin interview.

37. Newcomb Diary, Feb. 11–13, 1865.

38. Ibid., Mar. 11, 12, 1865.

39. Ibid., Jan. 28, Feb. 2, May 22–31, 1865.

40. Ibid., June 7–29, 1865; Irwin interview.

41. Matthews, *Interwoven*, 13–14; entries of Susan Newcomb in Newcomb Diary, Mar. 31, Sept. 27, Oct. 19, Nov. 18, Dec. 25, 1866; June 16, 1867. For women's views on the wilderness, homemaking, and social contact, see Julie Roy Jeffrey, *Frontier Women: The Trans-Mississippi West, 1840–1880*, 79–106ff., and, Sandra L. Myres, *Westering Women and the Frontier Experience, 1800–1915*, 12–36, 141–66, 167–76.

42. Newcomb Diary, Sept. 27, Oct. 19, 1866; Matthews, *Interwoven*, 13.

43. Matthews, *Interwoven*, 13, 41–42; Biggers, *Shackelford County Sketches*, 34.

44. Matthews, *Interwoven*, 5, 10, 20–21, 40; Newcomb Diary, May 2, 4, 6, 1865; McConnell, *West Texas Frontier* I, 94; Richardson, *Frontier of Northwest Texas*, 231–32.

45. Newcomb Diary, Jan. 2, Oct. 26, 27, 1865.

46. Matthews, *Interwoven*, 40–41. See also Myres, *Westering Women*, 129–30, 156.

47. *U.S. Census, 1870*, Shackelford and Stephens counties; Matthews, *Interwoven*, 67, 87–88.

48. Matthews, *Interwoven*, 5; Biggers, *Shackelford County Sketches*, 53. See also Myres, *Westering Women*, 37–38, 56–62.

49. Matthews, *Interwoven*, 3.

CHAPTER FOUR

1. Richardson, *Frontier of Northwest Texas*, 255; Cox, *Cattle Industry of Texas* II, 425.

2. Newcomb Diary, June 7–29, 1865.

3. Throckmorton to Stanton, Aug. 5, 1867, in Winfrey and Day, eds., *Texas Indian Papers* IV, no. 155, pp. 235–36.

4. McConnell, *West Texas Frontier* II, no. 509; Reynolds interview.

5. McConnell, *West Texas Frontier* II, no. 533; Irwin interview; Newcomb Diary, July 20–21, 1865; Reynolds interview.

6. McConnell, *West Texas Frontier* II, no. 500.

7. Newcomb Diary, July 23, Nov.–Dec., 1865; Jan. 7, Aug. 21, 1866; McConnell, *West Texas Frontier* II, nos. 559, 578.

8. McCulloch to Edmund P. Turner, Nov. 1, 1863; James Bourland to McCulloch, Apr. 25, 1864, *OR*, Ser. I, XXVI, pt. II, 378; Greer, *Buck Barry*, 156, 173, 201; William Richter, *The Army in Texas during Reconstruction, 1865–1870*, 5; W. C. Holden, "Frontier Defense, 1865–1889" *PPHR* 2 (1929): 58–60.

9. W. C. McGough, "Driving Cattle into Old Mexico in 1864," *WTHAY* 13 (1937): 133.

10. Ford, *Rip Ford's Texas*, 361; Newcomb Diary, Apr. 29, 30, June 5, 1865.

11. Howell, "Along the Texas Frontier," 85; Greer, *Buck Barry*, 173.

12. Cox, *Cattle Industry of Texas* II, 339–40; Matthews, *Interwoven*, 198–201.

13. Charles W. Ramsdell, *Reconstruction in Texas*, 33–41; Richter, *Army in Texas during Reconstruction*, 13; Holden, "Frontier Defense, 1865–1889," 43.

14. Holden, "Frontier Defense, 1865–1889," 47; Ramsdell, *Reconstruction in Texas*, 108–12; Richter, *Army in Texas during Reconstruction*, 66; Smith, *Frontier Defense*, 184; Sheridan to Throckmorton, Sept. 3, 1866, Throckmorton to Sheridan, Sept. 18, 1866, Sheridan Papers, Library of Congress, Washington, D.C.

15. Robert Wooster, *The Military and United States Indian Policy, 1865–1903*, 112–26ff.; "Report of Major General Philip H. Sheridan," Nov. 14, 1866, *OR*, Ser. I, XLVIII, pt. I, 301; P. H. Sheridan, *Record of Engagements with Hostile Indians within the Military Division of the Missouri, from 1868 to 1882*, 4–6.

16. McConnell, *West Texas Frontier* II, no. 579; Reynolds interview; Matthews, *Interwoven*, 34–36.

17. J. R. Webb, "Chapters in the Frontier Life of Phin W. Reynolds," *WTHAY* 26 (1945): 120–21.

18. Newcomb Diary, Mar. 22, June 7–29, 1865.

19. Jordan, *Trails to Texas*, 71; Newcomb Diary, July 1–19, 1865, entry of Susan Newcomb, Jan. 4, 1867; Matthews, *Interwoven*, 25, 77; Webb, "Life of Phin Reynolds," 117–18; Reynolds interview; Haley, *Charles Goodnight*, 119; Larry Earl Adams, "Economic Development in Texas during Reconstruction, 1865–1875" (Ph.D. diss., North Texas State University, Denton, 1980), 162.

20. R. C. Crane, "West Texas Trail Blazers," *WTHAY* 22 (1946): 60–61, 63; Irwin interview.

21. Richter, *Army in Texas during Reconstruction*, 66–68; "Sheridan Report," Nov. 14, 1866, *OR*, pp. 300–301; Sheridan to Heintzelman, Oct. 15; Sheridan to Rawlins, Oct. 15, 1866, Sheridan Papers, LC.

22. Richter, *Army in Texas during Reconstruction*, 88; Holden, "Frontier Defense, 1865–1889," 48, 51; George L. Hartsuff AAG, in "Report of the Secretary of War," H. Exec. Doc. 1, 40th Cong., 3d sess., serial set 1367, 211–13; PMH, July 1867, p. 1.

23. Matthews, *Interwoven*, 42.

24. Emmett Roberts, "Frontier Experiences of Emmett Roberts of Nugent, Texas," *WTHAY* 3 (1927): 53–54; Buell to AAG, Feb. 27, 1874, RG 393, FG, LS.

25. McConnell, *West Texas Frontier* II, no. 645.

26. Ibid., no. 649.

27. Ibid., nos. 653, 687.

28. Roberts, "Frontier Experiences," 48–50, 53; Reynolds interview.

29. Marshall L. Johnson, *Trail Blazing: A True Story of the Struggles with Hostile Indians on the Frontier of Texas*, 78–86.

30. Reynolds interview; McConnell, *West Texas Frontier* II, no. 616; Captain Davis to Post Adjutant, Aug. 6, 1869, RG 393, FG, Proceedings of Boards of Survey.

31. Commander to Sub-Assistant Commissioner, June 30, 1868, RG 393, FG, LS; *U.S. Census, 1870*, Shackelford and Stephens counties; Francis A. Walker, *A Compendium of the Ninth Census*, 346.

32. McWhiney, *Cracker Culture*, 51–53; McDonald and McWhiney, "Southern Herdsmen," 147; Newcomb Diary, June 7–29, 1865; *U.S. Census, 1860*, Buchanan,

Shackelford, and Throckmorton counties; *U.S. Census, 1870,* Shackelford and Stephens counties; Cox, *Cattle Industry of Texas* II, 313, stated that before the war, Bill Hittson and Joe Matthews possessed about three thousand head of cattle apiece. Dale, *Range Cattle Industry,* 31, quotes prices of "three-year-old steers and oxen" at much higher rates than does Cox.

33. *U.S. Census, 1860,* Buchanan, Shackelford, and Throckmorton counties; *U.S. Census, 1870,* Shackelford and Stephens counties; Adams, "Economic Development," 170; Cox, *Cattle Industry of Texas* II, 313; Dale, *Range Cattle Industry,* 28-30.

34. *U.S. Census, 1870,* Shackelford and Stephens counties.

35. Ibid.; Roberts, "Frontier Experiences," 56; Tommy J. Boley, ed., *An Autobiography of a West Texas Pioneer: Ella Elgar Bird Dumont,* 44.

36. Roberts, "Frontier Experiences," 43; Mrs. George Mendell, "A Texas Pioneer Tells of Early Days," *Dallas Morning News,* Aug. 26, 1928, Feature Section, p. 1; Henry Griswold Comstock, "Some of My Experiences and Observations on the South Western Plains during the Summers of 1871 and 1872," MS, n.d., NC; Limerick, *Legacy of Conquest,* 42, 44; Reynolds interview; Biggers, *Shackelford County Sketches,* 47.

37. Gammel, ed., *Laws of Texas* V, 1141-43; VI, 1014-23; Richardson, *Frontier of Northwest Texas,* 262-63; Roberts, "Frontier Experiences," 51-52; Cox, *Cattle Industry of Texas* II, 379; J. Marvin Hunter, comp. and ed., *The Trail Drivers of Texas* II, 704; Haley, *Goodnight,* 111.

38. Roberts, "Frontier Experiences," 44-46.

39. *U.S. Census, 1870,* Shackelford and Stephens counties; Reynolds interview; *Galveston Daily News,* July 13, 1878; Frances Mayhugh Holden, *Lambshead before Interwoven: A Texas Range Chronicle, 1848-1878,* 114-15.

40. Comstock, "Experiences and Observations." Comstock stated that he arrived in Texas in 1871; he actually arrived in 1872. His reference to a monument at Salt Creek Prairie as well as describing events related to the Panic of 1873 clearly indicated his dating error.

41. Ibid.

42. Buell to AAG, Jan. 23, 1874, RG 393, FG, LS.

43. Ibid.

44. Ibid.; Second Lieutenant E. P. Turner to Post Adjutant, January 6, 1874, RG 393, FG, LS.

45. Buell to AAG, Jan. 23, Turner to Post Adjutant, Jan. 6, 1874, RG 393, FG, LS; Irwin interview; Reynolds interview.

CHAPTER FIVE

1. For a succinct discussion of problems facing the postwar military, see Wooster, *Military and Indian Policy,* chaps. 1 and 3.

2. "Recent raids and outrages upon Citizens of Texas and in Chickasaw nation by bands of Kiowa and Comanche Indians," S. Exec. Doc. 60, 40th Cong., 2d sess., serial set 1317; Brevet Major General W. B. Hazen to Lieutenant General W. T. Sherman, Nov. 10, 1868, in "Indian Battle of the Washita River," S. Exec. Doc. 18, 40th Cong., 3d sess., serial set 1360, pp. 13-16.

3. General C. C. Augur to James B. Fry, in "Report of the Secretary of War," Sept. 28, 1872, H. Exec. Doc. 1, 42d Cong., 3d sess., serial set 1558, p. 55; McConnell, *West Texas Frontier* II, 563. Rister, in *Fort Griffin*, 60, wrote that the Comanches and Kiowas were trying to reclaim Texas. While they no doubt wanted to possess the Panhandle, they acknowledged that their home base was beyond the Texas frontier line. See block quote by Kiowa Chief Satanta in Richardson, *Comanche Barrier*, 302. The Penatekas, of course, had been removed from Texas during the Reservation War in 1859.

4. W. H. Wood to AAG, Feb. 20, 1872, RG 393, FG, LS.

5. Ibid.

6. Ibid.

7. *U.S. Census, 1870*, Shackelford and Stephens counties.

8. McConnell, *West Texas Frontier* II, no. 589; Biggers, *Shackelford County Sketches*, 54–55.

9. McConnell, *West Texas Frontier* II, nos. 603, 626.

10. Wood to AAG, Feb. 20, 1872, RG 393, FG, LS, NA.

11. A. B. Norton, Superintendent of Indian Affairs to D. N. Cooley, Commissioner of Indian Affairs, July 31, Sept. 28, 1866, in "Report of the Secretary of Indian Affairs," H. Exec. Doc. 1, 39th Cong., 2d sess., serial set 1284, pp. 145–46, 151; Augur to Fry, 42d Cong., 3d sess., H. Doc. 1, pp. 54–57; Charles L. Kenner, *A History of New Mexican-Plains Indians Relations*, 78. For a broad discussion of the Comanchero trade, see Kenner, chaps. 4, 8, and 9. See also J. Evetts Haley, "The Comanchero Trade," *SWHQ* 38 (Jan. 1935): 157–61; and Carl Coke Rister, *The Southwestern Frontier, 1865–1881*, 82.

12. Lieutenant Colonel S. B. Hayman to Sam Newcomb, Dec. 8, 1868; Hayman to AAAG, Jan. 17, 1869, RG 393, FG, LS; Captain Davis to Post Adjutant, Aug. 6, 1869, RG 393, FG, Proceedings of Boards of Survey.

13. Muriel H. Wright, *A Guide to the Indian Tribes of Oklahoma*, 249–51; Newcomb, *Indians of Texas*, 133; Nye, *Carbine and Lance*, 29–31.

14. Hayman to AAAG, July 30, 1868, RG 393, FG, LS; Throckmorton to General Oakes, Mar. 11, 1867, RG 393, FG, Miscellaneous Records, Tonkawa Indian Scouts.

15. Lee to AAG, June 12, 1869, RG 393, FG, LS; Throckmorton, "Extract from Executive Records," Aug. 8, 1867, in Winfrey and Day, eds., *Texas Indian Papers* IV, no. 157, pp. 240–41.

16. McConnell, *West Texas Frontier* II, no. 616; Reynolds interview; Johnson, *Trail Blazing*, 52–55.

17. Reynolds interview; Biggers, *Shackelford County Sketches*, 52–53, 101–102; McConnell, *West Texas Frontier* II, no. 617.

18. Reynolds interview; Biggers, *Shackelford County Sketches*, 52–53, 101–102; McConnell, *West Texas Frontier* II, no. 617.

19. Adjutant General's Office, *Chronological List of Actions, &c., with Indians from January 15, 1837 to January, 1891, 31*; McConnell, *West Texas Frontier* II, no. 618; Biggers, *Shackelford County Sketches*, 102; A. J. Sowell, *Rangers and Pioneers of Texas*, 256.

20. Wooster, *Military and Indian Policy*, 37–38.

21. Ibid., 41–48, 111–22ff.; "Testimony of General William T. Sherman," H. Rep. 384, 43d Cong., 1st sess., serial set 1624, pp. 270–84; Richardson, *Comanche Barrier*, 324–26.

22. Nye, *Carbine and Lance*, 123–24; Allen Lee Hamilton, *Sentinel of the Southern Plains: Fort Richardson on the Northwest Texas Frontier, 1866–1878*, 71; Neighbours, "Elm Creek Raid," 88–89; McConnell, *Five Years a Cavalryman*, 696–702; Wilbarger, *Indian Depredations in Texas*, 549–51.

23. "Testimony of General William T. Sherman," 43d Cong., 1st sess., H. Rep. 384, p. 270; "Indian Depredations in Texas," H. Misc. Doc. 142, 41st Cong., 2d sess., serial set 1433, pp. 1–7; Wilbarger, *Indian Depredations in Texas*, 551–55; Nye, *Carbine and Lance*, 124; McConnell, *West Texas Frontier* II, 704.

24. Nye, *Carbine and Lance*, 124–29; Wilbarger, *Indian Depredations in Texas*, 553; McConnell, *West Texas Frontier* II, 705; McConnell, *Five Years a Cavalryman*, 273–75; Benjamin Capps, *The Warren Wagon Train Raid: The First Complete Account of an Historic Indian Attack and Its Aftermath*, 44–54; Barbara A. Neal Ledbetter, *Indian Raids on Warren, DuBose, Feild [sic], Man Wagon Trains, 1871, in Young and Jack Counties*, 47, 57–59.

25. Nye, *Carbine and Lance*, 125; Capps, *Warren Raid*, 42–54ff.; Hamilton, *Fort Richardson*, 82; Wilbarger, *Indian Depredations in Texas*, 554; McConnell, West Texas Frontier II, 706; R. G. Carter, *On the Border with Mackenzie; or, Winning West Texas from the Comanches*, 76–80; "Testimony of General William T. Sherman," 43d Cong., 1st sess., H. Rep. 384, p. 273.

26. Carter, *On the Border with Mackenzie*, 81–82; Nye, *Carbine and Lance*, 131; M. L. Crimmins, "Camp Cooper and Fort Griffin," *WTHAY* 18 (1941): 42; Capps, *Warren Raid*, 42–54ff.

27. H. R. Clum, Acting Commissioner of Indian Affairs, to C. Delano, Secretary of the Interior, Nov. 15, 1871, pp. 415, 419; Lawrie Tatum, U.S. Indian Agent, to Enoch Hoag, Superintendent of Indian Affairs, Sept. 1, 1871, pp. 918–20, in "Report of the Commissioner of Indian Affairs," H. Exec. Doc. 1, 42d Cong., 2d sess., serial set 1505. See also Nye, *Carbine and Lance*, 132–36, and Richardson, *Comanche Barrier*, 342.

28. Clum to Delano; Tatum to Hoag, 42d Cong., 2d sess., H. Exec. Doc. 1, pp. 419, 918–20; Richardson, *Comanche Barrier*, 349–50.

29. McConnell, *West Texas Frontier* II, no. 711; Wood to AAAG, July 6, 1872, RG 393, FG, LS.

30. Wood to AAAG, Aug. 3, 5, 1872; July 3, Aug. 8, 12, 1873, RG 393, FG, LS; McConnell, *West Texas Frontier* II, nos. 716, 717, 734, 751, 752, 761, 762.

31. Wooster, *The Military and Indian Policy*, 152–53; Sherman testimony, 43d Cong., 1st sess., H. Rep. 384, pp. 270–84.

32. Sheridan, *Record of Engagements*, 5; Carter, in *On the Border*, 162–96ff., related his participation in the 1871 campaign and produced a detailed but sometimes suspect account. See also Hamilton, *Fort Richardson*, 108–19, 129–33; Richardson, *Comanche Barrier*, 361–65; AG, *Chronological List*, 49, 52.

33. Henry E. Alvord Report, in the "Report of the Commissioner of Indian Affairs," H. Exec. Doc. 1, 42d Cong., 3d sess., serial set 1560, p. 389; Nye, *Carbine and Lance*, 135.

34. Gammel, ed., *Laws of Texas* IX, 179; X, 87; Buell to AAG, Feb. 27, July 30, 1874, RG 393, FG, LS; Webb, *Texas Rangers*, 316–18.

35. Tom McHugh, *Time of the Buffalo*, 247–49, 253.

36. James Winford Hunt, ed., "Buffalo Days: The Chronicle of an Old Buffalo Hunter, J. Wright Mooar," *Holland's: The Magazine of the South* 52 (Jan. 1933): 13, 24; Don Biggers, *Buffalo Guns and Barbed Wire*, 8–11; Robert L. Moore, "Fort Griffin and the Buffalo Sharps," *The American Society of Arms Collectors Bulletin*, No. 52 (April 1985).

37. Biggers, *Buffalo Guns and Barbed Wire*, 7; McHugh, *Time of the Buffalo*, 273; Richard Irving Dodge, *The Hunting Grounds of the Great West*, 133, 143.

38. J. Wright Mooar, "The First Buffalo Hunting in the Panhandle," *WTHAY* 6 (1930): 109–11; Hunt, ed., "The Second Chapter of the Chronicle of J. Wright Mooar," *Holland's*, 52 (Feb. 1933): 10, 44.

39. "Report of the Secretary of War," H. Exec. Doc. 1, 43d Cong., 2d sess., serial set 1635, pp. 28, 40.

40. Sheridan, *Record of Engagements*, 40–45; AG, *Chronological List*, 58.

CHAPTER SIX

1. See list of garrison tenures in RG 94, FG, AG Reservation File, Box 47, Miscellaneous. See various monthly reports in PMH for troop strength.

2. Jacob Howarth, "Letter from an Ex-Soldier," *WTHAY* 2 (1926): 3–7.

3. Ibid.

4. Irwin interview; Lieutenant W. E. Worlow, Report of Buildings, Fort Griffin, Texas, May 31, 1870, RG 92, FG, Correspondence File of Quartermaster General; Hayman to General Potter, Sept. 4, 1868, RG 393, FG, LS; PMH, July 1867.

5. S. B. Holabird to AAAG, Dec. 4, 1872; William W. Belknap, Secretary of War, to House of Representatives, Jan. 14, 1873; Endorsement of General E. O. C. Ord, Nov. 8, 1875, RG 94, AG Reservation File, Box 47, Miscellaneous; Holabird Endorsement, Mar. 25, 1875, RG 92, FG, Correspondence File of Quartermaster General.

6. Report of Condition of Buildings, June 30, 1879, RG 92, FG, Correspondence File of Quartermaster General; Holabird to AAAG, Dec. 4, 1872, RG 94, AG Reservation File, Box 47, Miscellaneous; PMH, Apr. 1871.

7. PMH, Dec. 1869, Jan. 1870.

8. PMH, Nov. 1869, Feb. 1870.

9. PMH, Sept. 1869.

10. PMH, Mar. 1871.

11. Ibid.; "Statement showing the number, names, etc. of persons interred in the Post Cemetery at Fort Griffin, Texas," Apr. 10, 1873, RG 92, FG, Correspondence File of Quartermaster General.

12. PMH, Jan., Mar. 1872.

13. PMH, Sept. 1869; Hamilton, *Fort Richardson*, 122.

14. A. J. Sowell, *Rangers and Pioneers*, 254.

15. PMH, Dec. 1869, May 1870; Notes regarding construction of corral and guardhouse, n.d., RG 92, FG, Correspondence File of Quartermaster General.

16. PMH, Sept., Oct. 1869; Wood to AAG, Aug. 12, 1871, RG 393, FG, LS; "Semi-monthly report of civilians held in confinement," RG 393, FG, Miscellaneous Records; Monthly Reports, July 1869–Dec. 1872, RG 393, FG, Charges and Specifications.

17. PMH, Oct. 1869; *U.S. Census, 1870*, Shackelford County; Matthews, *Interwoven*, 51-52.

18. Hayman to AG, Oct. 1, 1868; Hayman to Colonel Starr, Nov. 2, 1868; Hayman to Commander, Fort Richardson, Feb. 11, 1869, RG 393, FG, LS; Matthews, *Interwoven*, 50-51.

19. Buell, draft of advertisement to the *Express* (San Antonio), Apr. 27, 1873, RG 393, FG, LS; Matthews, *Interwoven*, 50-51.

20. PMH, Dec. 1869, May 1870, Dec. 1874; Haley, *Fort Concho*, 315; McConnell, *Five Years a Cavalryman*, 210.

21. PMH, Sept. 1869; Monthly Reports, Aug. 1869, Apr. 1, 1876, RG 393, FG, Charges and Specifications.

22. Monthly Reports, Nov. 30, 1871; Aug. 16, 1876, RG 393, FG, Charges and Specifications; Buell to AAAG, May 8, 1873, RG 393, FG, LS; Roberts, "Frontier Experiences," 49; Comstock, "Experiences and Observations."

23. Aug. 16, 1871, RG 393, FG, Charges and Specifications.

24. PMH, Dec. 1870; Monthly Reports, Feb. 15, 1871, RG 393, FG, Charges and Specifications.

25. Monthly Reports, Feb. 22, 1875, RG 393, FG, Charges and Specifications.

26. Monthly Reports, Nov. 3, 1874, RG 393, FG, Charges and Specifications; Robert Wooster, *Soldiers, Sutlers, and Settlers: Garrison Life on the Texas Frontier*, 185.

27. Monthly Reports, Aug. 1869, RG 393, FG, Charges and Specifications.

28. Monthly Reports, Nov. 17, 1874, RG 393, FG, Charges and Specifications. See also Appendix 12-5.

29. Monthly Reports, Apr. 21, 1871; Mar. 4, 1873; July 29, Aug. 9, 1875, RG 393, FG, Charges and Specifications.

30. PMH, May, Dec. 1870; Mar., June 1871; Mar. 1872; "Statement showing the number, names, etc. of persons interred in the Post Cemetery at Fort Griffin, Texas," Apr. 10, 1873, RG 92, FG, Correspondence File of Quartermaster General.

31. Llerena Friend, ed., *M. K. Kellogg's Texas Journal, 1872*, 126; Roberts, "Frontier Experiences," 54; PMH, Oct. 1869, Apr. 1870, Mar. 1871; Wood to AAG, Aug. 12, 1871, RG 393, FG, LS.

32. Hayman to AG, July 27, 1868, RG 393, FG, LS.

33. Report of J. G. C. Lee, Oct. 16, 1868, RG 92, FG, Correspondence File of Quartermaster General.

34. Connor, *Peters Colony*, 160-64; Notes regarding efforts to lease land on Survey No. 478, RG 94, FG, AG Reservation File, Box 47, Miscellaneous. These notes acknowledge that "all the buildings at the post are located on Survey No. 478 containing 320 acres." Map illustrating the location of the post and town, both situated on Dowell Survey No. 478, RG 393, FG, Miscellaneous Records.

35. Webb and Grant, contribs., "Joe McCombs," 95-97; PMH, July 1867, Sept. 1869, June 1872; Irwin interview; "Frank E. Conrad," WP.

36. Hayman to AAG, Oct. 1, 1868; Schwann to Quartermaster, Oct. 15, 28, 1874, RG 393, FG, LS; Lieutenant Lewis Warrington to State of Texas, June 5, 1869, RG 393, Proceedings of Boards of Survey; Huckabay, *Ninety-Four Years*, 109; *The Flea* (Jacksboro), Apr. 15, 1869; McConnell, *Five Years a Cavalryman*, 161; Sophie Poe, *Buckboard Days*, 34–39.

37. Howarth, "Letter from an Ex-Soldier," 6; Webb and Grant, contribs., "Joe McCombs," 95–97; Haley, *Fort Concho*, 273; Carter, *On the Border*, 53–54; Aubrey A. Wilson, "A Soldier of the Texas Frontier: Brevet Major Robert Patterson Wilson, United States Army," *WTHAY* 34 (1958): 92; Jerry M. Sullivan, "Fort McKavett," *WTHAY* 45 (1969): 148; AG, *Chronological List*, 48–68ff.

38. Hamilton, *Fort Richardson*, 41–43; Henry H. Strong, *My Frontier Days and Indian Fights on the Plains of Texas*, 80; Huckabay, *Ninety-Four Years*, 109; *Frontier Echo* (Jacksboro), May 18, 1877.

39. Strong, *My Frontier Days*, 80–81; McConnell, *Five Years a Cavalryman*, 160, 296.

40. Howarth, "Letter from an Ex-Soldier," 6; Webb and Grant, contribs., "Joe McCombs," 95–97; Newcomb Diary, entry of Susan Newcomb, Jan. 28, 1871.

41. Friend, ed., *Kellogg's Journal*, 127; Anne M. Butler, *Daughters of Joy, Sisters of Misery: Prostitutes in the American West, 1865–1890*, 150–55.

42. Hayman to Sub-Assistant Commissioner, June 30, 1868; Wood to AAG, Dec. 1871, RG 393, FG, LS; Monthly Report, Aug. 1869, RG 393, FG, Charges and Specifications.

43. Biggers, *Shackelford County Sketches*, 41; PMH, May 1872; Reynolds interview; Webb, "Life of Phin Reynolds," 122; Rister, *Fort Griffin*, 129–32; John Creaton, "John Creaton: An Autobiography, 1856–1932," MS, CAH.

44. *U.S. Census, 1870*, Shackelford County; Wood to AAAG, Sept. 28, 1872, RG 393, FG, LS.

45. Wood to AAG, Feb. 20, 1872; Buell to AAG, Apr. 5, 1873, RG 393, FG, LS; PMH, Nov. 1874; Irwin interview.

46. W. G. Veal to C. K. Stribling and G. A. Kirkland, June 14, 1875, SP; Walker, *Compendium of the 1870 Census*, 435–37 (figures do not include Throckmorton County, which posted no returns in 1870); *U.S. Census, 1870*, Shackelford and Stephens counties; Hayman to Sub-Assistant Commissioner, June 30, 1868, RG 393, FG, LS.

47. *U.S. Census, 1870*, Shackelford and Stephens counties.

48. Monthly Reports, July 17, Oct. 23, 1875, RG 393, FG, Charges and Specifications; Buell to AAG, Jan. 23, 1874, RG 393, FG, LS.

49. Marcy, *On the Border*, 174; Hamilton, *Fort Richardson*, 21; McConnell, *Five Years a Cavalryman*, 49–50, 146; PMH, May 1872; Hayman to AAAG, July 30, 1868, RG 393, FG, LS.

50. Marcy, *On the Border*, 174–78.

51. Roberts, "Frontier Experiences, 57; References to various correspondence attesting to the Tonkawas' capture of horses from the Comanches, Sept. 21, 1875; Feb. 12, 14, 1874, RG 393, FG, Miscellaneous Records, Tonkawa Indian Scouts; Marcy, *On the Border*, 178; McConnell, *Five Years a Cavalryman*, 60.

52. Thomas Frank Schilz, "People of the Cross Timbers: A History of the Tonkawa Indians" (Ph.D. diss., Texas Christian University, Fort Worth, 1983), 196; Matthews, *Interwoven*, 46; Berta Hart Nance, "D. A. Nance and the Tonkawa Indians," *WTHAY* 28 (1952): 89–90; Friend, ed., *Kellogg's Journal*, 123–24; Mrs. George Wilhelm and Ida Grace to Etta Soule, Mar. 31, 1942, SL, NC.

53. Matthews, *Interwoven*, 46; Friend, ed., *Kellogg's Journal*, 130; Nance, "Nance and the Tonkawas," 90; Order issued by Buell, Sept. 14, 1873, RG 393, FG, Miscellaneous Records, Tonkawa Indian Scouts; Kenneth F. Neighbours, "Tonkawa Scouts and Guides," *WTHAY* 49 (1973): 98.

54. Nance, "Nance and the Tonkawas," 91–92; Thomas W. Dunlay, *Wolves for the Blue Soldiers: Indian Scouts and Auxiliaries with the United States Army, 1860–1890*, 119.

55. *Albany News*, June 14, 1978.

56. *Dallas Morning News*, Aug. 26, 1928.

57. Richard Henry Pratt, *Battlefield and Classroom: Four Decades with the American Indian, 1867–1904*, ed. Robert M. Utley, 55–56.

58. Friend, ed., *Kellogg's Journal*, 127; Schilz, "History of the Tonkawas," 189, 192, 196–97; Marcy, *On the Border*, 377–79; Dunlay, *Wolves for the Blue Soldiers*, 72.

59. List of "effects belonging to 'William' (Chil-la-iso), who died at Hueco Tanks," Feb. 14, 1873, Buell to AAG, June 1, 1873; Captain E. M. Heyl to AAG, June 24, 1875, unsigned, undated report regarding the death of "William," RG 393, FG, Miscellaneous Records, Tonkawa Indian Scouts.

CHAPTER SEVEN

1. Friend, ed., *Kellogg's Journal*, 128–33; Frank Collinson, *Life in the Saddle*, ed. Mary Whatley Clarke, 134; McConnell, *Five Years a Cavalryman*, 46–47; C. U. Connellee, "Some Experiences of a Pioneer Surveyor," *WTHAY* 6 (1930): 90–91; Reynolds interview; John R. Cook, *The Border and the Buffalo: An Untold Story of the Southwest Plains*, 168.

2. Biggers, *Buffalo Guns and Barbed Wire*, 169; Roberts, "Frontier Experiences," 47, 56; Jack Elgin, "Christmas Dinner on the Upper Brazos in 1872," *WTHAY* 14 (1938): 86.

3. *Dallas Morning News*, Aug. 26, 1928; Elgin, "Christmas Dinner, 1872," 88–89.

4. Friend, ed., *Kellogg's Journal*, 123; Comstock, "Experiences and Observations"; Roberts, "Frontier Experiences," 47.

5. Buell to AAG, June 29, 1873, RG 393, FG, LS; S. S. McKay, "Economic Conditions in Texas in the 1870s," *WTHAY* 15 (1939): 97; Friend, ed., *Kellogg's Journal*, 3–4; Walter Prescott Webb, "A Texas Buffalo Hunt with Original Photos," *Holland's Magazine*, Oct. 1927, pp. 10–11.

6. See Stribling Papers.

7. Stribling to M. Hurley, July 31, 1873, Stribling to W. R. Friend, Aug. 15, 1873, SP.

8. Irwin interview; Buell to AAG, Apr. 5, 1873, RG 393, FG, LS.

9. Kirkland to Dowell, May 4, 1874, SP.

10. Wood to AAG, Feb. 20, 1872, RG 393, FG, LS; Special Warranty Deed, Patent No. 478, conveyed to D. M. Dowell, Louisville, Ky., June 1, 1858, Deed Records, Shackelford County, Texas, Vol. B, p. 136; Kirkland to Dowell, May 4, 1874, SP.

11. Kirkland to Dowell, May 4, 1874; Stribling and Kirkland to Dowell, Oct. 7, 12, 1874, SP.

12. Dowell to Stribling and Kirkland, Apr. 26, 1875; Stribling and Kirkland to Dowell, Oct. 7, Nov. 21, 1874, SP; Circular, Feb. 9, 1875; Buell to AAG, Feb. 26, 1875; Buell to AG, Nov. 5, 1875, RG 393, FG, LS.

13. Stribling and Kirkland to Dowell, Oct. 11, 1874, SP; Schwann to AAG, Oct. 14, 1874, RG 393, FG, LS; PMH, Nov. 1874; Irwin interview.

14. Copy of Dowell lease, signed by S. B. Holabird, Quartermaster, Fort Griffin, Texas, May 6, 1875, RG 92, FG, Correspondence File of Quartermaster General; Circular issued by Buell, Feb. 5, 1875; Circular issued by Buell, Feb. 9, 1875; Buell to AG, Nov. 5, 1875, RG 393, FG, LS; Howarth, "Letter from an Ex-Soldier," 6.

15. Minutes of Commissioner's Court, Shackelford County, Vol. A, pp. 1–14, 17–18, 22, 28–29, 49–50, 86–93; Herron interview.

16. *Frontier Echo* (Jacksboro), Dec. 3, 31, 1875.

17. Biggers, *Buffalo Guns and Barbed Wire*, 13–14; Hunt, ed., "Mooar," 5, 22. Biggers mistakenly set the date at 1873, a year earlier than the hunters' arrival.

18. Frank M. Sherrod to J. Evetts Haley, Oct. 20, 1926, PPM; Wayne Gard, *The Great Buffalo Hunt*, 189–90; Marvin Shultz, "Hunters' Frontier: Exterminating the American Bison in the Concho River Region," *Fort Concho Report* 20 (Spring 1988): 11; Collinson, *Life in the Saddle*, 44–45; Webb and Grant, contribs., "Joe McCombs," 97–98.

19. Hunt, ed., "Mooar," 5, 22; Biggers, *Buffalo Guns and Barbed Wire*, 17–19; Cook, *Border and the Buffalo*, 128, 134.

20. Don Worcester, *The Chisholm Trail: High Road of the Cattle Kingdom*, 135–36; Wayne Gard, *The Chisholm Trail*, 227–31ff; Jimmy M. Skaggs, *The Cattle-Trailing Industry: Between Supply and Demand, 1866–1890*, 104–108; Joseph Nimmo, Jr., *Report in Regard to the Range and Ranch Cattle Business of the United States*, 27.

21. Skaggs, *Cattle-Trailing Industry*, 15–17, 90; Collinson, *Life in the Saddle*, 31, 35; *Frontier Echo* (Jacksboro), July 21, 1876; *Fort Worth Daily Democrat*, July 29, 1876.

22. Harold U. Faulkner, *American Economic History*, 515–16; Ray Ginger, *Age of Excess: The United States from 1877 to 1914*, 43; Felix Fruger and Harold U. Faulkner, *Readings in the Economic and Social History of the United States*, 685–90; Knight, *Outpost on the Trinity*, 85; Buell to AAAG, May 9, 1873, RG 393, FG, LS; Poe, *Buckboard Days*, 34–39.

23. *Frontier Echo* (Jacksboro), July 7, 1875; Feb. 4, 1876; *Fort Griffin Echo*, July 26, 1879; Herron interview.

24. Gammel, ed., *Laws of Texas* VIII, 31–32, 74–80, 144–49; J. L. Sellers to Stribling and Kirkland, May 12, 1875, Feb. 12, 1876, SP; McKay, "Economic Conditions," 118; *Frontier Echo* (Jacksboro), Oct. 13, 1876.

25. W. R. Baker to Stribling and Kirkland, Sept. 28, 1877, S. H. Darden, Comptroller, State of Texas, to Stribling and Kirkland, Jan. 16, 1875; C. R. Johns & Co., Texas Land Agency, Banking and Exchange, to Stribling and Kirkland, Jan. 22, 1875; D. D. Rosborough, State Representative, to Stribling, Jan. 15, 1875, SP.

26. *Frontier Echo* (Jacksboro), Sept. 29, 1876; Jan. 5, Mar. 2, 1877; Feb. 1, 1878; Stribling and Kirkland to S. J. Swenson, Nov. 21, 1876; Mar. 8, 15, 1878, SP; James T. Padgitt, "Early Days in Coleman," *WTHAY* 28 (1962): 63; Ruby L. Smith, "Early Days in Wilbarger County," *WTHAY* 14 (1938): 81.

27. *Frontier Echo* (Jacksboro), July 7, 21, Nov. 12, 1875; Aug. 11, Sept. 15, Nov. 3, 1876; Gammel, ed., *Laws of Texas* VIII, 1075.

28. *Frontier Echo* (Jacksboro), Apr. 14, Sept. 8, 1876; Feb. 8, 1878; Phin Reynolds to Webb, Jan. 21, 1947, WP; *Fort Worth Daily Democrat*, Sept. 14, 1876.

29. Buell to AAG, Apr. 5, 1873, RG 393, FG, LS; Biggers, *Buffalo Guns and Barbed Wire*, x-xi; Biggers, *Shackelford County Sketches*, 39; "Official Registry of Shackelford County and Griffin, Business Directory, Stribling and Kirkland, Land Agents, Fort Griffin, Texas," n.d., copy, NA.

30. *Fort Worth Daily Democrat*, Jan. 25, 1877; Notes of J. R. Webb, from Henry Herron interviews, compiled Sept. 29, 1939, WP; Veal to Stribling and Kirkland, June 14, 1875, SP; Miss Aught M. Ceil, comp., "Combination Map of the Town of Fort Griffin, Texas," n.d., map file, NC.

31. *Galveston Daily News*, June 6, 1876; Biggers, *Buffalo Guns and Barbed Wire*, 32; Irwin interview; James H. Cook, *Fifty Years on the Old Frontier*, 86.

32. Rex W. Strickland, ed., "The Recollections of W. S. Glenn," *Panhandle-Plains Historical Review* 22 (1949): 40-41; *Fort Worth Daily Democrat*, Jan. 25, Feb. 22, 1877; F. E. Conrad to Stribling, Aug. 8, 1877, SP.

33. McKay, "Economic Conditions," 108; Collinson, *Life in the Saddle*, 31; Strickland, ed., "W. S. Glenn," 22; Ben O. Grant, "Early History of Shackelford County" (M.A. thesis, Hardin-Simmons University, Abilene, Texas, 1934), 70; Biggers, *Buffalo Guns and Barbed Wire*, 28; Hunt, ed., "Buffalo Days: The Killing of the White Buffalo," *Holland's: The Magazine of the South* 52 (May 1933): 11; Herron, interview.

34. *Frontier Echo* (Jacksboro), Mar. 24, Oct. 27, 1876; Cook, *Border and the Buffalo*, 128, 133-34, 137.

35. Strickland, ed., "W. S. Glenn," 45; Cook, *Border and the Buffalo*, 185-86, 200; Webb, "Frank Conrad," WP; Naomi H. Kincaid, "Rath City," *WTHAY* 24 (1948): 40-46.

36. *Frontier Echo* (Jacksboro), July 21, Sept. 22, 1876; Feb. 16, Nov. 2, 1877; *Fort Worth Daily Democrat*, Sept. 22, 1876; Biggers, *Buffalo Guns and Barbed Wire*, 20, 32; Strickland, ed., "W. S. Glenn," 50; Hunt, ed., "White Buffalo," 12; Webb and Grant, contribs., "Joe McCombs," 99-100.

37. Cook, *Border and the Buffalo*, 188-95ff.; T. S. Lee, Commander to AAG, Mar. 8, 1877, RG 393, FG, LS; Strickland, ed., "W. S. Glenn," 44-46.

38. Lee to AG, May 25, 1877, RG 393, FG, LS. Three accounts by participants at the Yellow House Canyon fight offer varying interpretations. See Collinson, *Life in the Saddle*, 101-106; Strickland, ed., "W. S. Glenn," 43-63; Cook *Border and the Buffalo*, 202-32ff.

39. Lee to AG, May 25, 1877, RG 393, FG, LS.

40. Cook, *Border and the Buffalo*, 241–43.

41. Cook, *Border and the Buffalo*, 125; Herron interview.

42. Biggers, *Buffalo Guns and Barbed Wire*, 31; Cook, *Border and the Buffalo*, 134–37; *Frontier Echo* (Jacksboro), Nov. 2, 1877

43. Cook, *Border and the Buffalo*, 132, 166–67; J. Wright Mooar, "Frontier Experiences of J. Wright Mooar," *WTHAY* 5 (1929): 92.

44. Strickland, ed., "W. S. Glenn," 41; Conrad to Stribling, Aug. 8, 1877; Stribling and Kirkland to A. Goldstein and Co., July 12, 1878, SP.

45. Webb and Grant, contribs., "Joe McCombs," 100; *Frontier Echo* (Jacksboro), Oct. 18, 1878; *Fort Worth Daily Democrat*, May 8, 23, 1878; *Fort Griffin Echo*, July 12, 1879. The number of cowboys visiting Griffin was estimated by considering the volume of cattle traffic and the number of drovers and others who pushed the herds to market. Edward Everett Dale, in *Range Cattle Industry*, 62, contended that an optimum-sized herd was 2,500. Walter Prescott Webb, in *The Great Plains*, 262–68, commented that trailing outfits normally required one man for every 175 cattle; a cook and a wrangler accompanied every outfit.

46. Skaggs, *Cattle Trailing Industry*, pp. 87–88; Worcester, *Chisholm Trail*, 122–36; Jesse Gregory "Jet" Kenan to Soule, Oct. 24, 1945, SL.

47. *Fort Worth Daily Democrat*, Apr. 18, May 8, 23, 1878; *Fort Griffin Echo*, Apr. 19, May 24, 31, 1879.

48. *Fort Worth Daily Democrat*, Feb. 17, Apr. 4, 1877; Feb. 26, Mar. 7, Apr. 17, May 10, June 25, 1879; *Fort Griffin Echo*, Apr. 19, 26, May 17, 24, 31, Aug. 9, 1879; Wayne Gard, *Chisholm Trail*, 253.

49. *Frontier Echo* (Jacksboro), June 22, Aug. 24, 1877; Mar. 15, 1878.

50. Dowell to Stribling and Kirkland, Nov. 12, 1878, SP.

51. *Frontier Echo* (Jacksboro), Oct. 18, 1878; Stribling and Kirkland, "A Description of Shackelford County, Texas," Mar. 8, 1877 (circular), NC.

CHAPTER EIGHT

1. *Frontier Echo* (Jacksboro), July 27, Aug. 31, 1877.

2. *Fort Worth Daily Democrat*, Dec. 19, 1876; *Frontier Echo* (Jacksboro), Nov. 10, 1876; *Dallas Daily Herald*, Jan. 24, 1877.

3. James D. McCabe, "Pittsburg Riot of 1877," in Richard Maxwell Brown, ed., *Violence in America*, 85–89; *Frontier Echo* (Jacksboro), Aug. 16, 1879; *Dallas Daily Herald*, July 20, 1877; *Fort Worth Daily Democrat*, Aug. 10, 1877.

4. PMH, Mar. 1875; "Special Report of N. H. Davis," Inspector General, June 23, 1875, RG 92, FG, Correspondence File of Quartermaster General.

5. Circular issued by Buell, Feb. 5, 1875, RG 393, FG, LS; *Daily Cresset* (Denison, Texas), Oct. 27, 1875; Ben O. Grant, "Life in Old Fort Griffin," *WTHAY* 10 (1934): 37; Biggers, *Shackelford County Sketches*, 43; *Frontier Echo* (Jacksboro), Jan. 17, 1876.

6. See various cases filed 1st and 2d terms, 1875, District Court Minutes, Book A, 12th Judicial District Court, Shackelford County, Texas (hereafter cited as District Court).

7. Ibid.; file envelope, case no. 27, filed 1st term, 1875, District Court Papers (separate from District Court book). A number of envelopes containing papers from criminal cases (tried by the District Court) between 1875 and 1880 are extant; they are neither organized nor complete and are kept in two small file drawers in the Shackelford County courthouse.

8. See various cases filed 1st and 2d terms, 1876, District Court; Kenan to Soule, Sept. 15, 1945, SL.

9. *Fort Griffin Echo*, May 10, June 7, 1879; W. C. Holden, ed., *Rollie Burns; or, An Account of the Ranching Industry on the South Plains*, 54–55; Biggers, *Shackelford County Sketches*, 39; James Kimmins Greer, *Bois d'Arc to Barb'd Wire: Ken Cary, Southwestern Frontier Born*, 329.

10. J. W. Woody to Haley, Oct. 19, 1926; Jim Gordon to Haley, Feb. 1923, PPM.

11. Case no. 74, filed 2d term, 1876, District Court; Stribling and Kirkland, "Official Registry," NC; Herron interview with Webb, July 17, 1940; Phin Reynolds interview with Webb, 1945, WP; Kenan to Soule, Jan. 8, 1946, SL.

12. James W. Grahame, "Tales of the Texas Border," MS, 37–38, TSA. Grahame's reminiscences were full of errors; in this case he confused Fort Griffin with Jacksboro.

13. Herron interview with Webb, July 17, 1940, WP; Phillip D. Jordan, "Lady Luck," in *Frontier Law and Order: Ten Essays*, 53–54.

14. *Dallas Daily Herald*, Aug. 3, 1877; Kenan to Soule Jan. 28, 1946, SL.

15. Butler, *Sisters of Misery*, 42, 51–52, 55, 61–62, 67, 114–15, 150–55; *Fort Griffin Echo*, Jan. 25, 1879.

16. Butler, *Sisters of Misery*, 150–55; *Tenth U.S. Census, 1880*, Schedule I, Population, Texas, XXVIII (microfilm), Shackelford County, pp. 452–79, reel no. 1604; see District Court Index (separate volume from District Court book) for entries regarding William Martin; Herron interview; Reynolds interview; George Newcomb, Flood File, NC; Texas Ranger Lieutenant G. W. Campbell to Major John B. Jones, Apr. 3, 1878, AG Files, TSA.

17. Case no. 8, filed Nov. 1876, County Court; case no. 8, filed 1st term 1875, cases nos. 160, 161, 162, filed 1st term, 1879, District Court; *Frontier Echo* (Jacksboro), Jan. 14, 1875; June 30, 1876; *Dallas Daily Herald*, Apr. 23, 1876; Kenan to Soule Oct. 27, 1946, SL; Herron interview with Robert Nail, n.d., Map File, NC; Herron interview with Webb, July 17, 1940, WP; *Fort Worth Daily Democrat*, Sept. 22, 1876.

18. Four letters in the Stribling Papers established Deno's true identity: Stribling and Kirkland to William E. Friedlander, Oct. 2, Nov. 4, 1878, and Kirkland to Stribling, Apr. 2, 14, 1879. The Shackelford County Index to Real Property Records shows that Charlotte J. Tompkins leased lots "4 & 5, Blk 33" in the town of Fort Griffin, Mar. 15, 1878. She had purchased three other lots in 1877. In 1878 a county court judgment compelled her to turn over land to George Matthews and one "Wilson." See also Matthews, *Interwoven*, 109–10.

19. John Jacobs to Hunter, ca. 1927, in J. Marvin Hunter, *Lottie Deno: Her Life and Times*, 37; *Frontier Echo* (Jacksboro), Mar. 10, 1876; J. Evetts Haley interview with John Jacobs, Feb. 27, 1932, NMHL; Robert Nail interview with

Henry Herron, Sept. 20, 1939, NC; Herron interview with Webb, Apr. 8, 1941, WP; *Dallas Daily Herald,* Aug. 3, 1877; Stribling and Kirkland, "Official Registry," NC.

20. Butler, *Sisters of Misery,* 106; cases nos. 22, 26, 29, filed Jan., case no. 38, filed May 1878, County Court.

21. Stribling and Kirkland to William E. Friedlander, Oct. 2, Nov. 4, 1878; Kirkland to Stribling, Apr. 2, 14, 1879, SP.

22. J. Evetts Haley, *Jeff Milton: A Good Man with a Gun,* 20; Biggers, *Shackelford County Sketches,* 41–42, 91; Hutto, "Aunt Hank Smith," 42.

23. Case no. 17, 1st term, 1875; case no. 38, 2d term, 1875; cases nos. 59, 62, 1st term, 1876; cases nos. 87, 92, 1st term, 1877; case no. 124, 1st term, 1878; case no. 132, 2d term, 1878; cases nos. 154, 170, 1st term, 1879; case no. 180, 1st term, 1880, District Court; *Fort Griffin Echo,* June 14, 1879.

24. Case no. 62, 1st term, 1876, District Court; *Jacksboro Frontier Echo,* Dec. 24, 31, 1875.

25. Case no. 132, 2d term, 1878, District Court; *Jacksboro Frontier Echo,* Oct. 4, 18, 1878.

26. *Fort Griffin Echo,* Apr. 12, July 12, Aug. 2, 1879; case no. 170, filed 2d term, 1879, District Court.

27. Biggers, *Shackelford County Sketches,* 44; *Fort Worth Daily Democrat,* Jan. 26, 1877; Cook, *Border and the Buffalo,* 200–201, 233–34.

28. *Frontier Echo* (Jacksboro), Aug. 4, 1875; Feb. 22, 1878; *Fort Griffin Echo,* Jan. 4, 1879; see cases filed in various terms of both County Court and District Court, in particular, case no. 85, filed 1st term, and cases nos. 94, 105, 111, filed 2d term, 1877, District Court.

29. File envelope, case no. 21, n.d., District Court (misnumbered in District Court book); cases nos. 13, 14, 16, filed 1st term, 1875; case no. 71, filed 1st term, 1876; case no. 72, filed 2d term, 1876; cases nos. 16, 17, filed 1st term, 1877; District Court; case no. 31, 1879, County Court; Leon Claire Metz, *John Selman: Texas Gunfighter,* 79–80; Frank Collinson, "Jim White: Teamster, Buffalo Hunter, and Frontiersman, 1855–1881," MS, 1937, Frank Collinson Collection, PPM; S. P. Merry to Haley, Aug. 21, 1926, PPM; *Fort Worth Daily Democrat,* Sept. 22, 1876; Apr. 28, 1877; *Dallas Daily Herald,* July 20, 1877.

30. Herron interview; Roberts, "Frontier Experiences," 52; Connellee, "Experiences of a Pioneer Surveyor," 89.

31. *Frontier Echo* (Jacksboro), Jan. 19, 1877; Reynolds interview; *Dallas Daily Herald,* Jan. 24, 1877; Hutto, "Aunt Hank Smith," 42; Webb interview with Newton Joseph Jones, Mar. 15, 1947, WP (hereafter cited as Newt Jones interview).

32. Herron interview with Webb; Reynolds interview.

33. Kenan to Soule, Oct. 24, 1945, SP; Herron interview; see cases nos. 2, 3, 4, 17, 27, 35, filed 1st term, 1875; cases nos. 40, 42, 50, 51, 57, filed 2d term, 1875; case no. 58, filed 1st term, 1876; cases nos. 71, 76, 79, 80, filed 2d term, 1876; case no. 82, filed 1st term, 1877; case no. 102, filed 2d term, 1877; case no. 121, filed 1st term, 1878; case no. 128, filed 2d term, 1878; cases nos. 158, 159, filed 1st term, 1879, District Court.

34. Kenan to Soule, Oct. 24, 1945, SP; *Fort Worth Daily Democrat*, Sept. 22, 1876; *Dallas Daily Herald*, Aug. 3, 1877; Herron to Webb, Sept. 23, 1940, WP.

35. Grant, "Early History of Shackelford County," 77–78; *Fort Worth Daily Democrat*, Sept. 22, 1876.

36. Alwyn Barr, *Black Texans: A History of Negroes in Texas, 1528–1971*, 83–84; *Fort Griffin Echo*, Mar. 15, 1879.

37. Case no. 154, filed 1st term, 1879, District Court; *Fort Griffin Echo*, May 3, 24, 1879; Matthews, *Interwoven*, 115.

38. Cook, *The Border and the Buffalo*, 148–49.

39. J. M. Gordon to Haley, July 16, 1926, PPM.

40. Kenan to Soule, Sept. 15, 1945; Jan. 8, 1946, SP.

41. *Frontier Echo* (Jacksboro), Feb. 18, 1876.

42. *Fort Griffin Echo*, Aug. 16, 30, 1879; May 22, June 19, 1880.

43. *Fort Worth Daily Democrat*, Sept. 2, 1876.

44. Kenan to Soule, Jan. 8, 25, 1946, SP.

45. *Fort Griffin Echo*, Apr. 5, 1879.

46. *Fort Griffin Echo*, Jan. 11, Apr. 12, 1879.

47. *Frontier Echo* (Jacksboro), Oct. 25, 1878; *Fort Worth Daily Democrat*, July 19, 1877.

CHAPTER NINE

1. For other interpretations of this affair, see Metz, *John Selman*, 57–95, and C. L. Sonnichsen, *I'll Die Before I'll Run: The Story of the Great Feuds of Texas*, 150–66.

2. Richard Maxwell Brown, *Strain of Violence: Historical Studies of American Violence and Vigilantism*, 246–47; *Houston Telegram* article reprinted in *Frontier Echo* (Jacksboro), Mar. 8, 1878.

3. *Frontier Echo* (Jacksboro), May 19, 1876; Brown, *Strain of Violence*, 248–50, 317–18.

4. Commissioner's Court, 67, 112; Lieutenant Shipman to Post Adjutant, Apr. 11, 1876, RG 393, FG, LS; Pratt, *Battlefield and Classroom*, 59–60.

5. *Frontier Echo* (Jacksboro), Apr. 14, 28, 1876; *Dallas Daily Herald*, Apr. 23, 1876; *Fort Worth Daily Democrat*, Apr. 26, 1876.

6. *Frontier Echo* (Jacksboro), Apr. 14, 28, May 12, 1876; *Fort Worth Daily Democrat*, Apr. 26, 1876.

7. *Frontier Echo* (Jacksboro), Apr. 28, 1876.

8. Cases nos. 1, 5, 19, 24, 28, 37, filed 1st term, 1875, District Court. Board-certified trial attorney Tom Hall of Fort Worth proposed the argument for jury nullification.

9. *Frontier Echo* (Jacksboro), May 12, 1876.

10. Ibid., June 9, 1876.

11. Cases nos. 60, 63, 64, 65, 66, 67, 68, 69, 70, 72, filed 1st term, 1876, District Court; Shipman to Post Adjutant, Apr. 11, 1876, RG 393, FG, LS; *Frontier Echo* (Jacksboro), Apr. 28, June 9, 1876.

12. Hutto, "Aunt Hank Smith," 42; Howarth, "Letter From an Ex-Soldier," 6; Herron interview; Collinson, *Life in the Saddle*, 67–68.

13. *Frontier Echo* (Jacksboro), Nov. 10, 1876; *Fort Worth Daily Democrat*, Dec. 19, 1876.

14. A. C. Williams, "Cattle Raisers Association of Texas: Something of Its History," *The Cattleman* 10 (Mar. 1915): 13-14; Biggers, *Buffalo Guns and Barbed Wire*, 160-61; *Frontier Echo* (Jacksboro), Mar. 30, 1877.

15. *Weekly State Gazette* (Austin), Dec. 28, 1876.

16. Ibid.; Commissioners Court, 67, 112; Records of Official Bonds, Vol. B, 54-63, Shackelford County; Stribling and Kirkland, "Official Registry"; Emmett Roberts, "Frontier Experiences," 46-48; Newt Jones interview.

17. *Frontier Echo* (Jacksboro), Aug. 18, 1876; Tom Crum, "Camp Cooper, A Different Look," *WTHAY* 68 (1992): 68-69.

18. John Meadows interview with J. Evetts Haley, June 13, 1935, NHML; Reynolds interview; Newt Jones interview; Campbell to Jones, June 16, 1878, AG Files, TSA; *Galveston Daily News*, July 13, 1878.

19. Herron interview; telephone interview with Ramona Thompson, genealogist, South Solon, Ohio, by author, Oct. 14, 1991; Matthews, *Interwoven*, 136; Biggers, *Shackelford County Sketches*, 46-47; transactions involving James A. Brock, Shackelford County Index to Real Property Records, Vol. A, 114, 185, 209, 226, Vol. D, 661; *Madison County Democrat* (Ohio), July 8, 1891; *Frontier Echo* (Jacksboro), Jan. 28, Feb. 4, 1876; Mar. 30, 1877.

20. *Semi-Weekly Enterprise (London, Ohio), July 24, 1891; El Paso Times*, July 1, 1891; Matthews, *Interwoven*, 136-38; *The Nickel Plate* (London, Ohio), July 2, 1891; Herron interview.

21. Herron interview; Frank Collinson, "A Frontier Tragedy," *Albany News*, June 26, 1952, pp. 1, 10, reprinted from an article in a ca. 1935 series of reminiscences entitled "Range Romances," clippings file, NC; Biggers, *Shackelford County Sketches*, 47; *Madison County Democrat* (Ohio), July 8, 1891.

22. Herron interview; Biggers, *Shackelford County Sketches*, 47-48.

23. Cases nos. 108-10, filed 2d term, 1877, District Court; Meadows interview with Haley; John C. Jacobs to J. A. Matthews, Dec. 23, 1929, NHML; Grant, "Early History of Shackelford County," 89.

24. Cases nos. 25, 108, 109, 110, filed 2d term, 1877; case no. 175, filed 1st term, 1880, District Court; *Madison County Democrat* (Ohio), July 1, 8, 1891; Herron interview; Collinson, "A Frontier Tragedy," 10.

25. Cases nos. 93, 97, 100, 103, 107, 110, 112, filed 2d term, 1877; cases nos. 113-16, 120, filed 1st term, 1878; cases nos. 127, 131, 137, 138, 140-45, 147-49, filed 2d term, 1878, District Court.

26. For a good summary of the situation facing the Texas Rangers during this period, see W. P. Webb's *The Texas Rangers*, 307-42. Grant, "Early History of Shackelford County," 89; Newt Jones interview; *Frontier Echo* (Jacksboro), Aug. 18, 1876.

27. Newt Jones interview; Irwin interview; Campbell to Jones, Feb. 26, June 16, 1878, AG Files, TSA; *Galveston Daily News*, July 13, 1878.

28. J. R. Fleming to R. B. Hubbard, May 1, 1878; Campbell to Jones, Apr. 3, June 16, 1878, AG Files, TSA.

29. Sergeant V. E. Van Riper to Jones, June 15, 1878, AG Files, TSA.

30. Campbell to Jones, June 16, 1878, AG Files, TSA.

31. Newt Jones interview.

32. Phin Reynolds interview with Webb, n.d., in "Frontier History Notes"; Phin Reynolds to Webb, 1945, n.p.; Irwin interview; *Frontier Echo* (Jacksboro), July 5, 1878. No other single incident in the Clear Fork's history has provoked as much controversy as Larn's execution. Frank Collinson (*Life in the Saddle*, 96), to cite just one example, claimed that a relative of Larn's "put a mercy shot close to [his] head to make sure he was dead." In the brief (41 pp.) and myopic *John Larn*, Joe Blanton claimed to have produced the inquest papers that probed the slaying. The report seemed to cast doubt on much hearsay, such as that of Collinson's, but other details are certainly of dubious value. Whether the witnesses participated in the murder, were sympathetic to the vigilantes, or were cowed by them, their testimony cannot be considered reliable.

33. Newt Jones interview; Phin Reynolds interview with Webb, 1945.

34. Jones to Lieutenant G. W. Arrington, July 13, 1878; Arrington to Jones, Aug. 31, 1878, AG Files, TSA.

35. *Fort Griffin Echo*, May 17, 1879.

36. *Madison County Democrat* (Ohio), July 8, 1891; *Semi-Weekly Enterprise* (London, Ohio), July 3, 1891; *The Nickel Plate* (London, Ohio), July 2, 1891; telephone interview with Arlene Rainey (Woosley descendant), Benton, Arkansas, by author, Fort Worth, Texas, Aug. 6, 1991.

36. Herron interview; Biggers, *Sketches*, 48–49; Collinson, "A Frontier Tragedy;" *Madison County Democrat* (Ohio), July 1, July 8, 1891.

37. *Madison County Democrat* (Ohio), July 8, 1891; *The Nickel Plate* (London, Ohio), July 2, 1891.

38. *Madison County Democrat* (Ohio), July 8, 1891; *Semi-Weekly Enterprise* (London, Ohio), July 3, 1891.

39. *Madison County Democrat* (Ohio), July 8, 1891; *Semi-Weekly Enterprise* (London, Ohio), July 3, 1891; *The Nickel Plate* (London, Ohio), July 2, 1891.

40. *Madison County Democrat* (Ohio), July 8, 1891; *El Paso Times*, July 1, 1891; *Semi-Weekly Enterprise* (London, Ohio), July 3, 1891.

CHAPTER TEN

1. Biggers, *Buffalo Guns and Barbed Wire*, 27; Cook, *Border and the Buffalo*, 115.

2. Cook, *Border and the Buffalo*, 122–23.

3. Ibid., 128, 139–41, 148–49.

4. Kenan to Soule, Feb. 8, 1946, SL; Cook, *Border and the Buffalo*, 115; Biggers, *Buffalo Guns and Barbed Wire*, 26, 36–38, 40.

5. Herron interview; Biggers, *Buffalo Guns and Barbed Wire*, 43.

6. Cook, *Border and the Buffalo*, 79–81; Boley, ed., *Dumont*, 24. For an excellent essay comparing the experience of Dumont to other pioneer women, see Emily Cutrer's introduction in *Dumont*, ix–xvii. See also Jeffrey, Frontier Women, 79–106ff.; Myres, Westering Women, 167–212ff.

7. Carl Coke Rister, *Southern Plainsman*, 68–69; Boley, ed., *Dumont*, 24, 44–45; Myres, *Westering Women*, 141–46.

8. *Dallas Daily Herald,* July 20, 1877.

9. *Fort Worth Daily Democrat,* Aug. 10, 1877.

10. Deed Records, Shackelford County, vol. D, 157; *Fort Worth Daily Democrat,* Jan. 24, 1879; *Fort Griffin Echo,* Jan. 25, Feb. 22, Apr. 12, 1879.

11. *Fort Griffin Echo,* July 5, Oct. 4, 1879.

12. *Fort Griffin Echo,* Dec. 13, 20, 1879; Jan. 3, Dec. 25, 1880.

13. *Fort Griffin Echo,* Aug. 9, 1879.

14. Wilhelm and Grace to Soule, Apr. 6, 20, 1942, SL; Reynolds interview.

15. *Fort Griffin Echo,* Apr. 12, 1879.

16. Wilhelm and Grace to Soule, Mar. 31, 1942; Mar. 4, 1943, SL.

17. Wilhelm and Grace to Soule, Mar. 14, 1942; W. B. Champlin to Soule, Jan. 30, June 20, 1944, SL; *Fort Griffin Echo,* Jan. 18, 1879; Mrs. J. W. George interview with Joan Farmer, ca. 1950s, NC.

18. Wilhelm and Grace to Soule, Mar. 4, 1943, SL; *Fort Griffin Echo,* May 15, 1880.

19. *Fort Griffin Echo,* Jan. 11, Oct. 4, 1879; Jan. 7, 1882; George Newcomb, Flood File, NC; Champlin to Soule, Jan. 30, 1944, F. B. Conrad to Soule, Fall 1941; Feb. 16, 1942, SL.

20. Wilhelm and Grace to Soule, Apr. 6, Aug. 4, 1942, SL.

21. *U.S. Census, 1880,* Shackelford County; *Frontier Echo* (Jacksboro), Mar. 15, 1878; Hutto, "Aunt Hank Smith," 41; Kenan to Soule, Feb. 8, 1946, SL; Stribling and Kirkland, "Official Registry."

22. Kenan to Soule, Sept. 15, 1945; Jan. 8, Feb. 8, 1946, SL.

23. Matthews, *Interwoven,* 106, 114,; Jeffrey, *Frontier Women,* 72. For examples of early ranch houses, see illustrations and comments in Matthews, *Interwoven,* and F. M. Holden, *Lambshead before Interwoven.*

24. *Fort Griffin Echo,* Oct. 4, 1879; Matthews, *Interwoven,* 146, 162, 165, 186–87.

25. Matthews, *Intervowen,* 114, 118, 124, 131.

26. Matthews, *Interwoven,* 13, 41–42, 142–44; *Fort Griffin Echo,* Jan. 4, 11, 1879.

27. *Fort Griffin Echo,* Jan. 4, Aug. 30, 1879; Wilhelm and Grace to Soule, Mar. 4, 1943, SL.

28. Wilhelm and Grace to Soule, Apr. 6, 20, 1942, SL.

29. Wilhelm and Grace to Soule, Apr. 6, Oct. 12, 1942, SL; *Frontier Echo* (Jacksboro), Jan. 5, 1877; Sept. 6, 1878; *Fort Griffin Echo,* July 19, Aug. 9, Sept. 13, Dec. 6, 1879; *U.S. Census, 1880,* Shackelford County.

30. *Frontier Echo* (Jacksboro), Jan. 14, Sept. 11, Oct. 16, 1875; Dec. 15, 1876; Feb. 16, 1877; June 7, July 26, 1879; Gammel, ed., *Laws of Texas* VIII, 860.

31. *Frontier Echo* (Jacksboro), Aug. 18, 1876; Feb. 2, 1877; June 28, Aug. 2, 30, 1878; *Fort Worth Daily Democrat,* Sept. 26, 1876.

32. *Frontier Echo* (Jacksboro), Mar. 9, 1876; Jan. 19, Mar. 30, 1877; *Fort Griffin Echo,* Dec. 13, 1879; Reynolds interview with Webb, Oct. 2, 1944, WP.

33. Reynolds interview with Webb, Apr. 1, 1938; Oct. 2, 1944; Herron interview with Webb, Apr. 8, 1941, WP; *Frontier Echo* (Jacksboro), Aug. 30, 1878.

34. Gammel, ed., *Laws of Texas* VIII, 1074–76, 1078; Commissioner's Court, 98; *Albany Echo,* June 23, 1883.

35. McKay, "Economic Conditions," 111–12; Webb, *Great Plains*, 205–207; *Fort Griffin Echo*, June 21, 1879; *U.S. Census, 1880*, Shackelford County; Jordan, *Trails to Texas*, Fig. 6.7, p. 142.

36. *Frontier Echo* (Jacksboro), Nov. 1, 29, 1878; *Fort Griffin Echo*, Aug. 2, Sept. 13, 1879; Jordan, *Trails to Texas*, 142.

37. *Fort Griffin Echo*, May 3, 1879; Biggers, *Buffalo Guns and Barbed Wire*, 105; Stribling and Kirkland to John Hancock, Dec. 21, 1876, SP; Matthews, *Interwoven*, 110.

38. Newt Jones interview; *Fort Griffin Echo*, May 3, 1879; Matthews, *Interwoven*, 129; McKay, "Economic Conditions," 115–16.

39. See Stribling Papers; Gammel, ed., *Laws of Texas* VII, 11; County Court, Jan. 21, 1878; *Frontier Echo* (Jacksboro), Feb. 11, 1876; *Fort Griffin Echo*, Feb. 15, 1879.

40. E. D. Townsend, AG, to William G. Belknap, Secretary of War, in "Report of the Secretary of the Interior," 3–4, H. Exec. Doc. 102, 44th Cong., 1st sess., serial set 1689; Hayman to AAAG, July 30, 1868, RG 393, FG, LS; *U.S. Census, 1880*, Shackelford County and Throckmorton County, 290–306, reel no. 1328.

41. *Fort Griffin Echo*, Aug. 23, Oct. 11, 1879; Wilhelm and Grace to Soule, Mar. 31, 1942, SL; *Fort Worth Daily Democrat*, Apr. 6, 1877.

42. Champlin to Soule, Apr. 21, 1944, SL; Nance, "Nance and the Tonkawas," 92–93; *Fort Worth Daily Democrat*, May 12, 1877; Theodore Roosevelt, "Buffalo Hunting," *St. Nicholas* 17 (Dec. 1889): 138.

43. *Dallas Daily Herald*, Apr. 28, 1876; *Fort Griffin Echo*, Feb. 5, Apr. 16, 1881.

44. Veal to Stribling and Kirkland, June 14, 1875, SP; Kenan to Soule, Jan. 28, 1946; Feb. 15, 1949; Wilhelm and Grace to Soule, Mar. 4, 1943, SL. For a discussion of conditions under which Texas's African Americans lived during the post-Reconstruction era, see Barr, *Black Texans*, 70–111ff. *U.S. Census, 1880*, Shackelford County.

45. *U.S. Census, 1880*, I, XXVIII, 452–79; Poe, *Buckboard Days*, 40.

46. Barr, *Black Texans*, 90–93; *Frontier Echo* (Jacksboro), Sept. 6, 1878; *U.S. Census, 1880*, I, XXVIII, 452–79.

47. *Fort Griffin Echo*, July 12, 1879; Apr. 23, 1881; Barr, *Black Texans*, 83; Fred Cotten interview with Lawson Gratz, Feb. 1957, NC.

48. Kenan to Soule, Jan. 28, 1946, SL.

49. *Fort Griffin Echo*, Jan. 25, May 3, 24, 1879; April 23, 1881.

50. William H. Leckie, *The Buffalo Soldiers: A Narrative of the Negro Cavalry in the West*, 237–38; *Fort Griffin Echo*, June 14, 1879; June 12, 1880; Fred Cotten interview notes, NC.

CHAPTER ELEVEN

1. *Fort Griffin Echo*, Oct. 11, 1879; Jan. 3, 1880.

2. Ibid., Mar. 15, Apr. 5, 12, Sept. 6, 1879; July 24, 1880.

3. Ibid., June 14, Aug. 30, 1879.

4. Ibid., June 7, July 19, Nov. 15, 1879; Feb. 14, 1880; Mar. 5, 12, May 14, 1881.

5. Ibid., June 12, 19, 1880; Kenan to Soule, Feb. 15, 1949, SL.

6. *Fort Griffin Echo*, July 3, 1880; case no. 175, filed 1st term, 1880, District Court.

7. *Fort Griffin Echo*, Apr. 12, May 3, June 28, 1879; George Newcomb, Flood File, NC.

8. *Fort Griffin Echo*, Feb. 5, June 4, 1881; Captain J. B. Irvine to AG, May 31, 1881, RG 393, FG, LS; Special Orders, No. 64, RG 94, AGO Reservation File, Box 47, Miscellaneous, NA.

9. *Fort Worth Daily Democrat*, Aug. 6, 1879; *Fort Griffin Echo*, Jan. 4, July 26, 1879.

10. Charles H. Cole to Stribling and Kirkland, Oct. 8, 1878; Stribling and Kirkland to Henry Warren, Oct. 10, 1878; Henry Warren to Stribling and Kirkland, Oct. 11, 15, 1878; Stribling and Samuel Spears to Henry Warren, Dec. 17, 1878, SP; *Frontier Echo* (Jacksboro), Mar. 8, 1878; *Fort Griffin Echo*, Jan. 11, July 5, 19, 26, Sept. 20, Nov. 22, 1879.

11. *Fort Griffin Echo*, May 24, Sept. 20, 1879; *Callahan County Clarendon* (Belle Plain), Nov. 22, 1879, Jan. 3, 1880.

12. *Fort Worth Daily Democrat*, Aug. 14, Nov. 29, 1879; *Fort Griffin Echo*, Dec. 6, 1879.

13. S. G. Reed, *A History of the Texas Railroads*, 365.

14. *Callahan County Clarendon* (Belle Plain), Apr. 24, 1880; John Martin Brockman, "Railroads, Radicals, and Democrats: A Study in Texas Politics, 1865–1900" (Ph.D. diss., University of Texas, Austin, 1975), 226; S. B. McAllister, "Building the Texas and Pacific Railroad West of Fort Worth," *WTHAY* 4 (1928): 55; Reed, *Texas Railroads*, 365.

15. *Callahan County Clarendon* (Belle Plain), Nov. 20, 1880, Apr. 2, 1881; *Callahan County Clarendon* (Baird), Apr. 23, May 7, 1881.

16. *Fort Griffin Echo*, Feb. 19, 1881.

17. Ibid.

18. Ibid.

19. *Callahan County Clarendon* (Belle Plain), Apr. 24, 1880; *Callahan County Clarendon* (Baird), Apr. 23, 1881.

20. Reed, *Texas Railroads*, 217; *Fort Griffin Echo*, Apr. 23, 1881.

21. *Fort Griffin Echo*, Dec. 17, 24, 1881, Jan. 21, 1882; Skaggs, *Cattle-Trailing Industry*, 95.

22. *Fort Griffin Echo*, Dec. 10, 1881, Jan. 21, 1882; *Albany Echo*, Dec. 22, 1883; Skaggs, *Cattle-Trailing Industry*, 106–107.

23. *Fort Griffin Echo*, Feb. 5, 1881; Schilz, "History of the Tonkawas," 213–14; Nance, "Nance and the Tonkawas," 94–95; Biggers, *Shackelford County Sketches*, 84–85.

24. Biggers, *Buffalo Guns and Barbed Wire*, 40–43; Ralph A. Smith, "The West Texas Bone Business," 111–12, 116, 119; Gard, *Great Buffalo Hunt*, 300–301; *Fort Griffin Echo*, Dec. 17, 1881; Jan. 7, 21, 1882.

25. *Fort Griffin Echo*, Jan. 21, 1882; Wilhelm and Grace to Soule, Mar. 31, 1942, SL.

26. Rodman W. Paul, *The Far West and the Great Plains in Transition, 1859–1900*, 198–99; Biggers, *Buffalo Guns and Barbed Wire*, 144–45.

27. D. W. Hinkle to Joseph Nimmo, Jr., Mar. 21, 1885, in Nimmo, *Range and Ranch Cattle Business*, 144; Dale, *Range Cattle Industry*, 119–22; *Frontier Echo*, Aug. 6, 1879.

28. Dale, *Range Cattle Industry*, 122, 125; Biggers, *Buffalo Guns and Barbed Wire*, 123–25, 147.

29. For two particularly good studies on the drought, see J. W. Williams, "A Statistical Study of the Drouth of 1886," *WTHAY* 21 (1945): 85–109; and W. C. Holden, "West Texas Drouths," *SWHQ* 32 (Oct. 1928): 103–23; Michael Thomas Kingston, ed., *Texas Almanac and State Industrial Guide, 1984–1985*, 345; Peter Hart, *A Description of Shackelford County, State of Texas, U.S.A.*, pamphlet, cited in Skaggs, *Cattle-Trailing Industry*, 95; *Albany News*, Oct. 21, 1886.

30. *Albany News*, July 22, Dec. 28, 1886; Jan. 4, 1887; Holden, "West Texas Drouths," 106, 108–109, 112.

31. *Albany News*, July 22, Oct. 7, 14, 21, 28, Nov. 18, Dec. 2, 9, 1886; Mar. 31, 1887; Holden, "West Texas Drouths," 112–21ff.; Williams, "Drought Statistics," 100–103.

CONCLUSIONS

1. Edgar Rye, *The Quirt and the Spur: Vanishing Shadows of the Texas Frontier*, 7.

2. For a good discussion of the "new western" history, including recent historiography, see Patricia Limerick et al., *Trails: Toward a New Western History. The Oxford History of the American West*, by Clyde A. Milner II et al., provides the most recent comprehensive assessment of this field. Richard Etulain, in *Writing Western History*, crafted an introduction that traces the interpretive development.

3. Gerald Thompson, "Another Look at Frontier/Western Historiography," in Limerick et al., *Trails*, 94.

4. Donald Worster et al., "*The Legacy of Conquest*, by Patricia Nelson Limerick: A Panel Appraisal," *Western Historical Quarterly* 20 (Aug. 1989): 307–308.

5. Rye, *Quirt and Spur*, v–xvi.

6. See Seymour V. Conner's biographical essay about Don Biggers in *Buffalo Guns and Barbed Wire*, 193–239.

7. Charles Robinson III, *The Frontier World of Fort Griffin: The Life and Death of a Western Town*, 99–100.

8. Cynthia Rose, *Lottie Deno: Gambling Queen of Hearts*, 52–54, 60, 114.

9. D. W. Meinig, *Imperial Texas: An Interpretive Essay in Cultural Geography*, 104.

10. W. S. Adair, "Albany Found Real Frontier in Early Days," *Dallas Morning News*, June 1, 1930.

11. Robinson, *Frontier World*, 73; Hunter, *Lottie Deno*, 10; Carl Coke Rister, *Fort Griffin*, 132.

12. Collinson, *Life in the Saddle*, 84; Emmett Roberts, "Frontier Experiences," 52.

13. *Dallas Daily Herald*, Apr. 23, 28, 1876; Jan. 24, July 20, Aug. 3, 1877.

14. Case no. 170, filed 2d term, 1879, District Court; *Fort Griffin Echo*, Aug. 2, 1879.

15. J. W. Woody to Haley, Haley Papers.

16. W. C. Holden, "Law and Lawlessness on the Texas Frontier, 1875–1890," *SWHQ* 44 (1940): 202; *Jacksboro Frontier Echo*, Nov. 2, 1876; *Fort Griffin Echo*, Aug. 2, 1879.

17. John Myers Myers, *Doc Holliday*, 67–70; case no. 34, 1st term, 1875, District Court.

18. Milner II et al., *Oxford History of the West*, 395–96.

19. Although now somewhat dated, the Appendix (261–71) in Roger D. McGrath, *Gunfighters, Highwaymen, and Vigilantes: Violence on the Frontier*, provides a good assessment of this topic by separating authors into two camps, one arguing that the West was violent and lawless, the other representing the opposing view.

20. For a good rhetorical essay on this topic, see Frank E. Vandiver, *The Southwest: South or West?* For some more recent general queries about what constitutes the West, see White, *It's Your Misfortune*, 3–4, and, the introduction in Milner et al., *Oxford History of the West*, 1–7. The equally elusive question regarding what actually constitutes the South makes the task of identifying Texas's western-southern border especially difficult to pin down. A wide interpretive gulf, for example, separates Eugene Genovese's "planter hegemony" and Bertram Wyatt-Brown's concept of "honor" as the region's unifying principles. Forrest McDonald and Grady McWhiney have contended that a Celtic cultural heritage distinguishes the South. Of a body of Genovese's works, see particularly *The World the Slaveholders Made: Two Essays in Interpretation*. See also Bertram Wyatt-Brown, *Southern Honor: Ethics and Behavior in the Old South*; McDonald and McWhiney, "Southern Herdsman"; and McWhiney, *Cracker Culture*.

21. See Ewing, "Origins of Unionist Sentiment"; Ewing, "Unionist Sentiment on the Northwest Texas Frontier"; and Richardson, *Northwest Texas Frontier*, 226, 243.

22. Cook, *Border and the Buffalo*, 292–93.

23. *Frontier Echo* (Jacksboro), Aug. 30, 1878; Meadows interview with Haley, NHML.

BIBLIOGRAPHY

PRIMARY SOURCES

Manuscript Collections

Center for American History, University of Texas at Austin
    James H. Baker Diary, 1856–1920.
    Creaton, John. "John Creaton: An Autobiography, 1856–1932."
    Robert T. Hill Scrapbook.
    Diary of William R. Peveler.
    Cornelius Stribling Papers.
    Walter Prescott Webb Papers, 1857–1966, comp. Bruce Hupp, August 1968; rev. William H. Richter, 1972, Sara Clark, 1986.
Library of Congress, Washington, D.C.
    Sheridan Papers.
Robert E. Nail, Jr., Foundation Collection, Old Jail Art Center, Albany, Texas
    Henry Griswold Comstock manuscript (typed copy).
    Fred Cotten File.
    Flood File.
    Map Files.
    Newcomb Family Diaries (typed copy).
    Etta Soule Letters.
    Stribling and Kirkland File.
    J. R. Webb File.
National Archives, Washington, D.C.
    Combined Record Groups 94, Adjutant General's Office, and 393, Army Continental Command, in Post Returns, Camp Cooper, Texas, Microfilm 617, roll 253.
    Record Group 92, Office of the Quartermaster General, Consolidated Correspondence File, Fort Griffin.
    Record Group 94, AGO Reservation File, Box 47, Miscellaneous, Fort Griffin.
        Post Medical Returns, Fort Griffin.

Record Group 393, Charges and Specifications, Fort Griffin.
    General Orders and Circulars, Fort Griffin.
    Letters Sent, Fort Griffin.
    Miscellaneous Records, Tonkawa Indian Scouts.
    Narrative Reports and Scouting Expeditions, Fort Griffin.
    Proceedings of Boards of Survey, Fort Griffin.
    Records of U.S. Army Continental Commands, Miscellaneous
        Records, Fort Griffin.
    Post Returns, Fort Griffin. Microfilm 617, roll 429, Nita Stewart
        Haley Memorial Library, Midland, Texas.
  John Meadows interview.
  John C. Jacobs Letter.
Panhandle-Plains Historical Museum, Canyon, Texas
  Bugbee Files
  Frank Collinson Collection
  Bruce Gerdes Collection, Interview Files
  J. Evetts Haley Collection, Interview Files
  L. F. Sheffy Files
  Hank Smith Files
Rupert Richardson Research Center, Hardin-Simmons University,
    Abilene, Texas
  J. R. Webb Papers
Southwest Collection, Texas Tech University, Lubbock, Texas
  Eula M. Haskew Papers
  Carl Coke Rister Papers
Private holding of unpublished manuscripts, Sutherlin Family, Spokane,
    Washington
  Sutherlin, William. "A Partial Record of the Sutherlin Family."
Texas State Archives, Austin, Texas
  Bugg Collection
  Grahame, James W., "Tales of the Texas Border," manuscript.
  Texas Rangers, Adjutant General's Papers

Government Documents, Texas

Gammel, H. P. N., ed. *Laws of Texas.* 10 vols. Austin: Gammel Book
    Co., 1898.
Shackelford County.
  Criminal Court Case Envelopes.
  Deed Records.
  Index to District Court.
  Index to Real Property Records.

Minutes of Commissioner's Court, Volume A.

Minutes of County Court, Volume A,

Minutes of 12th Judicial District Court, Volume A.

Records of Official Bonds, Volume B.

Sumners, Bill, comp. *Inventory of County Records, Stephens County Courthouse*. Austin: Center for Community Services, North Texas State University and Archives Division, Texas State Library, 1975.

Winfrey, Dorman H., and James M. Day, eds. *The Indian Papers of Texas and the Southwest, 1825–1916*. 5 vols. Austin: The Pemberton Press, 1966.

Government Documents, United States

Department of the Interior. *Population of the United States in 1860: the Eighth Census*. Superintendent of the Census, Joseph C. G. Kennedy. Washington, D.C.: Government Printing Office, 1861.

———. *Population of the United States in 1870: the Ninth Census*. Superintendent of the Census, Frances Walker. Washington, D.C.: Government Printing Office, 1871.

———. *Population of the United States in 1880: the Tenth Census*. Superintendant of the Census, Frances Walker and Charles Seaton. Washington, D.C.: Government Printing Office, 1881.

Congress, House. H. Doc. 76, 29th Cong., 2d sess., serial set 500.

———, ———. H. Exec. Doc. 1, 34th Cong., 2d sess., serial set 864.

———, ———. H. Exec. Doc. 81, 36th Cong., 1st sess., serial set 1056.

———, ———. H. Exec. Doc. 1, 39th Cong., 2d sess., serial set 1284.

———, ———. H. Exec. Doc. 1, 40th Cong., 2d sess., serial set 1324.

———, ———. H. Exec. Doc. 1, 40th Cong., 3d sess., serial set 1367.

———, ———. H. Exec. Doc. 1, 41st Cong., 2d sess., serial set 1413.

———, ———. H. Misc. Doc. 142, 41st Cong., 2d sess., serial set 1433.

———, ———. H. Exec. Doc. 1, 41st Cong., 3d sess., serial set 1446.

———, ———. H. Exec. Doc. 1, 42d Cong., 2d sess., serial set 1503.

———, ———. H. Exec. Doc. 1, 42d Cong., 2d sess., serial set 1505.

———, ———. H. Exec. Doc. 1, 42d Cong., 3d sess., serial set 1558.

———, ———. H. Exec. Doc. 13, 42d Cong., 3d sess., serial set 1563.

———, ———. H. Exec. Doc. 1, 42d Cong., 3d sess., serial set 1560.

———, ———. H. Exec. Doc. 39, 42d Cong., 3d sess., serial set 1565.

———, ———. H. Exec. Doc. 1, 43d Cong., 1st sess., serial set 1597.

———, ———. H. Rep. No. 384, 43d Cong., 1st sess., serial set 1624.

H. Exec. Doc. 1, 43d Cong., 2d sess., serial set 1635.

———, ———. H. Exec. Doc. 1, 44th Cong., 1st sess., serial set 1674.

————, ————. H. Exec. Doc. 102, 44th Cong., 1st sess., serial set 1689.

————, ————. H. Exec. Doc. 33, 44th Cong., 2d sess., serial set 1755.

————, ————. H. Reports, No. 701, 45th Cong., 2d sess., serial set 1824.

Congress, Senate. S. Exec. Doc. 1, 30th Cong., 1st sess., serial set 503.

————, ————. S. Exec. Doc. 64, 31st Cong., 1st sess., serial set 562.

————, ————. S. Exec. Doc. 2, 36th Cong., 1st sess., serial set 1023.

————, ————. S. Exec. Doc. 60, 40th Cong., 2d sess., serial set 1317.

————, ————. S. Exec. Doc. 18, 40th Cong., 3d sess., serial set 1360.

Walker, Francis A. *A Compendium of the Ninth Census.* Washington, D.C.: Government Printing Office, 1872.

War Department. *The War of the Rebellion: A Compilation of the Official Records of the Union and Confederate Armies.* 128 vols. Washington, D.C.: Government Printing Office, 1880–1901.

Interviews by Author

Rainey, Arlene. Benton, Arkansas. Aug. 6, 1991.

Thompson, Ramona. South Solon, Ohio. Oct. 14, 1991.

Newspapers

Albany News, 1886–1887.

Austin Weekly State Gazette, 1876.

Baird Callahan County Clarendon, 1881.

Belle Plain Callahan County Clarendon, 1879–1881.

Clarksville (Texas) Northern Standard, 1859–1860.

Dallas Daily Herald, 1876–1878.

Dallas Herald, 1859–1860.

Dallas Morning News, 1928.

Denison (Texas) Daily Cresset, 1875.

El Paso Times, 1891.

Fort Griffin Echo, 1879–1882.

Fort Worth Daily Democrat, 1876–1880.

Fort Worth Democrat, 1875.

Fort Worth Star-Telegram, 1926, 1992.

Galveston Daily News, 1878.

Jacksboro Flea, 1869.

Jacksboro (Texas) Frontier Echo, 1875–1878.

Jacksboro (Texas) Whiteman, 1860.

London (Ohio) Nickel Plate, 1891.

London (Ohio) Semi-Weekly Enterprise, 1891.

Madison County (Ohio) Democrat, 1891.

Live Performances

Fandangle Parade, 1989, 1992, 1993
Fort Griffin Fandangle, 1989, 1991, 1992

Books

Adjutant General's Office, comp. *Chronological List of Actions, &c., with Indians from January 15, 1837 to January, 1891.* 1891. Reprint, Fort Collins, Colo.: Old Army Press, 1979.

Boley, Tommy J., ed. *An Autobiography of a West Texas Pioneer: Ella Elgar Bird Dumont.* Austin: University of Texas Press, 1988.

Carter, R. G. *On the Border with Mackenzie, or Winning West Texas from the Comanches.* 1935. Reprint, New York: Antiquarian Press, 1961.

Collinson, Frank. *Life in the Saddle.* Ed. Mary Whatley Clark. Norman: University of Oklahoma Press, 1963.

Cook, John R. *The Border and the Buffalo: An Untold Story of the Southwest Plains.* 1907. Reprint, New York: Citadel Press, 1969.

Dodge, Richard Irving. *The Hunting Grounds of the Great West.* London: Chatto & Windus, 1877.

Ford, John Salmon. *Rip Ford's Texas.* Ed. Stephen B. Oates. Austin: University of Texas Press, 1963.

Friend, Llerena, ed. *M. K. Kellogg's Texas Journal, 1872.* Austin: University of Texas Press, 1967.

Greer, James Kimmins. *Bois d'Arc to Barb'd Wire: Ken Cary, Southwestern Frontier Born.* Dallas: Dealy and Lowe, 1936.

Holden, W. C. *Rollie Burns; or, An Account of the Ranching Industry on the South Plains.* 1932. Reprint. College Station: Texas A&M University Press, 1986.

Johnson, Marshall L. *Trail Blazing: A True Story of the Struggles with Hostile Indians on the Frontier of Texas.* Dallas: Mathis Publishing Co., 1935.

McConnell, H. H. *Five Years a Cavalryman; or, Sketches of Regular Army Life on the Texas Frontier, Twenty Odd Years Ago.* Jacksboro, Texas: N. N. Rogers & Co., Printers, 1889.

Marcy, Randolph B. *Thirty Years of Army Life on the Border.* New York: Harper & Brothers, Publishers, 1866.

Matthews, Sallie Reynolds. *Interwoven: A Pioneer Chronicle.* 4th ed. College Station: Texas A&M University Press, 1988.

Nimmo, Joseph, Jr. *Report in Regard to the Range and Ranch Cattle Business of the United States.* 1885. Reprint, New York: Arno Press, 1972.

Parker, William B. *Notes Taken during the expedition commanded by Capt. R. B. Marcy, U.S.A., through unexplored Texas, in the summer and fall of 1854.* Philadelphia: Hayes & Stell, 1856.

Pratt, Richard Henry. *Battlefield and Classroom: Four Decades with the American Indian, 1867–1904.* Ed. Robert M. Utley. New Haven: Yale University Press, 1964.

Roemer, Ferdinand. *Texas: With Particular Reference to German Immigration and the Physical Appearance of the Country.* Trans. Oswald Mueller. San Antonio: Standard Printing Company, 1935.

Sheridan, P. H. *Record of Engagements with Hostile Indians within the Military Division of the Missouri, from 1868 to 1882.* Washington, D.C.: Government Printing Office, 1882.

Sowell, A. J. *Rangers and Pioneers of Texas.* 1884. Reprint, Austin: State House Press, 1991.

Strong, Henry. *My Frontier Days and Indian Fights on the Plains of Texas.* Waco: n.p., 1926.

Winkler, Ernest W., ed. *Journal of the Secession Convention of Texas, 1861.* Austin: Texas Library and Historical Commission, 1912.

Articles

Carriker, Robert C., ed. "Thompson McFadden's Diary of an Indian Campaign, 1874." *SWHQ* 75 (Oct. 1971): 198–232.

Connellee, C. U. "Some Experiences of a Pioneer Surveyor." *WTHAY* 6 (1930): 87–104.

Crane, R. C., contrib. "Report of Captain R. B. Marcy, of the Fifth Infantry, United States Army, on His Exploration of Indian Territory and Northwest Texas." *WTHAY* 14 (1938): 116–36.

Crimmins, M. L., ed. "Robert E. Lee in Texas: Letters and Diary." *WTHAY* 8 (1932): 3–24.

———, ed. "W. G. Freeman's Report on the Eighth Military Department." *SWHQ* 53 (Apr. 1950): 448–73.

Elgin, Jack. "Christmas Dinner on the Upper Brazos in 1872." *WTHAY* 14 (1938): 83–91.

Grant, Ben O., and J. R. Webb, contribs. "On the Cattle Trail and Buffalo Range, Joe S. McCombs." *WTHAY* 11 (1935): 93–101.

Howarth, Jacob. "Letter from an Ex-Soldier." *WTHAY* 2 (1926): 3–7.

Howell, D. S. "Along the Texas Frontier during the Civil War." *WTHAY* 13 (1937): 82–95.

Hunt, James Winford. "Buffalo Days: The Chronicle of an Old Buffalo Hunter, J. Wright Mooar." *Hollands: The Magazine of the South* 52 (Jan. 1933): 13, 24.

――――. "Buffalo Days: "The Second Chapter of the Chronicle of J. Wright Mooar." *Hollands: The Magazine of the South* 52 (Feb. 1933): 10, 44.

――――. "Buffalo Days: A Rendezvous with Death." *Hollands: The Magazine of the South* 52 (Apr. 1933): 5, 22.

――――. "Buffalo Days: The Killing of the White Buffalo." *Hollands: The Magazine of the South* 52 (May 1933): 11–12.

Mooar, J. Wright. "Frontier Experiences of J. Wright Mooar." *WTHAY* 4 (1928): 89–92.

――――. "Some Observations on the Cattle Industry." *WTHAY* 5 (1929): 124–25.

――――. "The First Buffalo Hunting in the Panhandle." *WTHAY* 6 (1930): 109–11.

Roberts, Emmett. "Frontier Experiences of Emmett Roberts of Nugent, Texas." *WTHAY* 3 (1927): 43–58.

Roland, Charles P., and Richard C. Robbins, eds. "The Diary of Eliza (Mrs. Albert Sidney) Johnston." *SWHQ* 60 (Apr. 1957): 463–500.

Strickland, Rex W., ed. "The Recollections of W. S. Glenn." *PPHR* 22 (1949): 15–64.

Sullivan, Jerry M. "Fort McKavett." *WTHAY* 45 (1969): 138–39.

Webb, J. R. "Henry Herron, Pioneer and Peace Officer during Fort Griffin Days." *WTHAY* 20 (1944): 21–50.

――――. "Chapters in the Frontier Life of Phin W. Reynolds." *WTHAY* 21 (1945): 110–33.

Williams, J. W. "Journey of the Leach Wagon Train across Texas, 1857." *WTHAY* 29 (1953): 115–77.

Wilson, Aubrey A. "A Soldier of the Texas Frontier: Brevet Major Robert Patterson Wilson, United States Army." *WTHAY* 34 (1958): 82–96.

SECONDARY SOURCES

Books

Adams, Ramon F. *Burs under the Saddle: A Second Look at Books and Histories of the West.* Norman: University of Oklahoma Press, 1964.

――――. *More Burs under the Saddle: Books and Histories of the West.* Norman: University of Oklahoma Press, 1979.

Barr, Alwyn. *Black Texans: A History of Negroes in Texas, 1528–1971.* 2d ed. Austin: Jenkins Publishing Company, Pemberton Press, 1982.

Bartlett, W. S.; Mabel Major; and Rebecca W. Smith, eds. *My Foot's in the Stirrup.* Dallas: Dealy and Lowe, 1937.

Biggers, Don H. *Buffalo Guns and Barbed Wire.* ca. 1902. Reprint, Lubbock: Texas Tech University Press, 1991.

————. *Shackelford County Sketches*. Ed. Joan Farmer. 1908. Reprint, Albany, Texas: The Clear Fork Press, 1974.

Billington, Ray Allen, and Martin Ridge. *Westward Expansion: A History of the American Frontier*. 5th ed. New York: The Macmillan Co., 1982.

Blanton, Joseph Edward. *John Larn*. Venture Press, 1994.

Bomar, George W. *Texas Weather*. Austin: University of Texas Press, 1983.

Brown, Richard Maxwell, ed. *American Violence*. Englewood Cliffs, N.J.: Prentice-Hall, 1970.

————. *Strain of Violence: Historical Studies of American Violence and Vigilantism*. New York: Oxford University Press, 1975.

————. "A History of Violence in the American West." In *Historians and the American West*. Ed. Michael P. Malone. Lincoln: University of Nebraska Press, 1983.

Butler, Anne M. *Daughters of Joy, Sisters of Misery: Prostitutes in the American West, 1865–1890*. Urbana: University of Illinois Press, 1985.

Caldwell, Clifton. *Fort Davis: A Family Frontier Fort*. Albany, Texas: Clear Fork Press, 1986.

Capps, Benjamin. *The Warren Wagon Train Raid: The First Complete Account of an Historic Indian Attack and Its Aftermath*. New York: The Dial Press, 1974.

Clarke, Mary Whatley. *Palo Pinto Story*. Palo Pinto, Texas: The Manney Co., 1956.

Conkling, Roscoe P. *The Butterfield Overland Mail, 1857–1869*. 2 vols. Glendale, Calif.: The Arthur H. Clark Company, 1947.

Connor, Seymour V. *The Peters Colony of Texas*. Austin: Texas State Historical Association, 1959.

Cox, James. *Historical and Biographical Record of the Cattle Industry and the Cattlemen of Texas and Adjacent Territory*. 1895. Reprint, New York: Antiquarian Press, 1959.

Crouch, Carrie J. *A History of Young County, Texas*. Austin: Texas State Historical Association, 1956.

Cullum, G. W., comp. *Biographical Register of the Officers and Graduates of the U.S. Military Academy at West Point, New York*. New York: J. F. Trow, Printer, 1850.

Curry, W. H. *Sun Rising on the West: The Saga of Henry Clay and Elizabeth Smith*. Crosbyton, Texas: Crosby County Pioneer Memorial, 1979.

Dale, Edward Everett. *The Range Cattle Industry*. Norman: University of Oklahoma Press, 1930.

Dunlay, Thomas W. *Wolves for the Blue Soldiers: Indian Scouts and Auxiliaries with the United States Army*. Lincoln: University of Nebraska Press, 1982.

Dykstra, Robert R. *The Cattle Towns*. New York: Alfred A. Knopf, 1968.

Emmons, David M. *Garden in the Grasslands: Boomer Literature of the Central Great Plains*. Lincoln: University of Nebraska Press, 1971.

Etulain, Richard W., ed. *Writing Western History: Essays on Major Western Historians*. Albuquerque: University of New Mexico Press, 1991.

Ewell, Thomas T. *History of Hood County*. 1895. Reprint, Granbury, Texas: Junior Woman's Club, 1956.

Faulkner, Harold U. *American Economic History*. New York: Harper & Brothers Publishers, 1960.

Fehrenbach, T. R. *Lone Star: A History of Texas and the Texans*. New York: American Legacy Press, 1983.

Frazier, Ian. *Great Plains*. New York: Farrar, Straus, Giroux, 1989.

Freeman, Douglas Southall. *Robert E. Lee: A Biography*. Vol. 1. New York: Charles Scribner's Sons, 1934.

Fruger, Felix, and Harold U. Faulkner. *Readings in the Economic and Social History of the United States*. New York: Harper & Brothers Publishers, 1929.

Gard, Wayne. *The Chisholm Trail*. Norman: University of Oklahoma Press, 1954.

———. *The Great Buffalo Hunt*. Lincoln: University of Nebraska Press, 1959.

———. *Rawhide Texas*. Norman: University of Oklahoma Press, 1965.

Genovese, Eugene. *The World the Slaveholders Made: Two Essays in Interpretation*. New York: Pantheon Press, 1969.

Gilbert, Miles. *Getting a Stand*. Tempe, Ariz.: Hal Green Printing, 1986.

Ginger, Ray. *Age of Excess: The United States from 1877 to 1914*. New York: MacMillan Publishing Co., 1975.

Greer, James K. *A Texas Ranger and Frontiersman: The Days of Buck Barry in Texas, 1845-1906*. Dallas: The Southwest Press, 1932.

Haley, J. Evetts. *Jeff Milton: A Good Man with a Gun*. Norman: University of Oklahoma Press, 1945.

———. *Charles Goodnight: Cowman and Plainsman*. Norman: University of Oklahoma Press, 1949.

———. Fort Concho and the Texas Frontier. San Angelo, Texas: San Angelo Standard-Times, 1952.

Hamilton, Allen Lee. *Sentinel of the Southern Plains: Fort Richardson and the Northwest Texas Frontier, 1866-1878*. Fort Worth: Texas Christian University Press, 1988.

Hilliard, Sam B. *Hog Meat and Hoecake: Food Supply in the Old South, 1840-1860*. Carbondale: Southern Illinois University Press, 1972.

Holden, Frances Mayhugh. *Lambshead before Interwoven: A Texas Range Chronicle, 1848–1878*. College Station: Texas A&M University Press, 1982.

Holden, W. C. *Alkali Trails, or Social and Economic Movements of the Texas Frontier, 1846–1900*. Dallas: The Southwest Press, 1930.

Hollon, V. Eugene. *Beyond the Cross Timbers: The Travels of Randolph B. Marcy, 1882–1887*. Norman: University of Oklahoma Press, 1955.

———. *Frontier Violence: Another Look*. New York: Oxford University Press, 1974.

Huckabay, Ida L. *Ninety-Four Years in Jack County, 1845–1948*. Austin: The Steck Company, 1949.

Hunter, J. Marvin. *The Trail Drivers of Texas*. 1925. Reprint, New York: Argosy-Antiquarian Ltd., 1963.

———. *Lottie Deno: Her Life and Times*. Bandera, Texas: The 4 Hunters, 1959.

Jeffrey, Julie Roy. *Frontier Women: The Trans-Mississippi West, 1840–1880*. New York: Hill and Wang, 1979.

John, Elizabeth. *Storms Brewed in Other Men's Worlds: The Confrontation of Indians, Spanish, and French in the Southwest, 1540–1795*. College Station: Texas A&M University Press, 1975.

Jordan, Philip D. *Frontier Law and Order: Ten Essays*. Lincoln: University of Nebraska Press, 1970.

Jordan, Terry G. *North American Cattle Ranching Frontiers*. Albuquerque: University of New Mexico Press, 1993.

———. *Trails to Texas: Southern Roots of Western Cattle Ranching*. Lincoln: University of Nebraska Press, 1981.

———, et al. *Texas: A Geography*. Boulder, Colo.: Westview Press, 1984.

Kenner, Charles L. *A History of the New Mexican–Plains Indians Relations*. Norman: University of Oklahoma Press, 1969.

Kingston, Michael Thomas, ed. *Texas Almanac and State Industrial Guide, 1984–1985*. Dallas: A. H. Belo Corp., 1983.

Knight, Oliver. *Fort Worth: Outpost on the Trinity*. Norman: University of Oklahoma Press, 1953.

Leckie, William H. *The Military Conquest of the Southern Plains*. Norman: University of Oklahoma Press, 1963.

———. *The Buffalo Soldiers: A Narrative of the Negro Cavalry in the West*. Norman: University of Oklahoma Press, 1967.

Ledbetter, Barbara Neal. *Indian Raids on Warren, DuBose, Feild [sic], Man Wagon Trains, 1871, in Young and Jack Counties*. Graham, Texas: Barbara A. Neal Ledbetter, 1992.

———. *Fort Belknap, Frontier Saga: Indians, Negroes and Anglo Americans on the Texas Frontier*. Burnet, Texas: Eakin Press, 1982.

Limerick, Patricia. *The Legacy of Conquest: The Unbroken Past of the American West.* New York: W. W. Norton & Co., 1987.

———, et al. *Trails: Toward a New Western History.* Lawrence: University Press of Kansas, 1991.

McConnell, Joseph Carroll. *The West Texas Frontier; or, a Descriptive History of Early Times in Western Texas.* 2 vols. Palo Pinto: Texas Legal Bank & Book Co., 1933.

McCoy, Joseph G. *Historic Sketches of the Cattle Trade of the West and Southwest.* Kansas City: Ramsey, Millett, and Hudson, 1874.

McGrath, Roger D. *Gunfighters, Highwaymen, and Vigilantes: Violence on the Frontier.* Berkeley: University of California Press, 1984.

McHugh, Tom. *The Time of the Buffalo.* Lincoln: University of Nebraska Press, 1972.

McWhiney, Grady. *Cracker Culture: Celtic Ways in the Old South.* Tuscaloosa: University of Alabama Press, 1988.

Meinig, D. W. *Imperial Texas: An Interpretive Essay in Cultural Geography.* Austin: University of Texas Press, 1969.

Metz, Leon Claire. *John Selman: Texas Gunfighter.* New York: Hastings House, 1966.

Milner, Clyde A., II, et al. *The Oxford History of the American West.* New York: Oxford University Press, 1994.

Murrah, David J. *C. C. Slaughter: Rancher, Banker, Baptist.* Austin: University of Texas Press, 1981.

Myers, John Myers. *Doc Holliday.* Boston: 1955. Reprint, Lincoln: University of Nebraska Press, 1973.

Myres, Sandra L. *Westering Women and the Frontier Experience, 1800–1915.* Albuquerque: University of New Mexico Press, 1982.

Neighbours, Kenneth F. *Robert Simpson Neighbors and the Texas Frontier.* Waco: Texian Press, 1975.

Newcomb, W. W. *Indians of Texas: From Prehistoric to Modern Times.* Austin: University of Texas Press, 1961.

Nunn, W. C. *Texas under the Carpetbaggers.* Austin: University of Texas Press, 1962.

Nye, W. S. *Carbine and Lance: The Story of Old Fort Sill.* Norman: University of Oklahoma Press, 1943.

Ormsby, W. L. *The Butterfield Overland Mail.* Ed. Lyle W. Wright and Josephine M. Bynum. San Marino, Calif.: The Huntington Library, 1954.

Owsley, Frank L. *Plain Folk of the Old South.* Baton Rouge: Louisiana State University Press, 1949.

Paul, Rodman W. *The Far West and the Great Plains in Transition, 1859–1900.* New York: Harper & Row, Publishers, 1988.

Poe, Sophie. *Buckboard Days*. Caldwell, Idaho: Caxton Printers, 1936.

Ramsdell, Charles W. *Reconstruction in Texas*. 1910. Reprint, Gloucester, Mass.: Peter Smith, 1964.

Reed, S. G. *A History of the Texas Railroads*. Houston: St. Clair Publishing Co., 1941.

Richardson, Rupert N. *The Comanche Barrier to South Plains Settlement: A Century and a Half of Savage Resistance to the Advancing White Frontier*. 1933. Reprint, Millwood, N.Y.: Kraus Reprint Co., 1973.

————, and Carl Coke Rister. *The Great Southwest*. Glendale Calif.: The Arthur H. Clark Co., 1934.

————. *The Frontier of Northwest Texas*. Glendale, Calif.: The Arthur H. Clark Company, 1963.

————. *Texas: The Lone Star State*, 4th ed. Englewood Cliffs, N.J.: Prentice-Hall, 1981.

Richter, William R. *The Army in Texas during Reconstruction, 1865–1870*. College Station: Texas A&M University Press, 1987.

Rister, Carl Coke. *The Southwestern Frontier, 1865–1881*. Cleveland: The Arthur Clark Co., 1928.

————. *Southern Plainsman*. Norman: University of Oklahoma Press, 1938.

————. *Fort Griffin on the Texas Frontier*. Norman: University of Oklahoma Press, 1956.

Robinson, Charles, III. *The Frontier World of Fort Griffin: The Life and Death of a Western Town*. Spokane, Wash.: The Arthur H. Clark Company, 1992.

Rye, Edgar. *The Quirt and the Spur: Vanishing Shadows of the Texas Frontier*. 1909. Reprint, Austin: Steck-Vaughn Co., 1967.

Shannon, Fred A. *Critiques of Research in the Social Sciences, vol. 3, An Appraisal of Walter Prescott Webb's "The Great Plains": A Study in Institutions and Environment*. New York: Social Science Research Council, 1940.

Skaggs, Jimmy M. *The Cattle-Trailing Industry: Between Supply and Demand, 1866–1890*. Lawrence: University Press of Kansas, 1973.

Smith, David Paul. *Frontier Defense in the Civil War: Texas' Rangers and Rebels*. College Station: Texas A&M University Press, 1992.

Smith, Henry Nash. *Virgin Land: The American West as Symbol and Myth*. Cambridge, Mass.: Harvard University Press, 1971.

Sonnichsen, C. L. *I'll Die before I'll Run*. 1962. Reprint, Lincoln: University of Nebraska Press, 1988.

Steffen, Jerome O. *Comparative Frontiers: A Proposal for Studying the American West*. Norman: University of Oklahoma Press, 1980.

Thompson, Jerry. *Colonel Robert John Baylor: Texas Indian Fighter and Confederate Soldier*. Hillsboro, Texas: Hill County Junior College Press, 1971.

——. *Henry Hopkins Sibley: Confederate General of the West*. Natchitoches, La.: Northwestern State University Press, 1987.

Turner, Frederick Jackson. *The Frontier in American History*. 1947. Reprint, Tucson: University of Arizona Press, 1986.

Van Deusen, Glyndon G. *Horace Greeley: Nineteenth Century Crusader*. Philadelphia: University of Pennsylvania Press, 1953.

Vandiver, Frank E. *The Southwest: South or West?* College Station: Texas A&M University Press, 1975.

Wallace, Ernest, and E. Adamson Hoebel. *The Comanches: Lords of the South Plains*. Norman: University of Oklahoma Press, 1986.

Webb, Walter Prescott. *The Great Plains*. New York: Grosset & Dunlap, 1931.

——. *The Great Frontier*. Lincoln: University of Nebraska Press, 1952.

——. *The Texas Rangers: A Century of Frontier Defense*. Austin: University of Texas Press, 1965. Reprint, Boston: Ginn and Co., 1978.

Weber, David J., ed. *New Spain's Far Northern Frontier: Essays on Spain in the American West, 1540–1821*. Albuquerque: University of New Mexico Press, 1984.

White, Richard. *Its Your Misfortune and None of My Own: A New History of the American West*. Norman: University of Oklahoma Press, 1991.

Wilbarger, J. W. *Indian Depredations in Texas*. 1889. Reprint, Austin: Eakin Press, Statehouse Books, 1985.

Wooster, Robert. *The Military and United States Indian policy, 1865–1903*. New Haven: Yale University Press, 1988.

——. *Soldiers, Sutlers, and Settlers: Garrison Life on the Texas Frontier*. College Station: Texas A&M University Press, 1987.

Worcester, Donald E. *The Chisholm Trail: High Road of the Cattle Kingdom*. Lincoln: University of Nebraska Press, 1980.

Wright, Muriel H. *A Guide to the Indian Tribes of Oklahoma*. Norman: University of Oklahoma Press, 1951.

Wyatt-Brown, Bertram. *Southern Honor: Ethics and Behavior in the Old South*. New York: Oxford University Press, 1982.

Articles

Bitner, Grace. "Early History of the Concho Country and Tom Green County." *WTHAY* 9 (1933): pp. 3–23.

Crane, R. C. "Early Days in Fisher County." *WTHAY* 6 (1930): 124–29.

——. "West Texas Trail Blazers." *WTHAY* 22 (1946): 60–68.

Crimmins, M. L. "Camp Cooper and Fort Griffin." *WTHAY* 17 (1941): 32–43.

Crum, Tom. "Camp Cooper, A Different Look." *WTHAY* 68 (1992): 62–75.

Dale, Edward Everett. "The Romance of the Range." *WTHAY* 5 (1929): 3–13.

Downs, Fane. "Fandangle: Myth as Reality." *WTHAY* 54 (1978): 3–9.

Duke, J. K. "Bad Men and Peace Officers of the Southwest." *WTHAY* 8 (1932): 51–61.

Ewing, Floyd F., Jr. "Origins of Unionist Sentiment on the West Texas Frontier." *WTHAY* 32 (1956): 21–29.

———. "Unionist Sentiment on the Northwestern Frontier." *WTHAY* 33 (1957): 58–70.

Grant, Ben O. "Life in Old Fort Griffin." *WTHAY* 10 (1934): 32–41.

———. "Citizen Law Enforcement Bodies: A Little More about the Vigilantes." *WTHAY* 39 (1963): 155–64.

Green, Robert. "The Free Range Era of the Cattle Industry." *WTHAY* 46 (1970): 204–10.

Griggs, William C. "The Battle of Yellowstone Canyon." *WTHAY* 51 (1975): 37–50.

Guice, John D. "Cattle Raisers of the Old Southwest: A Reinterpretation." *Western Historical Quarterly* 8 (Apr. 1977): 167–87.

Haley, J. Evetts. "The Comanchero Trade." *SWHQ* 38 (Jan. 1935): 157–61.

Hancock, William Box. "Trail Life." *WTHAY* 44 (1968): 106–16.

Haskew, Eula. "Stribling and Kirkland of Fort Griffin." *WTHAY* 32 (1956): 55–69.

Holden, W. C. "Frontier Defense in Texas during the Civil War." *WTHAY* 4 (1928): 16–31.

———. "West Texas Drouths," *SWHQ* 32 (Oct. 1928): 103–23.

———. "Frontier Defense, 1865–1889." *PPHR* 2 (1929): 43–64.

———. "Immigration and Settlement in West Texas." *WTHAY* 5 (1929): 70–73.

———. "Frontier Defense, 1846–1860." *WTHAY* 6 (1930): 39–71.

———. "Law and Lawlessness on the Texas Frontier, 1875–1890." *SWHQ* 44 (Oct. 1940): 188–203.

Hunter, J. Marvin. "The Lottie Deno I Knew." *WTHAY* 23 (1947): 30–35.

Hutto, John R. "Mrs. Elizabeth (Aunt Hank) Smith." *WTHAY* 15 (1939): 40–47.

Kincaid, Naomi H. "Rath City." *WTHAY* 24 (1948): 40–46.

Koch, Lena Clara. "Federal Indian Policy in Texas, 1845–1860." *SWHQ* 39 (July 1925): 19–35.

McAllister, S. B. "Building the Texas and Pacific Railroad West of Fort Worth." *WTHAY* 4 (1928): 50–57.

McDonald, Forrest, and Grady McWhiney. "The Antebellum Southern Herdsman: A Reinterpretation." *Journal of Southern History* 41 (Apr. 1975): 147–66.

McGough, W. C. "Driving Cattle into Old Mexico in 1864." *WTHAY* 13 (1937): 112–22.

McKay, S. S. "Social Conditions in Texas in the Eighteen Seventies." *WTHAY* 14 (1938): 32–51.

———. "Economic Conditions in Texas in the 1870s." *WTHAY* 15 (1939): 84–127.

McMillan, Edward L. "The Cowboy, Product of His Environment." *WTHAY* 31 (1955): 83–95.

McMurtry, Larry. "How the West Was Won or Lost." *New Republic*, Oct. 22, 1990.

Marchman, Watt P., and Robert C. Cotner. "Indian Agent Jesse Stem: A Manuscript Revelation." *WTHAY* 39 (1963): 114–54.

Meinig, D. W. "The Continuous Shaping of America: A Prospectus for Geographers and Historians." *American Historical Review* 83 (Dec. 1978): 1186–1205.

Moore, Robert L. "Fort Griffin and the Buffalo Sharps." *American Society of Arms Collectors Bulletin*, No. 52 (Apr. 1985).

Nance, Berta Hart. "D. A. Nance and the Tonkawa Indians." *WTHAY* 28 (1952): 87–95.

Neighbours, Kenneth F. "Chapters from the History of Indian Reservations." *WTHAY* 33 (1957): 3–16.

———. "The Assassination of Robert S. Neighbors." *WTHAY* 34 (1958): 38–49.

———. "Elm Creek Raid in Young County, 1864." *WTHAY* 40 (1964): 83–89.

———. "Tonkowa Scouts and Guides." *WTHAY* 49 (1973): 90–113.

O'Neal, Ben G. "The Beginnings of Fort Belknap." *SWHQ* 61 (Apr. 1958): 508–21.

Padgitt, James T. "Early Days in Coleman." *WTHAY* 28 (1962): 81–86.

Records, Ralph H. "At the End of the Texas Trail; Range Riding, 1878." *WTHAY* 19 (1943): 109–20.

Richardson, Rupert N. "Some Details of the Southern Overland Mail," *SWHQ* 29 (July 1925): 1–18.

———. "The Comanche Reservation in Texas." *WTHAY* 5 (1929): 47–71.

———. "Saga of Camp Cooper." *WTHAY* 56 (1980): 14–34.

———. "The Southern Overland Mail, Conveyor of News, 1857–1861." *WTHAY* 34 (1958): 25–37.

Ridge, Martin. "The American West: From Frontier to Region." *New Mexico Historical Review* 64 (Apr. 1989): 125–141.

Rister, Carl Coke. "Fort Griffin." *WTHAY* 1 (1925): 15–24.

———. "Social Activities of the Southwestern Cowboy." *WTHAY* 7 (1931): 40–55.

———. "The Border Post of Phantom Hill." *WTHAY* 14 (1938): 3–13.

Roland, Charles P., and Richard C. Robbins, eds. "The Diary of Eliza (Mrs. Albert Sidney) Johnston." *SWHQ* 60 (Apr. 1957): 463–500.

Roosevelt, Theodore. "Buffalo Hunting," *St. Nicholas* 17 (Dec. 1889): 136–43.

Sherill, R. E. "Early Days in Haskell County." *WTHAY* 3 (1927): 20–29.

Shirk, John H. "Mail Call at Fort Washita." *Chronicles of Oklahoma* 33 (1955): 22–28.

Shultz, Marvin. "Hunter's Frontier: Exterminating the American Bison in the Concho River Region." *Fort Concho Report* 20 (Spring 1988): 1–33.

Skaggs, Jimmy. "The Route of the Great Western (Dodge City) Cattle Trail." *WTHAY* 41 (1965): 131–43.

———. "The Economic Impact of Trailing: One Aspect." *WTHAY* 43 (1967): 18–30.

Smith, Glenn. "Some Early Runnels County History, 1858–1885." *WTHAY* 42 (1966): 111–27.

Smith, Ralph A. "The West Texas Bone Business." *WTHAY* 55 (1979): 111–34.

Smith, Ruby L. "Early Days in Wilbarger County," *WTHAY* 14 (1938): 52–72.

Studer, Floyd V. "Discovering the Panhandle." *PPHR* 4 (1931): 7–23.

Sullivan, Jerry M. "Fort McKavett, 1852–1883." *WTHAY* 45 (1969): 138–49.

Webb, J. R. "Chapters in the Frontier Life of Phin W. Reynolds," *WTHAY* 26 (1945): 110–43.

Webb, Walter Prescott. "A Texas Buffalo Hunt with Original Photographs." *Holland's Magazine* 46 (Oct. 1927): 10–11, 101–102.

West, G. Derek. "The Battle of Adobe Walls (1874)." *PPHR* 36 (1930): 11–36.

Whisenhunt, Donald W. "Frontier Military Life at Fort Richardson, Texas." *WTHAY* 42 (1966): 15–27.

Williams, A. C. "Cattle Raisers Association of Texas: Something of Its History." *The Cattleman* 10 (Mar. 1915): 13–16, 92.

Williams, J. W. "A Statistical Study of the Drouth of 1886," *WTHAY* 21 (1945): 85–109.

Worcester, Donald E. "The Spread of Spanish Horses in the Southwest, 1700–1800." *New Mexico Historical Review* 20 (Jan. 1945): 1–13.

Worster, Donald, et al. *"The Legacy of Conquest,* by Patricia Nelson Limerick: A Panel Appraisal." *Western Historical Quarterly* 20 (Aug. 1989): 303–22.

Theses and Dissertations

Adams, Larry Earl. "Economic Development in Texas during Reconstruction, 1865–1875." Ph.D. diss., North Texas State University, Denton, 1980.

Brockman, John Martin. "Railroads, Radicals, and Democrats: A Study in Texas Politics, 1865–1900." Ph.D. diss., University of Texas, Austin, 1975.

Frazier, Don. "Blood and Treasure." Ph.D. diss., Texas Christian University, Fort Worth, 1992.

Grant, Ben O. "An Early History of Shackelford County." Master's thesis, Hardin-Simmons University, Abilene, Texas, 1934.

Schilz, Thomas Frank. "People of the Cross Timbers: A History of the Tonkawa Indians." Ph.D. diss., Texas Christian University, Fort Worth, 1983.

Skaggs, Jimmy M. "The Great Western Trail to Dodge City, Kansas." M.A. thesis, Texas Technological College, Lubbock, 1965.

INDEX

Illustrations indicated by boldface type.

Abel, Cy, 265
Abilene, Kans., 88
Abilene, Tex., 7, 9, 23, 269, 270, 275
Adjutant General's Office, 104
African Americans, 60, 61, 87, 97–98, 119, 129, 131, 191, 204–205, 223–24, 283; art exhibit, 13; celebrate holidays, 241–42; as Comanche chief, 106; county seat election, 163; cowboys, 60; Fort Griffin community, 258–60; historians' view of, 286; Indian victims, 82, 107; mulattos, 258; population, 173; prostitution, 195–96; reenactors, 13; social significance, 292–93, 295; as subculture, 141–44; and violence, 140, 264–65; women, 247–48
Ainright, Sergeant, 154
Akers, Bill, 173
Albany, Tex., 8, 59, 163–65, 170, 211, 230, 240, 250–51, 253–55, 266–67, 274–75, 277–78, 291–92; cattle trail near, 167; commerce, 184; economy, 6, 9–10, 186; Larn killed at, 230–31; minorities in, 258, 260; railroad, 269, 271–72; vigilantes at, 215, 218, 229
Albany Tomahawk, 211, 240
American Express Co., 43
American Methodist Episcopal Church, 259
Anderson, John, 87
Anderson, Mitch, 72, 87
Andrews County, Tex., 253
Anglocentrism, 286
Anglo hegemony. *See* Racism
Apaches, 18
Appomattox, 118
Arkansas (state), 232, 238
Arrington, Captain G. W., 231
Atchison, Topeka, and Santa Fe Railroad, 167
Atrocities: Anglo, 37, 40, 87; Indian, 22, 28, 39, 65, 82–83, 91, 101–103, 107, 111, 181
Atwell, Tom, 98
Augusta, Ark., 232
Aunt 'Melia, 248
Aurora Borealis, 156
Austin, Stephen F., 22

Austin, Tex., 105, 230, 231
Austin Weekly Statesman, 220
Aztec Theater, 9–10

Bain, Charles, 171, 188
Baird, Tex., 270–71, 275
Baker, W. R., 170
Ballinger, Tex., 92
Banjo Bob, 190
Barker, Dave, 203
Barre, T. H., 164
Barrow, Dan, 203
Barry, Buck, 52
Barton, Clara, 279
Bass, Sam, 226
Bates, Henry, 44
Battle Creek, 105
Battle of the Pease River, 41, 47
Bayland Orphans Asylum, 169
Baylor, John R., 35–37, 39–41, 52, 61
Baylor County, Tex., 171, 253
Bee Hive Saloon, 11, 194, 202
Belknap, Tex., 38, 42, 48; 50, 57, 96. *See also* Fort Belknap
Belknap, William G., 26, 120
Bell, Dick, 264–65
Belle Plain, Tex., 170, 187, 267–68, 271
Belle Plain Clarendon, 271
Belton, Tex., 267
Bendenger, "Chips," 221
Benton, Ark., 232–33
Biggers, Don, 172–73, 254, 277, 283–84, 289
Big Nose Kate, 4
Big Spring, Tex., 269–70
Big Tree (Kiowa chief), 110
Birdwell, Sheriff John, 265, 270
Bishop, George, 91
Bison, 87, 113, 155; bone market, 274–75; extermination of, 158–59, 182–84; leave Southern Plains, 25, 236; market for products, 54, 191, 201; return to Southern Plains, 54. *See also* Buffalo hunting
Blackland Prairie, 60
Blanco Canyon, 112
Bland, Billy, 202–203, 220
Blanton, Joe, 334n

Index

361

Godwin, "Colonel," 277
Golden, Johnnie, 197–98, 204, 288–89, 291
Gonzalez, Tex., 263
Goodnight, Charles, 63, 88
Goodnight-Loving Trail, 88, 158
Gordon, Jim, 206
Gould, Jay, 268–69, 279
Grace, Ida, 243–44, **245**, 249
Graham, Lulu, 243, 250
Graham, Tex., 220
Grahame, "Comanche Jim," 194, 215, 288
Graham family, 250
Grant, Ulysses S., 89, 107, 115, 291
Great Depression, 10
Greathouse, Jack, 210
Greenback Party, 251, 295
Griffin, General Charles, 89–90
Griffin Avenue, 189, 191–92, 196–97, 202, 212, 249, 251

Hall, Prudy, 248
Hamby, James, 39
Hammin, Private John, 132
Hammond, John, 259
Hammond family, 244
Hamner, H. A., 55
Hardee, General William Joseph, 31
Hardin, John Wesley, 226
Harper, Hugh, 46, 48–49
Hart, Peter, 186
Haskell County, Tex., 87, 166, 248, 278
Haverty, Pete, 191, 260
Hayes, Bill, 97–99
Hayes, Rutherford B., 27–28
Hayman, Lieutenant Colonel S. B., 104, 133, 141
Hazelwood, George, 105
Hemphill, Zeno, 203, 253
Henderson, Bill, 218
Henderson, James, 124
Henrie, George, 141
Herding. _See_ Cattle raising
Herron, Deputy Henry, 176, 182, 192, 194, 196–97, 202–203, 218, 222; encounters women, 238; investigates Woosley disappearance, 223
Herron, J. M., 169
Hervey, Albert, 240
Hervey, Jules, 263
Heyl, Captain E. M., 154
Hickey, J. L., 176, 182–83
Hicks, W. B., 134–35, 162
Hidetown, Tex., 176
Hill Country, 213–14
Hilliard, A. A., 250
Hinkle, "Major," 185, 260
Hispanics, 286; Butterfield employees, 46; on cattle drive, 97; family, 258; trader, 105
Hittson, John, 59, 75, 82, 88, 92, 103
Hittson, William, 49, 75, 82, 93, 254

Hoeffle, Paul, 249–50, 270
Holabird, Quartermaster, 119–20
Holidays: Christmas, 240, 259, 278; Fourth of July, 240–41, 294
Holliday, Doc, 4, 190, 284, 289
Hood, John Bell, 32
Hoover, M. V. (Mart), 224, 254
Hoover, William G., 88
Horsehead Crossing, 88
Hough, Silas, 87–88
Houston, Sam, 20–21, 41; criticized, 48; and Stone Ranch, 52
Houston and Texas Central Railroad, 156, 272, 275
Houston Telegram, 214
Houston, Tex., 272
Howard County, Tex., 253
Howarth, Jacob, 119, 164, 218, 286
Howell, D. S., 56, 85
Hubbard Creek, 39, 83
Hubbard Creek Ranch, 102
Huber, Gus, 263, 265, 270
Hueco Tanks, 154
Hulltown, Tex., 278
Hunters' Retreat, 192, 263, 270
Hunting, 237–38, 243, 257. _See also_ Buffalo hunting
Huntington, Collis P., 268–69

Immigration, 251, 286, 294, 296; boom ends, 278; to Fort Griffin, 174, 263; from Ohio Valley, 23, 60–61; from Pennsylvania, 267; and railroads, 271; to Shackelford County, 186; to West Texas, 168–71
Indianola, Tex., 119
Indian policy: Texas, 30–31; U.S., 31–32, 36
Indian raids, 32, 39–40, 53–54, 81, 89–91, 177, 179, 181–82, 247, 278; during Civil War, 64–68; during 1868, 100, 105–106; during 1871, 107–109; fear of, 73–74, 159–60; near Fort Griffin, 291–92, 294; in North Texas, 102–103; on post–Civil War ranchers, 82, 85–87, 89–92, 94; Rangers' response, 171–72; white imposters, 45, 48–49
Indian trade, 21–22, 28, 103, 237
Indian-white relations, 34–35, 37; with cattlemen, 64–66, 87; with Indian agents, 31–32, 34–36; Penateka-Texas, 18–25, 27; Penateka-U.S., 24, 29; with Spanish and French, 19; Tonkawa-Texas, 104, 106
Iron Jacket (Comanche chief), 36
Irvine, Captain, 265–66
Irvine, Mrs. J. B., 266
Irwin, James F., 129
Irwin, John Chadbourne (son), 45, 47, 54, 163, 172, 228
Irwin, John G. (father), 46, 59, 62, 75, 93

Jack (Tonkawa), 256
Jack County, Tex., 36, 40